Rethinking Classical Indo-Roman Trade

Rethinking Classical Indo-Roman Trade

Political Economy of Eastern Mediterranean Exchange Relations

RAJAN GURUKKAL

OXFORD
UNIVERSITY PRESS

OXFORD
UNIVERSITY PRESS

Oxford University Press is a department of the University of Oxford. It furthers the University's objective of excellence in research, scholarship, and education by publishing worldwide. Oxford is a registered trademark of Oxford University Press in the UK and in certain other countries.

Published in India by
Oxford University Press
YMCA Library Building, 1 Jai Singh Road, New Delhi 110001, India

First Edition published in 2016

ISBN-13: 978-0-19-946085-4
ISBN-10: 0-19-946085-X

Typeset in ScalaPro 10/13
by The Graphics Solution, New Delhi 110 092
Printed in India by Rakmo Press, New Delhi 110 020

For the Ancient Mariners who lost
their lives in the Indian Ocean

Contents

Illustrations

Maps

Figures

Preface

This book is an attempt to understand the nature of the classical eastern Mediterranean transmarine commerce and the role played in it by the contemporaneous societies of the Indian subcontinent. A revaluation of the extant sources, including the latest archaeological findings in the coasts of peninsular India and Egypt, has been undertaken in this connection. This in turn has necessitated a historiographical reconsideration of some of the long-sustained assumptions about the role of the rulers and traders of the subcontinent. Examining the political economy of the early Mediterranean exchange relations and comparing it with that of the exchange practices of the Indian regions, especially those in the peninsula, it has been found necessary to revisit the expression 'Indo-Roman trade', widely used in the historiography of early India.

What turns up in the study is that the expression 'Indo-Roman trade' is a construct in Indian historiography, evolved under the epochal inspiration of national sentiments and the influence of neoclassical presumptions of trade. There has been no recognition of the fact among historians of early trade that neoclassical notions of production, markets, and exchange have no relevance to the forms, modes, and relations of exchange of ancient times. As a result, most historians have written about trade as a self-evident enterprise in time and space. Only a few historians working on early India seem to have bothered to situate exchange relations in their economy and society and to differentiate trade from other forms of exchange. This book seeks to try and make an attempt at situating the Graeco-Roman exchanges in their economy and society in the Mediterranean as well as in the Indian subcontinent. Having attempted a study in the nature of the exchange relations, the expression 'Indo-Roman trade' has been found to be a misnomer. The expression 'Roman–Indian trade' is a misnomer too.

I had this thought almost two decades ago while I was going through the historical sources of early south India, in connection with my doctoral research. Studying the socio-political conditions of early societies in the Tamil South, I happened to examine contemporary economic processes and forms of exchange, both internal and external. They hardly showed any match with the oft-hailed maritime civilization based on trade relations with the Mediterranean world. Ever since, it has been my interest to re-examine the sources closely, with a view to understanding the nature of the maritime contacts of the south-west coast of India. What the book embodies is the consolidated outcome of the exercise.

I am indebted to many experts for helping me in writing this book. Let me state at the outset that a book like this would not have been possible without their scholarly studies. I have been immensely benefited by my discussions with Romila Thapar, R. Champakalakshmi, and Shereen F. Ratnagar. I am particularly grateful to Y. Subbarayalu who liberally extended not only his rare scholarship in the source material but also his expertise in cartography. M.R. Raghava Varier, my long-term academic associate, has been significantly helpful in writing the book. I am thankful to Kesavan Veluthat who checked the manuscript and made valuable suggestions for improvement.

I should like to thank Raghavendra Gadagkar, Chairman, Centre for Contemporary Studies, Indian Institute of Science, Bengaluru, India; B. Balram and subsequently Anurag Kumar, Directors, Indian Institute of Science, for the honour done me by offering a Visiting Professorship, which enabled me to write the book. I am grateful to my colleagues at the Centre, Amruta Shah, Bitasta Das, and Uday Balakrishnan for all the support. I should like to acknowledge the technical help provided by P.M. Mohanan, my brother. Jalaja has always been the absent cause of my research and Krishnaraj, my purpose. Last but not the least, my indebtedness to the editors at the Oxford University Press for the professional quality in the production of the book is immense.

Rajan Gurukkal

1

Introduction

Theoretical Preliminaries and Methodology

India's maritime contact with the eastern Mediterranean in general and classical Rome in particular, celebrated as Indo-Roman trade, has been a prominent theme in her historiography, inspiring several historians of national sentiment to celebrate the phase as that of a maritime civilization. What has been sought to try and do here is a detailed study of the nature of the eastern Mediterranean overseas exchange relations with the coasts of the Indian subcontinent, especially with those of the peninsular region. It is a historiographical reconsideration and an interpretational reappraisal of the nature of 'classical Indo-Roman Trade' in the light of a fresh evaluation of the source material, including new archaeological finds at Myos Hormos (Quseir al-Qadim) and Berenike on the Red Sea coast and at Paṭṭaṇam on the southern west coast of India, from the perspective of political economy.

Recent reassertions of the established historiographical presumptions about the nature of the classical eastern Mediterranean overseas contacts, in view of new archaeological finds on the Red Sea coast of Egypt and the southern west coast of India, constitute the context of the present attempt. This encourages one to closely examine the fresh archaeological data in order to see whether they necessitate any revision of the extant presumptions about the features, processes, and dynamics of the Early Historic (2nd century BCE–3rd century CE) social formation of the region, and the nature of internal as well as external exchange relations thereof, because they foreclose the possibility of such scheduled commercial relations to have existed. A comparative appreciation of the political economy of Roman trade has also been attempted to ascertain the contrast. Adherence to the perspective of critical political economy in understanding the early Mediterranean exchange relations with the southern west coast, dependence on the analytical framework of social formation in characterizing the socio-economic aggregate of unevenly developed communities, and holistic integration of the multiple sources characterize the methodology of the attempt.[1]

It is well known in early Indian historiography that India had a bustling trade with the Mediterranean world long before the Graeco-Romans appeared on the scene. Any textbook chapter on the history of India's maritime contacts will inform us that ancient Egyptians from the days of the pharaohs onwards had trade relations with India and Indian merchants had sailed their vessels up to Alexandria to exchange their goods. Any specialized study would tell us that seasonal overseas traffic of goods from the coast of peninsular India to Egypt was not uncommon under the Ptolemies themselves. It has been pointed out that much before Hippalus had made out the seasonality of monsoon winds, ancient seafarers were aware of latitudinal parallels and corresponding destinations, as part of their inherited as well as experientially acquired professional wisdom. They must have recognized that sailing on a 12° latitude east from

[1] For a discussion of the theme from a holistic perspective, see R. Thapar, 'Early Mediterranean Contacts with India: An Overview', in *Crossings: Early Mediterranean Contacts with India*, eds F. De Romanis and A. Tchernia (New Delhi: Manohar Publishers and Italian Embassy Cultural Centre, 1997), 11–40. How theoretical insights help a deeper understanding of trade relations is well exemplified in S.F. Ratnagar, *Encounters: The Westerly Trade of the Harappan Civilisation* (New Delhi: Oxford University Press, 1981).

the Horn of Africa across the Arabian Sea would take them to the southern west coast of India.[2]

Nevertheless, it has been stated that it was to Augustus, who conquered Egypt at the end of the 1st century BCE and provided for the prosperity of trade under imperial protection, that the traders owed the phenomenal navigation based on monsoon winds and the sailing of their ships, huge in size and large in number, to the east. Augustus' conquest of Egypt, the hub of contemporary trade networks and caravan circuits from the Red Sea ports across the eastern desert to the Nile and beyond, was motivated by the huge potential of revenue offered by contemporary trade. It has been viewed that his patronage of overseas trade with the Indian coasts was due to the enormous pressure of the demand for the eastern goods.[3] Most historians agree that with the Augustan conquest of Egypt, the Indo-Roman trade became significantly different from what it used to be in the previous ages, especially at the organizational level where it showed features of scheduled commerce under imperial patronage.

Pliny the Elder's reference to the growing anxiety of the Roman Senate about the drain of gold due to the regular import of pepper and other spices from the Indian coasts is quoted in all books on ancient Indian overseas trade as clear evidence of the huge demand. This is famous and widely cited as proof of the influx of gold in bullion and as coins to India.[4] It has been noted by most historians that the heyday of

[2] *Periplus Maris Erythraei* (*PME*), 57. See L. Casson, *The Periplus Maris Erythraei: Text with Introduction, Translation, and Commentary* (Princeton: Princeton University Press, 1989), 83–5. Also A. Tchernia, 'Winds and Coins: From the Supposed Discovery of the Monsoon to the *denarii* of Tiberius', in *Crossings: Early Mediterranean Contacts with India*, eds F. De Romanis and A. Tchernia (New Delhi: Manohar Publishers and Italian Embassy Cultural Centre, 1997), 250–76.

[3] For a detailed discussion of the conquests, see C.R. Whittaker, *Rome and Its Frontiers: The Dynamics of the Empire* (London: Routledge, 2004), ch. 3, 52–61.

[4] See Pliny the Elder, *Natural History*, trans. J.F. Healy (London: Penguin Books, 1991), 6.21, 6.26, and 12.41. The trade in exotics is mentioned to have drained more than fifty million sesterces a year from the empire. This was a sum larger than the annual tribute that Caesar imposed on Gaul after his

Indo-Roman trade was the period between the beginning of the 1st century CE and the second half of the 2nd century CE.[5] Similarly, they saw the second half of the 2nd century CE, the period of the devastation of the empire's core as well as periphery by the Antonine Plague, as the point of the decline of Rome's easterly trade.[6]

Some of the specialized studies maintain that the Graeco-Roman vessels were not competent to cross the Indian Ocean during the monsoon and the major part of shipping of goods from the Indian coasts was done by the Arab and Indian merchants.[7] They have argued

---

conquest of the territory. See R. McLaughlin, *Rome and the Distant East: Trade Routes to the Ancient Lands of Arabia, India and China* (London and New York: Bloomsbury Academic, 2010), 2. The items of oriental goods were pepper, cardamom, cassia–cinnamon, nard, ginger, rice, lentil, cotton, ebony, citron, sesame oil and seeds, sugar, indigo, lycium, bdellium, woods, cotton products, *costus*-roots, gum, aloes, coconut, melon, peach, apricot, millet, frankincense, gum resins, myrrh, elephant, rhinoceros, lion, tiger, hound, monkey, python, parrot, peacock, fowl, ivory, wool, woollen products, hide, fur, silk, lac, pearl, oysters, onyx shell, conch shell, tortoise shell, *ghi* (clarified butter), musk, agate, carnelian, onyx, sard, nicolo, amethyst, rock-crystal, opal, ruby, sapphire, garnet, emerald, lapis-lazuli, zircon, tourmalines, jade, turquoise, iron, steel, copper, and Indian girls. For a catalogue of archaeologically documented merchandise of Indian, Arabian, and Mediterranean origins passing through Berenike, see Steven E. Sidebotham, *Berenike and the Ancient Maritime Spice Route* (California: University of California Press, 2011), 223–45.

5 Dating on the basis of inscriptional sources from the Indian side is shown in G. Fussman, 'The *Periplus* and the Political History of India', in *Crossings: Early Mediterranean Contacts with India*, eds F. De Romanis and A. Tchernia (New Delhi: Manohar Publishers and Italian Embassy Cultural Centre, 1997), 66–71.

6 The original source is Ammianus Marcellinus, a Roman historian of the 4th century, who reports on the Antonine Plague of 165–180 CE. See the discussion in D.S. Potter and D.J. Mattingly, eds, *Life, Death and Entertainment in the Roman Empire* (Michigan: University of Michigan Press, 1999), 105–6.

7 H.P. Ray, *The Winds of Change: Buddhism and the Maritime Links of Early South Asia* (New Delhi: Oxford University Press, 1994). Also 'A Resurvey of Roman contacts with the East', in *Athens, Aden, Arikamedu: Essays on the Interrelations between India, Arabia and the Eastern Mediterranean*, eds M.F. Boussac and J.F. Salles (New Delhi: Manohar Publishers, 1995), 97–114.

that the ship-building technology of ancient India was quite superior to that of contemporary Mediterranean world.[8] It has been argued in the light of allusions in ancient Tamil anthologies, popularly called Sangam Literature, that the Tamils had a major role in the organization of overseas trade with the Roman Empire and that some of their kings themselves were masters of the sea. Some of these views are reconsidered in the following chapters in the light of a fresh scrutiny of the source material and with the help of insights from anthropological theories of exchange.

Theoretical Preliminaries

What constitutes theoretical preliminaries for the study is drawn from the commendable body of literature on critical political economy, economic anthropology, and the history of ancient exchange. Its central component is the critical social theory of exchange relations in general and trade in particular. Theoretical engagement in the study of exchange relations requires us to try and understand, at the outset, the interconnection between the nature of social organization and forms of exchange. It helps us make sense of the homology between the nature of economy and forms of exchange. Insights from critical social theory make the connection explicable through the homology between the form of exchange and the formation of society. Studies in economic anthropology provide knowledge about the characteristics of various forms of exchange, their meanings, and implications. Historical studies in the ancient economy enable us to reconstruct out of the fragments the means, relations, and forces of production as well as distribution.

Society consists of multiple aspects or features that would appear to be a mere assortment so long as their interconnectedness is not explained theoretically. Critical social theory helps us make sense of society in terms of its structure and composition. It enables us to analyse its constituents, relations, institutions, ideas, practices, structures,

[8] R.K. Mukherji, *Indian Ship-building: A History of the Sea-Borne Trade and Maritime Activity of the Indians from Earliest Times* (Calcutta: Longmans Green and Co., 1912).

systems, and processes. This theoretical framework of analysis is largely called social formation that provides us a typological understanding of the socio-economic aggregate of people in time and space. It is based on historical materialism that defines a society in terms of the nature of means and relations of subsistence activities. Social formation is the sum total of economy, social relations, institutions, customs, rituals, cultural practices, governance, and law.

Integral to the theory of social formation, the concept of critical political economy applied here primarily means a critical understanding of the polity–economy interface, which involves an analysis of the homology between economic enterprises and social power relations. It is critical because the analysis, at the outset, starts off with the fundamental question as to which class owned and controlled the dominant economy of the period, how, and with what institutional forms, norms, and conventions. This critical component enables analytical differentiation between societies relatively classless and class-structured with the economic and the political remaining inseparable and separable respectively. This enables us to analyse who in the society has the capability to generate control over goods and services of a given time and place. In the case of the former society, whose economy and polity are informal and overlapping, there were no institutional and organizational means to achieve better functional efficiency. Whereas, in the case of the latter, whose economy and polity are separated from each other, complete in form and substance, the economy grows enterprising and the polity turns repressive, but as mutually reinforcing subsystems with structural and institutional means to make their functions efficient. Knowing this process theoretically helps us assess the nature and scope of economic enterprises as well as the capability of the political formation of a given society as realistically as possible. In the specific context of trade, the fundamental question is who were able to acquire more gains from trade and through what instruments. It helps us make out the problem of anachronism in attributing the conduct of overseas trade with instituted systems of tariff, treaties, and negotiations feasible only in a full-fledged state to a social formation in which the economy and polity overlap.

Certain niceties and nuances in the subject matter in question are not amenable to explanation within the central framework of critical political economy. They require insights from varied anthropological and sociological theories relating to the institution called exchange, which Adam Smith considered as part of the innate propensity of human beings to truck, barter, and exchange one good for another.[9] Long ago, Karl Marx and Bronislaw Malinowski, pointing out the correspondence between the type of social organization and its form of production, distribution, and exchange, had explained how trade differed from other forms of exchange in the pre-capitalist social formations in general and from trade in the capitalist society in particular.[10] Nonetheless, the use of the term 'trade' in historiography is as if it applies uniformly to all kinds of transactions in time and place, and this overlooks the relevance of differentiating trade from other forms of exchange. Such discussions, presuming trade as a universal phenomenon beyond time and place, necessitate no analytical differentiation of it in relation to the nature of peoples, economies, polities, institutions, and exchange practices.

Economic anthropologists, despite the formalist and substantivist divisions among them, identify reciprocity, a voluntary and spontaneous behaviour of equal sharing of goods and services, as the primeval form of exchange under non-market situations.[11] As a natural mode

[9] A. Smith, *An Inquiry Into the Nature and Causes of the Wealth of Nations*, 6th ed., 2 vols (London: Methuen, [1776] 1950), vol. 1, p. 15.

[10] For a broad theoretical perspective that helps us historicize the homologous connection, see K. Marx, *Economic and Philosophical Manuscript*, trans. M. Milligan (Moscow: Progress Publishers, [1844] 1959). B. Malinowski, *Argonauts of the Western Pacific: An Account of Native Enterprise and Adventure in the Archipelagos of Melanesian New Guinea* (London: Routledge and Kegan Paul, 1922).

[11] The substantivist perspective of economic anthropology took shape out of the theory of modes of exchange articulated in K. Polanyi, *The Great Transformation* (London: Beacon, [1944] 1957). It is empirically oriented and does not subscribe to the Western economic theory's claim of universality. G. Dalton and P. Bohannan were its early proponents. See P. Bohannan and G. Dalton, eds, *Markets in Africa* (Evanston, IL: Northwestern University Press, 1962). It acquired more strength in M. Sahlins, *Stone Age Economics* (Chicago and New York: Aldine-Atherton Inc., 1972). A formalist perspective of economics is what one finds in the writings of economists like R. Firth and H.K. Schneider, who sought to maintain the universality of neoclassical economic postulates and believed them applicable to any society on

of exchange it worked well in descent groups of close proximity in terms of clan–kin ties. As the descent group began to be complex due to the increase of people from outside the agnatic relationship or clannish affinity, the practice involved formalization affecting its pristine quality of being putatively altruistic. Naturally, the practice began to be standardized causing differentiation ranging between goods-for-goods exchange and forms of gift-exchange. Gift-giving began to be governed by expectations of returns. This led to a diversification of exchange into those implying social relationships of obligations, legitimacy of power, and political process as is evident in the case of the institution of redistribution, that is, an instituted form of reciprocity. Redistribution presupposes centralized pooling of goods and services, obviously at the chiefly residence in the case of a descent group, for eventual distribution to those in the clan–kin ties called the nexus of the redistributive relationship.[12]

Objects circulated among clan-based societies through reciprocity between two parties (individuals or households or two descent groups) as well as redistribution are not mere use-value goods and services of exchange but bonding objects of clan–kin ties. Their circulation through redistribution is symbolic of politico-cultural responsibility and hence generative of legitimacy to political authority. In stratified societies, gifts assume a form of self-deception and make domination invisible or disguised. They become almost as objects of exchange among people in a differentiated economy and stratified society, which generate exchange value and selfishness in the place of the use-value and generosity.[13] This

---

adaptation. R. Firth, *Economics of the New Zealand Maori* (New Zealand: R.E. Owen, Government Printer, 1959). H.K. Schneider, *Lifestock and Equality in East Africa: The Economic Basis for Social Structure* (Bloomington and London: Indiana University Press, 1980).

[12] See K. Polanyi, *The Great Transformation*, 247–9. Also see introduction of the concept in K. Polanyi, *Trade and Markets in the Early Empires*, eds K. Polanyi, C.M. Arensberg, and H.W. Pearson (Glencoe, IL: Free Press, 1957), 243–70. According to Polanyi, reciprocity and redistribution operate as culturally regulated practices based on trust that is inherent in descent groups of strong relationships as a contrast to markets that are self-regulating.

[13] See discussion in M. Mauss, *The Gift* (London: Routledge and Kegan Paul, 1925), 63–7.

is the point of the beginnings of trade, the structured form of exchange that precludes circulation of goods and services as gifts implying social obligations anymore. Instead they begin to circulate as merchandises or commodities presupposing exchange value and hence the notion of profit.[14] This hardly replaces the formalized or standardized system of goods-for-goods exchange, but carries it forward as transformed into the barter system, to the primordial market, a point of exchange integrated to the culture zone of the descent group, where producers of merchandise congregate periodically. In such barter markets the price of commodities is expressed in terms of a given measure of an essential commodity or one that is always in great demand, which in its turn would build inter-commodity exchange rates.

Karl Polanyi's formulation of forms of exchange is integral to the characterization of agro-pastoral economy that he distinguishes as a system of house-holding economy. He defines the system of house-holding economy as a cluster of small patrilineal households of kindred descendants with inalienable land functioning as independent but interdependent units of production and consumption. Polanyi conceives the rise of agro-pastoral house-holding economy as an independent social formation characteristically different from both the primeval economy of shifting cultivation and the subsequent peasant economy. He defines it as an economy of unity and stability, recurrent of its parts, integrated through three modes of exchange based on mutuality—gift, reciprocity, and redistribution. Reciprocity refers to movement of goods between corrective points of symmetrical groupings; redistribution, to appropriative movements towards a centre and from there to the dependants.[15] According to Polanyi, these forms of integration hardly represented any stages of development or sequence, since several subordinate forms often coexisted with the dominant, with ups and downs. In the ancient Indian context, the concept was first adapted and applied by Romila Thapar at

[14] For arguments differentiating commodities as antagonistic to gifts in political economy perspective, see C.A. Gregory, *Gifts and Commodities* (London: Academic Press, 1982).

[15] See Polanyi, *The Great Transformation*, 247–9. Also see his 'The Economy as Instituted Process', in *Trade and Markets in the Early Empires*, 243–70.

the instance of the later Vedic agro-pastoral social formation based on the labour of the family as well as that of the herders and craftsmen outside the kinship, paid in kind and maintained by each household.[16]

In the relatively evolved market, goods and services become commodities of prices determined at rates invariably higher than their estimated cost but with a tendency of incremental differentiation between the two, as allowed by the general elasticity of demand. This mode of exchange based on notions of exchange-value and price of commodities and the profit thereof is called trade. When goods and services of use-value are turned into commodities of exchange-value, the social process of their origins is masked by the market process of their transformation.[17] There commodities circulate by means of money as the medium of exchange for the people who use it as measure of value and means of payment. Non-monetized people, ignorant of the logic of monetized exchange, resorting to such markets for procuring condiments, require conversion of their goods and services into money first, a process that invariably deprives them of the market price for want of a variety of economic and social capabilities.

In the light of archaeological remains and anthropological conceptualization, archaeologists have analysed and classified archaic exchange practices into different modes of exchange without expecting them to have existed in any pure form at any point of time.[18] There are a few other such formulations too, to some extent drawing inspiration from systems theory, notwithstanding the limitations

[16] For details, see R. Thapar, *From Lineage to State, Social Formations of Mid-First Millennium BC in the Ganga Valley* (New Delhi: Oxford University Press, 1984), 38–40.

[17] See the discussion of K. Marx, 'Fetishism of Commodity', in *Capital*, vol. I (London: Penguin Classics, 1990), 165.

[18] C. Renfrew has identified ten archaic modes of exchange in the light of archaeological evidence, each of which is feasible in itself. See his 'Trade as Action at a Distance: Questions of Integration and Communication', in *Ancient Civilisation and Trade*, eds J.A. Sabloff and L.C.C. Karloski (Albuquerque: University of New Mexico Press, 1975), 3–59. Also see his 'Alternative Models for Exchange and Spatial Distribution', *Exchange Systems in Prehistory*, eds T.K. Earle and J.E. Ericson (New York: Academic Press, 1977), 71–89.

of being analytical classifications and diagrammatic representations. Geographical studies combined with scientific experiments, and ethno-archaeological investigations into artefacts, raw-material sources, networks of exchange, journey routes, points of exchange, and habitation sites have generated impressive knowledge about the localities of industries and the pattern of distribution. On the whole, the attempts in the field of theoretical archaeology of exchange have not gone beyond what Malinowski or Polanyi or Marcel Mauss could do, for the interest has been primarily in generating knowledge through scientific experiments with the localized data, rather than in theoretical generalization transcending the local. Among archaeologists in India too, there has been less theoretical preoccupation with ancient trade, since most of them prefer to describe the empirically given and be done with it. To a certain extent, this has disabled these archaeologists and historians of ancient modes of exchange from being conscious about the influence of the claim of universality about neoclassical economic meanings, measures, and parameters upon them and the entailing trap of anachronism. Hardly do they seem to have found it necessary to separate ancient forms of exchange from trade and refrain from using the term 'trade' indiscriminately in the context of exchange in ancient times. This has led to the application of the neoclassical notion of value in their discussions of ancient transactions, which is explicitly anachronistic.

It is indispensable to make a nuanced distinction in the concept of value in non-market modes of exchange among descent groups, and in the monetized market mode of other peoples. One has to recognize the compatible notions of value in exchanges between monetized and non-monetized peoples. In other words, it is necessary to theoretically differentiate the concept of value in the non-market modes of exchange, not only from the monetized market mode but also from the incompatible notions of value in the exchange between the monetized and non-monetized peoples. The concept of value expressed in terms of 'fair price' makes no sense in the context of an ancient descent group's exchange relations with the market of monetized people, which are bound to be unfair to the former who cannot experience value in terms of price and utility. It is important to bear in mind that notions of value would differ from people to people according to the nature of their social formations which determines the meanings, measures, and modes of their exchange.[19] What emerges as fundamental is the fact that economic activities become intelligible against the social formation that creates their value. Non-monetized people, who understand only the social logic of transactions based on use-value, are not benefited by trade that inevitably follows the market logic of exchange-value and price. The neoclassical theory of economic value cannot make this distinction, for it contemplates no difference between trade and exchange.

A critical anthropological perspective about the dominant economic processes alone can help us analyse the politico-cultural prejudices unavoidable in the principles of neoclassical economics. Therefore, it is necessary to free our thinking from the basic presumptions of neoclassical economics and liberal cultural anthropology, which equate value with exchange-value, in order to understand the concept of value embedded in exchange relations among the people of uneven economies and social organizations.[20] The quantitative price of a commodity in trade is not comparable to the qualitative value of an object in non-market forms of exchange such as gift, reciprocity, and redistribution. It is because the qualitative value of objects of transaction in non-market forms of exchange is not quantifiable unlike the price of commodities in trade. Often failing to take note of this has led most historians of ancient trade to miss the fact that the phenomenon they describe by using the term 'trade' in its generic sense was not trade but either an alternative form of exchange or a combination of different forms of exchange including trade.

It is a matter of tacit recognition among economic anthropologists and social historians that the present-day neoclassical theories of production and market exchange have no relevance to their forms,

[19] See G. Dalton, 'Traditional, Tribal and Peasant Economies: An Introductory Survey of Peasant Economy', *Modules in Anthropology*, ed. C.B. McCaleb (Reading, MA: Addison-Wesley, 1971). Also see his 'Aboriginal Economies in Stateless Societies', in *Exchange Systems in Prehistory*, eds, T.K. Earle and J.E. Ericson (New York: Academic Press, 1977), 191–212.

[20] For an attempt to unite the best insights of Karl Marx and Marcel Mauss at the instance of union of the economic, political, and cultural theories of value, see D.R. Graeber, *Toward an Anthropological Theory of Value: The False Coin of Our Own Dreams* (New York: Palgrave, 2001).

modes, and relations in ancient times, thanks to the studies by Marx, Malinowski, Mauss, Polanyi, and several others. Since the appearance of markets in any distinct form was a relatively recent phenomenon, efforts to extend the application of neoclassical theories of exchange, which owed their origins to the milieu of the evolved market-economy, to anterior contexts of exchange practices are bound to be anachronistic. In the primordial setting of transactions among descent groups, where the economic forces of supply and demand are least visible, postulation of markets itself is anachronistic. Economics of transactions in ancient societies was integral to community relations that had no comparison to market conditions of exchange. What economists have been sustaining as accepted truth about origins of money, market, value, and trade has been questioned in the light of reliable evidence and exposed as inaccurate.[21]

Anachronism has always been a major problem in historiography the world over, especially when the object of study belonged to the ancient period. This has been particularly true of specialists in economic history who have shown little or no consideration of the knowledge generated in the field of economic anthropology. Extrapolation of the nature, working, and motives of late medieval and early colonial trade to the context of early exchanges is a common practice among most historians of trade, which leads to anachronistic generalizations. The concept of nation state is an inescapable influence upon them. As a result, they liberally carry backward concepts of modern political economy such as national commerce, commercial policy, imports, exports, investment, tariffs, free trade, profit, commercial loan, banking, interest, and so on. Several economic historians treat such institutions, ideas, and practices of political economy as independent of the nature of the socio-economic aggregate, polity, and jurisprudence.

In Western historiography, this issue has been seriously debated by economic historians. Specialists either of the early or of the later periods have been debating the issue largely, notwithstanding the academic biases of their schools of thought. These scholars are labelled as 'modernists' and 'primitivists', the former adopting a synchronic

[21] See the discussion in D.R. Graeber, *Debt: The First Five Thousand Years* (Brooklyn, New York: Melville House Publishing, 2011), 26–34.

approach in their application of theoretical knowledge to explain the past phenomena and the latter adhering to the diachronic approach. Generally, labelling is intellectually non-productive, for it acts as a mutually exclusive strategy to contain the arguments of the other. It encourages them to withdraw from serious cognitive encounters and thereby pre-empts chances of production of fresh theoretical knowledge. Branding is an excuse for overlooking the other's critical strength and sticking on to one's own unrealistic exaggeration and loose generalization. However, this debate has considerably enriched the historiography of the West, as the studies of scholars such as M. Rostovtzeff, A.H.M. Jones, M.I. Finley, and others show.[22] The knowledge generated by them is profoundly enriching for anyone encountering the problems debated by them. They, in great detail, tell us empirically as well as theoretically how to characterize the nature of economy in the ancient society and determine the role played by trade in it. Their findings run counter to some of the widely accepted general assumptions regarding the position of trade and traders in the ancient economy. For instance, it has been convincingly shown in their studies that trade played too minor a role to be a prominent element in the ancient Roman economy that was primarily agrarian, unstable, and weakly integrated, making the traders 'typically small fries'.[23]

Most historians of trade in ancient India seem to have seldom bothered to characterize the economy before discussing trade and traders or to assess the part played by them in the economy. Trade in ancient India, and not trade in the ancient economy, was their object

22 See the discussion of the topic by K. Hopkins, 'Introduction', in *Trade in the Ancient Economy*, eds P. Garnsey, K. Hopkins, and C.R. Whittaker (Berkeley, Los Angeles: University of California Press, 1983), x–xviii. For specific details, see M. Rostovtzeff, *Social and Economic History of the Roman Empire*, 2 vols, revised by P.M. Fraser (Oxford: Oxford University Press, 1957); A.H.M. Jones, *The Roman Economy: Studies in Ancient Economic and Administrative History* (Oxford: Oxford University Press, 1974); and M.I. Finley, *The Ancient Economy*, 2nd ed. (Berkeley: University of California Press, 1985).

23 See Jones, *The Roman Economy*, 30. Also Hopkins, 'Introduction', in *Trade in the Ancient Economy*, xii. For a detailed analysis of the question, see Finley, *The Ancient Economy*, 17–34.

of narration because they took trade as an enterprise independent of the economy. Evidence of the existence of overland and overseas trade in ancient India was enough for them to consider trade predominant and its impact on the country substantial. An anachronistic element in their language of narration is the notion of the nation state, which exists as an inescapable influence in their perception and appreciation of the exchange operations of early periods. National labelling hardly makes any sense in the historical representation of activities and practices of regions anterior to the constitution of the national spatiality. It leaves historical imagination methodologically flawed and knowledge epistemologically invalid. Hence, it is a methodological prerequisite and theoretical need for historians of pre-modern India to sustain the subcontinental perspective with regional focus in their historical imagination. It is essential to conceive regions, peoples, and ruling lineages in their specific socio-economic and politico-cultural context for understanding the early history of exchange relations.

Methodology

As regards the discussion of the methodology, we state our preoccupation with the theory of social formation and critical political economy with a justificatory note on the advantages thereof and against the context of the logical problems of causation and generalization that most studies exhibit in the absence of a central framework of comprehension. We have relied on the holistic theory of historical explanation based on the insistence of economic causes as the ultimate instance, for methodologically characterizing the society as a coherent system of institutions, ideas, and relations of material processes. How this methodology helps us look at facts as pointers to a coherent whole by discriminating the anachronistic and recognizing the homologous linkages among them is made clear in the section. In order to understand and explain the niceties and nuances of exchange relations, how social theory, particularly what has been enunciated in economic anthropology, helps is an important component of our methodology.

What we have discussed as part of the theoretical preliminaries in the previous section is integral to this, for it contains the hermeneutic constituent of methodology. It is primarily heuristics that is discussed hereunder. As regards heuristics, the first component of methodology, the present study too seeks to follow the usual techniques of collection and critical analysis of the data from the primary and secondary sources. Similarly, hermeneutics, the other component of methodology, is based on the perspective of critical political economy, according to which consideration of the socio-economic and politico-cultural aggregate of a people is essential to understand the nature of their exchange relations. Analytical appreciation of the socio-economic and politico-cultural formations of the region during the time period under study, an exercise enabled by the aforesaid perspective of comprehension, is, therefore, fundamental to the project. Recognition of the data from primary as well as secondary sources and generation of evidences are enabled by this central perspective too. In short, it is an interpretational endeavour based on the theory of social formation supplemented by insights from critical social theory.

Social formation signifies a holistic theory of historical explanation based on the insistence of material causation as the ultimate instance, and helps us methodologically characterize the society as a coherent system of institutions, ideas, and relations based on the material processes.[24] Social formation means an aggregate of the economic, social, cultural, and political in their basic inter-connectedness. It refers to the essentially inseparable combination of economic activities and corresponding socio-political institutions, relations practices, and ideas of a people in a place and time. A social formation is a combination of several unevenly evolved forms of subsistence, with one form securing dominance over the rest, not necessarily always due to its advantages in terms of technological superiority and productivity. In short, a social formation emerges in the process of co-existence and interaction of multiple forms of subsistence involving different levels of technology. Formation, a metaphor like structure or system, is the conceptual category that sequentially orders and interrelates the multiple aspects of society.

An important advantage of this methodology is that it helps us look at facts as pointers to a coherent whole by discriminating the

24 For a detailed discussion, see R. Gurukkal, *Social Formations in Early South India* (New Delhi: Oxford University Press, 2010), 1–19.

anachronistic and recognizing the homologous linkages among them. It enables a relatively tenable interpretation based on the recognition of incompatibility among institutions, structures, relations, forms of exchange, norms, practices, and processes, at the instance of anachronism established by critical social theory. It is well known today that history does not exist out there in any pure form, for it exists only in the form of historians' interpretations, that is, as created and represented by historians. Hence, writing history by paraphrasing what is apparent in the sources needs no historian whose professional task is distinct for the intellectual depth of interpretation.

Another advantage of the methodology that enables the postulation of society as a coherent whole in the specific context of early southern India is convergence of data from multiple sources. Specialists have been following the practice of naming culture-types and their ages in terms of the source categories. Archaeologists made the label initially 'the Megalithic Age' and subsequently 'the Iron Age' based on the archaeology of burial monuments and iron artefacts respectively. Epigraphists identified an age of heterodox religious culture based on Jain/Buddhist inscriptions. Numismatists and specialists on classical Graeco-Roman accounts identified an age of maritime civilization. Specialists in ancient Tamil literature gave the label 'the Cankam Age'. Of course, these specialists did borrow facts from other sources, but only to supplement the characterization of the culture-type of their central source, notwithstanding the problem of overlap. But all of them seem to have overlooked the fact that the different sources point to one phase or the other of the same social formation. Instead of viewing them as segregated sources for the study of independent ages and cultures, we have used them as integrated ones shedding light on the ancient and early social formations of southern India.

Similarly, this methodology exposes the anachronism involved in the use of several ideas and expressions in the context of the past, which is rampant in the historiography of the subject matter under study. For instance, the use of the term 'trade' in historiography, as if it applies uniformly to all kinds of transactions, has precluded the possibility of differentiating trade from other forms of exchange. It has encouraged the discussion of trade, in a taken-for-granted sense, as a well-understood relationship of uniformity, precluding its analytical differentiation in terms of peoples, economies, polities, institutions, and practices. In historiography, trade has been a formally commissioned activity between two or more countries rather than an activity of organized merchants with or without the state's protection. It contains several uncritically accepted presumptions that are suggestive of trade as an open and balanced enterprise involving equal benefits rather than a relationship of unequal benefits. Another instance is the use of the name India in the context of a nation state, which defies historicizing. An important advantage is that the methodology helps us conceive ancient India as a subcontinent of unevenly evolved socio-economic and politico-cultural formations, ideas, institutions, groups, relations, practices, and processes, rather than as a politically integrated, geographical entity that is anachronistic. By way of self-justification for the present study, it may be pointed out that as of yet there is no study of the Mediterranean exchange relations with the Indian coasts in the perspective of critical political economy, though there are several studies on ancient Indian trade and trade-routes in historical and archaeological perspectives.

Chapters

A detailed consideration of the source material and historiography is what we have attempted in the second chapter, 'Sources and Historiography'. The review of the source material goes into the nature of the data available in archaeological as well as literary sources. It includes archaeological sources consisting of reports on the excavated remains of port-sites, Roman coins, Indian inscriptions, and Egyptian papyri. Literary material consists of direct and indirect types, of which the former is the classical Graeco-Roman maritime writings that provide practical knowledge about overseas routes to the Indian coasts and their ports, and the latter, the ancient Tamil poetic anthologies alluding to contemporary socio-economic and politico-cultural life. A discussion of these two categories has been done separately in two sections as the following. The discussion of relics of excavated ports includes the relics of Arikamedu and Azhakankuḷam on the south-eastern coast and Paṭṭaṇam on the south-western coast as well as those on the Red Sea coast, besides the Egyptian Red Sea ports. Inscriptions comprise mainly the Brāhmi-label inscriptions found at a few places in the Tamil region, the Muziris papyri and Egyptian epigraphs. Coins include the punch-marked coins from the Gangetic regions, Roman coins, and the coins of the Cēra, Pāṇḍya, and Cōḻa chieftains. A discussion of the literary sources has been done with a prelude to the traditional texts of northern India first and then by way of an extensive review of the literary sources directly relating to the subject matter, namely the classical Graeco-Roman maritime writings that provide practical knowledge about overseas routes to the Indian coasts and their ports with most of the relevant excerpts reproduced from the accounts left by Strabo's *Geography*, the unknown author's *Periplus Maris Erythraei* (*PME*), Pliny the Elder's *Natural History*, and Ptolemy's *Geography*. It involves a brief critical analysis of the question of their reliability and relative levels of veracity.

Discussions of the southern Indian literary sources also start with the northern Indian texts with references relating to exchange relations with the Tamil region before passing on to a detailed review of the ancient Tamil heroic literary source well known as the 'Cangan' works that contain specific allusions to Yavanas (Graeco-Romans) in the context of exchange of gold with spices. It contains a critical examination of the limitations of this source material, which forbid us from paraphrasing the anecdotes and events alluded to in the poems, for they belong to the genre of oral compositions noted for their uniformities, recurrences, regularities, stylized articulation, unconscious meanings, stock expressions, and stereotypes. We have reproduced most of the passages containing allusions to the subject matter relevant to our central theme. Since there are exaggerations about the purported content of these passages, we have tried to indicate the context of the poems and their literal as well as metaphorical meanings.

In the section on historiography, organized more or less in the chronological sequential order of the development of perspectives, we have begun the discussion after a brief review of colonial writings, and then passed on to the main task of doing a critical appreciation of the bearing of nationalism as well as the colonial parameters of greatness, in the writing of the history of early Indian trade. It is done at length with citations of appropriate excerpts from the writings of both the colonial and national historians. How the writings of the subsequent historians of materialistic perspectives facilitated a fresh appreciation of the source material amassed by the nationalist historians on the one side and added new data, particularly from the heterodox texts, forms part of the discussion of the subject matter in the chapter.

In the third chapter, 'Eastern Mediterranean Overseas Exchanges', the subject of discussion relates to antecedents, growth, and nature of the eastern Mediterranean exchange relations with the coasts of the Indian subcontinent. An overview of the land and sea routes of the pre-Roman times and the nature of contemporary transactions has been attempted as a background. How the Ptolemies had developed and maintained some kind of state-controlled exchange in the Red Sea region, east Africa, South Arabia, and the Persian Gulf besides north-western India forms part of the discussion. It critically examines the existing claim of Hippalus to have discovered the monsoon wind and explores the possibility of the utilization of the wind by the earlier coasting seafarers for their voyages. What circumstances had led to the establishment of Roman Egypt and the expansion of Graeco-Roman overseas trade have been summarized in the chapter. In this connection, the beginnings of cross-oceanic voyages to the coasts of the Indian subcontinent and the development of the necessary shipping technology in the Mediterranean have been reviewed. An important component of the chapter is the analysis of the nature of the Graeco-Roman exchange relations and their characterization as an ensemble of different modes of transactions from reciprocity and barter besides actual trade.

It is followed by the chapter 'Ports, Marts, and Ship Technology in Early South India' that deals with the characteristic features of contemporary ports and marts of north-western India as well as those on the south-western and south-eastern coasts. We owe almost entirely whatever we know about these ports/marts to the Graeco-Roman writings, particularly *PME*. What was the nature, structure, constitution, level of urbanism, and local base of contemporary ports; who were their inhabitants; and what were their functions—these are the main questions addressed in the chapter. A port was an emporium or mart as we understand from the writings of foreign navigators, geographers, and historians. Nevertheless, from archaeology we understand that ports in those times were multi-cultural assemblages and camps or temporary settlements of foreign merchants. These aspects are examined at some length as part of discussions in the chapter. In addition, an appraisal of the level of shipping technology of early India in general and of peninsular India in particular has been done against the background of the seafaring tradition of north-western and north-eastern India, considering it relevant to the chapter.

Exchange relations in early peninsular India constitute the subject matter of the fifth chapter, 'Exchange Relations in Early Peninsular India', that deals with their nature, modes, and forms in detail with special reference to characteristics of the social structure and dynamic of the political economy. It starts with an overview of the situation of contemporary northern Indian social structure and composition with its exchange network, before dealing with the situation of the Deccan as an extension of the formation in northern India in the form of recurrences as well as differences in the pattern of exchange relations and practices. In continuation of that, a detailed consideration of the social formation and forms of exchange of the Tamil region has been done. Another significant component of the chapter is the discussions of the coins and currency of peninsular India with a brief review of the pre-Mauryan and Mauryan backdrops of exchange practices in northern India. It consists of an analysis of the possible functions of coins in the Deccan and the Tamil region in the context of the notion of money and market. Yet another important component of the chapter is a general comparative examination of the contrasting political economies of Rome and peninsular India and a particular probing into the contrasts between Roman Britain and contemporaries in southern India. It also examines as to whether the Graeco-Roman exchange relations had any serious impact on the political economy of peninsular India, particularly of the deeper south.

What forms the subject matter of the last chapter, 'Polity, Statecraft, and Overseas Exchange', is the nature of the relation of contemporary polity and statecraft to overseas commerce. It starts with an overview of the conditions and processes of trade and trade routes in the Gangetic region, by way of the historical backdrops of what had prevailed in the Deccan and beyond during the period under study. A detailed consideration of the polity and statecraft of the Mauryas has been done in order to highlight how statecraft did matter in the successful operation of long-distance overland as well as overseas trade. Against this background, a critical review of the nature and structure of polity in the Deccan region at the instance of the Sātavāhanas as the lords of the southern trade routes has been attempted as a prelude to the detailed consideration of the political formation of contemporary Tamil region. This is followed by an analysis of the relation between contemporary polity and overseas exchanges as a general issue and the relevance of the poetic epithet of certain Tamil chieftains as the masters of the sea to the context of overseas navigation as a particular question. Making a comparative appraisal of the political formations of the Deccan as well as the Tamil South, their feasibility of administering a systematized and institutionalized control of contemporary exchanges has been examined. It has been argued that neither was it feasible nor necessary for reasons of the level of contemporary political economy of the regions.

A summary of the major arguments and observations is given at the end by way of a tentative conclusion of the study. It attempts at a recapitulation of the context, purports, questions, and methodological preoccupations of the book before stating the main arguments by way of tentative responses. We do not want to assert them as conclusions, for the arguments are open for critical reappraisals and improvements or even a total rebuttal. What has been sustained by way of self-justification for making a case for the arguments in the book is the methodological preoccupation ensuring transparency about the source-base of interpretations as well as harmony between premises and conclusions.

2

Sources and Historiography

Sources of the history of Mediterranean trade contacts with the coasts of the Indian subcontinent fall into two categories: archaeological and literary. Archaeological sources consist of reports on the excavated remains of port-sites, Roman coins, Indian inscriptions, and Egyptian papyri. Literary materials are of direct and indirect types, of which the former are the classical Graeco-Roman maritime writings that provide practical knowledge about overseas routes to the Indian coasts and their ports, and the latter, the ancient Tamil poetic anthologies alluding to contemporary socio-economic and politico-cultural life. A discussion of these two categories has been done separately in the two sections that follow.

Archaeological Sources

Archaeology of maritime trade contacts with the north-western coast of India goes back to the Harappan times. Remains of the Iron Age, relics of excavated port-sites, inscriptions, and coins constitute the archaeological material, the most valid primary source. Iron Age remains represent the most widespread archaeological relics of a single culture that had covered the whole of peninsular India during the first millennium BCE and a few centuries in the earlier part of the

Common Era. A discussion of the relics of excavated ports includes the relics of Arikamedu and Azhakankuḷam on the south-eastern coast and Paṭṭaṇam on the south-western coast, as well as those on the Red Sea coast. Inscriptions comprise mainly the Brāhmi-label inscriptions found at a few places in the Tamil region. Coins include the punch-marked coins from the Gangetic regions, Roman coins, and the coins of the Cēra, Pāṇḍya, and Cōḻa chieftains.

Though excavated Iron Age settlements are very few in peninsular India, Iron Age burial relics, often in thin debris of relatively uniform date, are found extensively.[1] Of the few habitation sites of Iron Age

[1] A. Bridget and F.R. Allchin, *The Birth of Indian Civilisation: India and Pakistan Before 500 B.C.* (Baltimore: Penguin Books, 1968), 223–38; B.K.G. Rao, *Megalithic Culture in South India* (Mysore: Prasaranga, 1972); L.S. Leshnik, *South Indian Megalithic Burials: The Pandukal Complex* (Wiesbaden: Franz Steiner Verlag, 1974); A. Sundara, *Early Chamber Tombs of South India* (Delhi: University Publishers, 1975). Of the several hundreds of Iron Age burial sites, very few have been subjected to systematic excavations, for instance, the sites of Tirukkāmpuliyur and Alagarai in the Tiruchchiṛappaḷḷi district. See *Indian Archaeology: A Review* (*IAR*), 1961–2 and *IAR* 1963–4. Also R. Champakalakshmi, 'Archaeology and Tamil Literary Tradition', *Puratatva* 8 (1975–6): 112. Korkai in the Tirunelveli District, *IAR*, 1964–5. For details regarding the Adichchanallur finds, see B. Nair, *The Problem of Dravidian Origins: A Linguistic Archaeological and Anthropological Approach* (Madras: Madras University Press, 1977), 166–72. Excavations at Korkai show the most archaic stratum which has a carbon dating pushing its antiquity to 795 BCE. See *Damilica*, vol. I, 1970, p. 52. Also, *IAR*, 1964–5. In a subsequent report the date assigned to period I is further late, that is, the 1st century BCE to 4th century CE. See *IAR*, 1965–6. At Tirukkāmpuliyur, Alagarai, and Uṛaiyur, the debris shows the antiquity of the 4th to 3rd centuries BC. Period I of Tirukkāmpuliyur is c. 500–400 BC. See *IAR*, 1961–2. The same is the case with Alagarai too. See *IAR*, 1963–4, 1964–5, and 1965–6. Kaveripattinam, Kānchipuram, Arikamedu, Sanur, Kunnattur, Amritamangalam, Cengamedu, Adichchanallur, and so on, provide chronological sequences roughly from the 3rd century BCE to the 2nd century CE. The sites at Kaveripattinam are dated tentatively between the 1st century BCE and 5th century CE. There is radio carbon date showing the 3rd century BCE as a strange case. See *IAR*, 1962–3, 1963–4, and 1964–5. Also see T.V. Mahalingam, *Report on the Excavations in the Lower Kavery Valley* (Madras: Madras University Press, 1970). Details on the Kānchipuram site have been given in *IAR*, 1954–5. For a discussion on

culture excavated so far, none deserves to be considered exhaustive. However, there are many sites identified and subjected to exploratory trial diggings all over southern India. Iron objects of a wide variety dominate the excavated goods. Different types of pottery of the black and red ware (BRW) tradition and black ware stand next. Among the iron objects spears, swords, tanged daggers, wedge-shaped blades, barbed arrow-heads, and horse fittings are notable. Sickles and hoes could be collected from certain graves. Sickles and socketed spades were there among the grave goods of the Nilgiri 'circles' and 'burrows'. Adichchanallur finds include iron hoe blades. A large number of knives, big and small, of varied shapes, tripods, bell-like objects, and lamps, besides a few unidentifiable artefacts, are there in the collection. A huge quantity of iron slag and ingots has been reported from many burial complexes in the lateritic as well as granite-rich megalithic zones. Bronze and copper objects have been found among the grave goods at a few excavated sites, but as very rare items. Metallurgical studies of the bronze objects have identified them as the high-tin type.[2]

Arikamedu, see R.E.M. Wheeler, 'Arikamedu', *Ancient India* (*A.I.*) 2 (1946). The Sanur site is discussed in N.R. Banerjee and K.V.S. Rajan, 'Sanur 1950 to 1952: A Megalithic Site in District Chinglepet', *A.I.* 15 (1959): 4–8. Kunnattur, Amritamangalam, and Sengamedu are discussed in *IAR*, 1956–7 and 1957–8; 1954–5; and 1961–2 respectively. Adichchanallur is ascribed to a very early period, that is, about 1000 BCE, by some scholars. See Nair, *The Problem of Dravidian Origins*, 182–9 and fn. 44. Radio-carbon dating of a sample at the site yielded 12th century CE, which is also questionable. This is a problem site. See the earlier studies of A. Rea, 'Adichchanallur Excavations', in *Annual Report of the Archaeological Department Southern Circle, Madras and Coorg* (*ARASMC*) (1902–3), 11–14.

[2] Archaeo-metallurgical analyses have shown that the high percentage of tin (23 per cent) was purposefully ensured primarily to overcome the problem of the bronze being brittle. For scientific details of the analysis, see S. Srinivasan, 'Megalithic and Surviving Binary High-tin Bronze Traditions in Southern India: Tracing Binary Bronze Usage to Harappan Times', *Transactions of the Indian Institute of Metals* 66, nos 5–6 (2013): 731–7. For a detailed ethno-archaeological and socio-economic analysis, see S.F. Ratnagar, *Makers and Shapers: Early Indian Technology in the Home, Village and Urban Workshop* (New Delhi: Tulika Books, 2007), 95–112.

Beads of semi-precious stones, horn, bone, glass, and terracotta are very commonly found in the grave debris. Among the beads of semi-precious stones, those made of carnelian and agate are extensively reported from megalithic monuments, especially huge rock-cut chambers and dolmenoid cists. Incidence of gold and silver beads, gold diadems, and some other minor ornaments have been reported too. A few punch-marked coins, most probably from the Magadhan region, and a small number of Roman coins have also been found at certain sites. Archaeological data thus generated are commendable and their empirical analysis quite extensive, which account for the availability of a fairly sound knowledge about the technology, economy, and material culture of the mainstream people of the age.[3]

Production and Exchange Sites

Archaeological data relating to the production and exchange sites of contemporary arts and crafts are commendable. Pot-making was the most widespread craft and hence extensively dispersed and practised, sometimes even at the household level in the case of commonly used wares. However, pottery was indeed a major industry of specialization too as its variety in terms quality, fineness, colour, shapes, and sizes indicate. Some of the ceramic varieties like BRW, red-slip ware, russet-coated ware, and rouletted ware involved rare skill and show extensive geographical distribution, presupposing the existence of their industries at places of the required clay types. A brittle object of everyday use in all households and on ritual occasions like the disposal of the dead in all settlements, pots were part of essential goods necessitating ceramic production as a regular enterprise.

Iron smelting and iron working were equally extensive all over the region and hence largely a part of the household enterprise. It appears that every settlement had its own iron-smelting and iron-working households. Archaeological relics of iron smelting and iron working have been found in all exchange centres including ports. Iron smelting was naturally quite extensive all over peninsular India where in most areas of concentration of megalithic monuments iron slag and

[3] See K. Rajan, *Archaeology of Tamil Nadu (Kongu Country)* (Delhi: Book India Publishing Co., 1994).

ingots in huge quantity have been collected. All the ancient ports were iron-working and bead-making centres. Archaeological remains show that bronze-making was another significant industry in terms of craftsmanship, but not so wide-ranging for the explicit reason of the scarcity of its constituent raw materials—copper and tin. Both copper and tin had to come from far-off places, and therefore, the bronze industry was not quite common. Bronze artefacts were mostly confined to chiefly households.

Remains of another craft object found extensively among the grave goods of the Iron Age are of beads. A highly specialized craft, bead-making was never diffuse but quite confined to places of the required raw materials. It is evident from the remains that bead-making was a major industry of importance among contemporary crafts production, next only to iron working. Kodumaṇal, praised by a couple of ancient Tamil poets as Kodumaṇam, a village of several megalithic monuments, now in the Periyar district, about 40 km from Erode, is a non-port-site of the bead industry, which has been thoroughly excavated and archaeologically appraised.[4] It is an area rich in beryl and rock crystals, which accounts for the existence of an industry of beads in gems, quartz, and crystals. Excavations have yielded a lot of material relating to the bead industry such as bead blanks, broken beads, waste pieces, and rough-outs. Archaeological data contain invaluable clues to craftsmanship, technology, and the level of material culture besides to the organization of manufacturing, the raw material source, the routes of distribution, and the points of exchange.[5] Many beads of various sizes, made of moonstone, cats-eye, rock crystal, beryl, and other stones, besides several prismatic objects of rock crystals perforated for using them as pendants, have been excavated from there. The site has yielded BRW shards with Tamil Brāhmi characters assignable to the 1st or

[4] See *Patirruppattu*, 6:7:1–5 and 7:4:6–7 in praise of the Cēra ruler, mentioning his gifts of jewels from Kodumaṇam. For the text and commentary, see A.D. Pillai, ed. *Patirruppattu* (Tirunelveli: The South India Saiva Siddhantha Works Publishing Society Ltd, 1949).

[5] For details, see the Excavation Report of Kodumaṇal kept with the Department of History, Pondicherry University, Pondicherry, and available with Y. Subbarayalu, Department of Indology, French Institute, Pondicherry.

2nd century CE, incised on them. Along with them, shards of terra sigillata and rouletted ware of Mediterranean origin have also been found, as clear proof of a Mediterranean presence at the site, which is a matter of some importance.

Kodumaṇal, as the relics show, was a major industry, predominantly of beads made of local stones but catering to the requirements of a very wide region, presupposing a larger distributive network around it connecting the main ports like Muziris, Korkai, Azhakankuḷam, Pukār, and Arikamedu which were themselves bead-making centres.[6] The raw material most commonly used in bead-making was quartz, citrine, and garnet, which are the widely available semi-precious stones in southern India. Nonetheless, beads made of two non-local semi-precious stones, carnelian and agate, available mainly in the Khambat region of Gujarat but quite famous for bead-making everywhere, have been found interned in many megalithic and urn burials all over the region.

It is evident that there was, indeed, a regular system for the circulation of beads made of non-local raw materials like carnelian and agate all over southern India. However, there were several bead-making centres in southern India during the Iron Age, using locally available raw materials and catering to the needs of the users of the time as excavation reports vouch for by showing the presence of stone beads, raw materials, and debitage albeit without much detailed information.[7]

All these production centres were probably linked up through a wide distributive network of long-distance itinerant merchants servicing the main ports. The contacts of long-distance traders with the production centres as well as ports are attested by the presence of shards of their characteristic pottery types such as russet-coated painted ware, red-slipped ware, rouletted ware, and so on, in the

6 See G. Kelly, 'Craft Production and Technology during the Iron Age to Early Historic Transition at Kodumanal, Tamil Nadu', *Tamil Civilization* 23 (October–December 2009): 1–14.

7 See details in K. Rajan, 'Traditional Bead Making Industry in Tamil Nadu', *Purātattva* 28 (1997–8): 59–63. Also P. Francis, 'South Indian Stone Bead making', in *Asia's Maritime Bead Trade: 300 B.C. to the Present*, ed. P. Francis (Honolulu: University of Hawaii Press, 2002), 112–25.

excavated goods of such sites.[8] A few other interior sites like Karur have yielded archaeological relics showing Mediterranean contacts. Karur on the Amravati River has yielded remains of BRW at the bottommost stratum and above that remains of brick flooring, an adjoining drain, several potsherds with Brāhmi labels on a few of them assignable to the beginning of the CE and, interspersed with them, shards of Roman amphorae, a piece of terra sigillata, and rouletted ware of Mediterranean origin, and the moulded pottery of kaolin (white clay) have been found. Above them an assemblage of shards of russet-coated painted black and red ware has been reported.

Port-sites in India

Archaeological data are available only from a very few sites such as Paṭṭaṇam on India's south-western coast and Korkai, Azhakankuḷam, Pukār, Arikamedu, and Kānchipuram on the south-eastern coast. Of these Paṭṭaṇam, excavated recently over eight seasons, and Arikamedu, excavated thrice at different points of time, are the only two ports with enough archaeological data as well as analytical studies for us to discuss them at some length. They have yielded considerable archaeological remains in the form of potsherds, beads, gems, a few pieces of gold ornaments, cameo blanks, tiles, bricks, terracotta spindle whirls, local coins, parts of built area, and so on. Excavations at Paṭṭaṇam, Korkai, Azhakankuḷam, Kānchipuram, and Arikamedu have yielded some cultural relics of foreigners as well as native goods as residues of ancient transmarine contacts.[9]

Paṭṭaṇam

Paṭṭaṇam, a village in the Ernakulam district and on the south-western coast of India, is situated on an ancient channel of the Periyar River that has changed its course over the past centuries, leaving the site 4 km away from the sea. Although local people had noticed bricks, tiles, potsherds, and beads scattered several years ago, it attracted

[8] B.K.G. Rao, *Megalithic Culture in South India*, 257–69.

[9] *Indian Archaeology: A Review, 1964–65* (New Delhi: Archaeological Survey of India, 1969); Wheeler, 'Arikamedu', *Ancient India*, no. 2.

archaeological attention only recently on the publication of the results of exploration and experimental digging done in 2003 showing evidence of Mediterranean contacts.[10] Having the antiquity established, detailed excavation began from 2007 onwards, stretching over eight seasons, notwithstanding the problems of the site full of households and heavy land-operations by way of filling up of water channels, levelling-up of the terrain, digging wells, construction of houses, opening of roads, and so on, which virtually scattered archaeological relics all over, precluding the survival of a mount to be excavated. Nonetheless, several trenches taken on the basis of surface remains have yielded a lot of archaeological remains relating to maritime contacts which, along with geo-morphological traces, have succeeded in convincingly identifying the site as Muziris.[11]

Like other excavated port-sites, Paṭṭaṇam has yielded relics of Iron Age habitat as the earliest assemblage consisting of BRW, superimposed by the ceramic assemblage of western Asia consisting of shards of Phoenician torpedo jars and turquoise glazed ware along with Indian rouletted ware and an unidentified ware presumably local, besides a variety of organic and inorganic categories of archaeological objects such as wood, plant-fibre, spices, vegetables, and nuts as well as beads and bead-materials, uncut gem-stones, copper, bronze and iron objects, several copper coins, baked bricks, triple-grooved roof tiles, and potsherds of different types including the early Roman such as amphorae and terra sigillata.[12] Shards of torpedo jars and turquoise

[10] V. Selvakumar, P.K. Gopi, and K.P. Shajan, 'Trial Excavation at Pattanam: A Preliminary Report', *Journal of the Centre for Heritage Studies* 2 (2005): 57–66.

[11] See K.P. Shajan, V. Sevakumar, and P.J. Cherian, 'Locating the Ancient Port of Muziris: Fresh findings from Pattanam', *Journal of Roman Archaeology* 17 (Cambridge: Cambridge University Press) (2004): 312–20. Also P.J. Cherian, V. Selvakumar, and K.P. Shajan, 'Evidence of the Ancient Port of Muziri at Paṭṭaṇam, Kerala', *Chemmozhi* 2, no. 1 (2007): 26–7. For an earlier hypothesis, see R. Gurukkal and C.R. Whittaker in our article 'In Search of Muziris', *Journal of Roman Archaeology* 14 (2001): 335–50.

[12] A comprehensive report of excavations done so far has not been published as yet. The *Interim Report of Paṭṭaṇam Excavations* for 2007, 2008, 2009, and 2010 is available at the Kerala Council for Historical Research (KCHR), Thiruvananthapuram. The report on the fifth season excavation, published by

glazed ware (jars and bowls) are indicative of the maritime contacts of the pre-Roman Egyptian phase. This thin debris apart, the majority of artefacts in the assemblage provide the latest archaeological evidence of the long-term regular transportation of spices, gems, beads, and so on, to the Mediterranean world and beyond in the age of the Roman Empire. Beads of semi-precious stones such as beryl, carnelian, quartz, agate, amethyst, garnet, chalcedony and onyx, and glass constitute the most voluminous quantity among the craft goods excavated.[13] A good quantity of beryl and carnelian raw material, a few stone moulds, their chips, broken pieces and abandoned defective ones have been collected. Shards of the Indian rouletted ware with a Brāhmi label, Amaṇa (Sramaṇa), incised on one of them, assignable to 2nd century CE, attest the presence of long-distance inland merchants, probably *upāsakas* of heterodox religious orders. Remains of spindle whorls, hop scotches, discs, and lamps have also been unearthed at the site. A huge quantity of local potsherds, mostly of the plain or coarse types, found all along the trenches as an assortment showing the ill-disposed state of the debris, has been unearthed, probably of suppliers of the necessities of life, commodities, and other accessories. Nonetheless, the most clinching remains from the site are shards of the Graeco-Roman ceramic variety such as amphora jars, *garum* jars, and huge grain jars, which prove beyond doubt the Mediterranean contacts.[14]

There are hardly any indications of built structures, except a platform made of lateritic rubble and lime with brick lining at the water

---

KCHR in 2011, contains a brief note on all the major archaeological finds. It has also compiled abstracts of papers presented by the Paṭṭaṇam research team in the Conference of the International Association for Asian Heritage, held at Colombo, Sri Lanka, in April 2011. For a more detailed account, see the sixth and seventh season interim report with a summary of findings, results of scientific tests, photographs of objects and the various technical registers, published by KCHR, Thiruvananthapuram, 2013.

[13] See P.J. Cherian, *Report on the Fifth Season Excavation at Pattanam* (Thiruvananthapuram: KCHR), 2011.

[14] For a study of the pottery, see R. Tomber, 'The Imported Pottery at Paṭṭaṇam: External Contacts and Trading Partners', in *The Living Dead and the Lost Knowledge* (Thiruvananthapuram: Department of Archaeology, Government of Kerala, 2008), 37–8.

level, presumed to be part of a wharf. Adjacent to it, a partly withered canoe has been found clogged in alluvial mire, giving the impression of a ferry. In the alluvial marsh were found seeds of bread-fruit, pulses, grape seeds, coconut shells, black pepper, cardamom, rice, wheat, green gram, lentil, mango seeds, bamboo, teak, gooseberry seeds, ladies' fingers seeds, gourd seeds, brinjal seeds, and palmyra palm.

Arikamedu

Arikamedu, situated at the mouth of the Āriyankuppam River, is about 4 km south of Pondicherry, probably the only ancient port-site that is right on the sea coast, rather than on the river bank in the interior. It is a site excavated a few times and studied very well by several scholars specializing in various aspects of the archaeology and history of ancient maritime exchange relations. The first excavation itself had unearthed archaeological debris consisting of shards of Mediterranean ceramics, particularly of Roman amphorae and terra sigillata, a variety of beads, certain structural remains—presumably of the warehouse, ring wells, tanks, terracotta spindle whorls, dye vats, some metal objects, Roman lamps, glassware, and so on.[15]

A subsequent excavation, more extensive, involving diggings at certain Iron Age megalithic burial monuments at Suttukkēṇi and Kōṭṭaimedu, two neighbouring villages, yielded remains like BRW, some beads, gems, and gold, obviously belonging to the period prior to the onset of Graeco-Roman trade.[16] Further excavation brought to light more archaeological data regarding the earlier settlements and their continuity and change.[17] More ceramic assemblages showing remains of Mediterranean amphora jars, terra sigillata, lived spaces,

[15] R.E.M. Wheeler, *Rome Beyond the Imperial Frontiers* (London: Bell and Sons, 1954).

[16] J.M. Casal, *Fouilles de Virampatnam-Arikamedu* (Excavation of Virampattanam-Arikamedu) (Paris: Imprimerie Nationale, 1949).

[17] V. Begley excavated the site during 1989–92. For a discussion of the relics in the context of cultural continuity in terms of ten phases, see V. Begley, P. Francis, N. Karashima, K.V. Raman, S.E. Sidebotham, and E.L. Will, eds, *Arikamedu: Ancient Port City*, Vol. II (Pondicherry: École Française d'Extreme-Orient, 2004). Also see V. Begley, P. Francis Jr., N. Karashima, K.V. Raman, S.E. Sidebotham, K.W. Slane, and E.L. Will, *The Ancient Port of*

and ceramic oil lamps were found in the northern sector that is closer to the port. Arikamedu was a major bead manufacturing centre, which has yielded as part of the debris the raw materials as well as many finished beads and the unfinished ones at different stages of their production, besides wastes and rough-outs.[18] A region rich in the raw material, Arikamedu was famous as an ancient industry of glass beads, which accounts for its importance as a port that shipped a lot of glass beads. However, most glass-bead types that Arikamedu has yielded as part of archaeological studies come under surface finds precluding a stratified context. Many beads found at the port-site were not locally made and they must have reached the port from various places like Azhakankuḷam and Sri Lanka, where alone are found the raw material for certain types, as scientific analyses would have us believe.[19]

Other Ports

An ancient port of the Pāṇḍya country excavated in the recent past is Korkai, a small village in the Srivaikunṭam *taluk* of the Tuticorin district in Tamil Nadu. It is celebrated in the epic, *Rāmāyaṇa* as Pāṇḍya-Kavāṭa, the gate to the Pāṇḍya country.[20] Situated originally on

---

Arikamedu: New Excavations and Researches 1989–1992, Vol. 1 (Pondicherry: École Française d'Extreme-Orient, 1996).

[18] See P. Francis, 'Beadmaking at Arikamedu and Beyond', *World Archaeology* 23, no. 1 (1991): 28–43. Also, V. Begley, P. Francis Jr., N. Karashima, K.V., Raman, S.E. Sidebotham, K.W. Slane, and E.L. Will, eds, *The Ancient Port of Arikamedu: New Excavations and Researches 1989–1992*, Vol. 2 (Paris: École française d'Extrême-Orient, 2004). For details of bead production debris at Kodumaṇal, see the unpublished report with the Tamil University and with Y. Subbarayalu, French Institute, Pondicherry, and K. Rajan, Central University, Pondicherry. For a later assessment by him, see K. Rajan, 'Further Excavations at Kodumanal', in *Man and Environment* 23 (1998): 65–76.

[19] For a scientific analysis, see 5.6.4 section on 'Arikamedu: The Best Studied Glass-Bead-Making in South Asia', in K.H.A. Janssens, ed., *Modern Methods for Analysing Archaeological and Historical Glass* (London: John Wiley & Sons Ltd., 2013), 406.

[20] See Vālmīki's *Rāmāyaṇa*, 'Kiṣkindhākāṇḍa', *adhyāya* 4:41–8: *tatō hēmamayam divyam muktā maṇi vibhūşitam / yuktām kavāṭam pāṇḍyānām gatā dṛukşyata vānara.*

the mouth of the Tāmraparṇi River that, over the centuries, changed its course to about 3 km south and the sea receded about 6 km, the port-site is in the interior today. This has been confirmed by palaeo-channel analyses based on the satellite image data on the course of the Tāmraparṇi, which shows that at the turn of the CE, the river had its course parallel to the coast and heading towards the north-east before reaching the sea on the south of Tuticorin. Archaeological excavation of urn burials close to the port-site has yielded Iron Age relics, mainly BRW along with some artefacts. Some of the potsherds have graffiti marks in Brāhmi characters along with a few pictorial signs of the sun, fish, bow and arrow, probably datable to the turn of the CE. Some shards of amphora and other Mediterranean ceramic showing Roman contacts have been discovered at the port-site. Shards of rouletted ware were also found, indicating the presence of long-distance inland traders who used to carry dishes often with personal marks incised on them. Split shells of pearl oysters have been found as part of the debris at the site as remains of the ancient pearl-processing unit.

Another port of the Pāṇḍya country, identified way back in 1838 by Caldwell and excavated recently, is Azhakankuḷam. Excavation at Azhakankuḷam, a village at the mouth of the Vaigai River, currently about 3 km interior from the eastern coast in the Ramanathapuram district, has yielded many shards of Mediterranean ceramics such as amphorae jars and rouletted ware along with remains of red ware with Tamil Brāhmi letters, assignable to the turn of the CE, incised on a few of them. Other objects like beads, grooved tiles, and bricks have been found across different strata. Among the debris of a later period, three copper coins of the Roman Empire were found, with the portrait of Emperor Valentine II (375 CE) on the reverse, made out on the basis of the female figure holding a globe, obviously the goddess of victory on the obverse.

Vāsavasamudram, a small village, probably on the erstwhile mouth of the Pālār River in the Kānchipuram district is a recently explored and excavated port of the Cōḻa country. Excavations have unearthed shards of amphorae, rouletted ware, bricks, drain pipes, conical jars, two ring-wells, a brick-lined tank probably used for dyeing, and an assemblage of red ware, red-slipped ware, black-slipped ware, and brown ware have been reported as excavated debris.

Red Sea Ports

Archaeological excavations at several Egyptian and Mediterranean sites have provided new evidence of the transport of Indian goods through the Red Sea ports of Berenike and Myos Hormos (Quseir al-Qadim). Some amount of archaeological data relevant to the study do come from the two main Red Sea ports of ancient Egypt, Berenike and Myos Hormos, constructed by the Ptolemies around the 3rd century BCE. It is said that Berenike was developed into a strategic harbour by Ptolemy II in 275 BCE to import elephants from Africa for his army. Excavations at the ancient port of Berenike seem to have uncovered a lot of archaeological data regarding the trade with the eastern world during the eight centuries of its existence. Many of the artefacts, particularly sail-goods and ceramics and flora and fauna remains, discovered through excavations, provide knowledge about the material culture of the people who had inhabited the port-settlement at the strategic point between the Mediterranean world and Asia.[21] A port-site noted for artefacts from different areas between the Mediterranean and Asia, a graveyard, and several wells providing drinking water is suggestive of a multicultural settlement like other contemporary counterparts elsewhere.

Excavations at Berenike and Myos Hormos, located on the Red Sea coast in the far south of the Egyptian eastern desert, have reportedly yielded, as part of the debris, some of the overseas exchange goods shipped from the ports of the south-western coast of India and ceramic assemblages consisting of shards of rouletted ware with indications of the presence of Indians, particularly Tamils, at the ports as well as along the caravan track on the Nile.[22] These reportedly include

[21] See S.E. Sidebotham, *Berenike and the Ancient Maritime Spice Route* (California: California University Press, 2011).

[22] For details of excavations at ancient port sites of Egypt, see S.E. Sidebotham and W.Z. Wendrich, eds, *Berenike 1997. Report of the 1997 Excavations at Berenike and the Survey of the Eastern Desert, including Excavations at Shenshef*, Research School of Asian, African and Amerindian Studies (CNWS) Special Series 3 (Leiden: CNWS, 1999); S.E. Sidebotham and W.Z. Wendrich, eds, *Report of the 1998 Excavations at Berenike and the Survey of the Egyptian Eastern Desert, including Excavations at Wadi Kalalat* (Leiden: CNWS, 2000); S.E. Sidebotham and W.Z. Wendrich, 'Berenike: A Ptolemaic Roman Port

shards of common Indian pottery in good quantity and a few shards of Indian rouletted ware, a couple of them with Tamil Brāhmi characters. One of the shards has two Tamil names Cātan and Kaṇṇan inscribed on it and the other shard has an inscription mentioning *koṟṟappumān*, a chieftain.[23] Other objects like brailing rings, remains of teakwood, and cotton sails probably of Indian weave have also been reported.[24] Berenike's strategic importance as the starting point for sailors bound to the east, coupled with the presence of teakwood among its archaeological goods, probably suggests, according to some enthusiasts, the possibility of an Indian boat-building centre on the Red Sea coast and the presence of Indian merchants and their ships in the Red Sea. Another significant item discovered is black pepper (*piper nigrum*) weighing 7.55 kg in a ceramic container, probably a southern Indian jar, along with various other goods from the southwestern coast of India. Excavations at Myos Hormos and Berenike have yielded shards reportedly of Indian fine ware and coarse ware, domestic wares probably of ancient Tamils, suggesting their extended stay in the place. Shards of storage jars, including the one containing the 7.55 kg of black pepper, red-slipped cooking pots, and casseroles were found as part of the debris.[25] These potsherds have taken to be corroborating the reference in *Periplus Maris Erythraei* (*PME*) to the sailors of 'Limryke' to the island of Soqotra in the Indian Ocean. The occurrence of Indian potsherds at a few sites along the Berenike–Koptos route encourages some archaeologists to presume the sojourn of Indian traders travelling to Alexandria with merchandise.

---

on the Ancient Maritime Spice and Incense Route', *Minerva* 13, no. 3 (2002): 28–31; S.E. Sidebotham, M. Hense, and H.M. Nouwens, *The Red Land: The Illustrated Archaeology of Egypt's Eastern Desert* (Cairo: The American University in Cairo Press, 2008). For a comprehensive interpretation of the archaeological data, see Sidebotham, *Berenike and the Ancient Maritime Spice*, 75–6.

23 For details, see R. Salomon, 'Epigraphic Remains of Indian Traders in Egypt', *Journal of the American Oriental Society* 111, no. 4 (1991): 731–6.

24 See Sidebotham and Wendrich, *Report of the 1998 Excavations*. Also see Sidebotham, *Berenike and the Ancient Maritime Spice Route*, 75–6.

25 For an analytical remark on the potsherds, see R. Tomber, 'From the Roman Red Sea to Beyond the Empire: Egyptian Ports and Their Trading Partners', *British Museum Studies in Ancient Egypt and Sudan*, 18 (2012): 201–15.

Some terracotta objects unearthed at Berenike, seemingly tokens (*ostraca*) of customs duty clearance given at Koptos for cargoes to be sent across the desert to the Red Sea ports, shed light on contemporary procedures of the legalization of goods on board.[26] However, it is too small a collection to provide details such as the volume and variety of cargoes.[27] Another set of ostraca (eighty-eight *ostracon*) known as the Nicanor Archive, consisting of caravan transport receipts, was excavated from Koptos.[28]

The earlier presumption was that the site of Quseir al-Qadim was a satellite port of Leucos Limen.[29] However, recent excavations have shown that the present-day site of Quseir al-Quadim (old Quseir), located 8 km north of the modern town of Al-Qusayr in Egypt, and Myos Hormos are the same. Like its satellite port at Berenike, Myos Hormos also has yielded archaeological remains relating to the ancient Egyptian trade, though mostly eroded by the sea, and of the subsequent Roman trade with India and the eastern world. Excavated goods comprise large volumes of finds relating to Graeco-Roman transmarine trafficking of the easterly trade goods, trader settlement, and naval artefacts. They are remains of ceramic goods, textiles, basketry,

[26] See R.S. Bagnall, C. Helms, and A.M.F.W. Verhoogt, *Documents from Berenike 1: Greek Ostraka from the 1996–1998 Seasons* (Bruxelles: Fondation Égyptologique Reine Élisabeth, 2000).

[27] See discussion in R. McLaughlin, *Rome and the Distant East* (New York: Hambledon Continuum, 2010), 15.

[28] For details, see A. Fuks, 'Notes on the Archive of Nicanor', *Journal of Juristic Papyrology* 5 (1951): 207–16. For details of excavation, see S.E. Sidebotham, 'Ports of the Red Sea and the Arabia–India trade', in *The Eastern Frontier of the Roman Empire: Proceedings of a Colloquium Held at Ankara in September 1988*, eds D.H. French and C.S. Lightfoot (Oxford: British Archaeological Reports, 1989), 83–92. Also see G.K. Young, *Rome's Eastern Trade: International Commerce and Imperial Policy, 31 BC–AD 305* (London and New York: Routledge, 2001), 64–5.

[29] For details, see D. Peacock and L. Blue, eds, *Myos Hormos—Quseir al-Qadim, Roman and Islamic ports on the Red Sea*, Vol. 1: *Survey of the Excavations 1999–2003* and Vol. 2: *Finds from the excavations 1999–2003* (Oxford, GB: Archaeopress, University of Southampton Series in Archaeology, 6 [BAR S2286]). Vol. 1 published in 2006 (Oxbow Books) and Vol. 2 published in 2011.

metal and wooden artefacts, glass, ship fittings, fishing material, flora and fauna items, and some written material. The naval objects consist of 169 brail rings, a deadeye, various sheaves from rigging blocks, and several fragments of sailcloth.[30] The written material consists of ostraca and paper documents.

Ceramics

Ceramic goods constitute an important archaeological source material for the study of early exchange practices. There is a commendable quantity of a variety of ceramic goods like the shards of Greek amphorae and Parthian glazed ware in the ports of Myos Hormos and Berenike of Ptolemian Egypt and Qana and Khor Rori of South Arabia. They include Greek, Rhodian, and Knidian amphora varieties, and Persian turquoise glazed pottery. Shards of these were discovered long ago at Hathab, Arikamedu, Azhakankuḷam, and recently at Paṭṭaṇam.[31] Similarly, shards of BRW, northern black polished ware, Indian rouletted ware, and coarse ware have been found at a few ports of South Arabia too. Distribution of shards of pottery of the Indian subcontinent in a few ports of Arabia suggests the prevalence of exchange relations between Arabia and the Indian subcontinent during pre-Roman times.[32] Shards of pottery from the Persian and the

30 For a detailed discussion on the material in the context of shipping technology, see J. Whitewright, 'Roman Rigging Material from the Red Sea Port of Myos Hormos', in *The International Journal of Nautical Archaeology* 36, no. 2 (2007): 282–92.

31 See D. Kennet, *Report on the TGP from Paṭṭaṇam Excavation 2007 Season* (Thiruvananthapuram: KCHR, 2009). His analysis shows that the turquoise glazed ware discovered at Paṭṭaṇam is later and could even be of the early Islamic period, c. 7th–8th century CE. Also see A. Pavan and H. Schenk, 'Crossing the Indian Ocean before the Periplus: A Comparison of Pottery Assemblages at the Sites of Sumhuram (Oman) and Tissamaharama (Sri Lanka)', in *Arabian Archaeology and Epigraphy* 23, no. 2 (2012): 191–202.

32 See A. Avanzini, 'Sumhuram: A Hadrami Port on the Indian Ocean', in *The Indian Ocean in the Ancient Period: Definite Places, Translocal Exchange*, ed. E.H. Seland (Oxford: International Series, Archaeopress, 2007), 29–31. Also A. Pavan, 'Sumhuram as International Centre: The Imported Pottery', in *Along the Aroma and Spice Routes: The Harbour of Sumhuram, Its and the Trade*

Red Sea coasts suggest the prevalence of pre-Roman exchange relations between West Asia and the Indian subcontinent. Much more extensively, the remains of the Graeco-Roman ceramic goods have been found at every identified port of both the Roman Empire as well as other dominions. Graeco-Roman and Italian amphora jars, storage jars, other containers, aristocratic tableware like terra sigillata, and so on, have been discovered mostly in shards and sparingly intact.

These ceramic relics provide valuable ideas about the circulation of goods, people, their sojourns, exchange relations, culinary practices, consumption culture, and so forth. Scientific analysis of their constituent material and location of source for over the last two decades have generated fresh knowledge about the distribution of the Mediterranean pottery types in the Indian subcontinent and the Indian pottery types at various sites along the Indian Ocean seaboards. Most of these remains are of terracotta containers of merchandise and some of domestic cooking pots and vessels. Therefore, it is reasonable to take all this as an indication of the short sojourn or relatively long stay of South Asian merchants at such places. There are several instances of local imitation of ceramics belonging to alien cultures and they seem to be suggestive of cross-cultural adoption of dietary items and culinary practices.

Inscriptions

A few Buddhist inscriptions from the sites of monastic establishments at Nasik, Karle, and Junnar in the western Deccan record votive observances of patronage by upāsakas, mainly merchants including those from the Graeco-Roman world, who are addressed as Yavanas, a word derived from the Old Persian word *yōna* that originally referred to Ionian Greeks. It is used in early Sanskrit, Prākrit, and Tamil texts to address the Graeco-Romans. Soon Sakas and Parthians were also referred to by the term. An inscription from Nasik registers the endowment by a merchant who addressed by himself as a Yavana named Indrāgnidatta, son of Dhamma Dēva, for a new relic chamber to be

---

between the Mediterranean, Arabia and India, ed. A. Avanzini (Roma: L'Erma di Bretschneider, 2011), 99–112.

built.[33] Another Yavana called Lēka Damacik Budik, a Saka writer, figures in an undated epigraph as the donor of a water cistern and yet another called Romanakas, probably a Prākrit rendering of the Latin name Romanus (Roman), figures in an epigraph of the same place, as a donor of some funds for the development of the monastery.[34] In the epigraphs of Karle caves, six Yavanas (Sinhadaya, Damma, Vitasangata, Dammadēva, Culayaka, and Yasavadana) of the 1st century CE, residents of Dhēnukakaṭaka and hailed as *vaṇikagāma* (settlement of merchants), appear as donors.[35] These Yavanas who, from the title, appear to have become upāsakas of the Buddha, are mentioned to have endowed the Karle monastery for carving out *tambo* (column) in the main relic hall. Inscriptions from the Buddhist monastery at Junnar are found registering donations by three Yavanas (Chanda, Irila, and Cita), for quarrying the cisterns, a façade, and the mess hall.[36] Two of these donors, called Cita and Irla, claim to have come from Gata.

Some of the Jain/Buddhist cavern sites in the region, mostly on the rocky hillocks, in the surroundings of Madurai have

33 See E. Senart, 'The Inscriptions in the Caves at Nasik', in *Epigraphia Indica*, ed. E. Hultzsch, Vol. VIII (Calcutta: Superintendent, Government Printing, 1906), 59–96. Also see no. 1140 in H. Luders, 'A List of Brahmi Inscriptions from Earliest Times to about A.D. 400 with the Exception of Those of Aśoka', Appendix to S. Konow, ed., *Epigraphia Indica*, Vol. X-1909-10 (Calcutta: Government Printing, 1912), 128–131. For updated full text, translation and historical details, see V.V. Mirashi, *The History and Inscriptions of Sātavāhanas and Kshatrapas* (Bombay: Maharashtra State Board for Literature and Culture, 1981), 66–8.

34 *Epigraphia Indica*, Vol. X, no. 1140.

35 See Sinhadhaya and Damma figuring in the inscription nos 7 and 10, respectively, of E. Senart, 'The Inscriptions in the Caves at Karle', in E. Hultzsch, ed., *Epigraphia Indica*, Vol. VII-1902-3, 47–74. Vitasangata, mentioned as hailing from Umehankataka figures in no. 1 and Dammadēva, Culayaka, and Yasavadana figure in nos 4, 6, and 7, respectively, of H.K. Sastri, ed., *Epigraphia Indica*, Vol. XVIII-1925-26, 1926, 325–9.

36 See E. Senart, 'The Inscriptions in the Caves at Nasik', in E. Hultzsch, ed., *Epigraphia Indica*, Vol. VIII-1905-06. Chanda and Cita figure in no. 1156 and Irila figures in no. 1154 of H. Luders, 'A List of Brahmi Inscriptions from Earliest Times to about A.D. 400 with the Exception of Those of Aśoka', Appendix to S. Konow, ed., *Epigraphia Indica*, Vol. X-1909-10, 1912, 128–31.

Tamil-Brāhmi-label inscriptions, the earliest even going back to the 3rd century BCE, incised on rock-beds, boulders, and so on.[37] Out of the fifteen cavern sites with labels belonging to the 3rd–1st centuries BCE, ten are on the trade routes from Madurai to its neighbouring towns, with a concentrated distribution in the north-east, on the routes to Tiruchchiṛappaḷḷi. Marugālttalai near Pālaiyamkōṭṭai on the Tāmbraparṇi, Kunnakkuṭi on the Tiruppattur–Karaikkuṭi route, Sittannavāsal on the Pudukkōṭṭai–Tiruchchiṛappaḷḷi route, and Pugaliyur on the Tiruchchiṛappaḷḷi–Erode route are the main sites outside the Madurai district. The Madurai sites are Annamalai and Varicciyūr on the route to Mēlur; Karungalkkuṭi on the route to Tiruchchiṛappaḷḷi; Kīḻvaḷavu on the Mēlūr–Tiruppattūr route; Vikkiramamangaḷam on the route to Sōḻavandan; Muttuppaṭṭi, Kongarpuḷiyankuḷam, and Tiruppaṛankunṛam on the route to Tirumangaḷam; Azhakarmalai and Mānkuḷam on the Azhakarkoil–Mēlūr route; and Sidharmalai on the Mēlūr–Tiruchchiṛappaḷḷi route.

The labels record mostly personal names of the donors of the caverns or rock-beds, often indicating their occupational status. In one of the label inscription of Mānguḷam, the accountant (*kāviti*) of the *nikamam* (organized body) of Veḷḷarai is mentioned.[38] The records of Azhakarmalai refer to a goldsmith (*ponkolavan*) of Madurai, a salt merchant (*uppu-vāṇikan*), a toddy merchant (*pānita-vāṇikan*), a ploughshare merchant (*koḻuvāṇikan*), and cloth merchant (*aṛikai-vāṇikan*) as donors.[39] The labels of Pugaḷur cavern refer to a gold merchant (*pon-vāṇikan*) of Karūr as the founder of the cavern and an *eṇṇai-vāṇikan* (oil-monker).[40] Certain labels have references to place names. One of the labels of Konkarpuḷiyankuḷam refers to Pākanūr, a village, which in later records figures as Pākanūr-*kūṛṛam*, a larger division almost equal to a *nādu* (a cluster of settlements, the counterpart of a *janapada*).[41] Pāṇḍyan Nedunjeḻiyan and Cēran Iḷamkaṭunko, son

[37] For an up-to-date reading and interpretation of these inscriptions, see I. Mahadevan, *Early Tamil Epigraphy from the Earliest Times to the Sixth Century A.D.*, Harvard Oriental Series 62 (Harvard: Harvard University Press, 2003).

[38] Mahadevan, *Early Tamil Epigraphy*, 319.

[39] Mahadevan, *Early Tamil Epigraphy*, 369, 372, 376–7, 381.

[40] Mahadevan, *Early Tamil Epigraphy*, 417, 419.

[41] Mahadevan, *Early Tamil Epigraphy*, 333.

of Perumkaṭunko and son of Ātan Cellirumpoṟai, figure in the labels of Mānkuḷam and Pukaḷūr respectively.[42] Chronology of the cave labels is fixed with the Arikamedu graffiti of the 1st century CE as the point of reference and on the basis of orthographic factors.[43] Labels of all of the above cavern sites are assigned to the pre-Arikamedu period, roughly the three centuries of BCE. There are two cave labels—one at Mamandūr on the Arcot–Kanchi route and the other at Aracalūr on the Erode–Coimbatore route referring to the name of a *taccan* (mason or carpenter) and a *malaivaṇṇakkan* (lapidary) respectively, belonging to the early 4th century CE.[44]

A few potsherds with label inscriptions in Brāhmi characters have been reported from the Red Sea coast, as part of the excavated debris. These inscriptions, assignable to the 1st or 2nd century CE on palaeographical grounds, have been discovered at Berenike.[45] One of the shards has two Tamil names Cātan and Kaṇṇan, probably of mariners from the Tamil region, inscribed on it. Another label inscription reportedly mentions *koṟṟan* (*koṟṟan pumān koṟṟan*), meaning chieftain.

Muziris Papyrus

The Muziris Papyrus, also known as the Vienna Papyrus discovered in 1985, is a portion of a maritime loan agreement on the recto and verso, dating back to mid-2nd century CE and relating to a shipment of goods from Muziris to Myos Hormos.[46] Its opening part, carrying the names of the parties to the contract, is lost. On the recto is an undertaking to transport the merchandise of Muziris unloaded at the

42 Mahadevan, *Early Tamil Epigraphy*, 315–17, 405–7.

43 For a detailed discussion, see Mahadevan, *Early Tamil Epigraphy*, 91–5.

44 Mahadevan, *Early Tamil Epigraphy*, 423, 441.

45 For details, see Salomon, 'Epigraphic Remains of Indian Traders': 731–6.

46 For the updated text, translation, and interpretation of the Muziris Papyrus in general and about the system of credit money in particular, see L. Casson, 'New Light on Maritime Loans: P. Vindob, G 40822', in *Zeitschrift fur Papyrologie und Epigraphik* 84 (1990): 195–206. Also see D. Rathbone, 'The "Muziris" Papyrus (SB XVIII 13167): Financing Roman Trade with India', in *Alexandrian Studies II in Honour of Mostafa el Abbadi* (Alexandria: Societé Archéologique d'Alexandrie, 2000), 39–50.

port on the Red Sea coast (Myos Hormos or Berenike) to Koptos across the eastern desert and from there along the Nile down to Alexandria, while on the verso is the quantity of nard, ivory, and textiles with an account of their value and a consolidated summary of the cargo for the purpose of customs duty:

> ... six parcels loaded aboard the vessel Hermapollon I will weigh and give to your cameleer another twenty talents for loading up for the road inland to Koptos, and I will convey [sc. the goods] inland through the desert under guard and under security to the public warehouse for receiving revenues at Koptos, and I will place [them] under your ownership and seal, or of your agents or whoever of them is present, until loading [them] aboard at the river, and I will load [them] aboard at the required time on the river on a boat that is sound, and I will convey [them] downstream to the warehouse that receives the duty of one-fourth at Alexandria and I will similarly place [them] under your ownership and seal or of your agents, assuming all expenditures for the future from now to the payment of one-fourth—the charges for the conveyance through the desert and the charges of the boatmen and for my part of the other expenses.[47]

Quite prominently signifying the legal basis of the whole transaction under Roman laws, it is mentioned that in the event of non-payment of the maritime loan, the debtor will forfeit the entire goods specified by way of security in the contract document. According to the scholars who first edited the Muziris Papyrus, the document was the security part of a maritime loan agreement signed at Muziris between a merchant (creditor) and ship-owner (borrower) by hypothecating the ship.[48] One of the subsequent studies shows that the contract was signed as two separate agreements—one dealing with the maritime loan and the other with the security stipulations that the Papyrus embodies—at Alexandria well before the ship set out on the voyage to Muziris. It also clarifies that the security was not the ship but the cargo. Another study taking the cargo as the security maintains that the original contract was drawn up at Muziris before the ship left the port and a supplementary agreement was signed at

47 Casson, 'New Light on Maritime Loans', 204.

48 Casson, 'New Light on Maritime Loans', 195–206.

Myos Hormos or Berenike on the arrival of the ship with the cargo from Muziris.[49]

A very significant contractual document under the Roman law, signed by agencies like an Alexandrian creditor, a transmarine trader, and a third person—probably a Greek stationed at Muziris—the Papyrus provides a set of strikingly fresh evidence of the highly formalized, document-based, widely networked, adventurous, and expensive nature of contemporary overseas transactions. At the instance of a ship called *Hermapollon* engaged in mercantile circuits between Berenike and Muziris during the mid-2nd century CE, the Papyrus gives a detailed account of merchandise and their prices. It contains a wide variety of information regarding the Mediterranean overseas trade with the west coast, particularly with Muziris, the major port to which ships from Berenike had sailed. One significant piece of information, incomplete though, relates to the cargo items and their prices. Taking clues from the available data regarding the price of the most significant items, mainly black pepper and Gangetic nard, the value and quantity of the aggregate cargo have been estimated as 20,500 talents of 95 Roman pounds each corresponding to more than 625 tons of which pepper and nard made 544 tons of pepper.[50] There are many details in the document regarding the conveyance of goods from the Red Sea port to Koptos through the desert, by using camels and from there to Alexandria by river. The Muziris Papyrus is, indeed, a significant source for understanding the financing system of maritime trade involving contractual monetary transactions and formal agreements based on legal documents; the shipping of goods involving high risks, huge liabilities, heavy customs tariff, expensive and adventurous land-transportation; and the exchange involving enormous profit.

Egyptian Records

A few label inscriptions datable to the turn of the CE, found in the caves at Wadi Menih on the route from Berenike as well as Myos

49 Casson, 'New Light on Maritime Loans', 195–206.

50 See F. De Romanis, 'Playing Sudoku on the Verso of the *Muziris Papyrus*: Pepper, Malabathron and Tortoise Shell in the Cargo of the *Hermapollon*', *Journal of Ancient Indian History* 27 (2012): 75–101.

Hormos to Koptos, provide some ideas about the movement of people and goods involved in Graeco-Roman exchange relations. The route being traversed by cameleers with full loads of low-volume but high-value goods like pepper, pearls, and gems, which were luxury items in contemporary Rome, these inscriptions with names of certain educated slaves of the ruling aristocracy and big merchants are extremely important.[51] An Egyptian stone inscription dated to c. 90 CE, known as the Koptos Tariff, deserves mention here as an important source that sheds light on the tolls to be paid by the caravan troupes leaving for Myos Hormos or Berenike.[52] The inscription helps us understand that tolls imposed on the travellers varied on the basis of their occupations, status, and ranking. Likewise, the tolls on cargoes were also charged differently depending on the items. It mentions the tolls imposed on the caravans, cameleers, donkey-men, and pack animals engaged in the trans-shipment of goods across the eastern desert. This inscription, being a matter of public notification, was incised on a big stone and installed at an open site at Koptos, suitable to catch the attention of the wayfarers. There are label inscriptions on the structures at watering stations and resting places along the desert routes, which contain names of wayfarers, particularly members of the caravan troupes, who travelled to the Red Sea ports. They included the names of the merchant-mariners who set out to distant destinations like the ports of India.

As noted earlier, the inscribed terracotta objects from Berenike, looking like tokens (ostraca) issued at Koptos after the clearance of customs duty imposed on the cargoes to be sent across the desert to the Red Sea ports, provide clues to contemporary procedures regarding the legalization of goods on board.[53] Some of the ostracons are receipts of customs duties imposed on commodities such as wine,

[51] For details of inscriptions, see D. Meredith, 'Eastern Desert of Egypt: Notes on Inscriptions: 2, Mons Claudianus Nos. 22–40', *Chronique d'Egypte* 29 (1954): 103–23. Also see his 'Inscriptions from the Berenice Road', *Chronique d'Egypte* 29 (1954): 281–7. For a better contextualization, see T. Judd, 'The Trade with India through the Eastern Desert of Egypt under the Roman Empire', University of Liverpool, Rev. Version, Special Paper, 2007, pp. 1–18.

[52] See the discussion in Sidebotham, Hense, and Nouwens, *The Red Land*, 187.

[53] Bagnall, Helms, and Verhoogt, *Documents from Berenike* 1.

olive oil, vinegar, onions, beets, and barley, mostly carried for the South Arabian and Persian ports.[54] These inscriptions attest the emperor's control over the movement of goods from the empire. They provide information about the personnel onboard in a contemporary Graeco-Roman merchant vessel, including its owners, financiers, and businessmen. These were mainly grains like wheat and barley besides other low-priced goods of high volume, shipped to the South Arabian ports. Some of the low-volume goods such as copper, antimony, tin, and other alloys that formed part of the cargo were for sending to the ports of the Indian subcontinent.

The Nicanor Archive (eighty-eight ostracons), excavated from Koptos, is another set of inscriptions written in Greek and dating back to 662 CE which provides valuable data relating to trans-shipment of goods through the desert route.[55] These are primarily the receipts of goods transported overland from Berenike and Myos Hormos to Koptos by cameleers. They are named after Nicanor who, according to the ostracons, was an Egyptian haulage contractor of the 1st century CE, owning many camels. He is mentioned as the son of Panes, and stationed at Koptos, contracting trans-shipment of goods across the desert routes to Myos Hormos as well as Berenike and back.[56] The Graeco-Roman merchants used to entrust him with the responsibility of transporting their goods across the desert to the Red Sea ports where the merchants certified the safe receipt of their consignments. The Nicanor ostraca are such receipts returned by the merchants to Nicanor at Koptos, through the cameleers. Ostraca mention the name of the members of Nicanor's family, particulars of the merchants who entrusted their cargoes for safe haulage, and details of the goods. Goods from Indian ports being seasonal, unlike those shipped to the Red Sea region and Arabia, the ostraca do not contain much information regarding them.

[54] See R.T.J. Cappers, *Roman Food Prints at Berenike: Archaeological Evidence of Subsistence and Trade in the Eastern Desert of Egypt*, Costen Institute of Archaeology Monograph Series 55 (Los Angeles, 2006), 6.

[55] For details, see Fuks, 'Notes on the Archive of Nicanor', 207–16. For details of excavation, see Sidebotham, 'Ports of the Red Sea', 83–92. Also see Young, *Rome's Eastern Trade*, 64–5.

[56] Fuks, 'Notes on the Archive of Nicanor', 207–16.

Coins

Coins constitute another significant category of source for studying the history of ancient economy and exchange. Many ancient coins have survived to modern times as a treasure trove, accidently discovered and subsequently preserved in numismatic museums. Some of the old coins surfaced in excavations, particularly among burial goods of megalithic and other grave sites of the Iron Age. Most coins of the ancient past have been found in hoards and they belong roughly to the period between the closing centuries of the first millennium BCE and the turn of the CE. They consist of punch-marked coins from the Gangetic region (c. 400 BCE–c. 180 BCE), Phoenician coins (c. 300 BCE), Sātavāhana coins (c. 200 BC–c. 200 CE), Roman coins (31 BCE–217 CE), and Tamilakam coins (c. 100 BCE–c. 200 CE).

A few hoards of punch-marked coins of uncertain chronology, sometimes called Magadhan or Gangetic coins, constitute the earliest collection of coins in southern India. Several of them probably date back to pre-Mauryan times and seem to have belonged to the pre-Mauryan Magadha. Some of them have been recovered as part of grave goods at a few burial sites of the Iron Age.[57] These are found all over the ancient trade centres, suggesting their circulation primarily among long-distance traders. The Mediterranean coins, found mixed up with the Roman coins, are next in antiquity. As many as over eighty hoards of gold and silver coins of the Roman emperors from Augustus of the 1st century BCE to Constantine of the 4th century CE constitute the chief numismatic material for the study of the classical Mediterranean trade along the south-western and south-eastern coasts of India. Plenty of copper coins are there in the collection too.

Collections by W. Elliot and Scott constitute the major pool of Roman coins found in India. Subsequently several hoards of coins surfaced at different places in different years. They are hoards of Roman coins from places such as Eyyāl, Poḷḷāchi, Karur, Veḷḷalur, Kalayamuttūr, Madurai, Vaḷḷuvaḷḷi, Panamkād, Koṭṭayathunādu, and Puthenchiṛa.[58]

[57] See W. Elliot, 'On the Sepulchral Remains of Southern India', *Report of the British Association for Advancement of Science Transactions* XIX (O.S.) (1857–8): 227.

[58] Roman coins have been found in India at over 130 sites, with a concentration in the Krishna valley in Andhra and the Coimbatore region in

Coins of the Eyyāl collection mostly belong to the period of Augustus, though a few are ascribed to the pre-Augustan period as well. Post-Augustan coins at Eyyāl are of Tiberius, Claudius, Nero, and Trajan. Coins of the Poḷḷāchi hoard are mainly of Augustus and Tiberius. Coins of Augustus, Darius, Germanius, Tiberius, Caligula, and Claudius constitute the Veḷḷalur hoard. The Karur hoard consists of the coins of Augustus, Antonia, Tiberius, Claudius, and Constantine. In the Kalayamuttūr hoard there are coins of Darius, Tiberius, Caligula, Claudius, Nero, Domitian, Nerva, Trajan, Hadrian, and Commodius. Coins of the Madurai hoards are mainly of Domitian, Theodosius, Eudocia, Constans, and Zeno. The Vaḷḷuvaḷḷi hoard contains inter alia the coins of Julius Caeṣar too. Some of these coins are preserved intact at the various museums of the country. The copper coins are mostly of Honorius and Arcadius, the chief collection of which is from the Vaikai bed in Madurai.[59] One-fourth of the total Roman coins found in India date from the time of Augustus and Tiberius. Some of these coins were in circulation for several centuries and the coins mentioned in the early medieval inscriptions of the kingdoms of southern India seem to be mostly old coins, often known as *paḻankācu*, were *dīnāra* of the Roman Empire. Some of the gold coins known as *tuḷaippon* were most probably of ancient period too.

Tamil Nadu. For early notices of finds, see W. Elliot, *Coins of Southern India* (London: Trubner, 1886); R. Sewell, 'Roman Coins Found in India', *Journal of the Royal Asiatic Society* (Cambridge), n.s., XXIII, no. 36 (1904): 591–637. Also his *List of Antiquities*, Vol. I. Find-spots are given in K.V.S. Aiyer, *Historical Sketches of the Dekhan*, Vol. I (Madras: Modern Print Works, 1917), 86–7. The Roman coins recovered from Kerala are discussed in P.L. Gupta, *The Early Coins from Kerala* (Thiruvananthapuram: Government of Kerala, Department of Archaeology, 1965). For a detailed catalogue of Roman coins, see S. Suresh, *Symbols of Trade: Roman and Pseudo-Roman Objects Found in India* (New Delhi, 2004), 18–20.

59 Sewell, 'Roman Coins Found in India', 200–15. All these coins need not be of genuine Roman mint but, probably, local imitations. R.H.C. Tufnell, *Hints to Coin Collectors in Southern India* (Madras, 1839), 27–31, quoted in B.D. Chattopadhyaya, *Coins and Currency Systems in South India* (New Delhi: Munshiram Manoharlal Oriental Book Publishers, 1977), 117.

Pāṇḍyan Coins

Several punch-marked silver and copper coins with a fish symbol on the reverse have been assigned to the Pāṇḍya chiefdom.[60] Silver punch-marked coins are found to be of six types while those made of copper are more or less of a uniform type. Their identification is solely based on a fish symbol on the reverse, well known as the totem of the Pāṇḍya chiefdom. The obverse is marked by any object like the sun, the trident, a dog, and so on. Most of these coins of different types have been recovered from the bed of the Vaikai River, close to Madurai. A single hoard of coins of uniform type, made of silver, reportedly containing a total of 1,124 coins, has been recovered from Bodynaykanur. A set of copper coins with a fish symbol on the reverse recovered from the Madurai area bear the name Peruvaḻūti incised on their obverse in Brāhmi characters. Peruvaḻūti is known from other sources as the chiefly suffix of a few Pāṇḍyas and some numismatists have assigned c. 200 BCE as the probable date to the coins. In fact, there is no reliable dating of any of these so-called Pāṇḍya coins, but some four types of silver coins have been assumed to be of the immediate post-Mauryan period, albeit without any convincing arguments. It is not reasonable to consider them pre-Roman, because it is well known that silver began to be available only with the arrival of the Graeco-Roman overseas traders on the western coast. Some of the coins have symbols, probably of a fire altar, pillar of the sacrificial shelter, or a sacrificial horse on their obverse. Several coins have symbols of animals like a tortoise, elephant, and bull on the reverse, and a few of them have a human figure on the obverse, presumably representing the ruler. Several coins have a representation of pearls for the rare variety of which the Pāṇḍya coast was famous.

Cēra Coins

Many copper coins, presumably of the Cēra chieftains of the initial two or three centuries of the CE, have been recovered from the bed of

[60] See R. Krishnamurthy, *Sangam Age Tamil Coins* (Madras: Garnet Publications, 1997). Also see his *Pāndyar Peruvaḻuti-nāṇayangal* (Coins of the Pāṇḍyan Peruvaḻūti) (Madras: Garnet Publications, 1991). P. Shanmugam, *Cankakāla Kācu Iyal* (Numismatics of the Sangam Age Coins) (Chennai: International Institute of Tamil Studies, 2003).

the Amarāvati River in Karur, the headquarters of the Cēras, and from a few places in the Coimbatore district. Most coins have a representation of a bow and arrow, the totemic symbol of the Cēra chiefdom on the reverse and a representation of certain animate objects such as elephants, horses, bulls, tortoises, and lions besides the snake and fish on their obverse. Several coins show the depiction of inanimate objects like arched hills, an axe, conches, a river, flowers, and the sun as well as symbols like the swastika and the trident. Archaeological excavations at Paṭṭaṇam in the Ernakulam district of Kerala have yielded several square and circular coins made of copper with a representation of a bow and arrow as well as an elephant facing to the right on the reverse, the symbol of the Cēras.

A Cēra silver coin with the portrait facing towards the left and wearing a bristled-crown helmet in Roman style on the obverse, assigned to the 1st century BCE, probably one of the earliest of the Cēra coins, has been recovered from Karur. A few coins have been found bearing, on the obverse, a human portrait with the names Mākkōtai or Kuṭṭuvan Kōtai incised in Brāhmi characters. Some of the numismatists assign these Cēra coins to the 1st century CE. The portrait coins are obviously imitations of the Roman coins as in the case of the silver portrait coins of the Sātavāhanas and Kshatrapas. Many Roman silver coins with the portrait of Augustus and Tiberius, recovered from the Coimbatore–Karur region, vouch for this influence. Graeco-Roman accounts contain references to the import of silver coins out of which the rulers of the Deccan must have made their coins. These portrait coins have a close resemblance with the Roman coins of Emperors Augustus and Tiberius. It is reported that a few seals with one side blank and the other side bearing the name Mākkōtai incised in the reverse direction in Brāhmi letters and the portrait facing the left have been recovered from the river bed of the Amarāvati.[61] While the incision on them remains the same, their portrait sizes and facial features vary from one another, as in the case of the coins of the western Kshatrapas. Some numismatists assign these coins to the period between the 1st century BCE and the 1st century CE. There are a few other portrait coins with the name Kuṭṭuvan Kōtai incised in Brāhmi

[61] See R. Krishnamurthy, 'Mākkōtai Coins', in A.V.N. Murthy, ed., *Studies in South Indian Coins*, Vol. II (Chennai: New Era Publications, 1992), 89–94.

characters using *puḷḷi* (a dot sign). They are assigned to the period between the 1st and 2nd century CE on palaeographic ground. A coin with a full human figure with the name Kollirumpoṛai incised in Brāhmi letters, datable to the same period and obviously referring to the Cēra chief Ko Perumcēral Irumpoṛai who is celebrated in ancient Tamil poetic literature as Kollirumpoṛai or the conqueror of Kolli, has been found at Karur.

Cōḻa Coins

Cōḻa coins recovered so far come to only a relatively small number. They are collected mostly from the Amarāvati River bed.[62] Some coins were recovered from the beds of the Peṇṇār River at Tirukkoilur. Some coins were collected from the debris excavated at the famous port of Arikamedu. A few coins were found in the stratified context at the time of the Pukār excavation too. Unlike in the case of the other two major chiefdoms, the Pāṇḍya and the Cēra, there are no portrait-type coins in the case of the Cōḻas. They are copper coins with the representation of a tiger on the reverse, the animal sign of the Cōḻas. Various other animate and inanimate objects common in the Pāṇḍya and Cēra coins on their obverse are seen on the Cōḻa coins too. Like most coins of the Pāṇḍyas and Cēras, there is no reliable chronology for the Cōḻa coins also. Some of the numismatists presume that a few Cōḻa coins could be of pre-Roman times, while others see them minted under the influence of the Roman coins. It is reasonable to assign the Cōḻa coins only to the post-Roman period.

Some of the hill chieftains (Malayamān) of Tamilakam are said to have issued coins too, with the representation of a flowing river on their obverse and their names incised on the reverse.[63] A coin bearing the name Tirukkaṇṇan, also known as Malaiyan Cōḻiya Ēnādi Tirukkaṇṇan, and Tirumuṭi Kāri is assigned to a Malyamān. Several coins bearing representation of a horse on the obverse and a flowing river on the reverse have been reported and proposed to be of

[62] See R. Krishnamurthy, *Cankakāla Cōḻar Nāṇayangal* (Cōḻa Coins of the Sangam Age) (Madras: Garnet Publications, 1991). Also Shanmugam, *Cankakāla Kācu Iyal* (Numismatics of the Sangam Age Coins).

[63] Krishnamurthy, 'Mākkotai Coins', 89–94.

the Malayamān chieftains.[64] Although the peak phase of exchange relations between the Roman Empire and the southern coasts of India was confined to the Julio-Claudian and Flavian reign periods, the Mediterranean trade with the coasts continued. Some of the late Roman copper coins have also been reported from Karur, Madurai, and Tirukkoilur areas, as an indication of the continuation of the Graeco-Roman trade with the southern coasts.[65]

Literary Sources

As regards the literary sources for understanding ancient maritime trade contacts of India, some at the outset refer to allusions in the *Old Testament* to Indian trade with Syrian coast as far back as second millennium BCE. Ancient Chinese literary texts are mentioned referring to maritime and trade activity between India and China as far back as the 7th century BCE. In the *piṭaka* and *nikāya* texts several Buddhist episodes of long sea voyages, one even of six months' duration, undertaken in a *nouka* (boat) are narrated.[66] Several *jātakas*, one jātaka is even named as 'Samudda Vaṇija' (sea trader), contain several stories recounting adventurous sea voyages to distant lands and mentioning the ancient ports of Supara and Bharukaccha.[67] A legend in its

64 Krishnamurthy, 'Mākkotai Coins'.

65 Although the state Department of Archaeology excavated the site for over a dozen seasons, there is no comprehensive report available. Only brief reports on excavations of the seasons 1986–7 and 1990–8 are available. The findings till 1992 are summarized in N. Kasinathan, A. Abdul Majeed, D. Thulasiraman, and S. Vasanthi, *Alagankulam: A Preliminary Report* (Madras: State Department of Archaeology, 1992). Also see S. Vasanthi, S. Selvaraj, D. Thulasiraman, and T. Śrītar, *Alagankulam: An Ancient Roman Port City of Tamil Nadu* (Chennai: State Department of Archaeology, Government of Tamil Nadu), 2005. For the study of coins, see R. Krishnamurthy, *Late Roman Copper Coins from South India: Karūur, Madurai and Tirukkoilūr* (Chennai: Garnet Publishers, 1994).

66 For a detailed discussion, see R.K. Mukherji, *Indian Shipping: A History of the Sea-Borne Trade and Maritime Activity of the Indians from Earliest Times* (Calcutta: Longmans Green and Co., 1912), 73.

67 Mukherji, *Indian Shipping*, 74–8.

Dipavamśa version talks about a woman sailing to an unknown island near the Persian Gulf and founding there a kingdom of women on an island. This has been interpreted as having beneath the story a trace of the maritime tradition of voyages between India and the Persian coasts in the days of the Buddha.[68]

There are several allusions to maritime activities of northern India in some of the ancient literary texts in Sanskrit. *Manusmṛiti* stipulates laws governing disputes in seaborne, inland, and overland traffic of merchandise.[69] It disqualifies a Brāhmaṇa who has gone on a sea voyage as unworthy of doing a *srāddha* (annual death-day ritual homage to the deceased). *Manusmṛiti* defines marine insurance holding the sailors collectively responsible for the damage caused to the goods of passengers. However, it absolves them from all responsibility if the damage is caused by an accident beyond human control.[70] Bottomry was marine insurance for a ship pledged as security for a loan for financing a voyage, according to which the lender would lose the loan amount in case of a shipwreck. In *Yājnavalkya Samhita*, there is a passage which indicates that some of the ancient people in northern India used to undertake adventurous sea voyages in pursuit of fortunes.[71]

Some of the astronomical texts also contain passages alluding to the prosperity of maritime trade, huge Indian ships, and the ancient craft of shipbuilding. Similarly, *Brihat Samhita* has a few passages alluding to huge ships, seafaring commerce, and sailors. The allusions are in the context of the forecast as to how the moon and stellar positions affect the health and fortunes of people of different walks of life such as the shippers, the sailors, the traders, the physicians, and

[68] Rev. T. Foulkes quoted from *Indian Antiquary* (1879), in Mukherji, *Indian Shipping*, 72.

[69] See *Manusmṛiti*, viii, 158 and 409. See the verse quoted in Mukherji, *Indian Shipping*, 60–1. For the translation of the full text of *Manusmṛiti*, see G. Buhler, *The Laws of Manu* (Oxford University Press, 1886; repr., Delhi: Motilal Banarsidass Publishers, 1984).

[70] *Manusmṛiti*, viii. See a discussion of this and related matters in Mukherji, *Indian Shipping*, 60–1.

[71] See discussion of this and related matters in Mukherji, *Indian Shipping*, 62.

so on.[72] In the same text, there is an allusion to maritime prosperity in the context of the prescription of a gold-flowing port where seamen are safely back ashore with their treasure, as an auspicious point to take a sea bath.[73]

Literary sources directly relating to the subject matter consist of the classical Graeco-Roman maritime writings that provide practical knowledge about overseas routes to the Indian coasts and their ports. They are mainly the accounts left by Strabo in his *Geography*, the *PME*, a sailors' manual describing sea routes and ports written by an unknown author, *Natural History* by Pliny the Elder, and Ptolemy's *Geography*.

Graeco-Roman Writings

Many of the writings of the Greaco-Roman navigators and geographers have survived only in fragments in the form of excerpts quoted by later writers. It appears that several writers like Apollodorus, Megasthenes, Eratosthenes, Ctesias, Onesicritus, Deimachus, Nearcus, Aristobulus, and so on, wrote on the conquest of India, its geographical measurements, climate, and crops. Most of such writers have been quoted by Strabo. Of the surviving accounts, the most relevant are the Graeco-Roman texts of the early imperial period (mid-1st century CE) such as Strabo's *Geography*, an anonymous merchant's experiential account called *PME*, Pliny the Elder's *Natural History* and Ptolemy's *Geography*, which give brief accounts on ports and marts on the south-western and south-eastern coasts of India.[74] The literature would show that

[72] Mukherji, *Indian Shipping*, 62–3.

[73] Mukherji, *Indian Shipping*, 63.

[74] The original text and translation of all these sources are now available online. See W.H. Schoff, *The Periplus of the Erythraean Sea* (New York: Longmans Green, 1912); McCrindle, *Ancient India as Described in Classical Literature* (repr., Patna: Eastern Book House, 1987). Also see his *Ancient India as Described by Ptolemy* (repr., Calcutta: Archaeological Survey of India, 1927); R.C. Majumdar, ed., *Classical Accounts of India* (Calcutta: Firma K.L. Mukhopadhyay, 1960); K.A. Nilakanta Sastri, *Foreign Notices of South India* (Madras: Madras University Press, 1939). The well-known classics that have contextualized and historicized their contents are E.H. Warmington, *The*

navigation between the East African coast and the Indian west coast was a common feature of the period. Conceived as an ensemble of excerpts from the various works quite relevant to the subject matter that constitutes the book, the section embodies statements of facts of their times.

Reliability established through critical analyses of the content and the context is the most important quality that any source material should possess and a historian is to appraise it independently. Often this is not possible for want of technical competence in the language of the source material. In the case of Graeco-Roman accounts, we cannot say that all of them are equally reliable, for they contain factual conflicts, exaggeration, mutual betrayal, and falsehood. Some of the writers, especially the earlier ones, seem to have been credulous and uncritical about what their informants rendered. Some of the later writers are understood to have tampered the accounts of their predecessors and distorted facts. Writers like Strabo, Pliny the Elder, the author of *PME*, and Arrian have been distinguished as more reliable due to their critical approach towards and rational judgement upon the accounts left by the preceding accounts, besides personal experience and first-hand knowledge.[75] Further, there are exaggerations, ambiguities, and conflicts of facts in their accounts. Strabo is one of the most cautious writers, methodologically committed to be reasonable and logically dismissive of exaggerations.

In the subsequent part of this section, we seek to reproduce extracts from the Graeco-Roman accounts in translation with a brief attempt at contextualizing them. Perhaps the earliest among foreign notices belongs to Herodotus who wrote in the 5th century BCE but with little or no knowledge about India. Nonetheless, whatever he did mention by way of observations, for instance, those about 'certain wild trees

---

Commerce between the Roman Empire and India (London: Cambridge University Press, 1928); M. Charlesworth, 'Roman Trade with India: A Resurvey', in P.R. Colman-Norton, ed., *Studies in Roman Economic and Social History in Honour of Allan Chester Johnson* (Princeton: Princeton University Press, 1951), 131–43; J.I. Miller, *The Spice Trade of the Roman Empire 29 B.C.–A.D. 641* (Oxford: Clarendon Press, 1969).

[75] For a discussion, see the 'Introduction' in Majumdar, *Classical Accounts of India*, xxiv–xxvi.

that bore wool which in beauty and quality excelled that of sheep and out of which the Indians made their clothing' helps us understand the nature of his curiosity.[76] It has been pointed out that 'the first direct notice of a South Indian kingdom occurs in Megasthenes whose quaint account of the Pāṇḍyan kingdom seems to be a mixture of facts and of contemporary fables relating to that kingdom'.[77] Arrian's quote of what Megasthenes said:

> In the sea which surrounds the islands, tortoises are bred of so vast a size that their shells are employed to make roofs for the houses; for a shell being fifteen cubits in length, can hold a good many people under it, screening them from the scorching heat of the sun, besides affording them a welcome shade. But, more than this, it is a protection against the violence of storms of rain far more effective than tiles, for it at once shakes off the rain that dashes against it, while those under its shelter hear the rain rattling as on the roof of a house. At all events they do not require to shift their abode, like those whose tiling is shattered, for the shell is hard and like a hollowed rock and the vaulted roof of a natural cavern.[78]

Strabo's accounts (23 CE), obviously of imperial approval and aristocratic acceptance, constitute the first reliable source for the subject matter, since they are mostly based on eyewitness accounts. A methodologically inclined Hellenic historian cum geographer of wider exposure to Greek intellectual tradition, he presents his findings as juxtaposed against what his precursors had put across, which he quotes extensively with specific reference to who maintains or dismisses what and why. This scholarly approach demonstrates his thorough comprehension of what the forerunners had written in the subject matter. His acceptance or rejection of the findings of the forerunners is methodologically tenable in the sense that the process involved rational inquiries into premises, inferences, evidence, and certain basic strategies of reasoning essential for the production of knowledge. There is a clear distinction between truth and myth or

76 McCrindle, *Ancient India as Described in Classical Literature*, 106, para. 4.

77 Sastri, *Foreign Notices of South India*, 1.

78 Arrian quoted in Sastri, *Foreign Notices of South India*, 4.

history and story in his accounts. He criticizes Megasthenes with a few others for having believed the stories of Heracles and Dionysus. Two excerpts given below illustrate his rational process of acceptance as well as rejection of observations made by the precursors:

> Megasthenes indicates the fertility of India by saying that it produces fruit and grain twice a year. And so says Eratosthenes, who speaks of the winter sowing and the summer sowing, and likewise of rain; for he says that he finds that no year is without rain in both seasons; so that, from this fact, the country has good seasons, never failing to produce crops; and that the trees there produce fruits in abundance, and the roots of plants, in particular those of large reeds, which are sweet both by nature and by heating, since the water from the sky as well as that of the rivers is warmed by the rays of the sun.[79]

Strabo takes these stories as fabrications by the sycophants of Alexander, and therefore does not treat them as reliable. It is also because of the weird nature of their content. He takes note of the disagreements among contemporary writers with regard to the reliability of the stories. Several of them just ignored it, while a few mention them, but as too unreasonable to believe. Most historians according to Strabo considered it utterly unreliable. Another notable feature is its unrealistic narration without any first-hand experience. If Dionysus and Heracles with their people had passed through the route to India, the account would have contained mention of some personal experience by way of evidence. In the words of Strabo:

> But that these stories are fabrications of the flatterers of Alexander is obvious; first, not only from the fact that the historians do not agree with one another, and also because, while some relate them, others make no mention whatever of them; for it is unreasonable to believe that exploits so famous and full of romance were unknown to any historian, or, if known, that they were regarded as unworthy of recording, and that too by the most trustworthy of the historians; and, secondly, from the fact that not even the intervening peoples, through whose countries Dionysus and Heracles and their followers would have had

[79] Sastri, *Foreign Notices of South India*, 15, 20.

to pass in order to reach India, can show any evidence that these made a journey through their country.[80]

It appears from the notes of Strabo that the traffic of goods to Alexandria through the Egyptian ports Berenike and Myos Hormos was well prevalent in the days of Ptolemies, but had involved months- or even over-a-year-long voyage since ships had to sail along the coasts of Arabia and Persia to reach India. Indeed, there were overland routes between India and the West, all along the Oxus to the Caspian and the Black Seas, or through Persia to Asia Minor or by way of the Persian Gulf and the Euphrates through Damascus and Palmyra to the eastern Mediterranean, although not quite frequently used. Strabo, describing the inception of trade by Eudoxus of Cyzicus in 130 BCE and the subsequent growth, mentions that soon after Augustus took control of Egypt, and while Gallus was prefect of Egypt (26–24 BCE), up to 120 ships were setting sail every year from Myos Hormos to India. It reads as the following according to two translations with a slight difference between each other:

> I was with Gallus at the time he was prefect of Egypt, and accompanied him as far as Syene and the frontiers of Ethiopia, and I found that about one hundred and twenty ships sail from Myos-Hormos to India, although in the time of the Ptolemies scarcely any one would venture on this voyage and the commerce with the Indies.[81]

There are always some differences in the translations of one and the same passage, although the central point remains. Niceties and subtle details left out in one translation or the other would really matter sometimes when we need to highlight certain implications. As regards the above passage, the translation of the initial portion makes no difference, although in McCrindle, Strabo is mentioned to have personally seen that 120 ships left Myos Hormos for India. But Carey takes the passage to mean Strabo to have learned the event through somebody, rather than witnessing it personally. Nevertheless, when

[80] Strabo, *Geography*, trans. H.L. Jones, eight volumes (Cambridge: Harvard University Press, 1917–32), Book 2, 15:9–10.

[81] McCrindle, *Ancient India as Described in Classical Literature*, 98.

it comes to the last part of the passage, there is a difference. While McCrindle gives us the impression that Strabo was saying that hardly anyone dared to venture on this voyage, Carey would quote Strabo to have said that a few ventured to undertake the voyage:

> At any rate, when Gallus was prefect of Egypt, I accompanied him and ascended the Nile as far as Syene and the frontiers of Ethiopia, and I learned that as many as one hundred and twenty vessels were sailing from Myos Hormos to India, whereas formerly, under the Ptolemies, only a very few ventured to undertake the voyage and to carry on traffic in Indian merchandise.[82]

There is a further difference in terms of nuances, when H.L. Jones translates the same passage. It is true that the main content is not lost in any of the translations, but being often trans-creations rather than translations, a historian does lose certain signifiers. What a historian really needs is a word-by-word translation. Jones takes Strabo to have meant that during the days of the Ptolemies only very few merchant-mariners dared to launch their ships:

> Up to a hundred and twenty ships make their way under sail from Myos Hormos to India, whereas previously, under the Ptolemies, very few people dared to launch their ships and trade in Indian goods.[83]

Same is the case with the translation of Strabo's mention of embassies sent by the rulers in the coastal region of the south-western part of the Indian subcontinent. Strabo is reported to have mentioned that embassies were sent by the Pāṇḍyan ruler to Augustus. In fact, the alleged mention of sending embassies or emissaries by rulers to the Roman emperors has to be viewed with some amount of scepticism for a variety of reasons. Some of the sources that repeat the mention exhibit uncertainty about the practice that was untenable:

> From one place in India and from one king, Pandion, but according to other writers, Poros, there came to Caesar Augustus' gifts and an embassy accompanied by the Indian sophist who committed himself

[82] Strabo, *Geography*, Book 2, 5:12

[83] Strabo, *Geography*, 2, 5:12.

to flames at Athens, like Kalanos, who had exhibited a similar spectacle in the presence of Alexander. If, however, one should dismiss these accounts and observe the records of the country prior to the expedition of Alexander, one would find things still more obscure.[84]

The embassies to Augustus are mentioned by various historians like Dion Cassius (c. 155–235 CE), Pius Annius Florus (c. 98–117 CE), and Paulus Orosius (c. 400 CE).[85] Dion Cassius mentions the embassies from India sent to Emperor Trajan too. What these writers really mean by that is, in fact, unclear, for there are two mutually incompatible factors involved. One fact is the irresistible economic compulsion of the Mediterranean traders for acquiring the eastern goods for the acquisition of which they would anyway have gone over to the eastern ports. The other factor is the rulers of the regions in the Indian subcontinent allegedly sending emissaries to persuade the emperor to have exchange relations. Historian Dion Cassius, mentioning the embassies from India sent to Emperors Augustus and Trajan, writes:

> ... ever so many embassies came to him from various barbarians, including the Indi [Indians]. And he gave spectacles on one hundred and twenty-three days, in the course of which some eleven thousand animals, both wild and tame, were slain, and ten thousand gladiators fought.[86]

From Strabo's quote of Nikolaos Damaskenos' definition, we understand that an embassy in those days meant just a couple of persons representing their lands or heads of tribes visiting the emperor with some gifts to gratify him and secure agreement on mutual collaboration. Questions like what kind of agreement, how and why are

84 McCrindle, *Ancient India as Described in Classical Literature*, 9, para. 4.

85 *Dio's Roman History*, Vol. IX, trans., E. Cary, Loeb Classical Library 117 (Harvard: Harvard University Press, 1927), 73; Florus, *Epitome of Roman History*, Vol. IV, trans. E.S. Forster, Loeb Classical Library Edition (Harvard: Harvard University Press, 1929), 12; *Orosius, Seven Books of History against the Pagans*, trans. A.T. Fear (Liverpool: Liverpool University Press, 2010), 18.

86 *Dio's Roman History*, Vol. IX (1929), 73.

unclear from the source material that refers to the embassy episodes and that it pertained to trade agreement is only a matter of imagination. There is no indication as to whether the embassy had consisted of personages of authority, who could negotiate with the emperor and formally execute any agreement regarding the exchange of goods. Instead, what appears is that the so-called embassies were ordinary persons who accompanied the mariners or some of the mariners themselves. In short, the whole matter is generally put in a fictitious language. For instance, look at the following embassy episode, quoted as follows:

> Eight naked servants presented the gifts that were brought. They had girdles encircling their waists and were fragrant with orpiment. The gifts consisted of a Hermes born wanting arms from the shoulders, whom I have myself seen, large snakes and a serpent ten cubits long, and a partridge larger than a vulture. They were accompanied, it is said, by the man who burned himself at Athens.... Numerous embassies came to him (Augustus at Samos, BCE. 21), and the Indians having first proclaimed a league of amity with him, obtained its ratification, and presented him, besides gifts, with tigers also—animals seen then for the first time by the Romans, and if I mistake not, even by the Greeks. They gave him also a stripling without arms (like the statues we see of Hermese), but as dexterous in using his feet as others their hands, for with them he could bend a bow, hurl a dart, and put a trumpet to his mouth. He also mentions the suicide by the envoy.[87]

It is interesting that while in certain references to the practice of sending embassies to the emperor by the rulers of alien societies are anecdotal, it is altogether empirical in certain others. For instance, there are details of gifts carried by the emissaries to the emperor in order to please and win his favour. Cassius Dio (c. 229 CE) writes:

[87] See McCrindle, *Ancient India as Described in Classical Literature*, 77–8, para. 73. See Florus, *Epitome of Roman History*, Vol. IV, 12. See McCrindle, *Ancient India as Described in Classical Literature*, 78–9. P. Orosius (c. 420 AD) is another historian who mentions the embassy that reached at the time when he was residing in the city. Since the dates do not match and the historian lacks credibility, K.A.N. Sastri rejects his account. See his *Foreign Notices of South India*, 47.

> Many embassies came to him (Augustus), and the Indians having previously proclaimed a treaty of alliance, concluded it now with the presentation, among other gifts, of tigers, animals which the Romans, and, if I mistake not, the Greeks as well, saw them for the first time ...[88]

Florus, a contemporary of Trajan (98–117 CE), says that the presents included jewels, precious stones, and elephants.[89] In fact, one would tend to ask the question as to what was the need for the rulers in the Indian subcontinent to send emissaries to the Roman emperors, since acquisition of oriental goods was the irresistible compulsion of the Graeco-Roman world. Accordingly, the merchant-mariners from there were adventurously reaching the south-western coasts of India to carry the goods catering to the high demand in the Mediterranean world. There was no reason for the regional ruling lineages to please the emperors with gifts and persuade them for the coming of the Graeco-Roman traders to the coasts. On top of it all, the regional political formations in the subcontinent were hardly evolved enough to have exchange relations with the empire diplomatically formalized.

Strabo was obviously addressing the Graeco-Roman mariners with the specific objective of providing them the benefit of first-hand information about sea routes, countries, ports, merchandise, and diplomacy, which even the experienced seafarers were not able to note down for others due to illiteracy.[90] He says:

> The merchants of the present day who sail from Egypt to India by the Nile and the Arabian Gulf have seldom made a voyage as far as the Ganges. They are ignorant men and unqualified for writing an account of the places they have visited.[91]

Written with a clear purpose and in response to the sailors' need, Strabo's accounts must have reached its primary clients. It was indeed

88 *Dio's Roman History*, Vol. IX, 73. Also see R.C. Majumdar, *The Classical Accounts of India* (repr., Calcutta: Firma KLM Private Ltd., 1981), 451–2.

89 Florus, *Epitome of Roman History*, Vol. IV, 12. The excerpt is quoted in Sastri, *Foreign Notices of South India*, 47n5.

90 Strabo, *Geography*, Book 2, 5:12.

91 Strabo, *Geography*, Book 2, 5:12.

a scholarly and methodologically refined work based on rational appraisal of works done by his predecessors:

> I must now begin with India, for it is the first and largest country that lies out towards the east ... for not only is it farthest away from us, but not many of our people have seen it; and even those who have seen it, have seen only parts of it, and the greater part of what they say is hearsay; and even what they saw they learned on a hasty passage with an army through the country. Wherefore they do not give out the same accounts of the same things, even though they have written these accounts as though their statements had been carefully confirmed. And some of them were both on the same expedition together and made their sojourns together, like those who helped Alexander to subdue Asia; yet they all frequently contradict one another. But if they differ thus about what was seen, what must we think of what they report from hearsay? Moreover, most of those who have written anything about this region in much later times, and those who sail there at the present time, do not present any accurate information either.[92]

Nonetheless, the immediate successors like Pliny the Elder or the author of *PME* or Ptolemy do not refer to his writing. It is surprising that a writer like Pliny the Elder who is well known for his thorough appraisal of previous works makes no reference to Strabo's accounts on Indian ports. Strabo's writing was largely unknown in Rome for a few centuries. Therefore, scholars think that it must have been written at Amasia, a place where his work was not quite appealing to the people. As a source material, Strabo's work has been of wider acceptance subsequently for its authenticity and credibility distinguished from the relative unreliability of predecessors like Megasthenes.

Gaius Plinius Secundus, well known as Pliny the Elder, is the next important authority on Graeco-Roman exchange contacts. His encyclopaedic *Natural History*, a huge compilation of knowledge about nature and people, running into 37 sizable volumes, prepared when he was serving as an advisor to the Emperor Vespasian around 75 CE and based on personal acquaintance with the Indian coasts, is a veritable source of information. These volumes embody bewilderingly diverse aspects, themes, anecdotes, and descriptive accounts of

[92] Strabo, *Geography*, 1–3.

the vast subject matter, besides critical appraisals of political and diplomatic significance, quite natural for an imperialist statesman like Pliny the Elder. It provides invaluable facts, relatively accurate and up-to-date, about the ports, marts, and merchandise of India's south-western and south-eastern coasts in the age of Roman Empire till the reign of Flavian. As regards the voyages to India, Pliny the Elder says:

> In after times it was considered an undeniable fact that the voyage from Sigerus, a cape in Arabia reckoned at 1335 miles, can be performed by aid of a west wind which they called Hippalus. The age that followed pointed out a shorter route that was also safer by making the voyage from the same cape to Sigerus, a seaport of India; and for a long time this route was followed until one still shorter was discovered by a merchant, and India was brought nearer through the love of gain. So then at the present day voyages are made to India every year; and companies of archers are carried on board because the Indian seas are infested by pirates ... If the wind called Hippalus be blowing, Muziris, the earliest mart of India, can be reached in forty days. It is not a desirable place of call, pirates being in the neighbourhood who occupy a place called Nitrias, and besides it is not well supplied with wares for traffic. Ships besides anchor at a great distance from the shore, and the cargoes have to be landed and shipped by employing boats. At the time I was writing this Caelobotras was the sovereign of the country. Another more convenient harbour of the nation is Neacyndon which is called Becare. There Pāndion used to reign, dwelling at a great distance from the mart, in a town in the interior of the country called Modura. The district from which pepper is carried to Becare in canoes is called Coṭṭanāra. None of these nations, ports, and cities is to be found in any of the former writers—from which it appears that the names of the places are changed. Travellers sail back from India in the beginning of the Egyptian month Mechir that is before the Ides of January. In this way they can go and return the same year. They sail from India with a south-east wind, and on entering the Red Sea catch the south-west or south.[93]

Pliny the Elder mentions three passages of chronological sequence, used by mariners suggestive of successive stages of improvement in the techniques of navigation. Earlier the route followed by the fleet of Alexander was long and time-consuming due to the coasting along

[93] McCrindle, *Ancient India as Described in Classical Literature*, 111–12.

the bay to Patala. It was found unsafe too. Thus, after a long period of experimental adventures, a better and shorter route was made possible with the introduction of sailing with the westward wind to reach the port of Sigerus on the north-western coast of the Indian subcontinent. After a long interval the shortest route across the ocean was discovered by a merchant, which turned out to be extremely profitable to the Roman Empire. There is a specific mention about the threat of pirates as a grave problem and hence soldiers from the imperial army contingent were deployed in Graeco-Roman vessels to guarantee safety. Pliny the Elder gives a clear account of the development of the routes:

> Such was the route followed by the fleet of Alexander; but subsequently it was thought that the safest line was to start from Sigerus cape (Ras Fartak) in Arabia with a west wind (the native name for which in those parts is Hippalus) and make for Patale, the distance been reckoned as 1332 miles. The following period considered it a shorter and safer route to start from the same cape and steer for the Indian harbour of Sigerus, and for a long time this was the course followed until a merchant discovered *Compendia*, and for the *lucrum* India was *admota*, indeed the voyage is made every year, with companies of archers on board, because these seas used to be very greatly infested by pirates. And it will not be amiss to set out the whole of the voyage from Egypt, now that reliable knowledge of it is for the first time accessible. It is an important subject, in view of the fact that in no year does India absorb less than fifty million sesterces of our empire's wealth, sending back merchandise to be sold to us at a hundred times its prime cost.[94]

As regards the stimulus behind the invention of better technology and the choice of passages, it has been pointed out that much more than the advantage of a short-cut or safety there is the motivation of better prospects of trade and profit.[95] For instance, the merchants taking the passage to Muziris obtained better gains that had been

[94] Pliny the Elder, *Natural History*, VI, 100–1.

[95] F. De Romanis, 'Rome and the *Nótia* of India: Relations between Rome and Southern India from 30 BC to Flavian Period', in *Crossings: Early Mediterranean Contacts with India*, eds F. De Romanis and A. Tchernia (New Delhi: Manohar Publishers and Italian Embassy Cultural Centre, 1997), 88–9.

impossible for those who sailed towards Palate or Sigerus, because the former provided goods of greater demand in Rome and of extensive distributive prospects all over Europe, which meant acquisition of huge profits. Muziris was indeed the most important centre of maritime contact during the peak phase of the Roman Empire. Pliny the Elder calls Muziris the *primum emporium Indiae*.[96]

It was not just a port of attraction for the Mediterranean traders alone but a centre of exchange for the northern Indian long-distance itinerants too, which predated the Roman period by two or three centuries. It was into this network of the Indian, Arab, and Phoenician traders that the Graeco-Roman merchants made their entry all by themselves as the consummation of Pliny the Elder's thesis of the three sequential shifts of routes over the ages.

However, Pliny the Elder is quite cynical about Muziris which, according to him, posed several problems to the merchant-mariners. First, it was not a port of attraction because of the presence of pirates in the neighbourhood at Nitrias, who were regularly plundering the ships approaching the port of Muziris. Second, the port was upstream precluding access to ships, and requiring them to anchor at a distance in the sea itself and transport cargoes by canoes with great difficulty. Due to these inconveniences, he expresses the advantages of ports like Becare and Nelcynda further south. Pliny the Elder describes it as follows:

> Coral is as highly valued among the Indians as Indian pearls. It is also found in the Red Sea, but there it is darker in colour. The most prized is found in the Gallic Gulf around the Stoechades Islands, in the Sicilian Gulf around the Aeolian Islands, and around Drepanum ... Coral berries are no less valued by Indian men than specimen Indian pearls by Roman ladies. Indian soothsayers and seers believe that coral is potent as a charm for warding off dangers. Accordingly they delight in its beauty and religious power. Before this became known, the Gauls used to decorate their swords, shields and helmets with coral. Now it is very scarce because of the price it commands, and is rarely seen in its natural habitat.[97]

[96] Pliny the Elder, *Natural History*, IV, 104.

[97] Pliny the Elder, *Natural History*, XXXII, chapters 21 and 23 quoted in J.F. Healy, *Pliny the Elder, Natural History: A Selection* (London: Penguin Classics, 1991), 281.

Pliny the Elder was critical of the craze of contemporary Roman aristocracy for the expensive goods from the East, for it had been draining a lot of gold and silver out of the empire. He estimated the annual value of Graeco-Roman trade with the east, especially India, as 100 million sesterces, which has often been thought to be an exaggeration in terms of coinage. This need not have been an exaggeration, for the demand for luxury goods of the East, the Chinese silk, and the Indian spices were in great demand in the West. Pliny the Elder observes:

> India, China and the Arabian Peninsula take one hundred million sesterces from our empire per annum at a conservative estimate: that is what our luxuries and women cost us. For what percentage of these imports is intended for sacrifices to the gods or the spirits of the dead?[98]

Obviously it is the total value rather than mere aggregation of the annual currency influx that his assessment reflects and in that sense the estimate appears to be quite reasonable. Indeed, Pliny the Elder was seriously critical of the Roman extravagance, especially of the aristocratic women whose craze for luxury had caused the drain of gold. Nonetheless, the value involved in trade was enormous as the case illustration given below endorses:

> For example, just one documented consignment from Muziris to Alexandria consisted of 700–1,700 pounds of nard (an aromatic balsam), over 4,700 pounds of ivory and almost 790 pounds of textiles. This has been calculated as worth a total value of 131 talents, enough to purchase 2,400 acres of the best farmland in Egypt. When it is borne in mind that an average Roman cargo ship would have held about 150 such consignments, Pliny's figure becomes entirely plausible. With such staggering profits it is little wonder that the Roman government in Egypt encouraged—and profited by!—the trade: a 25 per cent tax on all goods from India was levied by the Romans at the Red Sea port of Leuce Come.[99]

Pliny the Elder has given certain valuable observations about Taprobane. He says that gold and silver were held in high esteem in

[98] Pliny the Elder, *Natural History*, VI, 104.

[99] W. Ball, *Rome in the East: The Transformation of an Empire* (London and New York: Routledge, 2000), 123.

Taprobane. Likewise, pearls and precious stones were held in high honour too.[100] Speaking about the people of the island, Pliny the Elder says that the people had no courts of law and hence no litigation. He mentions about the arrival of ambassadors from there to the court of the Emperor Claudius and the way the mariners from Limyrike made their voyages to the coast of the island:

> Pliny mentions the embassy from Ceylon (Taprobane): '... in the reign of the Emperor Claudius ambassadors came to his court there from (Ceylon) ... The king (of Ceylon) particularly admired the Romans and their emperor as men possessed of an heard-of love of justice, when he found that among the money taken from the captive (a Roman revenue collector carried away by the gales of wind on his way from Arabia and wafted to Hippuri, a port of Taprobane, where he was humanely received) the denarii were all of equal weight although the different images stamped on them showed that they had been coined in the reigns of several emperors. This influenced him most of all to seek an alliance with the Romans, and he accordingly dispatched to Rome four ambassadors, of whom the chief was Rachia (Rajah).'[101]

It is said that the seafarers of Sri Lanka did not depend on the observation of stars to make sense of the direction in the sea to navigate to their destination. Maybe, it was due to the fact that the Great Bear was not visible to them. A technique widely used by them to identify the shore was keeping enough birds on board and letting each one fly away at spots in the sea where they required the way to the shore. They made their way by following the direction of the bird's flight. It appears that they were not used to sea voyages during the monsoon when the sea was rough, presupposing the fact that they had not evolved the appropriate naval technology for sailing in the outer sea. Virtually, they were active in the sea only during the seven months of summer. Pliny the Elder observes:

> In making sea-voyages, the Taprobane mariners make no observations of the stars, and indeed the Greater Bear is not visible to them, but they

100 Sastri, *Foreign Notices of South India*, 51.

101 Pliny the Elder, *Natural History*, 104. Also Sastri, *Foreign Notices of South India*, 50.

> take birds out to sea with them which they let loose from time to time and follow the direction of their flight as they make for land. The season for navigation is limited to four months, and they particularly shun the sea during the hundred days which succeed the summer solstice, for it is then winter in those seas.[102]

Of all the Graeco-Roman accounts, *PME*, a seafarers' manual of practical information packed into 66 short notes written by an unknown Greek mariner from Egypt, is the most significant source, distinct for the continuous and sequential description of overseas routes to and ports in the Gulf of Aden, the Persian Gulf, and the Indian Ocean. These oceanic regions were collectively called the Erythraean Sea in those days. It is the only work of its kind which has survived to the present. This rare account is now reliably dated to between 40 and 70 CE.[103] It is an account based on firsthand knowledge about overseas routes, landmarks, hazards, threats, ports, marts, merchandise, peoples, and ruling powers in each region. A set of practical information very useful for the merchant-mariners, it embodies crucial pieces of information relating to what items of goods are available at which mart, where, when, and under what conditions. It contains a table of seasons appropriate for ships to sail from Myos Hormos to the different ports on the Red Sea as well as the Indian Ocean. Most probably, the author of *PME* might have been a merchant-mariner well-versed in sailing between Myos Hormos on the coast of the Red Sea and Sopatma on the coast of the southern Bay of Bengal via the coast of north-western India from Barygaza on the Gulf of Cambay through the ports on the south-western coast down to the Cape and beyond along the ports on the south-eastern coast as well as Taprobane.

PME mentions the discovery of the monsoon wind by a sea captain named Hippalus, which obviously refers to the popularity of the dependence on the monsoon winds. It is clear that from the time of Emperor Augustus onwards, the sailors are mentioned to have been depending on the monsoon winds regularly for trans-oceanic

[102] Pliny the Elder, *Natural History*, VI, 104, trans. H. Rackham (Cambridge: Harvard University Press), 1938–63.

[103] G. Fussman, 'Le Periple et l'histoire politique del'Inde', *Journal Asiatique* (Paris) 279, no. 3/4 (1991): 37–8.

voyages towards the ports on the Indian west coast, as encouraged by the safety of sail and certainty of destination. We are made to believe that before the discovery of the use of the monsoon winds for sea voyages from Egypt to the coast of India, only about twenty ships could travel, for there was no certainty about when they would reach their destination and complete their journey back. Once the Winds became known, many ships could make their seasonal trips to the whole of the western coast of India.[104] As the author of *PME* says:

> The whole voyage ... from Cana and Eudaemon Arabia, they used to make in small vessels, sailing close around the shores of the gulfs; and Hippalus was the pilot who by observing the location of the ports and the conditions of the sea, first discovered.[105]

In ancient times mariners used to cover the whole distance from Cane to the eastern world in small vessels, coasting along the bays. A change in this began with the discovery of the possibility of utilizing the monsoon winds to reach the ports of the Indian subcontinent through a route far away from the coast and right across the Indian Ocean. This discovery is traditionally attributed to the Greek navigator Hippalus who had considerable experience in sea voyages and knowledge about the location of ports on the north-western coasts of the Indian subcontinent. It became common for the mariners to sail utilizing the south-west monsoon from the Gulf of Aden, to the north-western as well as the south-western coasts of the Indian subcontinent. *PME* provides a vivid account of this:

> This whole coastal route just described, from Cane and Arabia Felix, men formerly used to sail over in smaller vessels, following the curves of the bays. The ship captain Hippalus, by plotting the location of the ports of trade and the configuration of the sea, was the first to discover the route over open water ... In this locale the winds we call 'etesian'

[104] M. Carey and E.H. Warmington, *The Ancient Explorers* (Harmondsworth, Middlesex: Penguin Books Ltd., 1963), 73–7. Also see notes in Sastri, *Foreign Notices in South India*, 6.

[105] *PME*, 57. K.A.N. Sastri observes that Indian sailors must have known and used the monsoon wind much earlier than c. 45 CE, the date of Hippalus discovery. See Sastri, *Foreign Notices of South India*, 52–3.

> blow seasonally from the direction of the ocean, and so a south-westerly makes its appearance in the Indian Sea, but it is called after the name of him who first discovered the way across. Because of this, right up to the present, some leave directly from Cane and some from the Cape of Spices, and whoever are bound for Limyrike hold out with the wind on the quarter for most of the way, but whoever are bound for Barygaza and whoever for Scythis only for three days and no more, and, (carried along) the rest of the run on their own proper course, away from the shore on the high seas, over the (ocean) off the land, they bypass the aforementioned bays.[106]

PME then describes the sea route to the port of Barygaza, situated at the mouth of the Narmada River, the gateway to the other ports of Limyrike rich in pepper, cotton, and beryl. It is clear from the description that all these merchandises of the western coast of India were available in the port of Barygaza brought obviously by the coastal and inland traders, probably a practice continuing from the period prior to the arrival of the Graeco-Roman ships. There is a meticulous characterization of the entry track to the Scythian port called Barbarikon at the mouth of the Indus River distinct for its vast estuary. It has been observed:

> The northern seaboard of Scythia is very flat and through it flows the Indus, the mightiest of all the rivers along the Indian Ocean. It empties such a great volume of water into the sea that from far off—even before you reach land—you meet its lightly coloured waters. Those coming from the sea know that they are approaching the land near the river because of the eels emerging from the depths.[107]

PME gives an account in detail about the sea route to the many ports on the Indian west coast from Barbarikon at the mouth of the Indus down to Barygaza at the mouth of Narmada in the Gulf of Cambay and the south and south-east of the peninsula including Sri Lanka and right up to Sopatma, at the mouth of the Palar River in

[106] See the passage translated in L. Casson, 'The Sea Route to India: Periplus Maris Erythraei 57', *The Classical Quarterly*, n.s., 34, no. 2 (1984): 473–9.

[107] *PME*, 38.

the Chingelpet district in Tamil Nadu. It just mentions the route to further east till the mouth of the Ganges, but without details about ports, their countries, and the rulers. *PME* starts with a description of the sea route:

> Beyond the river Sinthus there is another gulf, not navigable, running in toward the north; it is called Eirinon; its parts are called separately the small gulf and the great; in both parts the water is shallow, with shifting sandbanks occurring continually and a great way from shore; so that very often when the shore is not even in sight, ships run aground, and if they attempt to hold their course they are wrecked. A promontory stands out from this gulf, curving around from Eirinon toward the East, then South, then West, and enclosing the gulf called Baraca, which contains seven islands. Those who come to the entrance of this bay escape it by putting about a little and standing further out to sea; but those who are drawn inside into the gulf of Baraca are lost; for the waves are high and very violent, and the sea is tumultuous and foul, and has eddies and rushing whirlpools. The bottom is in some places abrupt, and in others rocky and sharp, so that the anchors lying there are parted, some being quickly cut off, and others chafing on the bottom. As a sign of these places to those approaching from the sea there are serpents, very large and black; for at the other places on this coast and around Barygaza, they are smaller, and in colour bright green, running into gold.[108]

It must have been a very ancient port where the Egyptian and Arab vessels voyaging through the coasting route must have anchored for bartering their goods, the overland merchants bringing cargoes from India and China. Mediterranean ships had moored at Barbarikon for the same reason. *PME* continues the description of the route to Barygaza and beyond:

> Beyond the gulf of Baraca is that of Barygaza and the coast of the country of Ariaca, which is the beginning of the Kingdom of Nambanus and of all India. That part of it lying inland and adjoining Scythia is called Abiria, but the coast is called Syrastrene. It is a fertile country, yielding wheat and rice and sesame oil and clarified butter, cotton and the Indian cloths made there-from, of the coarser sorts. Very many cattle

108 *PME*, 40.

are pastured there, and the men are of great stature and black in colour. The metropolis of this country is Minnagara, from which much cotton cloth is brought down to Barygaza. In these places there remain even to the present time signs of the expedition of Alexander, such as ancient shrines, walls of forts and great wells. The sailing course along this coast, from Barbaricum to the promontory called Papica opposite Barygaza, and before Astacampra, is of three thousand stadia.[109]

PME gives a description of the heavy tides against the river flow, pushing sea water upstream, which makes the entry and exit of ships to the port extremely risky for the inexperienced sailors who arrive for the first time. Sailing to this port has been depicted as an extremely risky adventure, due to the most inhospitable characteristics of the sea. Due to the high-speed tidal current and flood, the vessels cannot easily enter or exit the bay. It is a markedly dangerous port to the inexperienced, for the irresistible rush of the tidal flow can divest the vessels of their direction, drag them into shoals or even capsize and wreck:

> For this reason entrance and departure of vessels is very dangerous to those who are inexperienced or who come to this port for the first time. For the rush of waters at the incoming tide is irresistible, and the anchors cannot hold against it; so that large ships are caught up by the force of it, turned broadside on through the speed of the current, and so driven on the shoals and wrecked; and smaller boats are overturned; and those that have been turned aside among the channels by the receding waters at the ebb, are left on their sides, and if not held on an even keel by props, the flood comes upon them suddenly and under the first head of the current they are filled with water. For there is so great force in the rush of the sea at the new moon, especially during the flood tide at night, that if you begin the entrance at the moment when the waters are still, on the instant there is borne to you at the mouth of the river, a noise like the cries of an army heard from afar; and very soon the sea itself comes rushing in over the shoals with a hoarse roar.[110]

A fairly thorough description of the surrounding landscape of gulfs and promontories is given as a broad background necessary for

[109] *PME*, 41.
[110] *PME*, 46.

the precise location of Barygaza that situated beyond a gulf and at the mouth of the Narmada River. What any sailor heading for Barygaza had to be aware of the gulf, its width, and navigability is beautifully portrayed in *PME* that shows how formidable a threat the Gulf of Cambay was to the Graeco-Roman sailors in those days:

> Beyond this there is another gulf exposed to the sea-waves, running up toward the north, at the mouth of which there is an island called Baeones; at its innermost part there is a great river called Mais. Those sailing to Barygaza pass across this gulf, which is three hundred stadia in width, leaving behind to their left the island just visible from their tops toward the east, straight to the very mouth of the river of Barygaza; and this river is called Nammadus.[111]

Observations in the *PME* are very sharp and often amazingly knowledgeable and precise as exemplified by the description of the features of the landscape, fertility of the soil, pattern of land-use, crops, and other resources of the region. It is interesting that the vestiges of Alexander's invasion in the form of Macedonian shrines, forts, and wells are noticed and commented on. Mentioning the distance from the port of Barbarikon to Barygaza, the focus shifts to the narrow and hazardous gulf of Barygaza and the eluding mouth of the river which makes access to the port extremely difficult:

> This gulf is very narrow to Barygaza and very hard to navigate for those coming from the ocean; this is the case with both the right and left passages, but there is a better passage through the left. For on the right at the very mouth of the gulf there lies a shoal, long and narrow, and full of rocks, called Herone, facing the village of Cammoni; and opposite this on the left projects the promontory that lies before Astacampra, which is called Papica, and is a bad anchorage because of the strong current setting in around it and because the anchors are cut off, the bottom being rough and rocky. And even if the entrance to the gulf is made safely, the mouth of the river at Barygaza is found with difficulty, because the shore is very low and cannot be made out until you are close upon it. And when, you have found it the passage is difficult because of the shoals at the mouth of the river.[112]

[111] *PME*, 42.
[112] *PME*, 43.

Since it was such a difficult port for any mariner to enter, the local ruler is said to have deployed local fishermen at the very entrance with large boats called *Tappaga* and *Cotymba*, who were to go up to Syrastrene and pilot the foreign vessels to Barygaza. This guidance had enabled them to safely reach the mouth of the bay and proceed to the deep basins and dock at the port. *PME* gives a meticulous description of this procedure in detail:

> Because of this, native fishermen in the King's service, stationed at the very entrance in well-manned large boats called tappaga and cotymba, go up the coast as far as Syrastrene, from which they pilot vessels to Barygaza. And they steer them straight from the mouth of the bay between the shoals with their crews; and they tow them to fixed stations, going up with the beginning of the flood, and lying through the ebb at anchorages and in basins. These basins are deeper places in the river as far as Barygaza; which lies by the river, about three hundred stadia up from the mouth.[113]

Descriptions of the shore, the interior, and the neighbourhood in terms of inhabitants, their rulers, strategic importance of the port, its historical indicators like inscriptions, and material remains of the Macedonian kings who reigned after Alexander are given. It is quite surprising to note how knowledgeable this unknown sailor was and how careful he was in noting down his knowledge as well as experience with an astounding brevity and precision:

> The country inland from Barygaza is inhabited by numerous tribes, such as the Arattii, the Arachosii, the Gandaraei and the people of Poclais, in which is Bucephalus Alexandria. Above these is the very warlike nation of the Bactrians, who are under their own king. And Alexander, setting out from these parts, penetrated to the Ganges, leaving aside Limyrike and the southern part of India; and to the present day ancient drachmae are current in Barygaza, coming from this country, bearing inscriptions in Greek letters, and the devices of those who reigned after Alexander, Apollodorus and Menander.[114]

[113] *PME*, 44.
[114] *PME*, 47.

Before recounting the goods available at the port, the nature and history of the inland from where the resources that ensured the prosperity of the port arrived is indicated. Then the goods of the merchant-mariners' attraction such as agate, carnelian, muslin, ordinary cotton cloth, and spikenard, which the port provides, are enlisted. It is obvious that several goods were brought to the port by the overland caravan troupes even from far-off places:

> Inland from this place and to the east, is the city called Ozene, formerly a royal capital; from this place are brought down all things needed for the welfare of the country about Barygaza, and many things for our trade: agate and carnelian, Indian muslins and mallow cloth, and much ordinary cloth. Through this same region and from the upper country is brought the spikenard that comes through Poclais; that is, the Caspapyrene and Paropanisene and Cabolitic and that brought through the adjoining country of Scythia; also costus and bdellium.[115]

PME, after describing the ports of Barygaza and Sopara as the gateway to the ports of the west coast of India, turns to the ports and marts of Limyrike, about which it provides information regarding sea routes, landmarks, geographical location, countries, rulers, and merchandise. It is with the location of Naura and Tyndis as the first ports of Limyrike that the description of Limyrike begins and passes on to the characterization of the importance of Muziris and Nelcynda. Tyndis, situated in a village just facing the sea, is mentioned as a port under the Cēra rulers. Muziris, on a river distant from Tyndis, is another port under the Cēras, and is mentioned to have been thronged by ships with cargoes from Arabia and the Mediterranean. Similarly, Nelcynda, situated on a river far away from Muziris, is mentioned as a port under the Pāṇḍya rulers, stationed in the interior. Another port located in the village of Bacare on a river, not quite far from Nelcynda, is mentioned to have been touched by ships sailing outwards from the latter and anchored off-shore to load the cargoes, due to the impediments of shoals in the river:

> ... Naura and Tyndis as the first ports of Limyrike, and Mouzeris and Nelcynda of leading importance. Tyndis is of the kingdom of

115 *PME*, 48.

> Cerabotros; it is a village in plain sight by the sea. Mouzeris of the same kingdom, abounds in ships sent there with cargoes from Arabia, and by the Greeks; it is located on a river, distant from Tyndis by river and sea five hundred stadia. Nelcynda is distant from Muziris by river and sea by about five hundred stadia, and is of another kingdom, the Pandian. This place is also situated on a river, about one hundred and twenty stadia from the sea ... There is another place at the mouth of this river, the village of Bacare; to which; ships drop down on the outward voyage from Nelcynda, and anchor in the roadstead to take on their cargoes; because the river is full of shoals and the channels are not clear. The king of both these market-towns live in the interior.[116]

Graeco-Romans sailed directly to these ports, lured by the huge quantity of pepper and malabathrum. They were able to barter a great quantity of gold coins, topaz, some thin clothing, figured linens, antimony, coral, crude glass, copper, tin, lead, realgar, and orpiment. *PME* makes it clear that these ships had carried enough wheat for the use of the sailors, for this staple grain of theirs was not available in these ports. It is noted that pepper available in these ports was produced in great quantity solely in a region called Coṭṭonāra, probably the present Kottanad in the interior of Thiruvalla. Other precious goods such as fine pearls, ivory, silk cloth, malabathrum, gems of all kinds like diamonds and sapphires, tortoise-shell, and spikenard were available at these Pāṇḍya ports. Excepting goods like pepper, ivory, malabathrum, and gems, other items were brought by overland merchants from distant places. *PME* specifically mentions that spikenard reached the port from the Ganges and tortoise-shell from Chryse Island, obviously through the sailors coasting between the Ganges bay and the Coromandel ports:

> They send large ships to these ports on account of the great quantity and bulk of pepper and malabathrum. There are imported here, in the first place, a great quantity of coin; topaz, thin clothing, not much; figured linens, antimony, coral, crude glass, copper, tin, lead; wine not much, but as much as at Barygaza, realgar and orpiment; and wheat enough for the sailors, for this is not dealt in by the merchants there. There is exported pepper, which is produced in quantity in only one region

116 *PME*, 53–4.

> near these markets, a district called Cottonara. Besides this there are exported great quantities of fine pearls, ivory, silk cloth, spikenard from the Ganges, malabathrum from the places in the interior, transparent stones of all kinds, diamonds, and sapphires and tortoise-shell; that from Chryse Island, and that taken among the islands along the coast of Limyrike. They make the voyage to this place in a favourable season who set out from Egypt about the month of July that is Epiphi.[117]

There are some differences in the translation of the passage by W.H. Schoff. For instance, when the goods are brought by the foreign ships to Limyrike, there is a mention about certain items of gifts like vessels of silver, singing boys, beautiful maidens, fine wines, thin clothing of the finest weaves, and the choicest orpiment brought for the king.[118] *PME* continues the description of the places towards the south beyond the port of Bacare, by identifying the Dark Red Mountain as the main landmark, belonging to the land stretching along the coast called Paralia. This could be most probably the Varkala cliff jutting out into the sea, as already proposed and accepted by most historians.[119] It is mentioned that the place has a fine port, Balita, in a village by the shore. Further south is a port called Comari, the cape, known as a cult spot and site of ritual importance:

> Beyond Bacare, there is the Dark Red Mountain, and another district stretching along the coast toward the south, called Paralia. The first place is called Balita; it has a fine harbor and a village by the shore. Beyond this there is another place called Comari, at which are the cape of Comari and a harbor; hither come those men who wish to consecrate themselves for the rest of their lives, and bathe and dwell in celibacy; and women also do the same, for it is told that a goddess once dwelt there and bathed.[120]

PME describes the places further south beyond Comeri where the region extends to another port, namely Colchis (Korkai) in the Pāṇḍya country, famous for the pearl fisheries worked by the captives. From

117 *PME*, 56.
118 Schoff, *The Periplus of the Erythraean Sea*, 40–66.
119 Sastri, *Foreign Notices of South India*, 59n39.
120 *PME*, 58.

there a sailor should cross the Gulf of Mannar to proceed further and reach an inland place called Argaru, famous for a fine variety of muslin, namely Argaritic:

> From Comeri toward the south this region extends to Colchis, where the pearl fisheries are; (they are worked by condemned criminals); and it belongs to the Pandian kingdom. Beyond Colchis there follows another district called the Coast Country, which lies on a bay, and has a region inland called Argaru. At this place, and nowhere else, are brought the pearls gathered on the coast thereabouts; and from there are exported muslins, those called Argaritic.[121]

There is a description in *PME* about Indian coastal sailors servicing from Sopatma in the south to the Gangetic bay and to the island of Chryse, whose vessels *Sangaram* as well as *Colandia* transported goods of the Gangetic region and Chryse respectively. These vessels carried cargoes from Limyrike, which included goods of the region as well as most things brought there by overseas merchants. It appears that the author of *PME* had probably no first-hand information about the eastern ports of India.[122] In fact, the Graeco-Roman ships generally did not sail beyond Sopatma, for it was difficult for overseas vessels to negotiate the shallow stretch between Sri Lanka and the Tamil coast and the alternative route around the island was quite a distance. It was unnecessary too since the Indian beach-combing sailors as well as long-distance inland traders were ensuring systematic supply of goods from the Gangetic region and the island of Chryse. If this facility had not been there, the Graeco-Roman sailors might have travelled all the way right up to the Ganges bay and Chryse Island but taking the risk of missing the seasonal wind for sailing back to Egypt.[123] A passage in *PME* is quite illustrative of the process of the movement of goods from the north-east to the south:

> Among the market-towns of these countries and harbours where the ships put in from Limyrike and from the north, the most important

121 *PME*, 59.

122 L. Casson, *The Periplus Maris Erythraei: Text With Introduction, Translation, and Commentary* (Princeton: Princeton University Press, 1989), 47.

123 Casson, *The Periplus Maris Erythraei*, 24, 83, 89.

> are, in order as they lie, first Camara Kaveri, then Poduca (it should be Aricamedu, Sastri suspects it to be Pondicherry), then Sopatma; in which there are ships of the country coasting along the shore as far as Limyrike; and other very large vessels made of single logs bound together, called *sangara*; but those which make the voyage to Chryse and to the Ganges are called colandia, and are very large. There are imported into these places everything made in Limyrike, and the greatest part of what is brought at any time from Egypt comes here, together with most kinds of all the things that are brought from Limyrike and of those that are carried through Paralia.[124]

It appears that the coasting along the Bay of Bengal was more or less the monopoly of the Indian vessels that were on sail throughout the year, thanks to the winds of a flexible type quite favourable to the voyages in different directions.

Then there is mention of Taprobane, rich in pearls, transparent stones, muslin, and tortoise-shell. Aelian identifies the Indian pearls as the best sort of pearls along with those from the Red Sea. The *Periplus* refers to 'those sailing out of "Limrike"' to Soqotra with rice, cloth, slaves, etc.'[125] Both Pliny the Elder and the author of *PME* knew nothing of the Far East; the merchants who frequented Barygaza and Muziris in their time knew little of the eastern navigation beyond India and they were still inquiring if Taprobane was an island or a continent communicating with Africa.

Claudius Ptolemy's *Geography* (139 CE) which comes next in the chronological order is a treatise on scientific cartography supplemented by a long list of important place names and coordinates. He gives no historical or political account of the places mapped by him, but for the brief notes here and there, which he owed to Marinos of Tyre, a knowledgeable contemporary of his times. It appears that Ptolemy makes a differentiation of places in terms of categories such as village, emporium, city and metropolis, albeit without any clear definition of each. He has referred to major ports like Muziris on the south-western coast and Korkai on the south-eastern coast as emporia. Khaberis (Kaveripattinam) is mentioned as a city or metropolis. His

124 *PME*, 60.

125 *PME*, 30–1. For details, see Casson, *The Periplus Maris Erythraei*.

mapping, as in the case of other contemporary geographers, seems to have failed to capture the peninsular shape of southern India, which he took to be a flat coast. In spite of such geo-morphological inaccuracies, Ptolemy's *Geography* is an invaluable source for the study of maritime history.

Ptolemy mentions Tyndis 116° 14° 10`, Bramagara 116° 45` 16°, Kalaikaris 116° 20` 14°, and Muziris 117° 50` 14° as ports of Limyrike. Ptolemy says that it was situated at the beginning point of Limyrike. After Ptolemy's attempt to put into scientific form the records and personal impressions of a number of merchants, travellers, and others of his time, there followed a long period without original observation or authorship—a period of copying, compilation, and imitation.[126]

Life of Appollonius of Tynana, a work on a charismatic teacher and miracle performer of the 1st century CE, by Philostratus (c. 170 CE–c. 247 CE), a Sophist, is an important source of information on the Graeco-Roman overseas exchange.[127] The work provides interesting details about contemporary trading vessels, their size, nature of the sail, the height of the mast, the capacity of the hull, the personnel who were on board, and so on. It describes the composition of the travellers in a Graeco-Roman vessel bound for the Indian ports. Philostratus quotes an Indian sailor who makes a comparative statement:

> The Egyptians construct ships for our ocean and they send them to sea to exchange Egyptian goods for Indian wares ... The Egyptians build these ships on a scale whereby one their vessels is equivalent in size to several of those used by the other races ... The rib the sides of the ship with bolts to hold the vessel together, and they raise its bulwarks and its mast to a great height, and they construct several compartments on the timber beams which run across the vessel.... They (Roman businessmen) set several pilots onboard the ship and subordinated them to the oldest and wisest man. They also post several officers on the prow and set skilled sailors to man the rigging.[128]

[126] Schoff, *Periplus of the Outer Sea*, 6. Also see Sastri, *Foreign Notices of South India*, 8.

[127] Philostratus, *Life of Appollonius of Tyana*, trans. F.C. Conybeare (London: William Heinemann, Loeb Classical Library, 1912), Book 3, p. 35.

[128] Philostratus, *Life of Appollonius of Tyana*, Book 3, p. 35.

Peutinger Table is another interesting source of information, the date of which is not quite certain but generally regarded as a work of c. 300 CE, which has survived in the form of a medieval copy. It provides us a cartographic representation of how ancient Graeco-Romans had conceived their trading world and the major overland routes, ports, overseas settlements, and other contact points. There is the 'Indis' region demarcated as the terminal segment of the *Table*. What has often been widely cited is the location of a temple of Augustus at Muziris. It is a huge diagrammatic map in colour on a parchment scroll of 3/4m × 7m which, of course, has no morphological correspondence to the real geography, for its cartographic perception of the landscape and the coastline is linear. Although a map of its own scale and dimension, but in fact a seriously prepared functional instrument of ancient journey designers and managers, the *Table* must have certainly made sense to contemporary users. As a source material, it is, indeed, a significant document.

A few Chinese writings of the 5th century CE representing the ancient conditions of the Mediterranean and Central Asian regions based on the records of the Han regime of the late 1st century CE give a reliable account of the Graeco-Roman contacts with China and the various Roman goods they exchanged with each other through the overland as well as overseas merchants. *Hou Hanshu*, recounting the later Han histories, which is the most important of such writings, has a chapter on 'the Western Regions'. Similarly, a 3rd century CE work, *Weilue* by Yu Huan, recounting the history of the Wei dynasty based on records dating between 116 CE and 165 CE, has a chapter on 'the people of the West', containing valuable information about the transactional relations between the two civilizations.

Ancient Tamil Poetic Anthologies

The earliest reliable literary reference to the trade goods of southern India is found in the *Arthaśāstra*. It mentions *pāndyakavāṭakam*, a variety of pearl, and *māduram*, a variety of muslin fabric, showing that both pearl fishing and cotton manufacturing were prosperous in the Pāṇḍya country. Ancient Tamil poetic anthologies, *Eṭṭuttokai* and *Pattuppāṭṭu*, popularly called the Cankam literature, constitute the richest literary source for understanding the socio-economic life of the Deep South.

Certain specific references to Yavana (Graeco-Roman) ships in the context of spice trade seen in a few poems have encouraged historians to imagine a glorious epoch of overseas transactions.[129]

It is now well known that episodes poetized in this class of ancient Tamil literature cannot be paraphrased as historical events, for it largely belongs to the genre of oral compositions noted for their uniformities, recurrences, regularities, stylized articulation, unconscious meanings, stock expressions, and stereotypes.[130] Moreover, it is well-established today that the poems are not contemporaneous to 'the academy of poets' (Cankam), which is believed to have undertaken the task of redaction and classification of the corpus in the present form. There is time lag of a few centuries between the composition and the compilation, the former taking place over a couple of centuries towards the end of the 1st millennium BCE down to two or three centuries CE and the latter taking place by about the mid-1st millennium CE. It has been detected that a few poems were composed and added to the old corpus at the time of redaction and classification of the verses in terms of their thematic or stylistic grouping at a later period. All this has made the period of the anthologies a big chronological mesh. Of the extant corpus of anthologies, the *Eṭṭuttokai* collection excluding *Kalittokai* and *Paripāṭal* is considered to be the

[129] References in ancient Tamil poems are very few and quite incidental. *Patirruppattu* 2nd Ten (*pattu*), 10th poem, lines: 1–3 refers to ship sailing for acquiring gold. For the original text and commentary, see A.D. Pillai, ed., *Patirruppattu* (Tirunelveli: The South India Saiva Siddhantha Works Publishing Society Ltd, 1949). *Puṛanāṉūṛu* 66:1–2 addresses Karikāl Peruvaḷattān Cōḻa as born in the lineage of the one who controlled the wind and set the ships on the vast ocean for sail. *Puṛanāṉūṛu* 126:14–16 refers to the inability of others to enter the western sea where the Cēra led his gold-giving ship. *Puṛanāṉūṛu* 343:4–6 mentions those bringing ashore in boats the gifts of gold given by the ships. For the text and commentary, see U.V.S. Iyar, ed., *Puṛanāṉūṛu*, with old commentary, 6th ed. (Madras: Thyagarajavilasam Publications, 1963). *Akanāṉūṛu*, 149:9–1 mentions the Yavana ships coming with gold and returning with loads of pepper and *Akanāṉūṛu* 152:5–7 mentions the ships of Tittan Veḷiyan bringing gold. For the text and commentary, see N.M.V. Nattar, ed., *Akanāṉūṛu*, Vol. 2 (Tirunelveli: The South India Saiva Siddhantha Works Publishing Society Ltd, 1950).

[130] See Kailasapathy, *Tamil Heroic Poetry* (Oxford: Clarendon Press, 1968).

most archaic, containing poems belonging to the period between the 3rd century BCE and 3rd century CE. Even in these anthologies embodying archaic poems, there are later compositions. Poems in the *Pattuppāṭṭu* collection are considered to be later than the *Eṭṭuttokai* collection. *Tolkkāppiyam*, which the traditional scholars ascribe to the 2nd century, is assigned roughly to the 5th–6th centuries by recent studies.

As a category of source material, the ancient Tamil literature thus poses certain serious problems other than its confused chronology. One is that it consists of heroic poems, the limitations of which are obvious as far as the purpose of historical reconstruction is concerned. So the use of this category of literature as source material has to be preceded by a series of rigorous methodological exercises of textual analysis starting from the syntagmatic analysis of the poems to their paradigmatic, psychoanalytical, and semiological analyses for grasping the techniques of versification as well as the genuine meaning often hidden below the apparent. A typical example is that of the *makaṭpārkāñcitturai* category of verses. Any poem in this category praises a chief by glorifying his daughter beautiful enough to attract many heroic chieftains including the three major ruling lineages (Cēra, Pāṇḍya, and Cōḻa). As part of the technique of versification, such poems allude to the arrival of all these heroes to marry her, making a battle among them imminent to the misfortune of the place, its people, and richness. What courses through the poem is this stock theme. If a historian goes about paraphrasing the ostensible, it ends up with an utterly wrong generalization.

Further the text, sub-text, hyper-text, and context of the poems have to be analysed before attaching referential significance to them. Usually, the corpus of Cankam literature is used for historical writing with little thought on its uncertain chronology and anthological nature comprising poems of disparate periods. It is significant to use this category of source very cautiously and with the help of all the available analyses of the structure, composition, and chronology of the productions classed under it.

There are a few direct references to some of the ports of the southwestern coast, such as Tondi and Muciṛi. *Akanāṉūṟu* (60:7), *Naṟṟiṇai* (8:9), and *Kuṟumtokai* (128:2) refer to *tin tēr poṟaiyan tonḍi* (Tonḍi of Poṟaiyan with the chariot). Likewise, *Akanāṉūṟu* (178:2–3) mentions *cenkōr kuṭṭuvan tonḍi* (Tonḍi of Kuṭṭuvan with sceptre) and *Akanānūṛu* (290:12–13), *virar pork-kuṭṭuvan ten tirḍip-parappin tondi munturai* (heroic fighter Kuṭṭuvan's Tonḍi of the expanse of sea waves). Tonḍi figures in a poem in *Puṛanānūṛu* (17:9–13), an ancient Tamil anthology, as meaning 'a landscape noted for groves of coconut palms bent due to heavy bunches of coconuts, wide paddy-fields fenced by mountains, moonlight like sand, extensive sea-shore and the inland water-body with fire-red flowers'.[131]

Kulaiyiṛainciya kōṭṭāḻai
Akalvayan malaivēli
Nilavu maṇal viyan kanar-
Renkaḻimicaiccutarppūvin
Tanṭonṭiyōraṭuporuna

Similarly, Muciṛi is mentioned in a poem of *Puṛanānūṛu* (343: 1–10), alluding to the bustling activities of exchange in the port:

mīnoṭuttu nelkuvai
Micai ampiyin manai maṛukkuntu
Manaik kuvai kaṛi mūṭaiyār
Kalic cummaiya karai kalakkuṛuntu
Kalam tanta por paricam
Kaḻittōṇiyār karai cērkkuntu
Malaittāramum kaṭattāramum
Talaip peytu varunarkkīiyum
Punanalam kaḷḷin polantōrk-kuṭṭuvan
Muḻanku kaṭal muḻavin muciṛiyanna

It alludes to the goods of the mountain and the goods of the sea, gifts of gold brought in by the ships, fishermen's boats with heaps of paddy, houses with pepper sacks piled up in the courtyard. In short, they all signify the riches of Muciṛi where the boat brings ashore the gold arrived in ships. By referring to the paddy heaped in the fishermen's boat looking like a small house and to a house with pepper sacks piled up looking like a ship, the prosperity of Muciṛi is signified. Similarly, the mention of toddy-rich Muciṛi owned by the Kuṭṭuvan

131 *Puṛanānūṛu*, 17:9–13.

Cēra with a gold chain, and the benevolence of the chieftain explicit in his act of giving gifts, the affluence of the land based on the resources from the hill and those from the sea is signified. It is important to be aware of the context of the poetic allusion, which seeks just to convey that the chieftain eulogized in the poem would give his daughter in marriage to none other than a great hero, even if the entire riches of Muziris are given.

A short poem praises Karikār Peruvaḷattān, a Cōḻa chieftain, to have belonged to the lineage of great navigational tradition. It mentions that the chieftain hails from the lineage of those mighty warrior chiefs who could command the wind to move the battleships hung in the sea wanting wind power:[132]

naliyirumunnīr nāvāyōṭṭi
Vaḻitoḻilānṭavuravōn maruka
Kaḷiyiyal yānai karikāl vaḷava

Literally, it only means that the chieftain belongs to the line of great naval fighters capable of commanding the wind to blow when the ship is halted in the sea, wanting the wind for it to move. Historians have elaborated upon this assuming the chieftains to be knowledgeable about the seasonal winds and skilful in utilizing them for overseas voyages. They have taken the passage as strong evidence of the Tamil chieftains' role in the conduct of transmarine commerce. There is an interesting incidental allusion to a Cēra chieftain's western sea with gold-yielding ship in a poem eulogizing Malayamān Tirumuṭik-Kāri, a hill chieftain.[133] It is a verse by a very humble singer who admits that he has nothing new to sing in praise of the chieftain, since all his exploits have already been eulogized by another well-known poet hardly leaving anything for others to sing. In the context, the poet uses a simile that his predicament is like that of the impossibility of any ship going after the gold-yielding ship in the Cēra's western sea:

cinamikutānai vānavan kuṭakaṭar
polantaru nāvāyōṭṭiya vavvaḻip-
piṛakalan celkalā tanaiyē mattai

[132] *Puṛanāṉūṛu*, 66:1–3.
[133] *Puṛanāṉūṛu*, 126:14–16.

Following the translation by Tamil scholars, historians in India and abroad have taken the above passage to mean that no vessel was able to sail in the western sea where the Cēra chieftain used to be sailing his gold-yielding ship. Literally, the verse means that no vessel can sail behind the gold-yielding ship that sails in the western sea of the Cēra chieftain. On the contrary, according to the prevailing translation, it means that no vessel can sail behind the gold-yielding ship that the Cēra chieftain navigates in the western sea. Actually, the verse is not referring to the Cēra chieftain navigating the gold-yielding ship but to the gold-yielding ship sailing in the Cēra chieftain's western sea.

Two poems in *Akanāṉūṟu* with passages referring to a battle of Pāṇḍya Ceḻiyan against the Cēra for capturing Muciṟi also allude to the richness of the port of Muciṟi. In one poem (57:14–15), the passage is about the suffering of the Cēra warriors tampered by the elephants of Ceḻiyan in the flagged chariot drawn by decorated horses rushing to capture the port of Muciṟi:

koy cuvar puravik koṭit-tērc-celiyan
mutunīr munturai muciṟi murri
kaḻiru pata cerukkiya kallen natpin
arum pun urunarin vauruntinal

The next poem (149:7–13) referring to the same episode alludes to the prosperity of Muciṟi as a bustling port where Graeco-Roman ships come with gold and return with pepper:

... cēralar
Cuḻḻiyam periyāṟru vennurai kalanka
yavanar tanta vinai man nan kalam
ponnoṭu vantu kaṟiyoṭu peyarum
valam elu muciṟi arpu ela valaiyi
arum samam kaṭantu patimam vaviya
neṭu nal yānai atu por ceḻiyan ...

The poem seeks to praise and please the Pāṇḍyan chieftain by extolling his victorious ride on the flag-bearing horse chariot and the march of mighty elephants tampering the Cēra warriors in defence against the attack on the port. He is celebrated to have surrounded the Cēra's prosperous Muciṟi situated on the great Cuḻḻi River full of white surf, won the battle, and seized the sacred icons of the port where the Yavana (Graeco-Roman) ships used to come with gold and leave with pepper. Both the poems, the second one in more explicit terms, use the episode for alluding to the richness of the port due to the Graeco-Roman trade that was the basis of irresistible temptation for the Pāṇḍyan to possess it. These are part of stock expressions, metaphors, and tropes integral to the techniques of versification followed in the ancient Tamil poetic tradition. Therefore, the events celebrated in the poem need not be historical as such. Nevertheless, the overall context of the poetic allusions is historical and essentially reflecting the political economy of the port. In fact, such a conflict between the Pāṇḍya and Cēra rulers over the control of the port was not unlikely in the wake of the rising significance of the Graeco-Roman contacts.

Ancient Tamil poems allude to the pearls of Korkai, expressed in the stock phrase for praising the glittering beauty of the lover's teeth.[134] A couple of poems allude to the pre-eminence of the port itself by way of eulogizing the Pāṇḍya ruler. One of them extols the fine chariot and the decorated horse of the Pāṇḍya chief, besides the fragrant port of Korkai.

... pu naru parappin
ivar tirai tanta irri katir muttam
kavar naṭaip puravi kal vaṭut-tapukkum
naltēr vaḻuti korkai mun tuṟai[135]

The poem praises the fragrance of the port of Korkai due to the beautiful flower. Its pearl-rich coast is surfed by the lashing waves, marked by the hoof of the horse of Pāṇḍyan Vaḻuti. There is an allusion to the features of the port in another passage:

vinai navil yānai virai porp pāndiyan
pukal ṃali ciṟappin korkai muntuṟai
avirkatir muttamotu valampuri coṟintu
talai anip polenta koṭu ēnāṭu alkul
palaiyar makaḷir panit-tuṟaipu parava[136]

[134] *Akanāṉūṟu*, 29:8–10 and *Ainkuṟunūṟu*, 185:1–2.
[135] *Akanāṉūṟu*, 201:3–7.
[136] *Akanāṉūṟu*, 201:3–7.

The passage alludes to the pearl-rich port of Korkai, the pride of the ever victorious Pāṇḍyan with trained war elephants. It mentions precious items like pearls and the conch shell of the *valampiri* type as common objects of oblation in the worship by fishermen's daughters. A passage in *Maturaikkāñci* signifies the prosperity of the pearl-rich port:

vilaintu mutirnta viḻumuttin
ilankuvalai iruncēri
kaṭkonṭik-kuṭippākkattu
narkorkaiyōr nacaipporuna[137]

The above passage alludes to the prosperity of the port based on the abundance of pearls by mentioning that 'the people of the fine port of Korkai drink toddy with the returns obtained by exchanging the mature bright pearls and celebrate'. A passage in *Maturaikkāñci* alludes to 'huge ships with flying sails attached to long posts, propelled by the wind blowing on the sheets which became bent on that account, brought to the Pāṇḍyan territory wealth-yielding articles of merchandise for consumption by the people of the inland districts'. Similarly, a passage in *Mullaippāṭṭu* describes a Tamil king's tent on a battlefield as follows:

> A tent with double walls of canvas firmly held by iron chains, guarded by powerful yavanas, whose stern looks strike terror into every beholder, and whose long and loose coats are fastened at the waist by means of belts, while dumb *mlēcchas*, clad in complete armour, who could express themselves only by gestures, kept close watch throughout the night in the outer chamber, constantly moving round the inner apartment, which was lighted by a handsome lamp.[138]

Two passages in *Paṭṭiṇappālai*, one of the long poems under *Pattuppāṭṭu* (Ten Idylls) and contemporaneous to most poems in

[137] *Maduraikkāñci*, 135–8. For the text and commentary, see 6th *pattu* in U.V.S. Iyar, ed., *Pattuppāṭṭu* with the commentary of Nāccinārkkiṉṉiyar, 6th ed. (Madras: Thyagarajavilasam Publications, 1961), 288–433.

[138] *Mullaippāṭṭu*, ii, 59–66. For the text and commentary, see 5th *pattu* in U.V.S. Iyar, ed., *Pattuppāṭṭu* with the commentary of Nāccinārkkiṉṉiyar, 263–87.

the *Akam* and *Puṟam* collections, contain extremely important data regarding the port of Pukār. One of them recounts the variety of goods arriving at the port of Pukār from various places and sources.

nīrin vanta nimir parip puraviyum
kalin vanta karun kaṟi mūṭaiyum,
vaṭamalaip piṟanta maṇiyum ponnum
kuṭamalaip piṟanta vāramum akilum
tenkaṭal muttum kuṇakaṭar tukilum
kankai vāriyum kāvirip payanum
īḻattu uṇavum kalakattākkamu
mariyavum periyavu neriya vīnṭi
valamtalai mayankiya nanantalai maṟuki[139]

This passage says that

horses were brought from distant lands beyond the seas; pepper was brought from a distant place by the caravans; gold and precious stones came from the northern mountains; sandal and *akil* came from the mountains towards the west; pearls from the southern seas, and coral from the eastern seas, besides the products from the regions watered by the Ganges; all that is grown on the banks of the Kāviri; articles of food from Elam or Ceylon; and the manufactures from Kalakam (in Burma).[140]

What the passage informs is about the commercial richness of Pukār as a pool of multiple resources arriving from regions far and wide. It mentions horses arriving through water and sacks of pepper reaching in caravan carts besides the coming of costly objects such as gems and gold of the northern mountains, sandal wood and *akil* of the western mountains, pearls of the southern sea, coral from the eastern sea, resources of the Gangetic regions, produce of the Kāvēri, foodstuff of Ceylon, artefacts of Kalakam, and so on.

139 *Paṭṭiṇappālai*, 185–93. For the text and commentary, see 4th *pattu* in U.V.S. Iyar, ed., *Pattuppāṭṭu* with the commentary of Nāccinārkkiṇṇiyar, 513–63.

140 *Paṭṭiṇappālai*, 1–40.

Historiography

It was the late medieval/early modern mercantile pressure of Renaissance Europe for the discovery of overseas routes to reach the Indian Ocean world, India, China, and the Far East which triggered research into the resuscitated classical wisdom for ancient maritime knowledge. In fact, it was this pressure that led to the detection, redaction, and publication of classical Graeco-Roman historical, geographical, and navigational manuscripts, mostly in the 16th century CE, and the heuristic interest they kindled generated several fresh editions and subsequently translations too.[141] Subsequently, it gave rise to historical geography, a special branch of knowledge which inspired inquiries into the classical understanding of the ancient Indian landscape and the identification of place names. Several articles of Francis Wilford (1761–1822) seeking to locate ancient Indian settlements mentioned in the Graeco-Roman accounts were published in the volumes of *Asiatick Researches* during the period between 1794 and 1822. Christian Lassen is said to have discussed the place names of classical Graeco-Roman settlements in India more exhaustively in his book *Indische Altertumskunde* (1847–53). Heinrich Kiepert (1818–99), the first major historical geographer of the classical world, is said to have identified and tentatively located most of them. Claudius Ptolemy's *Geographia* was interpreted and significantly improved upon in the perspectives of historical geography by the French geographer M. Vivien de Saint-Martin in 1860. Alexander Cunningham's *Ancient Geography of India* (1871), a landmark in the history of mapping the sites of antiquities, is still an invaluable source in historical geography. Henry Yule, in his *Map of Ancient India* (1874), substantially updated Saint-Martin's historical geography. James Burgess in his volumes of *Archaeological Survey of Western India*, published during the period between 1880 and 1905, incorporated significant archaeological data on classical Graeco-Roman settlements at certain coastal sites.

[141] For details, see Sunil Gupta, 'A Historiographical Survey of Studies on Indo-Roman Sea Trade and Indian Ocean Trade', *Indian Historical Review* XXXII, no. 1 (January 2005): 7.

With the aforesaid corpus of knowledge available and in the light of independent researches in traditional literary texts, Indologists like Sir William Jones and Lord Mount Stuart Elphinstone were the earliest to make historical comments on ancient maritime contacts of India. William Jones, quoting *Manusmṛiti*, is said to have opined that ancient Hindus must have been familiar with maritime practices in the age of Manu, as evidenced by his codes of law regarding bottomry.[142] Lord Mount Stuart Elphinstone commented: 'The Hindus navigated the ocean as early as the sage of Manu's Code, because we read in it of men well acquainted with sea voyages.'[143] Rhys Davids makes a general appraisal of ancient Indians' participation in overland and overseas trade in the light of the Brahamanical (Sanskrit) and Buddhist (Prakrit) sources as the following:

> The objective was probably the ports on the west coast, those on the sea-board of Sobira (the Sophir [Ophir] of the Septuagint) in the Gulf of Cutch or Bharukaccha. From here there was interchange by sea with Baveru (Babylon) and probably Arabia, Phoenicia, and Egypt ... Westward merchants are often mentioned as taking ships from Benares, or lower down at Champa, dropping down the great river, and either coasting to Ceylon or adventuring many days without sight of land to Suvannabhumi (Chryse Chersonesus, or possibly inclusive of all the coast of farther India).[144]

Vincent A. Smith has had a fairly good knowledge about the Mediterranean maritime contacts with India in general and South India in particular, thanks to his scholarship in the Graeco-Roman writings. This is evident in the following excerpt that summarizes the

142 See the discussion in R.K. Mukherji, *Indian Shipping: A History of the Sea Borne Trade and Maritime Activities of the Indians from Earliest Times* (Calcutta: Longmans Green and Co., 1912), 60–1.

143 M.S. Elphinstone, *History of India*, Vol. 1 (London: John Murray Publication, 1849), 166. Also see discussion of this in Mukherji, *Indian Shipping*, 60–1.

144 See Rhys David's statement published in 'Asoka and Buddha's Relics', *Journal of Royal Asiatic Society* (London) (July 1901): 397–410, quoted in Mukherji, *Indian Shipping*, 78. Also see economic conditions discussed in T.W. Rhys David, *Buddhist India* (London: T. Fisher Unwin, 1903), 94–103.

knowledge regarding the Roman trade with Southern India, which is expressive of contemporary western historiographical perspectives:

> Tamil land had the good fortune to possess three precious commodities not procurable elsewhere, namely pepper, pearls, and beryl. Pepper fetched an enormous price in the markets of Europe ... The pearl-fishery of the Southern Sea, which still is productive and valuable, had been worked for untold ages, and always attracted a crowd of foreign merchants. The mines of Padiyur in the Coimbatore district were almost the only source known to the ancient world from which good beryl could be obtained, and few gems were more esteemed by both Indians and Romans. The Tamil states maintained powerful navies, and were visited freely by ships from both east and west, which brought merchants of various places eager to buy the pearls, pepper, beryl, and other choice commodities of India, and to pay for them with the gold, silver, and art ware of Europe.[145]

Smith, after an appraisal of the entire sources of information on contemporary trade and commerce, observes that it is reasonable to believe that there were colonies of Graeco-Roman agents in all the main ports on the south-western and south-eastern coasts of India:

> There is good reason to believe that considerable colonies of Roman subjects engaged in trade were settled in Southern India during the first two centuries of our era, and that European soldiers, described as powerful Yavanas, and dumb *Mlecchas* (barbarians) clad in complete armour, acted as bodyguards to Tamil kings, while the beautiful large ships of the Yavanas lay off Muziris (Cranganore) to receive the cargoes of pepper paid for by Roman gold.[146]

Kanakasabhai Pillai gives a glorious picture of the ports of the coasts of Tamilakam, based on the allusions in poems of the ancient Tamil anthology. Quoting the passages, he describes that in the Cōḻa ports had lighthouses built of brick and mortar for showing light at night to the ships seeking their way to the docks. It is also said that the palace of the Cōḻa king in the city of Kāviripaṭṭiṇam was built by skilled artisans from Magadha, craftsmen from Maradam, smiths

[145] V.A. Smith, *Early History of India*, 4th ed. (London: Oxford, 1924), 400.
[146] Smith, *Early History of India*, 401.

from Avanti, carpenters from Yavana, and the cleverest workmen in the Tamil land.[147]

A scholarly work by R.K. Mukherji on India's overseas trade and maritime activities, based on an exhaustive search into the amazingly vast and varied corpus of literature, celebrates the country's mercantile presence all over the ancient world in the east and west:

> She [India] had colonies in Pegu, in Cambodia, in Java, in Sumatra, in Borneo, and even in the countries of the Farther East as far as Japan. She had trading settlements in Southern China, in the Malayan peninsula, in Arabia, and in all the chief cities of Persia and all over the east coast of Africa. She [India] cultivated trade relations not only with the countries of Asia, but also with the whole of the then known world, including the countries under the dominion of the Roman Empire, and both the East and the West became the theatre of Indian commercial activity and gave scope to her naval energy and throbbing international life.[148]

H.G. Rawlinson was first to do a specialized study on the subject matter of exchange relations between India and the Graeco-Roman world down to the fall of the Roman Empire.[149] In the light of the Asokan edicts mentioning the protection of trade routes and *Arthaśāstra* stipulating laws about the management of ferries, ports, the overland and overseas traders, frights, tolls, and so on, the continued progress in the prosperity of trade and commerce during the Mauryan period has been highlighted in the historiography on ancient India. R. Sewell's description of the post-Mauryan situation in the peninsular region during the Andhra–Sātavāhana period (200 BC to AD 250) shows how historians of his times characterized the early history of southern India:

> The Andhra period seems to have been one of considerable prosperity. There was trade, both overland and by sea, with Western Asia, Greece,

[147] V.K. Pillai, *The Tamils Eighteen Hundred Years Ago* (New Delhi: Asian Education Services, [1904] 1997), 16, 24–6.

[148] 'Introduction' in Mukherji, *Indian Shipping*, 4.

[149] H.G. Rawlinson, *Intercourse between India and the Western World* (Cambridge: Cambridge University Press, 1916), 1–26.

Rome, and Egypt, as well as with China and the East. Embassies are said to have been sent from South India to Rome. Indian elephants were used for Syrian warfare. Pliny mentions the vast quantities of specie that found its way every year from Rome to India, and in this he is confirmed by the author of the *Periplus*. Roman coins have been found in profusion in the Peninsula, and especially in the south. In AD 68 a number of Jews, fleeing from Roman persecution, seem to have taken refuge among the friendly coast-people of South India, and to have settled in Malabar.[150]

The same perspective of the flourishing commerce in the country is repeated in R.G. Bhandarkar's description of the great development of overseas trade between India and the Mediterranean worlds during the Kushan period:

> During the Kushana period the Roman influence on India was at its height. When the whole of the civilized world, excepting India and China, passed under the sway of the Caesars, and the Empire of Kaniska marched, or almost marched, with that of Hadrian, the ancient isolation of India was infringed upon, and Roman arts and ideas travelled with the stream of Roman gold which flowed into the treasuries of the Rajas in payment for the silks, gems, and spices of the Orient.[151]

K.V. Subrahmanya Aiyer gives an account of Roman intercourse with southern India with 'the civilized nations of the west especially with Rome' in the early centuries of CE. He is very much impressed by the fortunes of South India due to her ports of western contacts as distinguished from the North:

> Except in rare instances of invasion by foreign aggressive sovereigns northern India had less opportunities of coming in contact with outside nations than the south which had several ancient ports regularly visited by ships from Greece, Egypt, Rome, Persia, Arabia and China. Egyptian sailors had the benefit of Indian trade up to the time of its conquest by Rome which took place during the reign of Augustus in

[150] *Imperial Gazetteer*, new edition, Vol. ii, p. 325, quoted in Mukherji, *Indian Shipping*, 117.

[151] R.G. Bhandarkar, *Early History of the Deccan* (repr., Delhi: Asian Educational Services, 2001), 32.

about BC 30. Till then Rome had no direct communication with India but Indian products were received in Italy through Egypt.... This kind of busy interactions between two nations lasted till almost the beginning of 6th century AD, when the mighty Roman Empire became a prey to the Teutonic races who established independent kingdoms in Italy and elsewhere. The abundant finds of gold and silver coins throughout southern India of almost all the Roman emperors from Augustus to Zeno furnish us with links with the past of a kind that we look for in vain in the written records of the East or the West. They afford conclusive proof of the long maintained commercial relationship between two countries and supplement to a great extent the scraps of information supplied by the Roman historians.[152]

Aiyer quotes a Roman historian who mentions that every year about the time of the summer solstice, a fleet of 120 ships sailing from the Egyptian ports of Myos Hormos and Berenike arrived at the ports of India or Ceylon in forty days with the assistance of the monsoon wind and returned with rich cargo. The precious goods thus arriving on the Red Sea coast were transported on the camel's back to the Nile and through the river up to Alexandria and finally to the capital of the Roman Empire where they got exchanged at hundred times their cost. Aiyer says:

> Attracted by the hundredfold gain which trade with the east promised in those days, several people took to navigation, nothing daunted by the labour and risk involved in it.[153]

E.H. Warmington was the first to write a comprehensive book on ancient Mediterranean trade in the Indian Ocean with India conceived as part of the Roman monetary system and economically dominated through a series of trade colonies.[154] His scholarly work provided the historical basis for the postulation of the establishment of Graeco-Roman trading settlements in the port-sites of the south-western as well as south-eastern coasts of India from the time of the

152 Aiyer, *Historical Sketches of Ancient Dekhan*, 82–3.

153 Aiyer, *Historical Sketches of Ancient Dekhan*, 84.

154 Warmington, *The Commerce between the Roman Empire*, 131, 274–92, 319–20.

Ptolemaic dynasty and their continued existence there till the decline of the Roman Empire. His observation of the passion of the Roman aristocracy for ornaments with precious stones brought from the Tamil South is meticulous:

> Romans showed a taste for excessive decoration of the fingers and by the use of gems to cover conches, garlands, armour, walls, and so on. The practice of collecting gems became common during the 1st century BC and Scaurus, Julius Caesar, Marcellus, Maecenas, Vespasian, and Hadrian were collectors. All who could afford one obtained a gem signet from the guilds of ring makers, and the gem cabinet was an essential part of every rich home. The poor used glass imitations, the rich bought the largest and rarest genuine specimens and the imperial house encouraged the new art of cameo-engraving.[155]

The mention in the imperial records about the drain of gold and silver through the purchase of silk by the rich men of Rome to pamper their 'crazy' wives, and the mention in Pliny the Elder's *Natural History* about the problem of drain due to the purchase of pepper have inspired several writers. M.P. Charlesworth also followed the same colonial perspective, and later, more strongly, in the light of a re-evaluation of the source material in Greek and Latin.[156] Majumdar associated the history of the development of trade, industry, and commerce in India with the long tradition of the country's efforts to expand the political dominion and wealth. According to him, the material prosperity acquired by ancient Indians is reflected in the luxury and elegance of ancient Indian society. He shows archaeological evidence of the existence of regular trade between India on the one hand and Mesopotamia, Arabia, Phoenicia, and Egypt on

155 Warmington, *The Commerce between the Roman Empire*. Pliny the Elder talks about it as a major drain of gold currency. See *Natural History*, VI, 22. The *PME* endorses the fact that a large number of coins went out of Rome in exchange for the goods from Limyrike. Historians have noted the mention by Tacitus and Fenestella about the pepper and pearls changing the lifestyle of the Roman aristocrats of the Augustan period.

156 M.P. Charlesworth, *Trade-Routes and Commerce of the Roman Empire* (London: Cambridge University Press, 1928). Also see his 'Roman Trade with India', 131–43.

the other, both by land and sea as early as c. 800 BCE. He says that archaeological excavations in Philippines, the Malay Peninsula, and Indonesia have confirmed the persistence of extensive trade relations of India down to the early historic period. K.A. Nilakanta Sastri traces the antiquity of the overseas trade contacts of south India further back to the times of the Old Testament:

> ... the evidence of South Indian connections with the West drawn from references in his [Solomon's] reign to Ophir and Thar Shih to ivory, apes and peacocks is seen to be only a link in a more or less continuous chain of data suggesting such connections for long ages before and after ... and in any case the probability of very early maritime connections of Southern India with the West now rests on much broader grounds than the occurrence of a few words of doubtfully Tamil origin in one of the books of the Old Testament.[157]

It has been presumed that India's naval supremacy had enabled the country to colonize the islands in the Indian Archipelago. Majumdar says that in ancient times there was regular easterly trade traffic between India and China, both by land and sea and westerly trade relations between India and the Hellenic world:

> We learn from ancient authority that in the processions of Ptolemy Philadelphus (285–246 BC) were to be found Indian women, Indian hunting dogs, Indian cows, also Indian spices carried on camels, and that the yachts of the ruler of Egypt had a saloon lined with Indian stones. Everything indicates that there was a large volume of sea trade between India and the western countries as far as the African coast. From the coast the goods were carried by land to the Nile, and then down the river to Alexandria which was a great emporium in those days. There was a mercantile colony of Indians in an island off the African coast in the 1st century AD. The adventurous spirit of the Indians carried them even as far as the North Sea, while their caravans travelled from one end of Asia to the other.[158]

[157] K.A.N. Sastri, 'Southern India, Arabia and Africa', *The New Indian Antiquary*, Vol. I (Bombay: Karnataka Publishing House, 1938), 26–7.

[158] R.C. Majumdar, *Ancient India* (repr., New Delhi: Motilal Banarsidass Publishers, 2003), 210–16.

Majumdar edited the relevant excerpts from the classical Graeco-Roman accounts into a single compilation of the source material with a view to helping the researchers engaged in the reconstruction of the history of ancient India in general and overseas trade contacts in particular.[159] K.A. Nilakanta Sastri also did a similar exercise by editing a compendium of accounts drawn from the various source books referring to India in the context of the westerly as well as easterly trade contacts of over a long period. He defines the locale of ancient transmarine merchants' navigation as follows:

> The Indian Ocean is not a closed basin like the Mediterranean Sea; on the South it opens on an infinite expanse of water ... And in this system, Indian held a privileged, if not a preponderant, place by the advantage of her situation and the great length of her coasts; she is the centre towards which the many lines of this system converge. Doubtless, the documents are for the ancient period; but the race which carried civilization by the sea to Burma, to Siam, to Cambodia, Indo China, and Java and Madagascar was a race of navigators.[160]

K.M. Panikkar, much more self-consciously, wrote about Indian colonization of Sumatra, Java, and Borneo by the 2nd century CE, using the country's navy that was a formidable force of seamen excellent in oceanic navigation. He saw the flourishing overseas commerce an entailing aspect of the naval competency. The immense wealth of the Indian merchants, he says, is evident from their munificent endowments registered in the inscriptions of the Sātavāhana period.[161] Mortimer Wheeler, for example, put up the very strong postulation that the site of Arikamedu near Pondicherry was a Roman trade colony and compared the Roman presence in India with British trade factories.[162]

159 Majumdar, *Classical Accounts.*

160 Sastri, *Foreign Notices of South India.*

161 K.M. Panikkar, *India and the Indian Ocean: An Essay on the Influence of Sea Power on Indian History* (London: G. Allen & Unwin Ltd., 1947), 23–4. Also his *India through the Ages* (originally published by London: August, 1947; repr., Delhi: Discovery Publishing House, 1985), 84–93.

162 Wheeler, *Rome beyond Imperial Frontiers*, 124–5.

G.L. Adhya was perhaps the first economic historian to make a historiographic criticism of the major sources of knowledge about the Mediterranean trade relations. About the quality and nature of the organization of knowledge that the two major source books—Strabo's *Geography* and Pliny the Elder's *Natural History*—signify, he makes the following observation:

> In spite of their erudition, neither of these authors present facts in a properly systematic manner and they are almost silent about the sources of their information. Often we cannot determine whether they are quoting from old works or speaking about their own time on the basis of first hand information.[163]

He opined that the Indo-Roman trade, by and large, was trade by foreign merchants who reached the Indian centres of commerce through overland and overseas routes to carry goods of demand among foreigners, precluding the participation of Indian merchants in it, and hence it was an exchange not enterprising to the economy of India.[164]

Nonetheless, India's maritime contact with the eastern Mediterranean in general and classical Rome in particular, described as Indo-Roman trade, became a prominent theme in her historiography, inspiring several historians of national sentiments to celebrate the phase as that of a maritime civilization. It is against this context that one has to review the books by H.P. Chakraborti and B. Srivastava on ancient trade and commerce of India.[165] P.C. Prasad's book is specifically on ancient Indian foreign trade and commerce.[166] In the same year came Moti Chandra's well-researched book on ancient Indian

163 Wheeler, *Rome beyond Imperial Frontiers*, 7.

164 G.L. Adhya, *Early Indian Economics: Studies in the Economic Life of Northern and Western India, c. 200 B.C.–300 A.D.* (Bombay: Asia Publishing House, 1966), 136–7.

165 H.P. Chakraborti, *Trade and Commerce of Ancient India* (Kolkata: Academic Publishers, 1966). Also see B. Srivastava, *Trade and Commerce in Ancient India: From the Earliest Times to c. A.D. 300.* (Varanasi: Chowkhamba Sanskrit Series Office, 1968).

166 P.C. Prasad, *Foreign Trade and Commerce in Ancient India* (New Delhi: Abhinav Publications, 1977).

trade, trading organizations, route-systems, and their continuity and change, which the author has discussed up to the 11th century CE.[167] He says:

> From those land routes at least in the time of Augustus several Indian embassies reached Rome. At least four such embassies are mentioned in the Latin literature: 1) the embassy from Puru country (the territory between the Jhelum and Beas), took with it to Rome serpents, monals, tigers and a letter written in Greek language; 2) the embassy from Broach was accompanied by a Buddhist monk named Germanos; 3) an embassy from the Cēra country, where it was reported in Rome that at Muziris built a temple in honour of Augustus and; 4) embassy from the Pāṇḍya country brought with it precious stones, pearls and an elephant. We know that in the time of Augustus commercial relations between India and Rome grew but in this the balance of trade was in favour of India from the very beginning and as a result of this Roman gold poured into the country.[168]

He has studied the circuit of merchants and merchandises, the means and modes of transportation, and the main centres of exchange all over the entire Indian subcontinent, besides trade contacts with the islands of the East Indies, the Red Sea coast, and the shores of the Mediterranean.

Most historians recognize the fact that much before the Romans got interested in trade contacts with India, Greeks who were overseas traders had trade links with Ptolemaic Egypt, eastern Africa, but western Arabia and further in the Indian Ocean up to India's north-western coast, certainly not involving cross-oceanic voyages. They agree that in those days Aden was the transit port for ships coming with goods from the eastern world, particularly from the north-western coast of India. There is consensus among them about the expansion of the Mediterranean world's easterly trade after the Roman conquest of Egypt and the emperor's institution of state protection over the latter's trading zone. Even then the main traders were Greeks, many of whom had settled in Egypt. That this revolution of overseas trade

[167] M. Chandra, *Trade and Trade Routes in Ancient India* (New Delhi: Abhinav Publications, 1977).

[168] Chandra, *Trade and Trade Routes*, 111.

corresponded to the regular dependence on, if not discovery of, the monsoon winds, popularly called the Hippalus Wind, for cross-oceanic voyages is also a matter of general acceptance.

L. Casson's almost half-a-century-long studies of ancient mariners, commercial connections in the Indian Ocean, naval technology, and shipping of goods largely, which are thoroughly source-grounded and scholarly, represent more or less the up-to-date knowledge related to the history of the Indian Ocean commerce in general and the Mediterranean exchange relations with the coasts of peninsular India in particular.[169] One significant work specifically on south India is by R. Champakalakshmi, who discusses, briefly though, the features of trade and urban processes of the period under consideration, in the light of both archaeological remains as well as literary data.[170] Perhaps, the most up-to-date work, specifically on the question of Indo-Roman trade, is the scholarly anthology edited by F. De Romanis and A. Tchernia, which has presented a rigorously source-based analytical comprehension of the subject matter.[171]

Some historians maintain the strong presumption that Indian merchant-mariners were expert navigators of practical wisdom about

169 The following books (the old ones updated in the subsequent edition) and articles of L. Casson vouch for it. His first main book is *The Ancient Mariners: Seafarers and Sea Fighters of the Mediterranean in Ancient Times* (Victor Golancz, 1959; 2nd ed.: London: Princeton University Press, 1991). The next book, *Travel in the Ancient World*, first published in 1974 by George Allen & Unwin Ltd., had its second edition published by John Hopkins University Press in 1994. One of his seminal articles, 'P Vindob G 40822 and the Shipping of Goods from India', *BASP*, 23 came out in 1986. His other studies are *The Periplus Maris Erythraei: Text with Introduction, Translation, and Commentary* (Princeton: Princeton University Press, 1989); 'New Light on Maritime Loans: P Vindob G 40822', in *Zeitschrift fur Papyrologie und Epigraphik*, Vol. 84 (1990); 'Ancient Naval Technology and the Route to India', in *Rome and India: The Ancient Sea trade*, eds V. Begley and R.D. de Puma (Madison: University of Wisconsin Press, 1991), 8–11; and *Ships and Seamanship in the Ancient World* (Baltimore: John Hopkins University Press, 1995).

170 R. Champakalakshmi, *Trade, Ideology and Urbanization: South India 300 BC to AD 1300* (New Delhi: Oxford University Press, 1996), 117–30.

171 Romanis and Tchernia, eds, *Crossings*.

seasonal winds and positions of stars, and that they had trade relations with the Indian Ocean-rim countries, long before the establishment of the Roman Empire. They believe that the Mediterranean traders poured into the Indian Ocean by setting aside the Indian and Arabian traders. A few historians argue that even after the Roman occupation of the trading zone along the Red Sea coast and the Indian Ocean, the Arab as well as Indian seafarers were active.[172] It has been argued that the role of the Indo-Arab traders was not adequately represented in the Western writings and naturally the Indian writers under their influence thought that the trade in the Indian Ocean was mainly in the hands of the Mediterranean seafarers and under the control of the Roman Empire. Apart from the argument that the predominance of the Graeco-Roman seafarers in easterly trade was an exaggeration contingent upon the colonial historiography, it has been argued to be unlikely on technical grounds by proposing that the Mediterranean ships with their inadequate rigging system could not have sailed in the rough weather of the Indian Ocean. In contrast, Indian and Arabian ships with excellent masts and rigging systems have been highlighted as the most suitable.[173] Similar arguments, mainly emphasizing the appropriateness of the Indo-Arab and the inappropriateness of the Graeco-Roman sails and rigging systems, have been put forward to set aside the claims of predominance of the latter in the Indian Ocean.[174]

Archaeological and literary evidences of the Graeco-Roman presence in certain ports of the coasts of peninsular India have been seen as indicating the possibility of a few of them to have arrived as traders there in the Arab or Indian vessels. This perspective of stressing the

[172] H.P. Ray, *The Winds of Change: Buddhism and the Maritime Links of Early South Asia* (Delhi: Oxford University Press, 1994), 165–72. Also 'A Resurvey of Roman Contacts with the East', in *Athens, Aden, Arikamedu: Essays on the Interrelations between India, Arabia and the Eastern Mediterranean*, eds M.F. Boussac and J.F. Salles (New Delhi: Munshiram Manoharlal, 1995), 97–114. For a more assertive discussion notwithstanding the problem of being largely unfounded, see Ball, *Rome in the East*.

[173] See the arguments in Ray, *The Winds of Change*, 165–72 and in her 'A Resurvey of Roman Contacts with the East', 97–114. The arguments, though unfounded, are more assertive in the whole book of Ball, *Rome in the East*.

[174] Ball, *Rome in the East*.

Indian merchant-mariners' role has been pursued further in the light of the relatively recent archaeological finds from the excavations at the port of Berenike by S.E. Sidebotham.[175] Among the recent scholarly publications are F. De Romanis' deeper probing in the primary source, R. Tomber's studies on pottery, and McLaughlin's historical analysis, which have rendered an added strength and clarity about the features and dynamic of maritime transactions between the West and the East.[176]

In a recent assessment, it has been well sustained in the light of evidences that any effort to deny the Graeco-Roman presence in the Indian Ocean is not a tenable stance and that it is a fact that Graeco-Roman traders had navigated to India in ships with the Mediterranean type of sail and rigging system:

> Graeco-Roman traders could and did sail to India using their own ships, alongside Indian and Arab traders and their traditions. However, we do not have an exact idea about the intensity of Roman presence in the Indian Ocean. In this view, it is important to leave the question about Strabo's 120 ships unanswered: It is impossible to refute or confirm this number, unless referring to a broader hypothetical framework. Based on the sources, we can only state that Graeco-Roman traders were present in the Indian Ocean, having acquired a certain role within the old maritime networks.[177]

There is no doubt that traders of north-west India, Persia, and Arabia had a significant role, however infrequent it was, in the exchange relations with the Persian and South Arabian seaboards up to Aden for a few centuries before the Graeco-Roman mariners began

175 Sidebotham and Wendrich, *Report of the 1998 Excavations*. Also see Sidebotham, *Berenike and the Ancient Maritime Spice Route*, 75–6.

176 F. De Romanis, 'On Dechinabades and Limyrike in the Periplus Maris Erythraei', *Topoi*, Supplement 11 (2012): 329–40 and also Romanis, 'Playing Sudoku'; R. Tomber, *Indo-Roman Trade: From Pots to Pepper* (London: Gerald Duckworth & Co. Ltd., 2008) and also her 'Roman Red Sea to beyond the Empire: Egyptian Ports and Their Trading Partners', *British Museum Studies in Ancient Egypt and Sudan* 18: 201–15.

177 B. Fauconnier, 'Graeco-Roman Merchants in the Indian Ocean: Revealing a Multi-cultural Trade', *Topoi. Orient-Occident* (Lyon), Supplement 11 (2012): 75–109.

their activities in the Indian Ocean. It is also clear that when Graeco-Romans became active they made direct access to the south-western and south-eastern ports of India, making the anterior channel of distribution of goods irrelevant to them. We are quite convinced that the Graeco-Roman merchants had their temporary settlements in the ports, as necessitated by the dependence on the monsoon winds for the navigation across the Indian Ocean. The nature of evidences shows that extreme views related to the question of dominance or exclusion of one or the other was unlikely, for early overseas trade relations in the past were essentially based on use-value-based cooperation and mutuality across the unevenly developed communities and cultures, notwithstanding the entailing asymmetry about the gains.

In short, Indo-Roman trade is still a debated topic in spite of several scholarly studies, which have seldom probed into the exact nature of exchange. From the Indian side, the lack of clinching evidences is counterbalanced by overstatements and hasty generalizations. Although there is enough evidence to show the nature of the transactions, studies largely accept the presumptions of the Indian historiography for the obvious reasons of embarrassment in challenging them, which in the post-modern and post-colonial context would implicate such critics as colonial. Also, there is the problem of the dearth of linguistic competency for them in handling the ancient Tamil source, which precludes the possibility of overcoming the lacunae in the Indian translations. This is true of the writings by several historians of trade in India too, largely led by the values of nationalist historiography and a few of which go self-consciously biased under the influence of decolonization. A major limitation of most historians of ancient trade the world over is the inescapable influence of the ideas of the market economy of the present, the concept of trade as enunciated by neoclassical economics, the belief in its universality across time, and several notions of free trade. R. McLaughlin's book on the economy of the Roman Empire and the Indian Ocean trade, the most recent empirically well-grounded study on the subject, deserves mention in the context.[178] It reappraises the empire's economy, dependence on overseas trade, and links with the regions

178 R. McLaughlin, *The Roman Empire and the Indian Ocean* (Barnsley, South Yorkshire: Pen and Sword Military, 2014).

of Africa, Arabia, and India. But avowedly distanced from theoretical preoccupation, the study is largely deprived of methodological checks against anachronistic expressions.

A methodological critique would show that the historiography has been representing transmarine trade almost as a formal activity of state-level negotiations between countries of far-off lands, rather than an activity of merchant-mariners with or without the state protection. It has been represented generally as 'export' and 'import' between nations (*sic*) or as a transaction invariably advantageous to India or as an open and balanced exchange of equal benefits, and so on. Often such representations have been found based on several uncritically accepted presumptions, some explicitly anachronistic, about contemporary overseas trade. In the historiography of eastern Mediterranean trade relations with the Indian subcontinent, there has been little discussion of theoretical questions relating to the political economy of contemporary societies and efforts to apply theories of economic anthropology to early exchange practices. As a result, the predominance of Indian overseas trade and her maritime civilization based on spice export, particularly of pepper, has always been a case taken for granted in the country's historiography.[179] This has to be revisited with insights of theoretical meanings, measures, and parameters of critical political economy as well as economic anthropology, which show the term 'trade' inadequate to the context of the early eastern Mediterranean exchange relations with the regions of the Indian subcontinent.[180] Very few studies in Indian historiography have

[179] A scholarly overall assessment of the nature and extent of Indo-Roman trade is made in R. Thapar, 'Early Mediterranean Contacts with India: An Overview', in *Crossings*, 11–40. For specific details, see V. Begley and R.D. De Puma, *Rome and India: The Ancient Sea Trade* (Madison: University of Wisconsin Press, 1991). Also see Young, *Rome's Eastern Trade* and Tomber, *Indo-Roman Trade*.

[180] The projection of evolved economic institutions and practices into transactions of primordial communities is anachronistic. See M.J. Herskovits, *The Economic Life of the Primitive People* (London and New York: Knopf Publishers, 1940). The first detailed conceptualization of the issue is in Marcel Mauss, *The Gift: Forms and Functions of Exchange in Archaic Societies* (London: Cohen & West, 1954). Also see K. Polanyi, 'The Economy

used these insights for analysing the nature of exchange relations in ancient societies.[181] Many of our specialists in the history of trade have yet to learn much from Marx, Malinowski, Mauss, and Polanyi.

---

as Instituted Process', in *Trade and Market in Early Empires*, eds K. Polanyi, C.M. Arensberg, and H.W. Pearson (Illinois: Glencoe, 1957), 243–8. For a discussion on the context of social formation, see M. Godelier, *Marxist Perspectives in Anthropology* (London: Cambridge University Press, 1977). Other relevant studies are M. Sahlins, *Stone Age Economics* (London: Tavistock Publications, 1974); C.A. Gregory, *Gifts and Commodities* (London: Academic Press, 1982); C. Humphrey and S. Hugh-Jones, eds, *Barter, Exchange, and Value: An Anthropological Approach* (Cambridge University Press, 1992). C.A. Gregory, *Savage Money: The Anthropology and Politics of Commodity Exchange* (Amsterdam: Harwood Academic, 1997). Also his 'Exchange and Reciprocity', in *Companion Encyclopaedia of Anthropology: Humanity, Culture and Social Life*, ed. T. Ingold (London: Routledge, 1994), 911–39.

[181] Studies by R. Thapar and S.F. Ratnagar are examples. See R. Thapar, '*Dāna* and *Dakshiṇa* as Forms of Exchange', in *Ancient Indian Social History* (New Delhi: Orient Blackswan, 1978), 94–108; 'Black Gold: South Asia and the Roman Maritime Trade', *South Asia*, n.s. 15, no. 2 (1992): 1–27; and the introductory article, 'Early Mediterranean Contacts', 11–40. Also see S.F. Ratnagar, *Encounters: The Westerly Trade of Harappan Civilisation* (New Delhi: Oxford University Press, 1981).

3

Eastern Mediterranean Overseas Exchanges

Eastern Mediterrannean maritime contacts with India's north-west date back to the times of ancient Bronze Age civilizations. Ancient maritime routes from India had split around Hadhramaut into two streams: one towards the north into the Gulf of Aden and the Levant, and the other towards the south into Alexandria through the port of Axum on the Red Sea. Most parts of these routes, hugging the coastline, were in use from the times of the Egyptian, Sumerian, and Harappan civilizations. History of the eastern Mediterranean maritime relations with peninsular India goes back to the times of the Old Testament that contains several loanwords from Sanskrit and Dravidian languages.[1] During the reign period of the Ptolemies, Egypt had established trade network with India, by commanding the northern and western end of the routes for trading to India and southern

[1] The Hebrew *shan habbin* (Sanskrit, *ibha danta*, ivory), *kopha*, *kapi*, monkey, and *tukim*, *tokai*, peacock. V.R.R. Dikshitar, *Origin and Spread of the Tamils*, Adayar Library series, no. 58 (Madras: Adayar Library, [1947] 1971), 89–90. This list is carried on further from the Greek *oruza* (Tamil, *arisi* [rice]); Latin Zingiber, *srngivera*, ginger; corundum, Tamil, *kurundam*; and sandal, Sanskrit, *chandana*. See N. Subramanian, *The Sagam Polity* (Delhi: Asia Publishing House, 1966), 236.

Arabia, which was sustained by the Seleucid and the Parthian rulers. Traders of Egypt, Arabia, Persia, and India had jointly used the overseas as well as overland routes between Alexandria and Bharukaccha via Anatolia and Persia, which converged at certain points requiring trans-shipping of the cargoes through pack-animal caravans across deserts. It included the overland transactions across the extensive landscapes of West Asia that lay between the eastern Mediterranean and China through the Pamir Plateau to China, formed by the junction of the Himalayas with the Tian Shan, Karakoram, Kunlun, and Hindu Kush ranges. This history of contacts, vast in time and space, involved a series of antecedents of the opening up of routes connecting points of exchange between Egypt and the distant eastern world.

Antecedents of Contacts

It is an outmoded question as to where maritime trade originated, who dominated, when and how, for the present focus hardly has anything to do with the politics of claims thereof. Historians have debated the claims about whether trade began along the coast of the Aegean Sea or the Arabian Sea. Often in the debates national sentiments, rather than the political economy of contests for control over the coasts of exchange potential, came to the fore and hence coming to terms with questions of domination and subordination became important. One thing seldom contested is the great antiquity of exchange relations among societies in widely separated lands. Here we need to make only an overview of antecedents of exchange relations between the eastern Mediterranean world and the coasts of the Indian subcontinent.

Ancient Egyptians were foremost among those who opened up routes to settlements in far-off lands. Way back in the age of pharaohs they had gone over to the territories on the eastern frontiers of the Red Sea in search of aromatics that were indispensable for rituals and ceremonies as testified by hieroglyphic inscriptions. Such regular trips had led to the establishment of ports on the Red Sea and discovery of routes to farther regions in the years of the later pharaohs. Punt, a coastal region, somewhere between Somalia and the Red Sea coast of Sudan, was explored through a special voyage sent by Queen Hatshepsut. It is said that Nebuchadnezzar had obtained teak from the forests of India through the coasting mariners between the Indus and the Persian Gulf to build his Moon temple at Ur.[2] Though we know all this only with minimum facts, what turns up as extremely significant is the irresistible demand the ruling class had for objects of far-off lands, particularly from the eastern world. Many of the items that they had adventurously and expensively obtained from distant lands were of culturally or ritually contingent demand.

After over a millennium, long persistent voyages through the spice route along the coast of southern Arabia and beyond by the seafaring merchants accomplished a larger world of exchange relations that culminated in the making of the Persian Empire extending from the Red Sea to the north-west of the Indian subcontinent with the conquest of Egypt by Cambyses. Darius, by restoring to the channel linking the Nile with the Red Sea and by sending ships on voyages to explore routes to connect the distant places, expanded relations of exchange across his empire, as attested by his inscriptions. Sending Scylax on an expedition from the mouth of Indus to the Red Sea, across the Persian bays and along the coast of southern Arabia, Darius facilitated voyages between the Indian subcontinent and Egypt.

During the reign of the Ptolemies, most regions of the Persian Empire had gone into the hands of the Seleucids. While the former were eagerly guarding the Red Sea routes to the east African coasts for bringing wild elephants and to the southern Arabian coasts for obtaining aromatics, the latter were interested in maintaining the routes to the Indus to bring elephants to strengthen the royal army. Ptolemies developed Arsinoe, Myos Hormos, and Berenike as their major ports on the Red Sea, mainly to import wild elephants from the forests of east Africa. Merchants of Ptolemian Egypt as well as the Seleucidian Persia and north-western India had travelled only up to Aden for political reasons, although the route from Alexandria through the Nile, the eastern desert, the Red Sea, Aden, Socotra, the south Arabian Sea, Anatolia, and Persia to north-western India had already evolved. Mercantile navigation in the Arabian Sea was entirely through coastal routes for a long period. *Periplus Maris Erythraei* (*PME*) mentions a

[2] H.G. Rawlinson, *Intercourse between India and the Western World* (Cambridge: Cambridge University Press, 1916), 3–4.

place called Muza that was a nerve-centre of the coasting merchants, particularly the Arab ship-owners and merchants:

> Beyond these places in a bay at the foot of the left side this gulf, there is a place by the shore called Muza, a market-town established by law, distant altogether from Berenice for those sailing southward about twelve thousand stadia. And the whole place is crowded with Arab ship owners and seafaring men and is busy with the affairs of commerce; for they carry on a trade with the far side coast and with Barygaza, sending their own ships there.[3]

When the Greeks re-established their sway over the Persian Empire in 326 BCE with the invasion by the Macedonian King Alexander, the routes of exchange between the Indus bay and the Persian Gulf got re-explored through a new naval mission sent under Nearchus. In short, the routes of exchange were explored and re-explored through fresh expeditions from the east to the west and back, as the empires rose and fell, suggesting that voyages were quite infrequent, obviously for reasons of huge distance, high risk, total uncertainty, and long journey time to the tune of about thirty months for one way. Seemingly, it was only during the reign of strong empires that the long routes and passages got activated, primarily due to the political economy of greater demand for foreign goods and the possibility of better security under imperial protection. For example, during the reigns of the Mauryan and Seleucid empires the caravan routes passing through and connecting the two were safe and secure, thanks to their strong rule and the friendly relations between them. Likewise, it was only then the overland routes that supplemented overseas exchanges too could remain safe, thanks to the imperial garrisons, forts, and bastions in inhospitable terrain.

It is significant to note that several long overland caravan routes of very ancient times had existed connecting the West and the East, the most well known being the silk route between China and Rome. These were the channels through which the caravans carried the

[3] See *PME*, 21 as translated in W.H. Schoff, *The Periplus of the Erythraean Sea: Travel and Trade in the Indian Ocean by a Merchant of the First Century* (New York: Longmans, Green and Co., 1912).

Chinese goods to the west and north-west as well as the Mediterranean goods to the east. We understand from *PME* that from Bactria, a major centre of convergence of caravans, there were several caravan routes of great antiquity going to central Asia and the Mediterranean world on the one hand and to China through northern India on the other. Like Bactria, Taxila was another major centre of convergence for the caravans from different parts, to barter their goods that had a demand in the Mediterranean. Some of the routes from the northern and eastern India as well as those from central Asia converged at Taxila, where excavations have yielded Roman goods, particularly coins, affirming the circuit of merchants having exchange relations with Mediterranean seafarers.

In fact, the north-eastern trade route between the Indian subcontinent and China was anterior to the central Asian silk route.[4] Yet another equally important centre of convergence was Tamralipti that connected all important points of exchange in the northern part of the subcontinent. Routes from the Gangetic region in the east, which branched off into Srāvasti in the upper north, Champa, Vārāṇasi, Pāṭaliputra, Kauśāmbi, Ayodhya, Mathura, and Ujjain had three main points of convergence, namely Bharukaccha, Patala, and Puskalavati on the west and north-west. Along the Gangetic routes, there were several centres of exchange at strategic points where the routes intersected and most of them converged at ports used by the coasting seafarers. These routes with several points of exchange in central Asia supplemented the overseas traffic of goods by making cargoes from distant places available at the north-western ports of the Indian subcontinent and Persia. Overland Chinese merchants had been bartering their goods, including silk, with the Persian, Arab, and African seafarers at such ports, particularly those in central Asia from where the silks had been carried to Rome. In short, exchange relations in those days were largely built up and sustained over centuries by merchants themselves, rather than anything negotiated and formalized between rulers. The involvement of rulers was confined to assurance of security along the routes and collection of tolls, both depending upon the extent of their warrior power as well as institutional development.

[4] For details see H. Ray, *Trade and Trade Routes between India and China c.14 BC–A.D. 1500* (Kolkata: Progressive Publishers, 2003), 65–83.

Most routes passed through isolated tracts largely bereft of settlements and were hence unsafe all along due to the attack of wayside robbers and autonomous plundering tribes, not subdued and integrated by any of the organized ruling lineages or dynasties. Conflicts among chiefdoms of ruling lineages as well as battles among dynasties were other major hindrances for the march of caravan troupes. Due to adverse political circumstances in central Asia, the silk route got interrupted and was made largely non-usable by the close of the 1st century BCE, necessitating the opening up of an overseas silk route as an alternative. Its coincidence with the opening up of the wind-based cross-oceanic routes in the Indian Ocean by the Graeco-Roman maritime traders was not, in fact, accidental.

Hippalus' Discovery Fictitious

Whether the eastern Mediterranean sailors acquired knowledge about the use of monsoon winds from the earlier mariners of the Arabian Sea or discovered it afresh cannot be determined easily. It is quite likely that the coasting sailors of ancient times had acquired experiential lessons about the utilization of seasonal winds. Ancient seafarers had, anyway, awareness about latitudinal parallels and corresponding destinations, as part of their traditional working knowledge of contemporary overseas navigators. They knew that sailing from the Horn of Africa across the Arabian Sea by navigating the 12° latitude east would take them to the southern west coast of India.[5] Whether they were aware of the monsoon winds, now named after Hippalus, has been a question of debate with scholars accepting and rejecting the claim of the discovery of the winds by Hippalus. It is reasonable to believe that many Greeks and Arabs had already known and used the monsoon winds, though only for coasting along the seaboards and crossing the bays.

[5] *PME*, 57. See, L. Casson, *The Periplus Maris Erythraei: Text with Introduction, Translation, and Commentary* (Princeton: Princeton University Press, 1989), 83–5. Also, A. Tchernia 'Winds and Coins: From the Supposed Discovery of the Monsoon to the *denarii* of Tiberius', in *Crossings: Early Mediterranean Contacts with India*, eds F. De Romanis and A. Tchernia (New Delhi: Manohar Publishers and Italian Embassy Cultural Centre, 1997), 250–76.

Poseidonius (c. 130–51 BC), narrating a story of a shipwrecked Indian sailor, would have us believe that the monsoon winds were known to and utilized by sailors from the Indian coast, probably not for oceanic cross-voyages. The story narrates that the half-dead Indian sailor, brought to the King by coastguards on the Red Sea, promised to guide any of the King's navigators on a voyage to India. Accordingly, Eudoxus of Cyzicus, a Greek mariner, delegated by Ptolemy VIII for the mission, is reported to have been guided to India in 118 BCE. The next year Eudoxus himself is said to have led a direct voyage to India during the reign of Queen Cleopatra III, the wife of Ptolemy VIII. Strabo, rather sceptical about the role of the Indian sailor, dismisses the narrative by Poseidonius and reports the discovery of the wind by Hippalus.[6] Actually, there is nothing unlikely about the claim of the voyages of Eudoxus to India, because Alexandrian merchants well acquainted with the exchange network in the Red Sea, could barter for the precious goods from the east with their Indian and South Arabian counterparts experienced in the Indian Ocean. Hence, it is clear that Alexandrian sailors had knowledge about the monsoon winds in as early as the 2nd century BCE. Nevertheless, from *PME* we understand that vessels from India hardly used to travel beyond the Horn of Africa and those of Egypt hardly used to sail towards Indian Ocean until Aden became an accomplished port.[7] During the age of Ptolemies, Greek merchants had sailed only up to the port of Aden on the coast of south-west Arabia where they could barter with Arab as well as Indian mariners and acquire the eastern goods.

If at all Alexandrian ships ever dared to sail beyond Eudaemon Arabia, their journey was invariably along the coastline. Arab mariners also must have known about the monsoon winds, but they were hardly ever dependent on them for cross-oceanic voyages, probably due to the small size of their vessels, which would not suit the rough sea during the monsoon.[8] This was the situation till about the middle

[6] Strabo, *Geography*, Vol. I, tr. H.L. Jones (Cambridge: Harvard University Press, 1917), Book 2, 33.4–5.

[7] *PME*, 26.

[8] L. Casson, 'Ancient Naval Technology and the Route to India', in *Rome and India: The Ancient Sea Trade* V. eds Begley and R.D. de Puma (Madison: University of Wisconsin Press, 1991), 8–11.

of the 2nd century BCE when Roman financiers began to invest for gains from the Alexandrian money market. It is true that Alexandrian merchants had grown ambitious about their direct participation in the north–south exchange of oriental goods that had great demand in the Mediterranean world. Moved by the desire to gain direct access to the Indian ports by sidestepping the Arabian ports, Alexandrian navigators had felt the need for guidance from an Indian sailor, knowledgeable in the seasonal monsoon winds and experienced in wind-based voyages in the Indian Ocean.

It is only Strabo who has taken the episode of the Hippalus Wind seriously, which makes sense against his observations. The later writers like Pliny the Elder, the unknown author of *PME*, and Ptolemy have not given any importance to the tradition of the discovery by Hippalus. Strabo's intention was obviously to emphasize the phenomenal rise of the cross-oceanic voyages in the Indian Ocean by Graeco-Roman merchant-mariners as a major achievement of Gallus, the prefect of Egypt, who was the former's host and friend. He is said to have stated that

> in earlier times, not so many as twenty vessels would have dared to traverse the Red Sea far enough to get a peep outside the straits (Bab-el-Mandab), but at the present time, even large fleets are dispatched as far as India and the extremities of Ethiopia, from which the most valuable cargoes are brought to Egypt first and then sent forth to other regions.[9]

An external criticism of the statement against his position and relation with the ruling aristocracy makes the exaggeration of the increase in the number of ships during the Augustan reign and the intention explicit.

Writers like Pliny the Elder and Ptolemy have not attributed much significance to the episode of the Hippalus Wind. Pliny the Elder maintains that Hippalus was only a later discoverer, for monsoon winds had been part of the practical wisdom of the merchants in the Indian Ocean.[10] The author of *PME* says that at least half-a-century before the Roman conquest of Egypt, the knowledge about the monsoon winds

[9] Strabo, *Geography*, Vol. I, Book 2, 5.12

[10] Pliny the Elder, *Natural History*, 6:26.

had been utilized with the consequent expansion of exchange.[11] However, he gives credit of the discovery of the route to cross the Indian Ocean using the wind to the ship captain Hippalus after whom the mariners made it a regular feature for the sailing of ships, huge in size and large in number, to the east:

> The pilot Hippalus was the first to discover the direct route to India on the high seas. He thought to the location of the ports and to the shape of the sea and realised that the monsoon winds came from the sea and blow seasonally.... This wind is called 'Hippalus' after this navigator.[12]

Most historians have, therefore, considered the 'Hippalus episode' fictitious. E.H. Warmington, maintaining that the use of the trade winds was known in the early years of the CE, thanks to the adventurous sailors exploring shorter passages to the coasts of India from Aden, goes to the extent of saying that such a sailor called Hippalus hardly existed.[13] Archaeological excavations at Berenike, which establish the latter half of the first century BCE as the starting point of bustling commercial activity at the port, have prompted to predate Hippalus at least by a century. A recent study of a couple of inscriptions at Wadi Mineh in the eastern desert of Egypt mention Caius Numidius Eros, a wealthy Roman mariner, to have travelled regularly with his seamen to India in the closing years of the 1st century BCE.[14]

The Augustan conquest of Egypt, the hub of contemporary trade networks and caravan circuits from the Horn of Africa across the desert to the Nile and beyond, and his patronage of overseas trade with the East was a major factor that facilitated adventurous explorations. It is certainly true that the economic motive was the driving force behind it, for both the emperor as well as the merchants. The post-conquest affluence and the entailing incremental pressure of social

11 *PME*, 57 and Ptolemy, *Geography*, 4.7.41.

12 *PME*, 57.

13 E.H. Warmington, *The Commerce between the Roman Empire and India*, 2nd ed. (Cambridge: Cambridge University Press, 1928).

14 Therefore, S.E. Sidebotham believes Hippalus to have been a man who made a pioneering voyage around 110 BC, or possibly a little later. See S.E. Sidebotham, *Roman Economic Policy in the Erythra Thalassa, 30 BC–AD 217* (Leiden: E.J. Brill, Leiden University Press, 1986), 8.

demand for luxury goods intensified the urge of the merchant-mariners to discover a short route of direct access.[15] The explorations that culminated in the successful crossing of the Indian Ocean from the Horn of Africa to the southern coast of India, of course, involved a few stages of improvement, starting from the negotiation of the curved ways along the coasting route. Coasting about the Arabian Peninsula and crossing the northern Indian Ocean to Barygaza on the Gulf of Cambay must have been the first major improvement upon the traditional sailing route.

Subsequently, a route across the Indian Ocean became a reality, but to a great extent many sailors still sailed a long distance along the old sea route from the Red Sea ports via the Arabian port of Mouza, north of the strait of Bab-el-Mandeb, the port of Okelis, and the South Arabian coast to Kane, the strategic point of diversion to different routes to the coasts of the Indian subcontinent. It has been suggested that the gradual withdrawal from the coasting sea route connecting with north-west India to the cross-oceanic route connecting with south-west India was determined by a shift of priority of goods rather than the discovery of the monsoon winds.[16] However, this alone would not have been sufficient, for the development of naval technology for cross-oceanic voyage was a necessary precondition. Those ships destined for the ports of north-western India took a cross-oceanic route slightly towards the north-eastern direction from there while others destined for the ports of south-western India took an eastern route across the Indian Ocean. An alternative route to the south-west was from the Cape of Guardafui to the north-west India via the south-eastern tip of Arabia, which led the ships to the port of Barbarikon at the mouth of the Indus River or to the port of Barygaza on the Gulf of Cambay. Yet another route, the shortest and right across the Indian Ocean, was from Adan or the Horn of Africa to the port of Muziris

[15] For a detailed discussion of the conquests, see C.R. Whittaker, *Rome and Its Frontiers: The Dynamics of the Empire* (New York: Routledge, 2004), ch. 3, 52–61.

[16] F. De Romanis, 'Rome and the *Nótia* of India: Relations between Rome and South India from BC to the Flavian Period', in *Crossings: Early Mediterranean Contacts with India*, eds F. De Romanis and A. Tchernia (Delhi: Manohar Publishers and Italian Embassy Cultural Centre, 1997), 88–9.

on the Malabar Coast. Sasanian mariners must have depended on the monsoon winds to undertake cross-oceanic voyages from the Persian Gulf to the ports of south-west India during the turn of the CE.

This does not mean that the coasting route along the bays to the Persian Gulf and South Arabia had gone out of use, although it was so for the Greek merchant-mariners bound to the eastern world. In fact, the Indian and Arab merchant-mariners had continued to sail along the traditional routes even down to the 4th century CE, of course with the unavoidable long sojourns and intervals, which are well attested by their ceramic remains found at the ports of Arabia and the northwest India. A few Brāhmi inscriptions from the Hoq cave on the island of Sokotra (Yemen) vouch for the visit of Indian mariners to the South Arabian seaboard during the 3rd–4th century CE.[17] It is relevant to recall here the depiction of a ship with two masts, on a Sātavāhana coin, which, indeed, could be representations of the ship from north-western India. It has been suggested that the drawings of seagoing vessels with three masts seen adjacent to the inscriptions on the Hoq cave walls could be made by the mariners from north-western India.[18]

Voyages with the Winds

Although it makes no sense to assign the discovery of the monsoon winds to any particular mariner, their regular utilization to cross the Indian Ocean coincides with the establishment of the Roman outpost at Alexandria. It was possible for vessels to sail northward and eastward with the onset as well as conclusion of the south-west monsoon. Likewise, it became easy to sail southward and westward during the north-east monsoon. There is clear evidence of the prevalence of a systematized wind-based timetable among the Mediterranean sailors in the mid decades of the 1st century CE. *PME* mentions the month of

[17] I. Strauch and M.D. Bukharin, 'Indian Inscriptions from the Cave Hoq on Soquotra (Yemen)', *Annali dell 'Instituto Orientale di Napoli* 64 (2004): 126–30.

[18] S.E. Sidebotham, *Berenike and the Ancient Maritime Spice Route*, California World History Library, 18 (California: University of California Press, 2011), 203.

July as the ideal time for seafarers to set out from Egypt towards India, for the northern wind of summer would help them sail along the Red Sea until the south-western monsoon wind would enable them to sail through the Gulf of Aden and right across the Indian Ocean to land up on the western coast of southern India, called Limyrike (Map 3.1).[19] A vessel leaving Myos Hormos or Berenike in July could sail smoothly to enter at the right time in the Indian Ocean where the south-western monsoon wind would be at its highest velocity. *PME* shows how hard it was to sail with this wind but how swift it was to save time in crossing the ocean. A vessel leaving the Egyptian port in the third week of July could reach the destination towards the end of August.

Similarly, the month of November is mentioned as the ideal time to spread the sails for the return voyage along the same route in reverse, when the north-eastern monsoon wind starts blowing towards the Red Sea, enabling the vessels to reach the destination within the same duration. In the middle of the month of November the north-eastern monsoon wind slowly sets in for the vessels fully loaded with cargoes to spread their sails for the voyage back. It was possible for them to be in Berenike or Myos Hormos in early January. Easterly winds enabled them to negotiate the straits of Bab-el-Mandeb and sail part of the way up the Red Sea. Northerly winds prevailed in the Gulf of Suez and the north of the Red Sea, which helped the sailors up to Berenike and Leuke Come, where they had to terminate their voyages and proceed overland to Koptos through the desert. From Koptos, they continued their travel along the downstream in the Nile up to Alexandria, by using the current against the prevailing wind.

One should not carry the impression that voyages based on the monsoon winds had made the shipment of goods from the southern coasts of India always easy and safe. Actually, monsoon winds that often exceeded 70 km per hour were extremely dangerous at times, making the sea very rough and causing shipwrecks. *PME* has noted how hazardous it was for small Mediterranean ships to cross the Indian Ocean during the monsoon winds. The voyages were not time-saving either, for on certain occasions the bad weather could cause a lot of delay too. It took a vessel leaving Alexandria twelve days sailing

[19] 'They make the voyage to this place in a favourable season who set out from Egypt about the month of July that is Epiphi' (*PME*, 56).

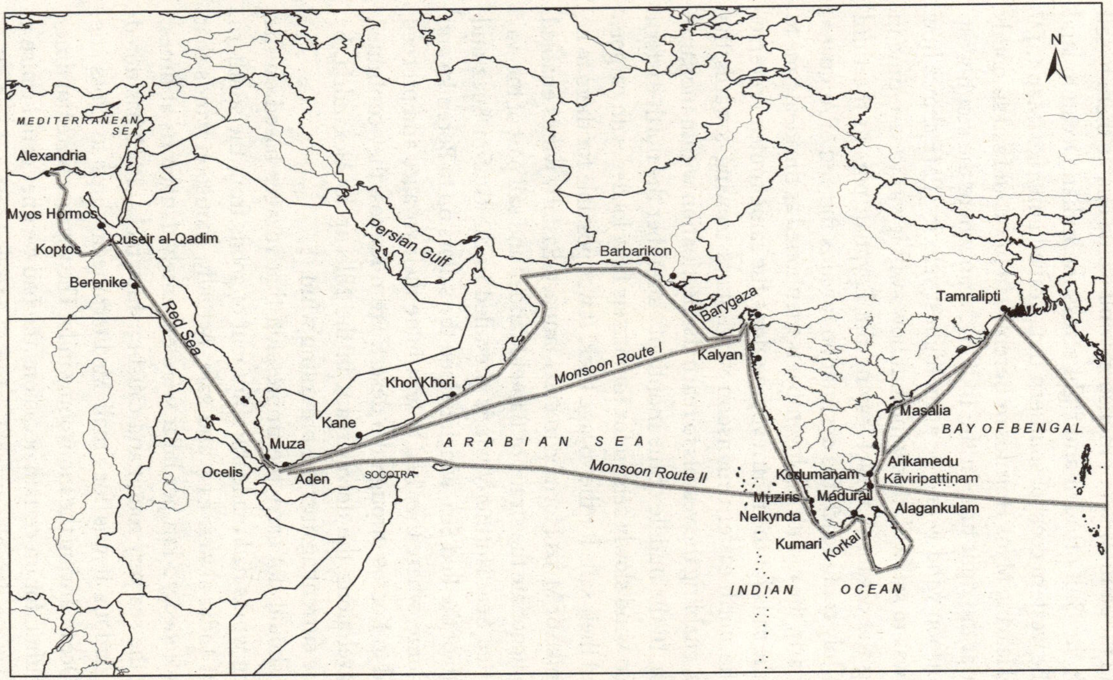

Map 3.1 Overseas Routes between the Mediterranean and Indian Coasts

Source: Author.

up the Nile to reach Koptos from where the goods took seven days to be trans-shipped across the desert by cameleers to Myos Hormos or twelve days to Berenike. Pliny the Elder has estimated the distance by the desert road from Koptos to Berenike as 257 miles long with eight intermediate stations, which the camel took twelve days to complete by travelling during the night, obviously to save them from the hot sun.[20] Strabo mentions that the route across the eastern desert from Myos Hormos to Koptos had eight watering stations and that it took the cameleers six to seven days to traverse the distance.[21] From either of the ports, the ships sailed straight down along the Red Sea in to the Indian Ocean. Of course, this was easy and short compared to the practice during the Ptolemaic regime when the vessels had to reach Aden and sail ahead to the Arabian port of Okelis on the strait of Bab-el-Mandeb or to the port of Mouza, just north of the strait, from where they had to sail along the coast of southern Arabia up to Karie (Map 3.2). Then the vessels destined to north-west India and those to south-west India had branched off each other. This long sailing along the coastline of Persia and Anatolia to north-western India and to the south must have taken two to three years.

An alternative route was used by those leaving from the harbour of Barbarikon at the mouth of the Indus for the port on the Arab–Persian Gulf, namely Forat and then to Charax from where the goods were carried on camels' back to Palmyra across the Syrian Desert. From Palmyra goods were transported to the Mediterranean for customs clearance and then carried forward to points of exchange in the Roman Empire. This was more hazardous than the longer sea voyage up to the Red Sea ports and then across the desert to Koptos because this overland route, unlike the Syrian Desert route bereft of any infrastructure, was with protected wells, cisterns, and road stations maintained by the imperial Roman state. It is quite unlikely that some of the merchants from north-west India who used to sail up to the Persian Gulf seaboards braved to cross the deserts of the Arabian Peninsula, rather than bartering their easterly goods with Arabs and

[20] Pliny the Elder, *Natural History*, 6.27.

[21] D.P. Peacock, 'Regional Survey', in *Myos Hormos Quseir al-Qadim: Roman and Islamic Ports on the Red Sea*, eds D.P. Peacock and L. Blue (Oxford: Oxbow Books, 2006), 6–7.

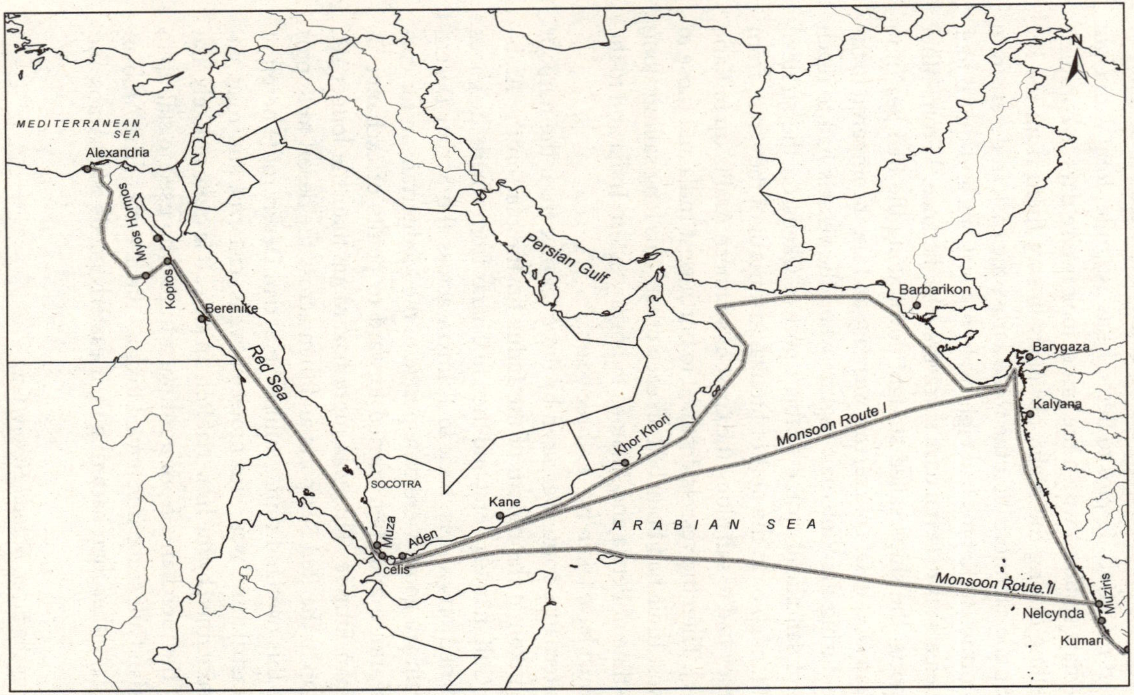

Map 3.2 Coastal and Cross-oceanic Routes

Source: Author.

be done with it. It is in comparison to all this that the monsoon-based voyage that took only less than three months becomes short and safe.

Graeco-Roman Expansion

Long before the Roman expansion, merchants of the north-western India and South Arabia had been maintaining exchange relations with the Indian Ocean world and the Red Sea coast. Some of the ports on the coasts of southern India also might have been active during the period. However, they were significantly infrequent and marginal, compared to what happened with the establishment of the Roman Egypt. Graeco-Roman involvement in trade is first attested by a maritime loan contract of the 2nd century BCE in which a creditor, a banker, five debtors, and five guarantors figure, who belonged to Rome, Carthage, Messalia, Elea, Thessalonica, Macedonia, and Greece. It is significant to note that the banker, whose bank managed the transaction, was Roman.

A few inscriptions of the period also vouch for the fact that they were well-established in Alexandria. Before the Roman financiers got involved in Mediterranean trade using oriental goods, especially spice goods and gems from India's south-western and south-eastern coasts, Greek merchants from Egypt had been active in bartering at the ports there. Graeco-Romans of Alexandria had bartered in spices and incense with the overland caravans of north-western India via Persia and Anatolia. It was, however, a small-scale enterprise in terms of the volume of transactions and with long intervals in terms of frequency, for there was no direct voyage between Egypt and India across the sea. Cargoes from Egypt as well as India could invariably reach only up to Aden beyond which their vessels would not sail. Strabo refers to the Arab and the Greek merchant-mariners active in bartering in aromatics and spice along the Red Sea coasts in the reign of the Ptolemies.[22] Merchants used to travel either overland by the tedious and inhospitable route of anterior times or by the sea route linking the ports of Aden and Socotra where Indian and Arab traders bartered with merchants from Alexandria who, in turn, carried them to the west for exchange.[23]

[22] Strabo, *Geography*, Book 2, 16.4.4.

[23] Warmington, *The Commerce between the Roman Empire and India*, 9.

When Roman Egypt was established by Augustus through conquest after the Battle of Actium (2 September 31 BCE), the Graeco-Romans expanded and regularized the overseas exchange network along the Red Sea ports of the Ptolemaic times with special attention to Indian Ocean to reach the south-western coast of India. Subsequently in 1 CE Augustus conquered Eudaemon Arabia too, which made Graeco-Roman merchant-mariners uncontested in the Indian Ocean and along the track to Indian ports. With the Augustan conquest of Egypt, the Indo-Roman trade became significantly different from what it used to be in the previous ages, especially at the organizational level where it showed features of scheduled commerce under imperial patronage. There was a major change in the political economy of the Roman Empire during the immediate post-Actian years in the wake of inflation caused by the booty from Alexandria. The extent of social demand for oriental goods is best expressed in Pliny the Elder's reference to the growing anxiety of the Roman Senate about the drain of gold due to the regular import of pepper and other spices from the East. This is famous and widely cited as proof of the influx of gold in bullion and as coins to the Indian west coast.[24] Driven by the enormous Roman demand for spices, gems, and textiles from the

[24] See Pliny the Elder, *Natural History*, 6.21, 6.26, and 12.41. The trade in exotics is mentioned to have drained more than fifty million sesterces a year from the empire. This was a sum larger than the annual tribute that Caesar imposed on Gaul after his conquest of the territory. See R. McLaughlin, *Rome and the Distant East: Trade Routes to the Ancient Lands of Arabia, India and China* (New York: Hambledon Continuum, 2010), 2. The items of oriental goods were: pepper, cardamom, cassia-cinnamon, nard, ginger, rice, lentil, cotton, ebony, citron, sesame oil and seeds, sugar, indigo, lycium, bdellium, woods, cotton products, *costus*-roots, gum, aloes, coconut, melon, peach, apricot, millet, frankincense, gum resins, myrrh, elephant, rhinoceros, lion, tiger, hound, monkey, python, parrot, peacock, fowl, ivory, wool, woollen products, hide, fur, silk, lac, pearl, oysters, onyx shell, conch shell, tortoise shell, ghee, musk, agate, carnelian, onyx, nard, nicolo, amethyst, rock-crystal, opal, ruby, sapphire, garnet, emerald, lapis-lazuli, zircon, tourmalines, jade, turquoise, iron, steel, copper, and Indian girls. For a catalogue of archaeologically documented merchandise from Indian, Arabian, and Mediterranean origin passing through Berenike, see Sidebotham, *Berenike and the Ancient Maritime Spice Route*, 223–45.

Indian ports, Graeco-Roman vessels in a substantial number sailed to India every year, though not as many as 120, which could be a number slightly inflated by Strabo in his assessment. Nevertheless, the sudden fillip in demand for luxury goods, which the Roman Empire owed to the extra affluence after the conquest of Egypt and the congenial circumstances of direct navigation across the Indian Ocean, had led to a remarkable presence of Graeco-Roman merchant vessels on the coasts of peninsular India.

It was a process of expansion of the Graeco-Roman financiers, businessmen, and merchant-mariners in search of oriental goods to meet the social demand of their empire. They went straight into the source-ports on the south-western coast of India in their own vessels. Soon there was a substantial increase in the number of ships and the volume of goods shipped from the Indian subcontinent, particularly from the south-western and south-eastern regions of the Tamil chiefdoms under the Cēras, Pāṇḍyas, and Cōḻas. Sri Lanka was also significantly linked to this exchange network. All this accounts for the significant presence of Graeco-Roman merchant vessels in the south-western ports of India during the period between the 1st century BCE and 3rd century CE, as indicated by archaeological remains and literary references. The ships set out from Myos Hormos and Berenike with enough gold and silver in bullion as well as coins besides goods of exchange and provisions for their subsistence. Goods of self-subsistence were extremely important for the merchant vessels because they were constrained to stay ashore for four to five months waiting for the return winds, at places where their staple grains, condiments, wine, olive oil, fish fat, sauce, and so on, were not available. Naturally, it was inevitable for them to settle down at a safe and convenient spot not far away from the ships offshore, which inevitably made the port a site of their settlement too.

The Augustan conquest of Egypt and Eudaemon Arabia was certainly motivated by commercial revenue prospects. It had, indeed, fatally affected the economy of Aden. Similarly, the bypassing of Alexandrian merchants had a negative impact on the South Arabian merchant intermediaries, who were involved in the transit of goods from the Indian subcontinent. Further, this must have considerably reduced the trafficking of exchange goods through the coastal sea-route and almost entirely supplanted the overland route of exchange.

However, the unhindered possibility of oriental and southern exchange in incense, spices, aromatics, precious stones, and so on, had not urged the Graeco-Roman merchants to establish their monopoly in the Indian Ocean and easterly exchange relations. Moreover, the demand for goods was too high to have deprived other seafarers of their opportunities either. The Phoenician, Philistine, Arab, and Indian merchants were active in their own limited way, independently as well as collaboratively. Hence, the often exaggerated question of Graeco-Roman dominance over the Indian Ocean exchange relations is not quite relevant. Also, it is inappropriate to historicize the classical Graeco-Roman maritime activities in the Indian Ocean and their exchange network with the south-western ports of India in terms of the late medieval and early modern experiences of trade rivalry, domination, and colonization.

It was easier for the overland caravans to gain access to the Indian subcontinent after the expansion of the Kushans into north-western India during the 1st century CE, and then down the Ganges Valley in the early 2nd century.[25] Indian merchants overland as well as overseas were integral to the Mediterranean networks as cargo suppliers to the Graeco-Roman vessels. They were the main agents who supplied the non-local goods, especially those from the Gangetic, Himalayan, and the south-east Asian regions, brought overland to the ports on the south-western coast and overseas to the ports on the south-eastern coast. It was the period between the beginning of the 1st century CE and the beginning of the second half of the 2nd century CE when the Graeco-Roman vessels made extensive utilization of the monsoon winds for their voyages to India; the Indian merchants and mariners had a boom in their enterprises.

[25] See the chapter on the 'Western Regions from Hou Hanshu 88', in John E. Hill, ed. and trans., *The Western Regions according to the Hou Hanshu The Xiyu juan*, 2nd ed. (Washington: University of Washington Press, 2003), 11–18. Also 'The Peoples of the West', in John E. Hill, ed. and trans., *The Weilüe: A Chinese Description of the West*, including the Roman Empire (Da Qin), especially Sections 11–21 (Cooktown, Australia, 2004), 23–38. Also J.E. Hill, *Through the Jade Gate to Rome: A Study of the Silk Routes during the Later Han Dynasty, First to Second Centuries CE.*, Sections 11–16 (North Charleston: Book Surge Publishers, 2009), 28–36.

> ... [T]here are ships of the country coasting along the shore as far as Limyrike; and other very large vessels made of single logs bound together, called *sangara*; but those which make the voyage to Chryse and to the Ganges are called *colandia*, and are very large. There are imported into these places everything made in Limyrike, and the greatest part of what is brought at any time from Egypt comes here, together with most kinds of all the things that are brought from Limyrike and of those that are carried through Paralia.[26]

It was the Indian *Sangaram* that transported the goods from the Gangetic and the Himalayan tracts to the ports on the south-eastern coast and carried the goods of the Mediterranean vessels as well as those of the south-western region. *PME* mentions that 'these put into them vessels which sail out of both Limryke and the North ... in them are local craft that follow the coast as far as Limryke, as well as others, made out of very big dugout canoes held together by yoke called *Sangara*'. These coasting merchants had a kind of monopoly over the trans-shipment of western goods, during every season during the months of September–October. It is significant to note that the period of the bustling business of the coastal seafarers of northern India corresponded to the peak time of the Graeco-Roman exchange relations, the heyday of the Roman Empire when the economy of Rome was most resplendent.[27] This affluence of Rome, which it owed to the conquest of Egypt did not last more than three centuries, due to luxury and extravagance rampant among the rich.

The Augustan era (27 BCE–14 CE) marked the zenith of Rome's glory and, to a great extent, that affluence persisted during the reign of Tiberius (14 CE–37 CE) too. Reigns of the Emperors Caligula (37 CE–41 CE), Claudius (41 CE–54 CE), and Nero (54 CE–68 CE) somehow managed to sustain the prosperity of the empire. Nevertheless, towards the closing decades of the first century CE, the economy of the empire began to show signs of decline. Graeco-Roman trade

[26] *PME*, 60.

[27] Dating on the basis of inscriptional sources from the Indian side is shown in G. Fussman, 'The *Periplus* and the Political History of India', in *Crossings: Early Mediterranean Contacts with India*, eds F. De Romanis and A. Tchernia (New Delhi: Manohar Publishers and Italian Embassy Cultural Centre, 1997), 66–71.

based on the goods from the eastern world, particularly the Indian subcontinent, continued to flourish till the first half of the 2nd century CE. A decline in Rome's easterly trade began by the second half of the 2nd century with the epidemic devastation of the empire as a whole by the Antonine Plague during the period between 165 and 180 CE.[28] However, Graeco-Roman exchanges with the East continued, though by fits and starts probably till the close of the 4th century CE.

Goods of Exchange

PME and the Alexandrian Tariff of Marcus Aurelius (176–180 CE), a document of Marcus Aurelius and Commodus preserved in Justinian's *Digest*, constitute the main literary source that contains information about the goods that moved in and out of the Red Sea ports. Most of the goods that moved in were plants, leaves, flowers, seeds, oils, fruits, wine, roots, barks, woods, resins, and gums from Arabia and the Indian subcontinent.[29] *PME* lists thirty-four items while the Alexandrian Tariff lists fifty-four items of external goods to have been subjected to the imposition of customs duty at Alexandria. Only a few items of one are found repeated in the other and the rest in aggregate make a little lower than eighty. Together, they mention forty-five different trade items, of which only nine are mutual trade items ranging from sources in Arabia and India. Items loaded from the Arabian harbours were mainly aloe, frankincense, and myrrh, while items gathered from India were mainly black pepper, nard, malabathrum, indigo, long pepper, lykion, costus, and bdellium.

PME, the firsthand account on the goods available at different ports, gives the most exhaustive list of items that were shipped from

[28] The original source is Ammianus Marcellinus, a Roman historian of the 4th century, who reported on the Antonine Plague of 165–180 CE. See the discussion in D.S. Potter and D.J. Mattingly, eds, *Life, Death and Entertainment in the Roman Empire* (Michigan: University of Michigan Press, 1999), 105–6.

[29] R.T.J. Cappers, *Roman Food Prints at Berenike: Archaeobotanical Evidence of Subsistence and Trade in the Eastern Desert of Egypt*, Costen Monograph Series 55 (Los Angeles: Costen Institute of Archaeology Publications, 2006), 3.

the coasts of peninsular India.[30] Although there is no archaeological corroboration of most items, the information that *PME* provides is eminently reliable, for the account was a manual meant for the practical purpose of seafarers, especially the Greek merchant mariners. It is essential for the merchants to know in detail about how much quantity of the goods of their demand would be available at each port during which season and in exchange of what goods. *PME* notes that the Graeco-Romans went to the ports and marts of Limyrike in large ships to carry in great quantity pepper and malabathrum, the two major items that filled most part of the Graeco-Roman vessels. Other items were great quantities of ginger, cardamom, cotton fabrics, fine pearls, ivory, silk cloth, spikenard from the Ganges, transparent stones of all kinds, diamonds and sapphires, and tortoise-shell.[31] Other accounts like the Alexandrian Tariff add to this list teakwood, sandal, steal, muslin, cotton, ordinary textiles, ebony, and indigo, besides cloves and other products of Malaya and Chinese silk. A detailed list includes cardamom, cassia-cinnamon, rice, lentil, citron, sesame oil and seeds, sugar, lyceum, bdellium, woods, cotton products, *costus*-roots, gum, aloes, coconut, melon, peach, apricot, millet, elephant, rhinoceros, lion, tiger, hound, monkey, python, parrot, fowl, wool, woollen products, hide, fur, lac, onyx shell, conch shell, ghee, musk, agate, carnelian, onyx, nard, nicolo, amethyst, rock-crystal, opal, ruby, sapphire, garnet, emerald, lapis-lazuli, zircon, tourmalines, jade, iron, steel, copper, and Indian girls. In short aromatics, pepper, ginger, cardamom, cloves, and similar spices, goods of wild fauna including ivory; wild woods such as teak and sandal; cotton fabrics, precious stones, pearls, gems, and iron are enumerated as the items of goods carried from the coasts of peninsular India.

Generally several goods of different regions of the Indian subcontinent were available in the ports of the north-west, the south-west, and the south-east; for instance, ivory, Chinese silk, and long pepper (*piper longum*) were available both at Barygaza and Limyrike, while the ordinary black pepper (*piper nigrum*) was available only at Muziris and Nelcynda of Limyrike. Long pepper was a culinary item of demand in Rome and, naturally, was carried in a great quantity from the ports of

[30] The references are scattered in *PME*, 39–63.

[31] *PME*, 56.

south-western India.[32] In fact, black pepper, which, of course, had a very high ceremonial value among the aristocratic women of Rome, was more a preservative spice, especially for storing meat, than a culinary item. It is not accidental that the Graeco-Roman accounts do not include black pepper among food items. In fact, it had become an essential part of the everyday life of their households by the turn of the CE.[33]

Silk and pearls were available mainly at Kolchis on the south-east coast, but they were available at Muziris on the Limyrike coast as well. Similarly, the ports of the south-east coast had provided goods of the Gangetic plains and the Himalayas. It is clear from the Muziris Papyrus that Gangetic nard was available at the ports even in the south-west.[34] This is obviously indicative of a continuation of the practice from the earlier times of coastal seafarers who had required convergence of overland merchants with goods drawn from different parts of the Indian subcontinent and beyond. It is said that Mediterranean goods like Italian bronze objects, Roman glassware, and fine ceramics were distributed through ports of north-western India to Scythian Asia along the ancient overland routes. Explicitly, it was the direct access to the source ports begun by the Graeco-Roman ships which brought about a shift in the conventional system of entrepôt. Many of the goods loaded from the ports of Limyrike were brought from far away places including northern India, which presupposes the existence of a well-established overland distributive network of caravan goods. *PME* prominently notes the operation of the coastal cargo-supply by the local sailors who were servicing around the southern tip of India with goods carried from the Ganges and places beyond in south-east Asia:

32 See the discussion in Cappers, *Roman Food Prints at Berenike*, 117.

33 For an alternative opinion, see Marijke van der Veen, *Consumption, Trade and Innovation: Exploring the Botanical Remains from the Roman and Islamic Ports at Quesir al-Qadim, Egypt* (Frankfurt am Main: Africa Magna Verlag, 2011), 2.

34 For details, see D. Rathbone, 'The "Muziris" Papyrus (SB XVIII 13167): Financing Roman Trade with India', in *Alexandrian Studies II in Honour of Mostafa el Abbadi* (Alexandria: Societé Archéologique d'Alexandrie, 2000), 39–50.

> Of the ports of trade and harbours in these parts at which vessels sailing from both Limyrike and the north call, the most important, lying in a row, are the ports of trade of Kamara, Poduke, and Sopatma. They are the home ports for local boats that sail along the coast as far as Limyrike and others, called *sangara*, that are very big dugout canoes held together by a yoke, as well as for the very big *kolandiophonta* that sail across to Chryse and the Ganges region.[35]

Archaeological corroboration of textual references to most exchange goods brought from the ports on the Indian coasts is enabled by the excavation at the Red Sea ports, particularly Berenike. Excavated objects from Berenike confirm that goods shipped from Muziris to Berenike were mainly forest products like teak, ivory, peacock feather, aloe wood, and medicinal herbs; spices such as black pepper, cardamom, *costus, bellium, lykion*, nard, and malabathrum; marine products like corals, pearls, and tortoise shells; and fabricated products such as gems, well-worked glass, semiprecious stone beads, cameo-blanks, and textiles including silk. A significant discovery from the south-western coast of India is that of black pepper (*piper nigrum*) weighing 7.55 kg in a ceramic container, along with various other goods datable to around the 1st century BCE/1st century CE.[36] Studies have shown that the pepper container is a terracotta jar from south-west India, quite possibly shipped from Noura, Tyndis, or Muziris.[37] Excavation at Pattanam has yielded a few signs of aromatics, but not any concrete samples of the goods for which Muziris was famous. Various organic relics such as *moong* beans (green gram), gooseberry, sesame seeds, and coconut have been found as clogged in alluvial marsh precluding stratified context, but adjacent to the wharf-like space. However, none of these being items of interest for the Mediterranean people,

[35] *PME*, 60.

[36] For a catalogue of archaeologically documented merchandise of Indian, Arabian, and Mediterranean origins, passing through Berenike, see Sidebotham, *Berenike and the Ancient Maritime Spice Route*, 223–45. Also see R. Tomber, 'From the Roman Red Sea to Beyond the Empire: Egyptian Ports and Their Trading Partners', in *British Museum Studies in Ancient Egypt and Sudan* 18 (2012): 201–15.

[37] For details see Cappers, *Roman Food Prints at Berenike*, 117.

they would not have formed part of the goods carried by the Graeco-Roman ships.

At Myos Hormos and Berenike archaeological excavation had yielded black pepper among the Roman deposits.[38] Nevertheless, long pepper that is mentioned as a food product in written sources has not been discovered in any of the sites so far, although it was an important item of demand in Rome.[39] Likewise, cardamom (*ellettaria cardamomum*) has also not been found among the Roman deposits and wherever it has surfaced, it invariably shows an association with early Islamic West Asian goods.[40] Cardamom has been reported from the site of Paṭṭaṇam, but as an item among a variety of botanical objects clogged in alluvial mire precluding stratified context. Therefore, its early West Asian Islamic association is not altogether undeniable in the case of the find at Paṭṭaṇam too. Shells of coconut, *nargilos* of *PME*, have been found in the Roman deposits at Berenike, obviously carried from the Malabar cost by the Graeco-Roman vessel.[41] Anyway, coconut was only an accidental item that had never been an attraction for Egyptians or Greeks or Romans. Moong pulses were found at Myos Hormos and Berenike, as an equally inadvertent item among Roman deposits. They have been reported from among the assortment of the alluvial marsh at the Paṭṭaṇam site as well. As in the case of coconut, probably moong pulses had nothing to do with the dietary items of Graeco-Romans. The presence of such items in the marsh of the Paṭṭaṇam ferry is no evidence of taking them to be part of the items shipped from there. Similarly, rice has been discovered at the Berenike site as another alien item, for it is well known that Graeco-Romans were not rice eaters.[42]

38 Marijke van der Veen, *Consumption, Trade and Innovation*, 41.

39 Cappers, *Roman Food Prints at Berenike*, 117–18.

40 Marijke van der Veen, A. Cox, and J. Morales, 'The Plant Remains Evidence of Trade and Cuisine', in *Myos Hormos—Quseir al-Qadim, Roman and Islamic Ports on the Red Sea, Vol. 2: Finds from the Excavations 1999–2003*, eds D.P.S. Pracock and L. Blue, University of Southampton Series in Archaeology No. 6 (Oxford: Archaeopress, 2011), 3.

41 Cappers, *Roman Food Prints at Berenike*, 78–9.

42 Cappers, *Roman Food Prints at Berenike*, 104–5.

At Arikamedu, Azhakankuḷam, and Paṭṭaṇam we have plenty of archaeological evidence of beads of semi-precious stones, gems, and well-worked glass objects. Beads of semi-precious stones such as beryl, carnelian, quartz, agate, amethyst, garnet, chalcedony and onyx, and glass constitute the most voluminous quantity among the craft-goods excavated at Paṭṭaṇam.[43] A good quantity of beryl, carnelian, agate, and glass beads, their raw materials, a few stone moulds, their chips, broken pieces, and abandoned defective ones have been collected from the different trenches there. A huge quantity of glass beads has been found as part of the excavated goods at Arikamedu as well as Muziris. Remains of spindle whorls, hop scotches, discs, and lamps unearthed at the site are suggestive of the existence of textile production at both the ports.

The items that these ships brought to the Indian coasts were a great quantity of coin and topaz; a good amount of copper, tin, and lead; a relatively small quantity of mineral powders like grey antimony sulphide, red realgar, and yellow orpiment; and some crude glass.[44] Other sources add to this list Egyptian fabric, bronze, peridot gemstones, and high-quality coral. Precious objects like peridot and high-quality coral must have been brought in a small quantity, for they were primarily personal goods of the rich Greeks and Romans on board or meant to be given as gifts to the chieftains. What the Graeco-Roman ships brought in a relatively big quantity were the goods that the mariners bartered mainly for malabathrum and spikenard brought by the itinerant merchants of northern India, particularly of the Gangetic region. It is important that coins, obviously, the Roman silver and gold coins, constituted an item bartered in all the Indian ports against spices. R.K. Mukherji has made an altogether different interpretation of this:

> The chief reasons for the dearth of coins in the north are that the export to Rome of which we have mention in classical writers, in exchange for which Roman coins were brought to India, was mostly of products of South India and the Deccan, while the Kushan kings had the Roman

[43] P.J. Cherian, *Report on the Fifth Season Excavation at Pattanam* (Thiruvananthapuram: KCHR), 2011.

[44] Cherian, *Report on Fifth Season Excavation.*

coins melted down in a mass and new coins issued from the metal having exactly the weight of the *aurei*.[45]

At Barygaza and Sopara these coins collected by the merchants were sent to the mints for re-minting as the coins of the Kshatrapas and Sātavāhanas. But the coins were bartered for pepper at the ports of Limyrike, especially at Muziris and Nelcynda, where they formed part of the objects of treasure as well as raw material for the production of ornaments, rather than money.

The mere presence of a given raw material in an area need not necessarily mean that it was processed and used by the people there. On the contrary, people in a given place would procure certain raw materials from far-off places, and convert them into products using technology unknown to the source region. Hence, it is significant to understand what raw materials of the ancient Mediterranean world circulated were in contemporary India through overseas exchanges. In different periods, different areas could have supplied raw materials, and knowledge about that has helped some archaeologists and historians of exchange studies identify the direction of routes of the circulation of artefacts across continents. Such integrated scientific and technological studies' crucial role in the production of reliable knowledge about the past pattern of exchanges has been widely recognized today. Some attempts to use the range of equipment available for the kind of analysis which is potentially useful to the archaeology of trade and trade routes have also been made. Scientific studies of elemental composition of raw materials of archaeological objects like metallic artefacts are of immense help and several scientists-turned-archaeologists have generated knowledge providing strikingly fresh insights.[46] Antimony, used in ancient Egypt mainly

[45] R.K. Mukherji, *Indian Ship-building: A History of the Sea-Borne Trade and Maritime Activity of the Indians from Earliest Times* (Calcutta: Longmans Green and Co., 1912), 119.

[46] To cite only a few instances: Petrographic analysis in R.V. Karanth, K. Krishnan, and K.T.M. Hegde, 'Petrography of Lime Plaster', *Journal of Archaeological Science* (London) 13, no. 6 (1986): 543–51; Spectroscopic techniques including atomic absorption spectroscopy, X-ray fluorescence analysis in D.P. Agrawal, R.V. Krishnamurthy, and S. Kusumgar, 'New Data on the Copper Hoards and the Daimabad Bronzes', *Man and Environment* II

for the cosmetic purpose of blackening the eyes, and for the medical purpose of treating some skin diseases, must have been probably brought for the needs of the Yavana women in the country as well as the Graeco-Roman mariners. A purpose of some relevance to the artisans and craftsmen of the country was its use in alloying lead and tin for quality improvement in the context of bronze-making. It was used as a ceramic enamel and in glass polishing too. Realgar and orpiment were minerals used in ancient times mainly for painting, and hence were objects of artisan's interest. Copper needs no explanation regarding its past uses, but the mention of tin and lead along with it shows the context of bronze-making. Pliny the Elder mentions that copper was bartered by the Graeco-Roman merchants for gems and pearls of Limyrike.[47] Coral and crude glass objects, some of the raw materials for bead-making, were certainly items of interest for the lapidary craft.

Items of goods going out to Arabia and India constituted a remarkably small number, which in the case of the former consisted of oil, grain, and wine in exchange for aloe, frankincense, and myrrh; and in the case of the latter, metals like copper, tin, antimony, and so on, in exchange for incense, aromatics, spices, textiles, pearls, and gems. Since the goods in demand in the Indian subcontinent were only a few, most goods were bartered against gold and silver. In short, most items that the Graeco-Roman merchants brought and bartered with indigenous merchants were raw materials of artisans and craftsmen, who were functioning as occupational bodies established at the sites of their industries and points of exchange. The presence of almost all the items mentioned in the source texts as brought by the Graeco-Roman ships has been corroborated by the archaeological finds from the excavated ports like Arikamedu, Azhakankuḷam, and Paṭṭaṇam, besides a few other port sites. Antimony, realgar, orpiment, copper, tin, lead, bronze, cameo blanks, coral, and crude glass objects have been found at all these sites.

Most of the goods, bulky and space-consuming, carried in the incoming ships were grains filled in several huge storage jars; wine,

---

(1978): 41–6; and lead isotope analysis by K.T.M. Hegde, 'Scientific Studies in Archaeology', in *Recent Advances in Indian Archaeology*, eds S.B. Deo and K. Paddayy (Pune: Deccan College Publications, 1985), 100–4.

[47] Pliny the Elder, *Natural History*, 34: 48.

olive oil, fish-fat, sauce, and *garum* filled in a number of amphorae jars; and other provisions and condiments filled in many containers for the consumption of sailors during the period of sailing both ways and the sojourn in the ports. Several historians have taken these goods as items of import, which hardly makes any sense, for they were of no use for the people in India. Although wine was an item of demand in central Asia, it was not an object of exchange in Limyrike.[48] A fairly good quantity of Italian wine amphorae shards recovered at Arikamedu has encouraged some of the historians to presume that the Graeco-Roman merchants were able to reap a lot of profit by exchanging the Italian wine, too cheap in Rome, as an item of luxury among the Tamils.[49] The mariners were compelled to stay ashore for three to four months until the return winds started blowing. It appears that some thin clothing and figured linens, which they brought, were for their own use. *PME* specifically mentions that the Graeco-Roman vessels carried in them enough wheat for the people on board, for such goods were not dealt in by the merchants in the ports of Limyrike.[50]

Modes of Exchange

What has been usually described as classical Indo-Roman trade or Roman–Indian trade was not trade as such but a combination of dif-

[48] *PME*, 56.

[49] See the discussion in P. McLaughlin, *Rome and the Distant Past: Trade Routes to the Ancient Lands of Arabia, India and China* (London: Bloomsbury Academic, 2010). However, *Puṟanāṉūṟu*, 56:18–21 (see U.V. Saminathaiyar, ed., *Puṟanāṉūṟu*, 6th ed. [Madras: Thyagarajavilasam Publications, 1963]) cited in support of the argument is a passage of poetic embellishments, which cannot be paraphrased as history. There are several references to toddy as the favourite beverage of the Tamil chieftains. Wine must have been a yavana gift to them and hence an item not very common. This would hardly mean that it was a luxury item of the chieftains and that it had great demand among them. What the passage 'yavanar nankalantanta tankamal teral poncaipunai kalattentinalum ontotimakaḷir...' literally means is that the fragrant and chilled honey brought by the Yavanas served daily in golden vessels by young women with beautiful bangles.

[50] *PME*, 56.

ferent forms of exchange which included trade as well. It was not an exchange relation solely between India and Rome either. Merchants from various regions of the rim-world of the Indian Ocean and the Bay of Bengal besides the Chinese and the Far Eastern lands participated in it. Often the goods moved amazingly long distances both overland and overseas as bartered and carried forward by merchants of multiple cultures. In fact, the movement of goods covered the huge distance between the Indian coasts and Rome, with Alexandria the main distributive harbour. But before reaching Alexandria there was the trans-shipment across the eastern desert of Africa. All this involved transactions at different levels and of various modes. In short, to most of the people who were participants in the exchange, it was not trade in the strict sense of the term that technically means profit-oriented transactions using money as the medium of exchange, measure of value, and means of payment. An aspect to be noted here, which is largely ignored by historians of trade, is the predominance of the non-trade mode in exchange relations across unevenly evolved societies of ancient times.

It was trade for Roman/Egyptian financiers, investors, shipping contractors, business agents, overseas Greek merchants, and the marketers dealing with the aristocratic buyers in Rome.[51] But to the local servicemen like the cargo packers and loaders at the ports on the Red Sea as well as on the Indian coasts, and the movers like the donkey men on the Egyptian village routes and cameleers in the deserts, involved in the trans-shipment of goods, it was standardized reciprocity. To many coastline merchants on the Red Sea, southern Arabia, Persia, Anatolia, and India, it was barter. As far as the chieftains of the Indian subcontinent were concerned, it was gift exchange. In short, the modes of exchange varied from reciprocity, gift, and barter to trade among unevenly developed peoples like descent groups, ranked societies, aristocrats, chieftains, coastal seafarers, overland

[51] The Nicanor Archive, a haulage contractor's accidentally survived set of documents, gives a sample of the different actors involved in the trade. They contain references to at least a minimum of twenty trading companies, twenty-five investors, and almost thirty business agents involved in the conduct of trade in Indian goods. See A. Fuks, 'Notes on the Archive of Nicanor', *Journal of Juristic Papyrology* 5 (1951): 209–10.

merchants, overseas merchants, financiers, and bankers, implying different types of values such as those implying social relationships of obligations, legitimacy of status, ranking, political power, use-value, and exchange value. Value in the non-market modes of exchange is incompatible with that of the market mode, for the concept of value expressed in terms of 'fair price', invariably crucial to the latter makes no sense to the former. Exchange relations with the latter are bound to be unfair to the former who cannot experience value in terms of price and utility.[52]

It is significant that the Graeco-Roman merchants were of the milieu of the monetized market mode of exchange, whereas the coastline seafaring and overland itinerant merchants of the Indian subcontinent were of the non-monetized and non-market modes of exchange, which meant a fundamental difference in their notions of value. This would mean that the value-goals of the Indian merchants were incompatible with those of the Graeco-Roman merchant-mariners. The Indian merchants of an altogether different social formation, and accustomed to the social logic of use-value-based transactions, would not get much benefit out of exchange relations with the Greco-Roman merchants motivated by the market logic of exchange-value and price. The neoclassical theory of economic value, despite its claim to universality in time and space would hardly help us perceive this distinction, for it makes no difference between exchange and trade. It is hard to resolve the problem unless we distinguish between the notions of value in non-market and market forms of exchange.

Nature of Trade

It is important to examine the nature of the trade component in the ensemble of contemporary Graeco-Roman system of exchange relations, which had certain fundamental constituents of a market

[52]G. Dalton, 'Traditional, Tribal and Peasant Economies: An Introductory Survey of Peasant Economy', in *Modules in Anthropology* (Reading, MA: Addison-Wesley, 1971), 28–34. Also see his 'Aboriginal Economies in Stateless Societies', in *Exchange Systems in Prehistory*, eds Earle and Ericson (New York: Academic Press, 1977), 191–212.

economy.[53] It was a tremendously profiteering, massive enterprise involving heavy investment in the form of money as the medium of exchange, means of payment, and measure of value; organized and controlled by royal personages, big financiers, and bankers of Rome; and networked and operated by overseas merchants mainly of Greece. From the names seen in the *ostraca* it has been pointed out that the main actors in the trade were Romans, Greeks, and Egyptians.[54] In the ostraca from Berenike, some ten rich Romans are mentioned in administrative and organizational capacities. Similarly, some seven rich Romans, who had trading firms in Egypt and trusted agents at Myos Hormos and Berenike, looking after transactions, figure in the Nicanor Archive. Several Roman aristocrats were rich enough to own the ship or hire the whole ship and post their business agents and service staff on it. Various intermediaries such as cargo suppliers of the Mediterranean world, southern Arabia, and India; shipping agents; and haulage contractors besides several others like cameleers and donkey men of Egypt were participants in this huge enterprise of which the principal investors were Roman aristocrats who had their slaves or freedmen as trusted agents in Egypt. Though some of the royal personages and their close kinsmen were involved in the trade, there is no evidence to believe that the trade was ever directly under the control of the Roman state unlike the practice in the age of the Ptolemies who had exercised de facto control over long-distance mercantile transactions.[55]

However, it appears that many in the ruling aristocracy were not against this trade in luxury goods, since they were very much involved in the enterprise and hence it meant that it was highly remunerative for them. Some of the label inscriptions in the caves at Wadi Mineh on the caravan route in the eastern desert of Egypt, which mention personages, presumably educated slave-turned-merchants who travelled

[53] For details, see C. Parker, 'Classical Antiquity: The Maritime Dimension', *Antiquity* (Cambridge) 64, no. 243 (1990): 335–46.

[54] R.S. Bagnall, C. Helms, and A.M.F.W. Verhoogt, *Documents from Berenike 1: Greek Ostraka from the 1996–1998 Seasons* (Bruxelles: Fondation Égyptologique Reine Élisabeth, 2000).

[55] G.K. Young, *Rome's Eastern Trade: International Commerce and Imperial Policy 31 BC–AD 305* (London: Routledge, 2001), 213.

seasonally to India and Sri Lanka to bring the luxury goods.[56] For instance, one of the inscriptions mentions a certain Caius Numidius Eros, a wealthy Roman mariner of Greek origin, presumably involved in the voyages to bring luxury goods from the ports of southern India during the late 1st century BCE. He claims to have just returned from India, probably from the north-western port. Another inscription mentions one Annius Plocamus, a freedman–turned–rich mariner of Rome who, according to Pliny the Elder, was the emperor's first contact of Taprobane, quite accidentally through a shipwreck and subsequently he had held the Red Sea *vectigal* (the grain tax contract).[57] He seems to have been a participant in the Indian Ocean trade with the coasts of southern India. Likewise, some of the ostraca also contain names of certain prominent Roman, Greek, and Egyptian personages who were participants in the Graeco-Roman trade in the eastern luxury goods. A frequently occurring name is that of Marcus Julius Alexander, the brother of Tiberius Julius Alexander who was the governor or *epistrategos* of the Thebaid. He was obviously a personage of high-level connections and part of the ruling aristocracy. A few plaster amphorae plugs with the stamps of high aristocratic Romans have been found at Koptos. A Greek inscription of mid-2nd century CE at an Egyptian temple at Medamoud registers huge donations by two Alexandrian businesswomen who were Red Sea ship-owners commanding a fleet.

It is quite clear that the emperor was eager to protect and promote the heavily profiteering trade for the huge revenue benefits by way of tariff on the luxury goods from the ports of India, an agenda evident in the conquest of Egypt. Tariff duties (*portoria*) imposed on goods brought from the Indian ports were at a rate as high as 25 per cent of their estimated cost. These goods, unloaded at the Roman Egyptian ports of Berenike and Myos Hormos, the frontier gateways to the empire, were sealed and tariff was levied before the merchants could

56 T. Judd, 'The Trade with India through the Eastern Desert of Egypt under the Roman Empire', Rev. version, Special Paper (England: University of Liverpool, 2007), 1–18.

57 Pliny the Elder, *Natural History*, VI: xiv. For an authentic epigraphical study, see D. Meredith, 'Annius Plocamus: Two Inscriptions from the Berenice Road', *Journal of Roman Studies* (Cambridge) 43, nos 1–2 (1953): 38–40. Also see the detailed analysis in Judd, 'The Trade with India'.

trans-ship them to Koptos. The fact that a tariff duty at the same rate was levied on the goods brought both from the south as well as the east when they landed at the port of Leuke Come on the Arabian shore of the Red Sea, which was the gateway to Nabataea, a kingdom under Roman domination, further underlines the empire's economic interest.[58] Tariff duties were levied on the goods at the empire's borderline ports on the Red Sea when they were shipped out as well, but at a relatively low rate of 2.5 per cent, for they were mostly subsistence goods.

Transactions of luxury goods from the coasts of southern India, such as pearls, gems, silk, fine cottons, pepper, nard, and other similar items had involved very huge investment and generated enormous profit. Most items were fancy-priced low-volume goods; although they would take a relatively small space on the ship, the merchants who jointly owned them had to pay the ship-owner a rent proportionate to the anticipated profit. A Graeco-Roman ship of moderate size when fully loaded was a massive investment pooled by the Roman aristocrats as the ship-owner, the banker, and the financier, and the Greek merchants who were borrowers of the former. It is said that a shipment from Alexandria carried from southern India roughly between 700 to 1,700 pounds of nard, about 4,700 pounds of ivory, and about 790 pounds of textiles, worth '131 talents, a mighty sum, one that could have purchased almost 2400 acres of Egypt's best farmland'.[59] Values of some of these items have been assessed on the basis of the survived data in the Muziris Papyrus and by multiplying either the number of containers or their ascertained weights in terms of their prices per unit.[60] Accordingly, the price of sixty containers of Gangetic nard loaded in the ship *Hermapollon* has been estimated to have been priced 270,000 drachmas. Similarly, one mina of sound ivory was priced at 100 drachmas and one mina of *schidai* at 70 drachmas. It gives an idea of the scale of trade items in Rome's eastern trade. McCrindle says:

[58] *PME*, 19.

[59] Casson, 'Ancient Naval Technology', 8–11.

[60] F. De Romanis, 'Playing Sudoku on the Verso of the Muziris Papyrus', *Journal of Ancient Indian History* 27 (2012): 75–101.

> The amount of cargo carried by ancient ships was generally computed by the talent or the amphorae, each of which weighed about a fortieth of a ton. The largest ships carried 10,000 talents or 250 tons. The talent and the amphora each represented a cubic foot of water, and as the Greek or Roman foot measured about 97 of an English foot, the talent and the amphora each weighed very nearly 57 lbs.[61]

Several such ships, though not as many as 120 as estimated by Strabo but at least half the number, carrying cargo worth a minimum of 7,800 talents, must have reached Alexandria during every season.

The high tariff duty on luxury goods has been seen in the context of the drain of gold and silver, which was raised by Pliny the Elder as a matter of serious concern. According to him, the empire had been incurring about 50 million sesterces annually as the cost of these luxury items that the traders brought.[62] Another statement of Pliny the Elder, made in the same context, saying that the Graeco-Roman traders were selling in Rome the alleged goods from the Indian subcontinent at hundred times their original price is generally ignored by historians. It is a fact that the easterly trade had drained a lot of the empire's gold, but the implication of the statement of Pliny the Elder is that far more than what went into the hands of traders of the Indian subcontinent or China reached the hands of Greek merchants. A lion's share of the trade profit belonged to the Roman ship-owners, bankers, and financiers themselves. Nonetheless, the gold and silver that reached the Indian subcontinent was indeed a drain, for it never returned and went out of circulation under inapt economic circumstances such as the absence of a widespread aristocratic group with extensive demand for Roman products, the largely non-monetized set-up, the dominance of barter, and the common use of coins as part of valuables, store of

[61] C. Torr, *Ancient Ships* (London: Cambridge University Press, 1895), 25. Also see R.K. Mukherji, *Indian Ship-building: A History of the Sea-Borne Trade and Maritime Activity of the Indians from Earliest Times* (Calcutta: Longmans, Green and Co., 1912), 104.

[62] Pliny the Elder, *Natural History*, VI, xxvi. One gets the relative gravity of the value of the sum when it is examined against an instance at the disaggregate level. It is said that a contemporary Roman soldier was paid 900 sesterces per year, and a small estate in Italy might be worth 1 million sesterces. See Young, *Rome's Eastern Trade*, 213.

wealth, and ornaments. Such a situation pointing to an onset of deflation might have probably acted as a reason for the imposition of a very heavy tariff duty on the luxury goods. It is evident from the remarks of Pliny the Elder that there was strong opposition from the literati and the traditional rich against the aristocratic extravagance with luxury goods from the Indian subcontinent, especially by women.

An outstanding feature of the trade component in the ensemble of Graeco-Roman transactions is its highly document-based organization and operation. All affairs about the shipping of goods in and out were governed by written laws prevalent in the Roman Empire. The occurrence of some terracotta objects unearthed at Berenike, seemingly tokens (ostraca) of customs-duty clearance given at Koptos for cargoes to be sent across the desert to the Red Sea ports, shed light on contemporary procedures of the legalization of goods on board.[63] The set of ostraca in the Nicanor Archive, consisting of caravan transport receipts, excavated from Koptos is another clinching proof of document-based transactions.[64] Nicanor was an Egyptian caravan owner and haulage contractor at Koptos who provided pack animals for transporting goods across the desert from Berenike. These ostraca were the receipts signed and returned to Nicanor by the merchants on the safe acceptance of their goods from the camel men.

Moreover, the Muziris Papyrus, a very significant contractual document of detailed stipulations executed by an Alexandrian creditor, a transmarine trader, and a third person, under the Roman law shows how highly formalized and document-based contemporary overseas transactions were.[65] The document makes explicit the fact that the overseas

[63] Fuks, 'Notes on the Archive of Nicanor', 207–16. See Bagnall, Helms, and Verhoogt, *Documents from Berenike 1*.

[64] For details, see Fuks, 'Notes on the archive of Nicanor', 207–16. For details of excavation, see S.E. Sidebotham, 'Ports of the Red Sea and the Arabia-India trade', in *The Eastern Frontier of the Roman Empire: Proceedings of a Colloquium Held at Ankara in September 1988*, eds D.H. French and C.S. Lightfoot (Oxford: British Archaeological Reports, 1989), 83–92. Also see Young, *Rome's Eastern Trade*, 64–5.

[65] D. Kessler and P. Temin, 'The Organization of the Grain Trade in the Early Roman Empire', *Economic History Review* 60, no. 2 (2007): 313–32. M.P. Fitzpatrick, 'Provincialising Rome: The Indian Ocean Trade Network and Roman Imperialism', *Journal of World History* 22, no. 1 (2011): 27–54. For a

transactions had required a document-based, law-bound, juridico-political set-up of an empire. It proves that the Graeco-Roman trade was never an informal individualistic enterprise. The Papyrus says:

> With regard to there being—if, on the occurrence of the date for repayment specified in the loan agreements at Muziris, I do not then rightfully pay off the aforementioned loan in my name—there then being to you or your agents or managers the choice and full power, at your discretion, to carry out an execution without due notification or summons, you will possess and own the aforementioned security and pay the duty of one-fourth, and the remaining three-fourths you will transfer to where you wish and sell, re-hypothecate, cede to another party, as you may wish, and you will take measures for the items pledged as security in whatever way you wish, sell them for your own account at the then prevailing market price, and deduct and include in the reckoning whatever expenses occur on account of the aforementioned loan, with complete faith for such expenditures being extended to you and your agents or managers and there being no legal action against us [in this regard] in any way. With respect to [your] investment, any shortfall or overage [se. as a result of the disposal of the security] is for my account, the debtor and mortgager ...[66]

It is not only a legal agreement between the debtors and creditors with their names, as well as those of the witnesses, stipulating contractual obligations/responsibilities but also a detailed record of everything relating to the transactions such as the items of exchange and their prices, the tariffs and taxes to be paid at the port, the payments to be made to the cameleers, and so on.[67]

A portion in the Papyrus is quite revealing:

> ... and I will weigh and give to your cameleer another twenty talents for loading up for the road inland to Koptos, and I will convey [the goods]

---

detailed account of organization of trade and trading vessels, see Sidebotham, *Berenike and the Ancient Maritime Spice Route*, 195–205.

66 Rathbone, 'The "Muziris" Papyrus', 39–50.

67 K. Hopkins, 'Rome, Taxes, Rents and Trade', in *The Ancient Economy*, eds W. Scheidel and S. Von Reden (Edinburgh: Edinburgh University Press, 2002), 190–232.

> inland through the desert under guard and under security to the public warehouse for receiving revenues at Koptos, and I will place [them] under your ownership and seal, or of your agents or whoever of them is present, until loading [them] aboard at the river, and I will load [them] aboard at the required time on the river on a boat that is sound, and I will convey [them] downstream to the warehouse that receives the duty of one-fourth at Alexandria and I will similarly place [them] under your ownership and seal or of your agents, assuming all expenditures for the future from now to the payment of one-fourth-the charges for the conveyance through the desert and the charges of the boatmen and for my part of the other expenses.[68]

In short, the trade component of the Graeco-Roman system of exchange was a highly formalized, extensively document-based, elaborately networked, heavily investment-intensive, amazingly adventurous, and extremely risky enterprise jointly run by multiple agencies with the dominance of the Roman aristocrats including the ruling class and rich Egypto-Greek merchants under the protection of the imperial Roman army.

Mediterranean Ships

Egyptian mariners were the earliest innovative craftsmen in shipbuilding who had built vessels by lashing planks together into the hull, using woven straps, and sealing the seams with grass stuffed between planks, as early as in the 3rd millennium BCE. They had a long history of sailing from north-eastern Africa to the coasts of India, Sri Lanka, and Nubia, in hulled cargo ships, the archaeological proof of which dates back to c. 1300 BCE. The Phoenicians come next in shipping technology of galleys having square sails made more powerful with oars, which had enabled them to dominate the Mediterranean Sea for trade. Following them, the Greeks inherited and improved the Mediterranean sail fore and aft through the 2nd century BCE to sail around the eastern Mediterranean, and later across the Indian Ocean for trade. It is said that the vessels of Roman Egypt were 180 feet on an average and each with a capacity to carry a thousand tonnes of Egyptian grain.

[68] Rathbone, 'The "Muziris" Papyrus', 39–50.

Nonetheless, such large ships were not necessary for trade in the Indian Ocean because the cargo from the east invariably used to be of goods of low volume and high value. Nevertheless, they were quite huge according to the Mediterranean scale, as noted by the author of *PME*, for the rough weather in the Indian Ocean necessitated it. Moreover, the three principal merchandises, black pepper, nard, and malabathram, were items of very high demand and had to be carried in maximum quantity. Black pepper and nard, packed in sacks, weighed quite heavy, while malabathrum, though light but bulky, required more space. Other items like ivory, sandalwood, and teak were heavy too. All this naturally necessitated the vessels going to the Malabar Coast to be exceptionally huge and technologically superior. These ships were noted for their efficiency and endurance, thanks to their well-rigged sails appropriate to resist the south-west monsoon wind and the huge hulls strong enough to stand the rough sea without being swamped by tall waves. Philostratus describes a Graeco-Roman ship with a mast of great height, the bulwarks fully raised, the hull of big size with bolted ribs, and several compartments built on the timber beams which run across the vessel.[69] Their method of rigging with the facility to shorten the sail, though conservative, was so designed as to prefer safety over velocity. The widespread practice of building the hull in ancient times was laying the keel first and fixing ribs to form the skeletal structure for planking. However, the Mediterranean method was just the other way round.[70] It is said that the hull of Graeco-Roman ships was built by lashing together the planks with slots and projections at ends and sides alternately to insert and lock them against one another. All joints were then transfixed with dowels and the hull was made stronger by putting a frame inside, precluding the possibility of the planks falling apart. Hulls were reinforced externally with lead sheets from the bottom to the water level, which could protect the planking from degradation, as the excavated remains at

[69] See his *The Life of Appollonius of Tyana*, tr. F.C. Conybeare (London: William Heinemann, Loeb Classical Library, 1912), 3.35.

[70] L. Casson, *The Ancient Mariners* (Princeton: Princeton University Press, 1991), 10. Also see his *Ships and Seamanship in the Ancient World* (London: John Hopkins University Press, 1995), 34–46.

Myos Hormos indicate.[71] Archaeological explorations there have yielded a number of lead sheets and parts of condemned ships reused as beams of certain later buildings at the site, shedding light on the shipping technology of ancient times. Moreover, remains of several shipwrecks in the Black Sea, the Mediterranean Sea, and the Red Sea, recovered and preserved in the various museums of Europe, provide data for technological studies in ancient ship-building.[72]

A few pieces of wooden planking with signs of pegging with wooden nails recovered from Berenike and Myos Hormos constitute the remains of a hull, which help us imagine the strength and capacity of a Mediterranean ship. Planking remains from Berenike show them to have been reused while those recovered from Myos Hormos appear intact. Similar in design and dimension, they clearly signify features of the Mediterranean ship-building technology.[73] Remains of rigging components such as block sheaves, brail rings, sailcloth, wooden toggles, and deadeye have been recovered from Myos Hormos.[74] Such remains shed light on contemporary Mediterranean square sail and rigging technology appropriate for withstanding the weather of the Indian Ocean. Half-a-dozen of the block sheaves made of wood dating to the 2nd century CE, which, by functioning like a pulley, meant to provide a mechanical advantage for pulling the rope attached to the

[71] See a detailed discussion of hull construction in R.J. Whitewright, *Maritime Technological Change in the Ancient Mediterranean: The Invention of the Lateen Sail*, Vol. 1 (PhD dissertation, University of Southampton, 2008), 167–74.

[72] Maritime archaeological finds are appended in R.J. Whitewright, *Maritime Technological Change*, Vol. 2, 221–61.

[73] L. Blue, R.J. Whitewright, and R. Thomas, 'Ships and Ships' Fittings', in *Myos Hormos—Quseir al-Qadim Roman and Islamic Ports on the Red Sea*, eds D.P.S. Peacock and L. Blue, Vol. 2: *Finds from the Excavations 1999–2003*, BAR International Series 2286 (Oxford: Archaeopress, 2011), 179–80.

[74] R.J. Whitewright, 'How Fast Is Fast? Technology, Trade and Speed under Sail in the Roman Red Sea', in *Natural Resources and Cultural Connections of the Red Sea*, Red Sea Project III, British Archaeological Reports, International Series 1661, eds J. Starkey, P. Starkey, and T. Wilkinson (Oxford: Archaeopress, 2007), 83–4.

sail, have been recovered. Several brail rings made of wood, mostly with two pairs of eyes or holes, used for tying the rope to the sail for furling it, were recovered too, of which one had a small remnant of the sail cloth, obviously manufactured in the Indian subcontinent, and dating back to the beginning of the 2nd century CE.[75] It is well known that the Mediterranean square sail rig in the age of the Roman Empire was of a very high efficiency.[76]

We understand from specialized studies that hulls of certain Graeco-Roman ships were huge enough to carry up to a maximum of 500 tons, even though the weight of exchange goods was relatively low and volume proportionately very small, particularly regarding what the vessels carried while heading towards the ports on the Indian coasts (Figure 3.1).[77] Actually, the main weight was of the huge stock of provisions essential for the mariners while on board as well as during the stay at the ports. The mariners, service personnel, and personal goods also constituted a substantial portion of weight. It is easy to generalize them as mariners, but there were helmsmen, sailors, look-outs, guards, and pilots, sometimes belonging to different cultures and continents. According to Philostratus, the Graeco-Roman ship-owners 'set several pilots onboard the ship and subordinated them to the oldest and wisest man. They also post several officers on the prow and set skilled sailors to man the rigging.'[78] Several artisans and craftsmen like carpenters, weavers, and smiths experienced in repairing the hull, sail, rigging system, the metal fittings, and other activities, relating to ship-building accompanied a big Graeco-Roman vessel. There were imperial soldiers offering armed protection to the

75 L. Blue, 'Boats, Routes and Sailing Conditions of Indo-Roman Trade', in *Migration, Trade and Peoples, Part I: Indian Ocean Commerce and the Archaeology of Western India*, eds R. Tomber, L. Blue, and S. Abraham (London: The British Association of South Asian Studies, The British Academy, 2009), 7; also Blue, Whitewright, and Thomas, 'Ships and Ships' Fittings', 191.

76 Whitewright, 'How Fast is Fast?', 83–4.

77 K. Hopkins, 'Models, Ships and Staples', in P. Garnsey and C.R. Whittaker, eds, *Trade and Famine in Classical Antiquity* (Cambridge: Cambridge University Press, 1983), 98–9. Also Casson, *The Ancient Mariners*, 10.

78 See his *The Life of Appollonius of Tyana*, tr. F.C. Conybeare (London: William Heinemann, Loeb Classical Library, 1912), 3.35.

Figure 3.1 Model of an Ancient Graeco-Roman Ship

Source: Author.

vessel as well as its precious cargo and slaves serving their masters who were ship-owners, big merchants, and business agents. In short, it was the people on board and their goods including the provisions which occupied the major part of the vessel's space.

Graeco-Roman ships engaged in easterly exchange were mostly built at the Egyptian ports, Myos Hormos and Berenike, which probably had shipyards, as indicated by archaeological remains of ship-building. Remains of teak, the best tropical hardwood ideal for ship construction; cotton, most appropriate for making the sail; rigging artefacts such as brailing rings made of wood as well as horn; and lead sheets recovered through excavations at the ports suggest the presence of an attached shipyard there for the regular repair and maintenance besides occasional manufacture of vessels.[79] *PME* makes a reference to the Indian vessels bringing ship-building materials like teak and copper alloy nails to the Persian Gulf.[80] This would

[79] S.E. Sidebotham, M. Hense, and H.M. Nouwens, *The Red Land: The Illustrated Archaeology of Egypt's Eastern Desert* (Cairo: The American University in Cairo Press, 2008), 195.

[80] *PME*, 36.

have us believe that the Graeco-Roman ships were made of weather-resistant and durable hardwood like teak.

Common Sail Technology

Square sail, universal in the ancient maritime technology, was what the Egyptians, Arabs, Indians, Phoenicians, and the Graeco-Romans too had followed. It is said that at times the Graeco-Roman navigators used a spritsail attached on a small foremast for raking up and sailing with a beam wind. In order to achieve a balanced-lug, a small square sail tilted down a bit was attached to the fore and at times another sail was rigged towards the stern of the ship. Although it was natural for the balanced-lug to try and shorten the fore portion of the sail, and to raise the back for gaining more wind power, that development was achieved soon. It has been shown that Mediterranean mariners had started using a new form of sailing rig, the lateen, from at least the 2nd century CE, the utilization of which began to be common all over since the 5th century CE.[81] The lateen sailing rig proved so popular that the square sail was eventually abandoned in the Mediterranean during the medieval period.[82] Experts maintain that there was no fundamental change in the sail technology anywhere in the world till the late medieval or early modern times.

It appears from the existing archaeological indications as well as literary allusions that the square sail continued in the ships of the seafarers in the Indian subcontinent till the medieval period. Indian cotton sail and rigging material are said to have been so superior that such goods had great demand in the Western world. Sail fragments and reinforcement strips of cotton, dated to the 1st and late 4th century CE, collected as part of excavated relics at Myos Hormos and Berenike, have been identified as Indian on the basis of the direction and design of spin, which was invariably clockwise.[83] The closely

81 For a specialized study, see Whiteright, *Maritime Technological Change*, 66–126.

82 Whiteright, *Maritime Technological Change*.

83 The cotton and textile industry had existed in Egypt in the 1st century CE, but they were spun anticlockwise. For details, see J.P. Wild, 'Cotton in Roman Egypt: Some Problems of Origin', *Al-Rafidan* 18: 287–98. Also J.P. Wild and F.C. Wild, 'Sails from the Roman Port of Berenike', *International*

woven Indian cotton fabric was found stronger and more enduring than the Egyptian linen that was widely in use in the Red Sea.[84] By and large the Mediterranean mariners were depending on the linen-made sails, the predominant practice in the Red Sea, for the Egyptian linen fabric was readily available in the region. A Graeco-Roman ship had a large square sail tied to a high mast fitted at the middle of the vessel ensuring maximum wind resistance and velocity. A small sail was fitted near the prow as well (Figure 3.2).

Cotton sails not being prevalent in the Mediterranean ships, scholars presume that the sail fragments found at Myos Hormos and Berenike could most probably be of Indian ships, the voyages of which between the Gulf of Cambay and the Horn of Africa were not unlikely in ancient times. It appears that the sails were of a Graeco-Roman ship itself, for they are found attached to the Mediterranean rigging system. Probably, the vessel might have got its sail and rigs repaired at Myos Hormos or Berenike with those made out of cotton brought from India. Such replacements and repairs of ships used to be carried out on contingency at Myos Hormos and Berenike with the material from east Africa and India.[85] The wooden blocks that formed part of the rigging system attached to the square sail and the brail rings were made of the east African and Indian wood. It is even likely that some of the Mediterranean vessels were fully built at the Red Sea ports with the wood and cotton brought from these places. Mere availability of the material in a region need not necessarily presuppose the development of technology required for using it in all the possible ways, as a natural process, in the given culture. Abundance of teakwood and

---

Journal of Nautical Archaeology 30, no. 2 (2001): 211–20. For another related study, see F.C. Wild, 'The Webbing from Berenike: A Classification', *Archaeological Textiles News Letter*, 34 (Spring): 9–16. Also J.F.L Handley, 'The Textiles: A Preliminary Report', in *Myos Hormos—Quseir Al-Qadim: A Roman and Islamic Port on the Red Sea Coast of Egypt*, Vol. 2, *Finds from the 1999–2003 Seasons*, BAR International Series 2286, eds D.P.L. Peacock and L. Blue (Oxford: Archaeopress, 2011), 321–34. For a subsequent discussion, see Whiteright, *Maritime Technological Change*, 89.

[84] For an analysis of the advantages of cotton sails, see E. Black and D. Samuel, 'What were Sails Made Of?', *Mariner's Mirror* 77, no. 3: 217–26.

[85] Handley, 'The textiles', 321–34.

Figure 3.2 A Cross-oceanic Ship of Roman Times on Sail

Source: Author.

cotton in a region is not enough to presume development of superior shipping technology there, which is a factor determined by a variety of socio-economic and politico-cultural demands. In ancient times, technology spread widely across cultures through mutual sharing and borrowing under the pressure of demands, but as adapted to the socio-economic conditions of each region. The demands would ensure the availability of the raw materials through exchange or acquisition even most adventurously. It is known from the sources that cotton was a major item of exchange and that the Graeco-Roman vessels themselves must have carried from India the thickly woven stuff appropriate for the making of sails.

Keeping in view the political economy of exchange in the pre-Roman Egypt and the Roman Empire, anyone would hardly refute the fact that the Mediterranean seafarers had a long tradition of seafaring activities and that they had a well-developed shipping technology. The relative weakness of the sail-rig had never made the Mediterranean shipping technology incompetent to cruise in the Indian Ocean, a fact archaeologically and historically established. It is equally indisputable that they had played a significant role in the Indian Ocean trade during the turn of the CE and that they had established their settlements at the major ports in the south-western and south-eastern coasts of the Indian subcontinent.

4

Ports, Marts, and Ship Technology in Early South India

This chapter is intended to discuss the characteristic features of the major ports and marts of peninsular India as portrayed in the extant source material. It is appropriate to review the ship technology of early India in this chapter along with the nature of ports and marts. The exact constitutive structure of a port in early India has to be examined realistically, for the picture that most of us sustain is that of a modern harbour with an attached city. How far do the data from the literary and archaeological sources tally with what has been construed under the contemporary empirical consciousness is an issue to be critically analysed.

Several ports of ancient India, of which those on the west coast alone, coming to about twenty-two, have been known to us from their descriptions in the Graeco-Roman writings. Barygaza, Akabaru, Suppara, Kalliena, Semylla, Mandagora, Palaipatmai, Melizeigara, Byzantion, Toparon, Tyrannosboas, Naura, Tyndis, Muziris, Nelcynda, Bakare, Balita, Komar, Kolchoi, Kamara, Poduke, and Sopatma are the ports listed in *Periplus Maris Erythraei* (*PME*).[1] Although most of these

[1] *Periplus Maris Erythraei* (*PME*), 49 and 52–60. See W.H. Schoff, trans. and ed., *The Periplus of the Erythraean Sea: Travel and Trade in the Indian Ocean*

ports have been tentatively located on the basis of historical studies, only a very few of them could be correctly identified in the light of archaeological evidence. Several of these ports were not opened for the first time in the wake of the eastern Mediterranean or Roman trade. They had existed before and the antiquity of certain ports like Barygaza and Sopara might go even to the pharaohs' period of beach-combing tracks or coastal sea routes (Map 4.1).

Barygaza

Barygaza, identified as Bharukaccha of ancient records or Broach of more recent records, is perhaps one of the oldest and the landmark port on the Indian west coast, described in *PME*, the most informative among the Graeco-Roman writings regarding marine routes and marts of peninsular India and Sri Lanka.[2] This port was situated at the mouth of the Narmada River in Gujarat. *PME* provides a cartographic representation of how the Graeco-Roman navigators had conceived the landscape terminal where the coastal trade routes and transmarine routes converged, and how efficiently the anonymous author had made a practical manual for the mariners of his times. *PME* begins with a description of Eirinon beyond the Indus and far off from the shore, which existed as a non-navigable gulf of small and large parts invariably shallow and notorious for the shifting sandbanks. Even before sighting the shore, the ships touch the ground and they are wrecked in case of holding their course. A headland protrudes from the gulf curving around towards the east, then south and west, and enclosing the gulf of Baraca that has seven islands. Showing how treacherous the gulf sea, unexpectedly shallow at certain points and deep at others with rocks, eddies, and whirlpools, to be crossed in order to reach Barygaza is, *PME* cautions the sailors against the misleading and entrapping landscape as well as the perilous gulf sea abruptly shallow, rocky, and sharp with violent waves, eddies, and whirlpools.[3]

---

by a Merchant of the First Century (New York: Longmans, Green and Co., 1912), 40–50.

[2] Schoff, *The Periplus of the Erythraean Sea*, 40–50.

[3] *PME*, 40.

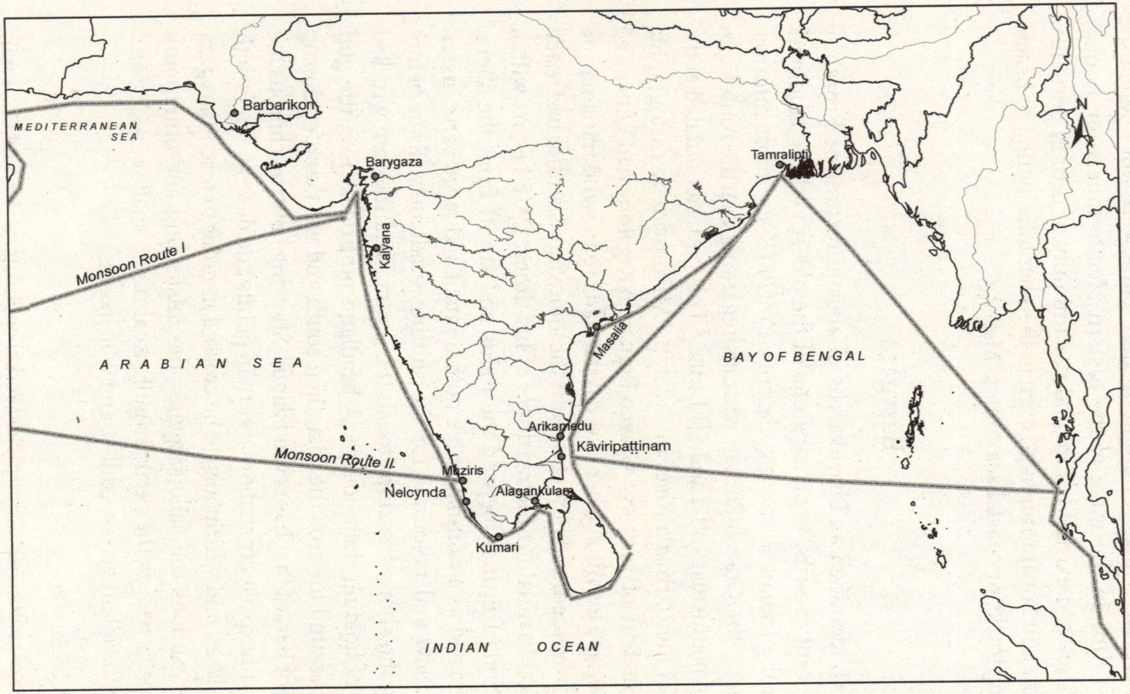

Map 4.1 Sites of Peninsular India

Source: Author.

PME then gives a description of the landscape of Ariaca, the opening fertile stretch of inland adjoining Scythia and the littoral called Syrastrene, which precedes India, a rich agro-pastoral country producing clarified butter and growing wheat, rice, sesame oil, and cotton out of which the thick cloths are manufactured at Minnagara, the main metropolis, from where they are brought down to Barygaza for shipping. There is a picturesque depiction of another gulf of 300 stadia in width running up towards the north, and an island called Baeones, which the sailors heading for Barygaza had to cross. Leaving behind the island just visible towards the east, they enter straight in to the two narrow and rocky passages on the right and left—the former too hard to navigate compared to the latter with a bad anchorage due to strong currents. Even after successfully negotiating the adverse passage, it was still difficult to reach the port right at the mouth of the river called Nammadus, which could not be made out unless the service of the fishermen stationed by the ruler was sought. *PME* informs the sailors that even if they would be successful in entering the gulf, to attain the bay was hard due to the low-lying shore not visible until drawing closer. Moreover, the shoals at the mouth of the river would impede the ship's movement. Therefore, the boats called *Tappaga* and *Cotymba*, manned by the local fishermen and deployed by the ruler, used to pilot the ships from Syrastrene (Saurashtra) straight to the port of Barygaza and drag them to fixed points for docking at anchorage of appropriate depth.[4]

Further due to the intense ebb and flow of the tides the passage of the ship through the bay would be hazardous. At times the bay becomes shallow due to the low tide, making its bottom visible, and at other times it gets flooded heavily due to the inrush of the tidal sea waves driving the river many stadia upwards. Therefore, *PME* cautions in picturesque detail the sailors who reach the port for the first time about the danger due to the irresistible rush of waters of the incoming tide that the anchors could not withstand. Even the large ships would be caught up by the force of it and get driven on the shoals and wrecked. It further cautions that even if the waters are still at the entrance, a sudden rush of the sea over the shoals with a noise resembling the cries of an army at a distance is quite likely.[5]

[4] *PME*, 44.
[5] *PME*, 46.

It is mentioned that the ships unloaded goods such as copper, tin, lead, coral, topaz, storax, sweet clover, flint glass, realgar, orpiment, antimony, gold, and silver coins at Barygaza. For the ruler they are said to have brought silver vessels, singing boys, beautiful maidens, fine wines, thin clothing, and the choicest ornaments like bright-coloured girdles a cubit wide. They loaded spikenard, costus, bdellium, ivory, agate and carnelian, lyceum, cotton cloth of all kinds, silk cloth, mallow cloth, yarn, long pepper, and other such things brought overland by caravans as well as by the coasting merchants from the ports further south down to the cape and even beyond. Barygaza's proximity to Ujjain, a point where several northern overland routes, including the trans-Himalayan, converged, had made it the port of greatest attraction to the Egyptian, Mediterranean, Arab, Persian, and central Asian merchants for a long period.

Sopara or Opara

After Barygaza, *PME* records that the adjoining coast extends straight to the south securing the region the name Dachinabades, meaning the southern course. It is mentioned that the inland towards the east was largely barren with hills and forests full of 'wild beasts like leopards, tigers, elephants, enormous serpents, hyenas, and baboons of many sorts; and many populous nations, as far as the Ganges'. This description shows the anonymous author's knowledge about the nature of the Deccan plateau and the forested landscape beyond. Such explicit acquaintance with the land and people, however tenuous, would have us accept *PME* as much more than just a sailors' manual recounting sea routes to ports and marts of India.

> Among the market-towns of Dachinabades,... Paethana, distant about twenty days' journey south from Barygaza; beyond which, about ten days' journey east, there is another very great city, Tagara', from where carnelian in great quantity and all kinds of muslins and mallow cloths besides other merchandises were carted to Barygaza through rough tracts along the sea-coast. It is mentioned that 'the market-towns of this region are ... in order, Suppara, and the city of Calliena, which in the time of the elder Saraganus became a lawful market-town; but since it came into the possession of Sandares the port is much obstructed,

and Greek ships landing there may chance to be taken to Barygaza under guard.' PME notes that, 'beyond Calliena there are other market-towns of this region; Semylla, Mandagora, Palaepatms, Melizigara, Byzantium, Togarum and Aurannoboas'.[6]

What *PME* calls the first major mart towards the south of Barygaza is Sopara situated at Thane near Mumbai on the coast of Maharashtra. It provided the strategic outlet for the Deccan. This equally ancient port of long continuity is variously mentioned in different sources as Supparaka in the Pali texts; Surparaka in the epics, Puranas, and inscriptions; and probably Sophir or Ophir in the Old Testament. Studying archaeological, historical, topographical, and textual data of this north Konkan port, scholars have attempted to precisely locate its exact site but so far in vain. It is well known that the port of Kalliena situated at the mouth of the Ulhas River was one of the main centres of commerce in the western Deccan during the reign of the Sātavāhanas, in spite of its subjugation by the Saka ruler Nahapana for a brief period. According to *PME*, ordinary cotton cloth, coloured onyx, and wild beasts were shipped from the Kalliena port by the Graeco-Roman merchants.[7] It appears that several Graeco-Roman business personnel and merchants had stayed in the port over a relatively long duration to mobilize and stock the cargoes to be shipped. A settlement of these people is supposed to have existed at Dhenukakata in the neighbourhood. In some of the inscriptions of the Buddhist institutions at Nasik, Karle, and Junnar in the western Deccan, they figure as Yavana (Greek) or Raumaka (Roman) donors richly endowing the *caityas* (Buddhist shrines) and *vihāras* (monasteries). They were probably *upasakas* of the Buddhist religion, but never the convert unlike some historians presumed, for Buddhism was hardly a proselytizing religion but only an order of monks precluding the laity within it.

Southern Ports

All along the whole coast till the end of Limyrike, measuring a distance over seven thousand stadia, there were several ports and marts

[6] *PME*, 51.
[7] *PME*, 49–52.

mentioned by the Graeco-Roman writers. Our focus in this section is on the ports along the coasts of the deeper south of the peninsular India. *PME* mentions:

> ... then come Naura and Tyndis, the first markets of Lymrike, and then Muziris and Nelcynda, which are now of leading importance. Tyndis is of the kingdom of Keprobotos it is a village in plain sight by the sea. Muziris, in the same kingdom, abounds in ships sent there with cargoes from Arabia, and by the Greeks; it is located on a river, distant from Tyndis by river and sea 500 stadia, and up the river from the shore 20 stadia ...[8]

From the pairing of Tyndis and Naoura in *PME* it is clear that they were situated more or less adjacently. Ptolemy mentions four ports of Limyrike with their latitudes and longitudes, namely Tyndis at 116° 14° 10', Bramagara at 116° 45' 16°, Kalaikaris at 116° 20' 14°, and Muziris at 117° 50' 14°.[9] A port that *PME* mentions beyond Muziris is Nelcynda situated on a different river 500 stadia away in the land of the Pāndion and at a distance of 120 stadia from the sea.[10] Becare is another port on the same river, which finds mention in *PME* as an interior village before reaching the Dark Red Hill and the Paralia coast where appears the port of Balita and then Comeris, the southernmost point. Beyond Comeris was the Pāṇḍya port of Colchois, famous for pearls.[11] Further was the Cōḻa port Argaru in the interior, famous for the muslin called Argaritic, named after the village.[12] Taprobane rich in pearls, transparent stones, muslin, and tortoise-shell is the port mentioned next. Then ports on the Coromandel Coast, namely Camara, Poduca, and Sopatma are mentioned.[13]

Among these ports Naoura, Bramagara, and Kalaikaris have not been identified as yet, although Naoura is often presumed to have been on the Kannur coast in the Kannur district. Muziris has been convincingly identified with Paṭṭaṇam on an ancient channel of

8 *PME*, 54.
9 Ptolemy, *Geography*, VII, I, 7–8.
10 *PME*, 54–5.
11 *PME*, 59.
12 *PME*, 59.
13 *PME*, 61.

the Periyar River with the help of Mediterranean ceramic remains unearthed through archaeological excavation. Nelcynda and Becare have been reliably identified with Nakkida on the upper reaches and Purakkad at the mouth, respectively, of the Pampa River. Balita, probably Bammala of Ptolemy's *Geographia*, could be Varkkala, landmarked as the Dark Red Hill of *PME*. Comeris is Kanyakumari, as the name suggests. Colchois has been identified with Korkai on the Tambraparni River. Argaru has been taken for Uṛaiyur in the Cōḻa country. Camara is believed to be Pukar on the Kaveri River. Poduca has been identified with Pondi in the light of archaeological evidence from Arikamedu. Although most ports have been largely identified in terms of their places, very few among them have archaeological evidence of precisely locating them. All the ports mentioned in the sources are not discussed separately for want of details. Some of them figuring in the sources quite prominently with more details and having been subjected to detailed archaeological excavations and historical studies are dealt with independently.

Tyndis

Tyndis is mentioned in *PME* as the first major mart next to Naoura that marks the northern boundary of Limyrike. It appears that these two were located in coastal villages close to the shore in the land of Cerobotros and a major emporium, next only to Muziris. *PME* mentions that Tyndis and Muziris are on two rivers in the land of Cerobotros, distant by 500 stadia (about 250 km). A port of prominence celebrated in ancient Tamil anthology as the abode of the ruling chieftains, Tyndis seems to have had an independent existence, probably under a collateral branch of the Cēras.

The exact location of the port is still unknown in the absence of archaeological indications. It has been generally presumed to have existed somewhere at the mouth of the Kadalundi River. Some scholars think that it was at the mouth of the Ponnani River. Its strategic importance must have been the proximity to the Palghat gap of about twenty miles width across the Western Ghats, which provides easy access to the eastern parts of the Tamil land. Moreover, it is believed that the port was on the northern border of the land of the Cēras.

Tyndis could be the Greek rendering of Tondi that figures in a poem in *Puṟanāṉūṟu*, an ancient Tamil anthology, as:

Kulaiyiṟaiñciya kōṭṭāḻai
Akalvayan malaivēli
Nilavu maṇal viyan kānar-
Renkaḻimicaiccuṭarpūvin
Tanṭonṭiyōraṭuporuna

The lines mean 'a landscape noted for groves of coconut palms bent due to heavy bunches of coconuts, wide paddy-fields fenced by mountains, moonlight like sand, extensive sea-shore and the inland water-body with fire-red flowers'.[14]

Poets have praised the paddy harvested in Tondi and the fish captured from its sea. A poem composed by Kapilar mentions Tondi where the Cēra ruler Selva Kadumko Vali Atan, the hero of the seventh *pattu* of *Patirruppattu*, had his residence. Another Cēra ruler Kanaikkal Irumporai is said to have planted the teeth of his vanquished enemy chieftain at the gates of Tondi. Kōthai Mārpan is another Cēra ruler mentioned to have been stationed at Tondi.

Muziris

Greco-Roman writings mention Muziris as the most prominent port and emporium in the Limyrike, with which many Greeks, Phoenicians, and Romans had a sustained trade engagement. *PME* hails Muziris, with a fairly big settlement, the main mart as well as port of Limyrike. The author believes that the land of Keprobotos owed its prosperity to the bustling overseas commerce under the Roman Empire, which involved shipping of Arabian and Greek cargoes to and the Indian cargoes from Muziris, mainly by the Greek merchants. *PME* associates the port with black pepper, a spice in great demand all over the Mediterranean world and beyond. It mentions the spice in huge loads as brought by the local suppliers and stored in the warehouse well

[14] *Puṟanāṉūṟu*, 17:9–13. For the text and commentary, see U.V.S. Iyar, ed., *Puṟanāṉūṟu* with commentary, 6th ed. (Madras: Thyagarajavilasam Publications, 1963).

before the arrival of the Graeco-Roman merchants. A port indeed of worldwide attraction, Muziris was thronged by merchants not only from the eastern Mediterranean, but also from the upper west coast, north, and north-east of the country.[15]

Pliny the Elder, though he calls Muziris the *primum emporium indiae*, was sceptical about Muziris for a variety of problems such as the unfavourable location due to the presence of pirates in the neighbourhood, the shallowness of the port bay quite up the river denying access to deep-hulled vessels, and the hardships about transporting the cargoes in boats to the port upstream. He says:

> To those who are bound for India, Ocelis (on the Red Sea) is the best place for embarkation. If the wind, called Hippalus (south-west Monsoon), happens to be blowing it is possible to arrive in forty days at the nearest market in India, Mouzeris by name. This, however, is not a very desirable place for disembarkation, on account of the pirates which frequent its vicinity, where they occupy a place called Nitrias; nor, in fact, is it very rich in articles of merchandise. Besides, the road stead for shipping is a considerable distance from the shore, and the cargoes have to be conveyed in boats, either for loading or discharging. At the moment that I am writing these pages, the name of the chief of this place is Caelobotras.[16]

Ptolemy locates Muziris emporium towards north of the river mouth, *pseudostomos* (false mouth), a Greek word referring to the landscape, which might have in due course become a synonym of Periyar.[17] The Peutinger table marks a large lake behind the Muziris emporium and puts an icon denoting *templum Augusti*, which is generally made out as a temple of Augustus.[18] This indirectly suggests the

[15] *PME*, 54.

[16] Pliny the Elder, *Natural History*, VI, 104.

[17] Ptolemy, *Geography*, VII, I, 7–8. Some scholars take the term *pseudostomos* for the name of a river. See V.K. Pillai, *The Tamils Eighteen Hundred Years Ago* (Madras: Asian Education Services, [1904] 1979), 17. Also Peter Francis, *Asia's Maritime Bead Trade: 300 B.C. to the Present* (Honolulu: University of Hawaii Press, 2002), 119. In fact, the term refers to the morphology of the landscape at the river mouth that looks like a split lip.

[18] For a reproduction of the table at 2:3 scale, see A. Levi and M. Levi, *Itineraria picta: Contributo allo studio della Tabula Peutingeriana* (Picturesque

presence of Graeco-Romans in a considerable number at the port site, as settlers, who were constrained to stay there several months waiting for the monsoon winds and also engaging themselves in various activities relating to the mobilization of goods and their stocking up for shipping. Some of the Graeco-Roman subjects must have lived at their port settlement for a longer duration too, for their trade-related preparations before and after every shipping season were manifold.

A passage in *Puṟanāṉūṟu* (343: 1–10), one of the ancient Tamil anthologies, does vouch for what the core of Graeco-Roman accounts describes. It poetizes the riches of Muciṟi by referring to the ship bringing gold and the boat bringing it ashore (*Kalam tanta por paricam/Kaḻittōṇiyār karai cērkkuntu*). The poem alludes to the prosperity of Muciṟi by referring to the people mistaking for a house the paddy heaped in the fishermen's boat after exchanging the fish (*mīnoṭuttu nelkuvai*), and the house with pepper sacks piled up for a ship (*micai ampiyin mania maṟukkuntu/manaikkuvai kaṟi mūṭaiyār*). Further, the poetic embellishment about the toddy-rich Muciṟi owned by the Kuṭṭuvan Cēra with a gold chain (*Talaip peytu varunarkkīyum/Punanalam kaḷḷin polantōrk-kuṭṭuvan/Muḻanku kaṭal muḻavin muciṟiyanna*) alludes to the chiefly munificence in redistributing the wealth of the land from the hill and the sea (*malaittāramum kaṭattāramum*). All this is to praise a small chieftain by regretting the imagined devastation of the fortified household and the village on its owner's refusal to give his daughter in marriage to none other than the one of might and mien, even if the entire wealth of Muciṟi was offered. It is actually a poem belonging to the *makaṭpārkkāñcituṟai* category that invariably adopts the stereotypical poetic strategy of pleasing the hero by extolling his daughter as so beautiful that even the three major ruling lineage heads are at the door ready to fight against one another to win her, and hence the poet laments about the possible destruction of the settlement in the imminent battle.

There are two poems in *Akanāṉūṟu* with passages referring to a battle of Pāṇḍya Ceḻiyan against the Cēra to seize Muciṟi. We have

---

Itineraries: Contribution to the Study of Peutinger Tables) (Rome: L'Erma di Bretschneider, 1967). Also, R. Talbert, *Rome's World: The Peutinger Map Reconsidered* (Cambridge: Cambridge University Press, 2010).

no idea about the historical background of the event, although it was, indeed, a historical possibility. As a poem in praise of a Pāṇḍya chief, it would glorify only the hero in the poem. There is a good possibility of the Pāṇḍya ruler waging a battle to gain control over Muciṛi that was not too far from the two ports of the Pāṇḍyas, Nelcynda, and Bacare. It is only reasonable to think that the Pāṇḍya ruler had an eye upon Muziris, the greatest emporium of the times. Of the two poems, the first has the passage about the suffering of the Cēra warriors trampled by the elephants of Ceḻiyan riding the flagged chariot drawn by decorated horses to seize Muciṛi.[19] In the other poem too, the episode mentioned is the same but the passage contains reference to the prosperous status of Muciṛi as a port of bustling transactions where Graeco-Roman ships turn up with gold and set out with pepper (*yavanar tanta vinai man nan kalam/ponnoṭu vantu kaṛiyoṭu peyarum/ valam elu muciṛi arpu ela valaiyi*). The reference is, indeed, very important in the context of the eastern Mediterranean exchange relations with the south-west coast of India.[20]

This poem praises the Pāṇḍyan chieftain by glorifying his triumphant ride in the flag-bearing chariot with elegant horses and the huge elephants tampering the Cēra warriors trying to resist the attack on the port. He is eulogized to have won the battle waged for securing the Cēra's prosperous Muciṛi on the surfing Cuḷḷi and seized the icons of the port where the Yavana ships arrived with gold and departed with pepper. Using the same episode, both the poems refer to the prosperity of the port based on the Graeco-Roman trade. The second poem explicitly shows the riches of the port as the veritable source of irresistible temptation for the Pāṇḍyans to besiege it. What is significant here is the allusion to a battle between the Pāṇḍya and the Cēra chieftains, the historicity of which remains unclear, wanting corroborative evidence. However, it is not altogether unlikely that they fought each other for Muziris, and it could well have been historical as well, because the port was foremost among the rest in the context of

19 *Akanāṉūṛu*, 57:14–15. For text and commentary, see N.M.V. Nattar, ed., *Akanāṉūṛu*, with detailed commentary, in 3 volumes (Tirunelveli: The South India Saiva Siddhantha Works Publishing Society Ltd), 1949–51.

20 *Akanāṉūṛu*, 149:7–13.

contemporary Graeco-Roman transactions and a powerful competitor against the Pāṇḍyan ports of Nelcynda and Bacare.

Scholars have been taking Muziris for some unknown and eluding part of Kodungallur (Cranganore) ever since the decipherment of the Jewish Copper Plate that mentions Muyirikkōde as the place from where the King Bhāskara Ravi of the 10th century CE signed the charter. Mahōdayapuram, the Sanskrit equivalent of Koṭumkōḷur that subsequently became Kodungallur, being the capital of the Cēra kings, the location of Muyirikode at Cranganore became easy and the Muyiri–Muciṛi equivalence then made scholars think Muziris to be somewhere near.[21] But so far there is no archaeological indication of an ancient port anywhere in or around Cranganore to support the scholarly postulate that has been accepted by many as self-evident. Archaeological remains excavated and geo-morphological traces identified at Paṭṭaṇam, a coastal village in the Chirrārrukara Panchayat (North Parur *taluk*, Ernakulam district) on the southern west coast of India, point to the great possibility of its being Muziris.[22] Relics, especially of the Mediterranean ceramic goods and items clearly identified as Graeco-Roman, prove it as a site where overseas merchants camped. If they had camped there, it must have been for collecting goods for their ship and this would mean that it was a port. We know from the Graeco-Roman accounts that Muziris was a port in the interior, not accessed directly by seagoing vessels. Significantly enough, this geographical position is true of Paṭṭaṇam. Moreover, excavations conducted so far give us to believe a ferry surrounded by the camp of overseas merchants as the core of Paṭṭaṇam. If Paṭṭaṇam is not Muziris, the Graeco-Roman writings would have mentioned the former by some name. It is important that they do not mention any port other than Muziris, as located between Tyndis

21 For the earliest attempt at locating Muciṛi in Kodungallur, see R. Caldwell, 'Introduction', in *A Comparative Grammar of the Dravidian or South-Indian Family of Languages* (London: Harrison and Sons, 1856), 97.

22 See K.P. Shajan, V. Sevakumar, and P.J. Cherian, 'Locating the Ancient Port of Muziris: Fresh findings from Paṭṭaṇam', *Journal of Roman Archaeology* (Cambridge: Cambridge University Press) 17 (2004): 312–20. For the old hypothetical assumption, see R. Gurukkal and D. Whittaker, 'In Search of Muziris', *Journal of Roman Archaeology* 14 (2001): 335–50.

and Nelcynda. Further, it is not reasonable to believe that there was another port at Cranganoṛe, a place only about 6 km away. Keeping in view all this, it appears that the identification of Paṭṭaṇam as Muziris is quite tenable.

Nelcynda

Strabo mentions Nelcynda and Becare, often paired in references, as the northern limit of the Pāndion region. Of the pair, Pliny the Elder takes the former for the name of the inhabitant tribe (Nelcyndes tribe) and the latter for the emporium, a long way off from Modura, the headquarters of the Pāndion located inland. A port famous for the best variety of pepper brought from Coṭṭanāra and transported in small mono-trunk boats through the tiny river to the ship anchored at the bay far ahead, Becare seems to have attracted Pliny the Elder. He certifies it to be a port better navigable than Muziris, where transportation of cargoes was hazardous.[23] According to him, Becare was richer than Muziris in goods of Graeco-Roman demand. *PME* on the contrary takes Becare for a separate settlement and a rather inconvenient port to which cargoes had to reach through unclear channels and with the small river full of shoals. It locates the port at a strategic point on the course of the journey down the south beyond Muziris, at a distance of 500 stadia and a bit before a dark red mountain:

> There is another place at the mouth of this river, the village of Becare, to which ships drop down on the outward voyage from Nelcynda, and anchor in the roadstead to take on their cargoes; because the river is full of shoals and the channels are not clear. The kings of both these market-towns live in the interior. And as a sign to those approaching these places from the sea there are serpents coming forth to meet you, black in colour, but shorter, like snakes in the head, and with blood-red eyes.[24]

The passage 'serpents coming forth ... black in colour, but shorter, like snakes in the head, and with blood-red eyes' could be a description

[23] Pliny the Elder, *Natural History*, VI, 104–5.
[24] *PME*, 58.

of the crocodiles that were in plenty in the rivers of Kerala. It is interesting that like Strabo, Ptolemy also takes Nelcynda and Becare as two ports or emporia on the same river called Baris.[25] In fact, the connection between the two places is explicit. What appears to be true is that the port of Nelcynda was on the upper reaches of the river while Becare, both a port and a mart, was at the mouth of the river. It is evident that ships were not able to enter Nelcynda due to sandbanks and shoals, and hence they had to anchor at Becare at the mouth of the river. There is nothing unusual about Pliny the Elder's mention of Nelcyndes as the name of the local tribe, for it has always been a common practice to address the inhabitants with the name of the locality.

Scholars have identified Nelcynda variously by developing on one indicator or the other that is present in the Graeco-Roman source. Depending on the description in *PME*, Sastri had suggested the location of Nelcynda in the Kottayam district and subsequently a few scholars put forward different proposals to precisely locate the port.[26] Scholars have presumed Becare to be Vaiskara on the Mīnachil River and in the Kōṭṭayam district, but it is not tenable in the light of Graeco-Roman writings. Nonetheless, most people tend to believe the port to be somewhere on the backwaters, for hardly any of the proposals seems to satisfy the features, landmark, and distance given in the *PME* and Ptolemy's location of the port at the mouth of the Baris River. There is no mention of any place resembling Nelcynda or Becare mentioned in the ancient Tamil anthologies, for exploring better clues of identification.

Recently, a proposal seeking to determine the location of Nelcynda and its identification with Nākkida at 30° 55' 76° (ELL) and 20° 30' 9° (NLL) in the Tiruvalla taluk has been convincingly put across, although without any archaeological proof.[27] It satisfies landscape features and landmarks along the course of navigation described in *PME*. Like Muziris, Nelcynda was famous also for shipping the fine variety of pepper grown at Coṭṭanāra figuring in the Graeco-Roman writings. Coṭṭanāra is taken for Kuṭṭanād on the backwaters, by a few

[25] Ptolemy, *Geography*, VIII, 1, 8.

[26] Pillai, *The Tamils Eighteen Hundred Years Ago*, 19–20.

[27] A. Mathew and S. Raju, 'Inching towards *Nelcynda*', *Rational Discourse* (Thiruvalla: Marthoma College Publications) XII, nos 1 and 2: 5–17.

historians, in spite of the inappropriateness about conceiving the wetland region that has never been known for pepper production. In those days, the region could have been famous only for the varieties of fish endemic to wetlands, rather than for any of the spices. It has been suggested that Korranād, a place near Nākkida with a long tradition of growing fine-quality pepper, could well be Coṭṭanāra in Greek rendering. Ethnographic tradition reveals that Korranādu was famous for pepper production and exchange, and this turns up good evidence of the identification of Nelcynda with Nākkida. According to tradition, pepper used to be transported through an old-time channel with surviving traces, which connects Korranādu with the Maṇimala River and then to the Pampa River.

Nākkida, a place name that literally means the space between the tongues, is a confluence of the three rivers, namely Maṇimala, Pampa, and Achenkovil, which provides for a bay suitable for big boats to stay anchored. This strategic importance of the place has also encouraged a few historians to try and identify Nelcynda with it. So far the attempt of identification, largely based on literary mentions matching landscape circumstances, has not succeeded in mustering archaeological finds to corroborate it.

Becare has been convincingly proposed to be identified as Purakkad at the mouth of the Pampa River.[28] Now the arguments confirm that Purakkad, where the main stream of Pampa joins the Arabian Sea, is an appropriate locale to be Becare, for it satisfies the landmarks of the navigational course specified by Strabo as well as the features in *PME*, besides the geographical location by Ptolemy.

Ports on the Coromandel

There were a few ports on the Coromandel coast visited mainly by the west Asian, Arab, and Graeco-Roman merchant-mariners. *PME* describes the sailors' course beyond Becare, the place distinct for the dark red mountain that is a significant landmark on the route. One after the other, it gives the precise location of these ports on the

[28] K.A.N. Sastri, *Foreign Notices of South India* (repr., Madras: Madras University Press, 2001), 57.

Coromandel coast, details about the items of merchandises available there, and particulars of the rulers of the region:

> Beyond Becare there is the Dark Red Mountain, and another district stretching along the coast toward the south, called Paralia. The first place is called Balita; it has a fine harbour and a village by the shore. Beyond this there is another place called Comari, at which are the Cape of Comari and a harbour; hither come those men who wish to consecrate themselves for the rest of their lives, and bathe and dwell in celibacy; and women also do the same; for it is told that a goddess once dwelt here and bathed.[29]

It is clear that the dark red mountain is the lateritic cliff of Warkkala jutting out right into the sea, precluding the possibility of a beach. We do not know the exact location of the village called Balita and the port there. What appears from the description in *PME* is that it could be close to the Warkkala cliff itself. The next landmark mentioned is the Cape of Comari where a port seems to have existed. As is evident from the excerpt, nothing except the ritual importance of the place is known. *PME* describes the strategic points of the mariners' attraction, which lay beyond the Cape:

> From Comar toward the south this region extends to Colchoi, where the pearl-fisheries are (they are worked by condemned criminals); and it belongs to the Pandion Kingdom. Beyond Colchoi there follows another district called the Coast Country, which lies on a bay, and has a region inland called Argaru. At this place, and nowhere else, are bought the pearls gathered on the coast thereabouts; and from there are exported muslins, those called Argaritic.[30]

It cannot be towards the south from Comar in the strict sense of direction from the land but what *PME* describes being the mariners' practical perception, inevitably based on how they navigate in negotiation with the sea-reality, wherein the initial set-off direction may be different. Nonetheless, where the region extends is to Colchoi (Kolkkoi–Korkai), the main port of the Pāṇḍya country, renowned widely in the Indian subcontinent as well as the Mediterranean world

[29] *PME*, 58.
[30] *PME*, 59.

since very ancient times for the finest pearls available there. Multiple sources mention the extensive pearl fishing along the coast, seemingly under the direct control of the ruling authority. *PME* mentions the practice of deploying convicts as pearl divers, which is indicative of the ruler's control over the pearl fishery. The overall signification of what Arrian quotes from *Indica*, though pertaining largely to mythical notions not worth reproducing as part of history, is to the Pāṇḍya country's reputation for its abundance of luxury goods such as pearls, precious stones, ivory, and silk that attracted the Mediterranean aristocracy. Such mythical accounts with embedded facts of practical relevance must have delightfully informed the merchants and seamen certain truth about trade, trade routes, ports, marts, and goods. They must have inspired them to venture onboard in search of pearls to the coasts of southern India.[31] Pliny the Elder, whose personalized notes are generally critical, cynical, and satirical, provides better insights into historical reality. He observes:

> I once saw Lollia Paulina, the wife of the Emperor Gaius—it was not any solemn ceremonial, but only at an ordinary betrothal entertainment—covered with emeralds and pearls, which shone in alternate layers upon her head, in her hair, in her wreaths, in her ears, upon her neck, in her bracelets and on her fingers, and the value of which amounted in all to 40,000,000 sesterces; indeed she was prepared at once to prove the fact by showing the receipts and acquaintances.[32]

A lot of these luxury goods of enormous value as assessed by Pliny the Elder, adorning the queen's body, indeed, had reached Rome from the ports of Muciṟi and Korkai. With this level of royal opulence as the highest index, we are able to reasonably guess the extent of the craze that contemporary aristocratic women sustained at the enormous cost of being recklessly extravagant in the use of such luxurious items.

[31] See the implications of the myth of Indian Heracles, the Pāṇḍyan Queen, and Kaṇṇaki discussed in F.D. Romanis, 'Rome and the *Nótia* of India: Relations between Rome and Southern India from 30 BC to the Flavian Period', in *Crossings: Early Mediterranean Contacts with India*, eds F. De Romanis and A. Tchernia (New Delhi: Manohar Publishers and Italian Embassy Cultural Centre, 1997), 110–13.

[32] Pliny the Elder, *Natural History*, IV, 104.

> Our ladies glory in having pearls suspended from their fingers, one, two or three of them dangling from their ears, delighted even with the rattling of pearls as they knock against each other; and now, at the present day, the poorer classes are even affecting them as people are in the habit of saying that 'a pearl worn by a woman in public is as good as a lector walking before her: Nay even more than this, they put them on their feet, and that not only on the laces of their sandals, but all over the shoes; it is not enough to wear pearls, but they must tread upon them, and walk with them under foot as well.'[33]

Pearls and silk of the Pāṇḍya country is celebrated in the *Arthaśāstra* too, which mentions *pāndyakavāṭakam* as the finest variety of pearls procured by the divers obviously of the Korkai fishery and *māduram*, the best-quality silk.[34] This reputation of the Pāṇḍyan pearls was widespread in the regions of the Mauryan Empire and beyond. Among the kinds of pearls listed in the text, *tāmṛapaṛnikam* and *pāndyakavāṭakam* belonged to the Pāṇḍya country and *caurṇēyam* to the Cēra land. An inscription of Khāravēla, the ruler of Kalinga, mentions the variety of pearls and gems brought to his country from the Pāṇḍya region.[35]

In ancient Tamil anthologies there are a few references to the pearls of Korkai, expressed in the stock phrase for praising the glittering beauty of a lover's teeth.[36] A couple of poems refer to the pre-eminence of the port itself by way of eulogizing the Pāṇḍya ruler. One of them seeks to please the Pāṇḍya by extolling his fine chariot and horse (*naltēr vaḻuti korkai mun tuṛai*) besides the fragrant port of Korkai (*pūnāṛu parappin ivar tiṛai tanta īrn katir muttam*).[37]

33 Pliny the Elder, *Natural History*.

34 R.S. Sastri, ed., *Arthaśāstra* of Kautilya, *Bibliotheca Sanskrita* 37 (Mysore: University of Mysore Oriental Library Publication Series, 1909), chapter II, verses 11:2.

35 K.P. Jayaswal, 'The Hathigumbha Inscription of Kharavela', in H. Sastri, ed., *Epigraphia Indica* XX (1929–30; repr., New Delhi: Archaeological Survey of India, 1983), 72–4.

36 *Akanānūṛu*, 29:8–10. For text and commentary, see Nattar, ed., *Akanānūṛu*, Vol. I; *Ainkuṛunūṛu*, 185:1–2. For text and commentary, see U.V.S. Iyar, ed., *Ainkuṛunūṛu* with commentary, 5th ed. (Madras: Thyagarajavilasam Publications, 1957).

37 *Akanānūṛu*, 201:3–7.

Its pearl-rich ground, made wet by the lashing waves, leaves marks on the hoof of the horse of Pāṇḍyan Vaḻuti who owns a fine chariot. Another poem alludes to the features of the port. Literally, the verse sings, 'fishermen's daughters dressed in leaves on their rounded hips and dazzling waists, worship by offering conch shell of the *valampiri* type and shining pearls, in the port of Korkai, the pride of the battle winning Pāṇḍyan with trained elephants'.[38] Invocation of precious items like pearls and the conch shell of the valampiri type as common objects of oblation in the worship by fishermen's daughters signifies the prosperity of the port.

A passage in *Maturaikkānci* provides another similar example of signifying the opulence of the port based on the abundance of pearls. The verse, in order to praise the Pāṇḍya chief, sings about 'the people of the fine port of Korkai who drink toddy with the returns obtained by exchanging the mature bright pearls and celebrate', signifying the settlement's affluence based on the profusion of pearls.[39] What comes up central in the references is the pearl-oyster-rich sea coast of Korkai port with good returns, accounting for the prosperity of the ruler as well as the fisherfolk, the former earning gold in exchange with the Graeco-Roman merchants and the latter earning subsistence goods through haggling with the local people.

After Korkai, the port mentioned in *PME* is Argaru, belonging to the coast country ruled by the Cōḻas, which comes next to Korkai for pearl fishing and the production of a fine type of muslin that became famous among the Graeco-Roman merchants as argaritic. Argaru has been taken for Uṛaiyur, the early headquarters of the Cōḻas. We do not have any further details about the port and commercial activities there, from any source including the ancient Tamil anthologies.

It is well known that Sri Lanka was very much a part of the Graeco-Roman mariners' overseas circuit. Many mariners who visited the ports of Limyrike had taken a deviation probably from Kanyakumari, the southernmost point of Limyrike, and gone to the ports of Sri Lanka, a place mentioned as Taprobane in the Graeco-Roman writings. *PME*

[38] *Akanāṉūṛu*, 201:3–7.

[39] *Maturaikkāñci*, 135–8. For text and commentary, see U.V.S. Iyar, ed., *Pattuppāṭṭu* with the commentary of Nāccinārkkiṉṇiyar, 6th ed. (Madras: Thyagarajavilasam Publications, 1961), 288–433.

describes the route to the port of Taprobane, famous for pearls, semi-precious stones, muslin, and tortoise-shells:

> About the following region, the course trending toward the east, lying out at sea toward the west is the island Palaesimundu, called by the ancients Taprobane. The northern part is a day's journey distant, and the southern part trends gradually toward the west, and almost touches the opposite shore of Azania. It produces pearls, transparent stones, muslins, and tortoise-shell.[40]

PME resumes the description of the route along the coast of south-east India and the other ports such as Camara, Poduca, and Sopatma in the Cōḻa land, which had attracted the Graeco-Roman merchants not only for the local products but also for the goods brought from the regions beyond by the coastal traders of India:

> Among the market-towns of these countries, and the harbours where the ships put in from Limyrike and from the north, the most important are, in order as they lie, first Camara, then Poduca, then Sopatma ...[41]

A major port in the Cōḻa country that the mariners reach after Argaru, according to *PME*, is Camara, identified as Pukār. It is Caberis of Ptolemy's *Geography*, which is mentioned as a big emporium.[42] Apart from the local goods like pearls and muslin, the spice goods from the forests of the upper reaches of the main rivers, including those of the Gangetic region, and the products of the Himalayas reached the port. This indicates a shift in the nature of the functions of the ports in the north-east of Korkai, which appear to be more like transit points of consignments brought from places far and near through land and sea. Unlike the ports on the south-western coast, the ports on the south-eastern coast were points of convergence for goods arriving through land routes from the relatively near and far-off places including the Himalayan tracks as well as through sea routes. They were meeting points of inland and overseas traders. In a way, this was the case with all ports in the sense that the trade of the

40 *Maturaikkāñci*, 61.

41 *PME*, 60.

42 Ptolemy, *Geography*, VII, 1, 13.

mariners was dependent to a certain extent on the goods transported by coastal seafarers as well as inland traders. There were seafaring merchants servicing along the coast between Broach and the Cape, well supplemented by the long-distance inland traders meeting them mainly at Broach and Sopara. In the peak phase of Graeco-Roman trade, the overseas merchants seem to have preferred direct access to the resource regions for obvious economic reasons. However, ships returning from the ports of the south-west must have certainly depended on itinerant merchants for products of northern India. This dependence was far more in the ports on the south-eastern coast, for it was feasible in the region that was well connected to the pan-Indian trading networks.

One of the interesting passages in *Paiṭṭnappālai* gives a somewhat realist account of the nature of convergence of goods at Pukār. The passage describes Kāviripaṭṭiṇam as the port where

> horses were brought from distant lands beyond the seas; pepper was brought in ships; gold and precious stones came from the northern mountains; sandal and *akil* came from the mountains towards the west; pearls from the southern seas, and coral from the eastern seas. The produce of the regions watered by the Ganges; all that is grown on the banks of the Kāviri; articles of food from Elam or Ceylon; and the manufactures from Kalakam (in Burma).[43]

It refers to the commercial richness of Pukār as a pool of multiple resources arriving from regions far and wide. It mentions horses arriving through water and sacks of pepper reaching in caravan carts besides the arrival of costly objects such as gems and gold from the northern mountains, sandalwood and akil from the western mountains, pearls from the southern sea, coral from the eastern sea, resources of the Gangetic regions, produce of the Kāvēri, food stuff of Ceylon, artefacts of Kalakam, and so on.

Poduke, archaeologically located in a coastal village near modern Pondicherry, was another major port of the Cōḻa country, an important mart of spice goods, muslin, gems, and so on, and a settlement of Graeco-Roman mariners. Graeco-Roman writings do not provide

[43] For text and commentary, see U.V.S. Iyar, ed., *Pattuppāṭṭu*, 6th ed., 513–63.

much information about the port and the goods shipped from there. Ancient Tamil anthologies also do not contain any mention of Poduke. Archaeology helps us understand the nature of settlements and material cultures at the port site and at the habitation sites in the neighbouring villages.

PME then mentions Sopatna, generally identified as Marakkāṇam at the mouth of the Pālār River in the Chinglepet District, as the next important port from where the Indian merchant ships, made up of single logs bound together and called Sangāra, serviced the coast up to Limyrike.[44] Although, the Graeco-Roman navigators had not regularly extended their voyages beyond Sopatma, it is noted in *PME* that the large vessels of India called *Colandia* made voyages to Chryse and to the Ganges.[45] These vessels carried cargoes from Limyrike, which included goods of the region as well as most things brought there by overseas merchants.

Little Local Base

In the case of Arikamedu, the Iron Age settlements at Sūttukkēṇi situated on the banks of the Gingee River and Kottaimēdu, at a distance of about 30 km, have been often mentioned as neighbouring villages, which they are not, although there existed several megalithic sites like Nāṭṭamēdu, Karaikkādu, Tiruvakkarai, and Cenkamēdu in a radius of about 80 km. This is true of Paṭṭaṇam too where, in a radius of 40 km, there are several sites of dolmenoid cists and urn burials, which yielded black and red ware (BRW), iron artefacts, and carnelian beads. However, there is a marked difference about the relics of the sites such as Tiruvakkarai, Karaikkādu, Sūttukkēṇi, Kōṭṭaimedu, Tirukkoilur, and Cenkamēdu, where the archaeological remains show some links with the port of Arikamedu. Archaeological remains of Karaikkādu are distinct for the shards of the wares of local imitation of the Graeco-Roman ceramics, especially amphora, in the form of big conical jars and Roman-type rouletted ware besides iron slag and glass beads. Along with shards of BRW, Sūttukkēṇi, Kōṭṭaimedu,

[44] *PME*, 60.
[45] *PME*, 60.

Tirukkoilur, and Cenkamēdu have yielded beads, gems, Roman coins, and other objects with obvious links with the material culture and context of Roman contacts. Tirukkoilur is said to have yielded several square copper coins reportedly of Malaimān, a chieftain of the 1st century CE. This settlement was probably connected to Arikamedu, Karur, and Uṛaiyur by routes of exchange.[46]

Most of these sites of craft production at their earliest stratum show signs of the Iron Age and were anterior to the onset of Graeco-Roman trade. Sūttukkēṇi and Kōṭṭaimedu were evidently settlements of craft production, but without any local source of the raw material with which craftsmen had worked.[47] Some of the inland sites like Kodumanal, Karur, and Poruntal were manufacturing cum exchange centres that must have provided artefacts to the overseas merchants of the Roman times. Antiquities like coins, rings, seals, and so on, collected from Karur show that it was an important exchange centre. Although there is no evidence of exchanged objects, Kodumanal and Poruntal were most probably manufacturing cum exchange centres. Archaeological remains of Kodumanal are coeval with the Roman period and it is quite likely that the site supplied beads and other gemstone objects for the overseas merchants, although no Roman coins have been reported from there. Similarly, Poruntal must have supplied gemstones and glass beads to the ports.[48]

It is clear that the raw material was reaching the ports from source sites like Karur. This would suggest that these settlements had owed their emergence as craft-production centres to the strategic importance of their locality, probably due to the easy accessibility or proximity to people of consumption practices. As has been made out by archaeologists, the port was not the causal factor for their emergence since they predate the Graeco-Roman arrival. Moreover, there is ethno-archaeological evidence of lapidary showing long

[46] For details, see B. Suresh, *Arikamedu: Its Place in the Ancient Rome–India Contacts* (New Delhi: Embassy of Italy and Manohar Publishers, 2007), 70–1.

[47] J.M. Casal, *Fouilles de Virampatnam-Arikamedu* (Excavation of Virampattanam-Arikamedu) (Paris: Imprimerie Nationale, 1949).

[48] Y. Subbarayalu, 'Pottery Inscriptions of Tamil Nadu—A Comparative View', in *Airavati: Felicitation Volume in Honour of Iravatham Mahadevan*, eds R. Kalaikkovan, and M. Maldini (Chennai: Varalaru.com, 2008), 209–48.

continuity of stone-working in these villages even after the decline of Mediterranean contacts. There is some indication of production–exchange relations with Arikamedu in the case of some of these sites, although there is no clinching evidence as yet to identify them as the hinterland base for the port. Excavations of the port site have yielded evidence of the existence of a major industry of glass beads, the raw material of which existed abundantly right on the coast. Shipping of beads made of carnelian and certain other semi-precious stones is also attested by the remains unearthed from there. Excavated relics like terracotta spindle whorls, dye-vats, and so on, suggest the presence of a textile manufacturing unit at the port site, but without any evidence of the hinterland base.

Raw material source sites in the case of precious and semi-precious stones are quite well known, thanks to archaeological as well as ethno-archaeological evidence. Garnet must have been brought to the southern sites from the Trichinopoly, Salem, Nīlagiri, and Tirunelvēli areas. Caravans from Ajmer, Merwar, Jaipur, and Udaipur also must have made it available at the ports of the north-west. Agate in association with chalcedony might have been obtained mainly from the beds of the Krishna, Bhīma, and Narmada rivers. Long-distance overland merchants from Ahmedabad, Mōṛi, Jabalpur, Rajmahal, and Rudok also could have supplied it. Craftsmen in lapidary must have brought both agate and carnelian, their raw material, mainly from Rajpipla in Rajasthan and some of the rocky regions of Gujarat. Rock crystal must have been brought primarily from the beds of the Krishna and Godavari rivers besides the Thanjavur rock belt. Craftsmen itinerants must have brought it to the south from Jaipur and Rajpipla as well. Amethyst and beryl were available mainly at Coimbatore and Palghat hillocks of the Western Ghats for the south Indian craftsmen.

Archaeological excavations at Paṭṭaṇam have yielded lapidary waste, swindle whorls, crucibles, and fragments of iron slag, evidently indicative of bead, textile, and iron industries. There are no clues in the source to know who owned and controlled these seasonal industries, be it of bead-making or spinning. Likewise, there are no clues regarding who worked the gems and who the bead-makers were. However, except perhaps in the case of iron working, none of these industries was based on locally available raw materials. This would mean that the artisans and craftsmen engaged in crafts production were not permanent settlers of the locality but non-local people camping at the port site seasonally, because the related remains look temporary and fully induced by overseas exchange. Unlike the case of Arikamedu, there is neither archaeological evidence of crafts production nor ethno-archaeological evidence of its tradition anywhere in the neighbourhood. None of the crafts except silk-weaving and pearl-fishing attested by literary evidence seems to have local base to make Paṭṭaṇam a strategic point of crafts-production. As regards the production of textile artefacts of distinction, namely muslin or silk and precious objects like pearls, we have no knowledge as to who had proprietorship over them, how and where.

Distinguished by the absence of the remains of any permanent structures, Paṭṭaṇam cannot be called an urban site in the strict sense of the term, which denotes a strategic point of convergence of goods and services with enough infrastructures for transport, communication, and governance, sustained by the hinterland.[49] Paṭṭaṇam was a bazaar where transmarine and overland merchants converged for exchange. Many artisans and craftsmen with a good stock of their products and raw-material must have camped there drilling, chiselling, polishing, and finishing their artefacts. Pliny the Elder calls Muziris *the primum emporium* which, though not archaeologically corroborated as yet, cannot be an exaggeration altogether. Being a long exposed and heavily damaged site, Paṭṭaṇam cannot be expected to provide any clear picture of the port of Muziris. Much of the remains there has been shattered all over and even transported to fill in depressions at different parts of the village of the waterlogged landscape. Most probably like Arikamedu, Muziris too must have had two sectors, one occupied by the foreign merchants and the other by long-distance itinerant merchants, the various craftspeople, and many retailers. A bazaar, or what Pliny the Elder calls an emporium, might have existed adjacent to this sector of overland merchants, retailers, hawkers, and peddlers. Predominantly a littoral landscape (*neytal*) inhabited by fisherfolk and salt-makers (*paratavar* and *umaṇar*), the local people had no role in the bazaar, other than bartering their products.

[49] For a scholarly examination of the nature of trade enclaves, see R. Champakalakshmi, *Trade, Ideology and Urbanization. South India 300 BC to AD 1300* (New Delhi: Oxford University Press, 1996), 117–40.

The locality of the port hardly seems to have been producing any of the craft-goods and rendering expert services, except common pottery and iron implements of daily use, besides maintenance services like blacksmithy and carpentry. There are references in some of the ancient Tamil poems to households of hereditary craftsmen such as potters, ironsmiths, and goldsmiths attached to the chieftains. A wide distribution of carnelian and glass beads has been archaeologically attested by their presence as part of burial goods in the megaliths, clusters of which survive at places, not too far from the port site of Paṭṭaṇam and quite accessible through water bodies. Nevertheless, these do not seem to indicate local craft production, for the bead material is non-local and habitation remains are absent. There is no lapidary tradition of ethno-archaeological significance in the locality or in its neighbourhood either. However, archaeological indication of craft production has been found at the port site, most probably suggestive of the activity by migrant craftsmen during their seasonal sojourn. It appears that specialists in craft production like gem-cutters and bead-makers were non-local, mostly drawn from far-off places, who must have been seasonal migrants arriving with their products and raw material and camping at the port temporarily.

We know that the technology, material culture, and consumption practices of the local people contemporaneous to the port were of the Iron Age/megalithic culture and early historic period from archaeological studies. Supplemented by references in the ancient Tamil poems, we have a tentative idea about contemporary ways of life, economy, staple grains, other main dietary items, housing, costumes, ornaments, burial practices, rituals, worship, polity, and so on. At the lowest stratum of the Paṭṭaṇam site, early Iron Age non-burial remains have been unearthed. Shards of BRW dominate these remains that appear in their stratified contexts as superimposed by the multicultural relics of overseas trade.[50] Certain features of discontinuity are explicit in

50 For details, see K.P. Shajan and V. Selvakumar, 'Paṭṭaṇam: The First Iron Age Early Historic Settlement of Kerala', in *Archaeology in Kerala: Past and Present*, ed. M.R. Manmathan (Kozhikode: Feroke College Publishers, 2007), 30–45. Also see P.J. Cherian, G.V. Raviprasad, Koushik Datta, Dinesh Kumar Ray, V. Selvakumar, and K.P. Shajan, 'Chronology of Paṭṭaṇam: A Multi-cultural Port Site on the Malabar Coast', *Current Science* 97, no. 2 (2009): 236–40.

these relics, signifying a culture not evolved out of the BRW people's life. They are relics of an alien culture that had, in fact, replaced the BRW settlers, as the superimposition clearly shows. Apart from the sequential disposition of the two strata, there is no archaeological evidence at the site to presume the transformation of the BRW people into craft specialists like bead-makers or gem-cutters. This precludes the possibility of a general transition of the social formation from the Early Iron Age/Megalithic to the Early Historic consequent on the overseas trade.[51] Nevertheless, the presence of local people in the port is well attested by shards of local ware in substantial quantity, but in what capacities and functions is not certain. It is reasonable to presume that many were providers of local provisions and services like manual labour.

In short, a port of the period, as already pointed out, was not a socio-economic outcome of the surrounding villages. It was the geography and related strategic advantages together with the availability of goods or the possibility of their easy mobilization that made the place a port. It became a point of convergence of other merchants and craftsmen because the merchant-mariners camped there for a few months. This made it a site of demand for certain goods and services attracting some people from the neighbourhood as their caterers. A site where several people crowded, it turned out to be a bazaar, but of a temporary nature looking more like a seasonal fair. People called it a coastal town, but without permanent townsfolk. Indeed, it was primarily a centre of consumption but camped by people least dependent on the local people's resources. The local economy, as discussed elsewhere, was not resourceful enough to sustain a dependent people. Historians, inspired by poetic allusions to paddy heaped in front of certain households on the coast, have presumed it to be a rich economy of wet-rice agriculture and spice trade. It is true that there was rice cultivation during the period but as a community enterprise limited to small pockets, as shown elsewhere. None of the chiefdoms

[51] V. Selvakumar, P.K. Gopi, and K.P. Shajan, 'Trial Excavations at Pattanam, Paravur Taluk, Ernakulam District, Kerala—A Preliminary Report', *Journal of the Centre for Heritage Studies* 2 (2005): 57–66. Also see R. Tomber, 'Amphorae from Pattanam', *Journal of the Centre for Heritage Studies* 2 (Cochin: Hill-Palace Museum): 67–8.

in the region had an economy based on agricultural surplus capable of sustaining a population of full-time artisans, craftsmen, and traders.

Port as Ferry and Bazaar

As already noted, we understand from *PME* that Barygaza had a huge bay with specific points of anchorage. Being the earliest entry point to the Indian subcontinent for the vessels and mariners from Persia and Arabia first and then from the Graeco-Roman world, it is reasonable to presume that Barygaza had some built structures essential to meet the needs of their vessels, persons, and goods. Moreover, it was a major point of convergence for many long-distance overland routes, and naturally the port must have had arrangements for receiving, storing, and shipping of goods besides accommodating the caravans, cargo suppliers, craftsmen, and so on. Similarly, although we do not know the details about the built nature of the port, Tamralipti had a huge and deep bay enabling ships to enter and get anchored. It must have had a larger wharf and allied structures to meet the requirements of the ships arriving from the eastern regions near and far. It is well known that the huge Graeco-Roman ships had seldom ventured beyond the ports on the south-east India and their naval accounts hardly speak about the port in detail.

A few of the ports on peninsular India too, such as Poduke, seem to have had some built features like wharfs, a few allied structures, and a big bay. Excavations at Arikamedu have shown remnants of a few structures, probably of a wharf and warehouse. It appears that the port had two sectors, one occupied by the Graeco-Romans and the other by the miscellaneous crafts-folk and inland traders as discussed at length earlier. However, what could be the exact nature of a port of the period is much of a figment of our imagination, for archaeology hardly helps us reconstruct a realistic map of even the most thoroughly excavated site. From the extant source material, it appears that most ports of early India were boat-ferries rather than built harbours with warehouses, wharfs, customs toll rooms, and predetermined anchorage. They were devoid of docking facilities and invariably ships had to be moored offshore.

Muziris, the most prominent among the emporia of Limyrike, is a good example. Located in the interior constraining the ships to be offshore and dependent on boats for the conveyance of goods, Muziris was basically a trans-shipment ferry precluding docks and anchorage, but presupposing warehouses, camps of overseas traders, a bazaar of merchandise, convergence of overland merchants, craftsmen, and so on, with multiple service personnel hanging around. As argued earlier, there is every possibility that Muziris could be the site now known as Paṭṭaṇam where excavations have distinguished the space with Mediterranean ceramic goods, remains of a platform made of lateritic rubble and lime with brick lining at the water level, probably part of a wharf, and relics of a small canoe, mostly withered and clogged in the alluvial mire, its core. This is indeed a ferry site from where the boats might have carried the cargoes to the ship moored offshore. However, the canoe, probably used for inland fishing by somebody, is too small to have anything to do with the trans-shipment of goods between the ferry and the ship. Archaeological remains, especially of the ceramic goods, suggest that the overseas merchants had their camps adjacent to the ferry site itself. Ceramic remains of overland itinerant merchants are relatively too limited to presume them to have camped at the site. As noted earlier, archaeology testifies activities of metal smelting and lapidary at the site, suggestive of the existence of a set-up of workshop and exchange in temporary stalls. Lack of remains of permanent structures shows the site to have been a seasonal bazaar mostly spread out on the ground in the open and the rest in temporary stalls, as a place of exchange fair.

Indications in a couple of passages in *Paṭṭiṇappālai*, one of the long poems of contemporary Tamil anthology, give us a different picture in the case of a port on the south-east coast of the subcontinent. The passages describe a few of the features of the port, which are relevant to our discussion. One of them describing the port of Pukar mentions functionaries in charge of the protection of the Chieftain's wealth (at the port) (*nalliṛaivan poruḷkākkun-tollicait-toḻinmākkaḷ*), levying tax without fault (*vaikaṛoṛu macaivinṛi pulkucaik kuṛaipaṭātu*) on the various goods that are showered on to the shore from the waters and from the waters to the shore (*māripeyyum paruvampōla/nīrininṛu nilattērravu/ nilattininṛu nīrpparappavu /maḷanta niyāppala paṇṭam*) and heaped up in boundless quantity (*varampaṛiyāmai vantīṇṭi*), and the check-post measuring and stamping the ruler's tiger seal (the emblem of the Cō<u>l</u>a ruler) on the goods so glorious that they fill one's heart with joy (*yarukaṭip perunkāppin/valiyuṭai vallaṇankinōn puliporittup-puṛampōkki matiniṛainta malip-paṇṭam*) and sending them out.[52]

The other passage gives a beautiful account of what goods reach the port from where or which source. It lists the horse, pepper, gold, gems, sandal, akil, pearls, coral, conch shells, and so on, with their source regions. They include various goods produced in the regions watered by the Ganges and grown on the banks of the Kāviri (*kankai vāriyum kāvirip payanum*), besides the items of food from Elam (Ceylon) and the manufactures from Kalakam (Burma) (*ī<u>l</u>attu uṇavum kalakattākkamu*). As regards the sources of goods, the passage mentions the horse to have reached from the land beyond the seas (*nīrin vanta nimir parip puraviyum*), pepper from a distant place as brought by the caravans (*kālin vanta karun kaṛi mūṭaiyum*), gold and precious stones from the northern mountains (*vaṭamalaip piṛanta maṇiyum ponnum*), sandal and akil from the mountains in the west (*kuṭamalaip piṛanta vāramum akilum*), pearls from the southern seas and coral from the eastern seas (*tenkaṭal muttum kuṇakaṭar tukilum*).[53]

Some passages in *Cilappatikāram*, a later text, give an interesting description of Pukār of the Buddhist times, which is quite helpful in imagining the features of a port of the Graeco-Roman times. They give the picture of a port-town with all sorts of people like hawkers of cosmetics, perfumes, flowers, and incense; tailors who worked on silk, wool, and cotton; traders in sandal, akil, coral, pearl, gold, and precious stones; dealers in grain, fish, and salts; washermen, butchers, blacksmiths, braziers, carpenters, coppersmiths, painters, sculptors, goldsmiths, cobblers, and toymakers. It is mentioned that there were settlements of the Yavana traders speaking alien languages and exhibiting many types of merchandise to attract the local merchants. It is further described that in the Cō<u>l</u>a port the lighthouse built of brick and mortar showed blazing light at night to guide ships to ports.[54]

52 *Paṭṭiṇappālai*, 120–36.

53 *Paṭṭiṇappālai*, 185–93.

54 Pillai, *The Tamils Eighteen Hundred Years Ago*, 24–6. In the discussions the author has integrated the content of references from *Paṭṭiṇappālai* and *Cilappatikāram*; for him both the texts belonged more or less to the same

Actually, every port on the coast of the Indian subcontinent in those days was just a strategic point for the overseas vessels mostly moored offshore to load the goods they wanted. Goods of their choice were available at all the ports, probably in varying quantity, and hence none of them had exclusive command over any of the items. Goods produced in various places converged wherever the ships reached. Ports on the north-west, south-west, and south-east India were, to a great extent, shipping points of most items of the eastern world that had demand in the Mediterranean. Most spices and forest goods of the Himalayas and the Western Ghats were shipped from the ports of north-west India during pre-Roman times. We learn from *PME* that Gangetic nard and malabathrum were available in the ports of the south-west as well as south-east India.[55] Intimation about the arrival of ships at various ports might have made the cargo suppliers move towards them with goods of demand procured even from far-off places. In fact, the overseas circulation of goods of the period was dependent heavily on the extensive network of overland merchants. They were the people who made the ports emporia of multiple goods. None of the ports had owed its origins to the economic surplus of the hinterland. Ports were just convenient points for mariners to camp, to fill their vessels with cargo, and set out when the wind began blowing.

In short, ancient ports were mostly not sea ports but ferries on the river mouth and located at safe points aloof from the tidal waves. A few of them that were sea ports had problems like the formation of sand-beds and silting, which caused the bay running into disuse. It is said that in ancient times even in big ports like Alexandria, silting was beyond what contemporary dredging could contain. Most ports on the coasts of the Indian subcontinent were mostly upstream without a quay for the big ships to be moored. Therefore, the ships had to anchor offshore from where the cargo was to be lightered ashore

period and the impression one gets is that the entire details are drawn from the former. For instance, the reference to the two divisions of the port into Maruvam Pākkam and Yavanaccēri, the lighthouse, and details about the people and activities is found only in *Cilappatikāram*. However, he has cited both the texts in the footnotes.

[55] *PME*, 56.

in smaller vessels. They must have required tugboats and barges for their safe movement offshore and to be closer to the shore for a relatively easy trans-shipment of goods upstream. Excavated sites show that the ancient ports on the Indian coasts were very simple with minimum structures and wharf features. However, all of them have relics of multicultural settlers, mainly of merchant-mariners and their agents. It is true that this must have converted a coastal village into a pool of multiple goods, services, and personnel across cultures. Definitely, it might have created some amount of effective demand, but too insignificant for bringing about any structural change in the clan-kin-based local economy.

Multicultural Assemblages

Archaeological excavations reveal multiple ceramic assemblages suggestive of the co-existence of several cultural groups of varied livelihoods at the ports on the south-western and south-eastern coasts of the Indian subcontinent. Material culture goods of Graeco-Roman settlers have been found at all the excavated port sites, and significantly at Arikamedu and Paṭṭaṇam. Archaeological studies have shown some differentiation of material culture in the northern and southern sectors of Arikamedu in the case of ceramic goods. Archaeological debris of the northern sector comprised shards of Mediterranean ceramics, particularly of the Mediterranean amphorae jars, Roman aristocratic tableware like terra sigillata, variety of beads, certain structural remains presumably of the warehouse, lived space, ring-wells, tanks, terracotta spindle whorls, dye-vats, some metal objects, ceramic oil lamps, glassware, and so on.[56] They are suggestive of wealth and an advanced material culture which distinguish the northern sector, closer to the port, from the southern, a little away, characterized by shards of ordinary ceramics and other remains, presumably of non-Mediterranean ethnic groups engaged

[56] R.E.M. Wheeler, *Rome beyond Imperial Frontiers* (Harmondsworth, London: Pelican, 1954), 124–5. Also see G.L. Adhya, *Early Indian Economics: Studies in the Economic Life of Northern and Western India, c. 200 B.C.–300 A.D.* (Bombay: Asia Publishing House, 1966), 126–7.

in gem cutting, bead manufacturing, textile weaving, and metal working, as objects in the debris indicate.[57]

At Paṭṭaṇam too, the multicultural goods are indicated by shards of Phoenician torpedo jars and the pre-Roman Egyptian turquoise glazed ware (jars and bowls), the Graeco-Roman tableware such as terra sigillata and other wares such as amphorae jars, *garum* jars, gems, cameo blanks, and so on, have been discovered, as distinguished from other Indian fine ware found interspersed. Shards of Indian rouletted ware with a Brāhmi label, Amaṇa (Sramaṇa), incised on one of them, assignable to the 2nd century CE, attest to the presence of long-distance inland merchants, probably *upāsaka*s of heterodox religious orders. Beads of semi-precious stones such as beryl, carnelian, quartz, agate, amethyst, garnet, chalcedony, and onyx, and glass found in a substantial quantity with raw material, stone moulds, chips, broken pieces and abandoned defective goods, and rough-outs suggest lapidary at the site. Remains of spindle whorls, hop scotches, discs, and lamps indicate spinning and cotton works there. All this signifies the presence of crafts-folk and artisans.[58] Local ceramic shards in huge quantity, mostly of the plain and coarse types and of daily use for cooking food and storing water, indicate the presence of inhabitants, probably from the neighbouring villages. Since they are found interspersed with other ceramic goods and without any indication of a separate settlement, these could be the goods of local supply to the site or what the potters stocked for exchange. Being a totally disturbed site with very little remains of built structures, one cannot expect the discovery of indications of different sectors at Paṭṭaṇam.[59]

[57] See P. Francis, 'Beadmaking at Arikamedu and Beyond', *World Archaeology* 23, no. 1 (1991): 28–43. Also V. Begley, P. Francis Jr., N. Karashima, K.V., Raman, S.E. Sidebotham, K.W. Slane and E.L. Will, eds, *The Ancient Port of Arikamedu: New Excavations and Researches 1989–1992*, Vol. 2 (Paris: École Française d'Extrême Orient, 2004). For details of bead-production debris at Kodumaṇal, see the unpublished report with the Tamil University and with Y. Subbarayalu, French Institute, Pondicherry and K. Rajan, Central University, Pondicherry.

[58] P.J. Cherian, ed., *Report on Fifth Season Excavation* (Thiruvananthapuram: KCHR Publications, 2011).

[59] A comprehensive report of excavations done so far has not been published as yet. See the *Interim Report of Paṭṭaṇam Excavations*

Mediterranean seafarers of cross-oceanic voyages in the Indian Ocean, dependent on monsoon winds, were not the only merchants present in the peninsular Indian ports of the period. There were many fellow seafaring merchants following coastal routes from Egypt, southern Arabia, and Persia, with a longer history of exchange relations with the region. Several overland merchants from various other regions of the Indian subcontinent were also there bartering their goods with the Mediterranean merchant-mariners. In those days, a port was, therefore, a confluence of different cultures as represented by overland merchants from the Gangetic, the north-west, and the Deccan regions and overseas traders from the Mediterranean world, northern Africa, South Arabia, and Persia. Although the main people were Greeks and Romans, there were Phoenicians, Philistines, Egyptians, Arabs, and Persians too, as coasting merchant-mariners of longstanding tradition had contacts with the ports on the western coasts of the Indian subcontinent.

This status of the port as a place of multicultural assemblage gave the feeling that it was a cosmopolitan centre. But that may certainly be a loose generalization, for the term 'cosmopolitan' presupposes a city culture distinct for its sophistication that transcends regional identities. It is not a mere assortment of people from different cultures congregating at a given site for a while but settled for good with permanent assets and vocations. On the contrary, any port of the time was an enclave of temporary arrangements for the seasonal sojourn for several overseas merchants, overland itinerants, craftsmen, and artisans who conducted their businesses in stalls, sheds, and open grounds. It was basically a site of consumption necessitating goods and services for the subsistence of the people camped there. Most

---

(Thiruvananthapuram: KCHR Publication, 2007–10). The report on the fifth season excavation has been published by KCHR in 2011, with a brief note on all the major archaeological finds of previous seasons. It has also compiled abstracts of papers presented by the Paṭṭaṇam research team in the Conference of the International Association for Asian Heritage held at Colombo, Sri Lanka, in April 2011. There is a more detailed account given as part of the seventh season interim report with a summary of findings, results of scientific tests, photographs of objects, and the various technical registers, published by KCHR, Thiruvananthapuram, in 2013.

goods that overseas merchants required, not being available locally, were brought by them in sufficient quantity in their ships. Others who could sustain themselves on local goods had to procure them from the local people through goods-for-goods exchange. The place, perhaps, looked almost like a fair with many people thronging there, but certainly distinct for the few built structures there; any ancient port indeed deserved to be called a *nagaram* or *paṭṭaṇam*, meaning a town. However, this hardly means that it was a cosmopolitan city. Those historians and archaeologists who tend to view an ancient port as cosmopolis have in their minds a modest harbour city.

Several archaeologists and historians conceive ancient ports almost close to full-fledged harbours with dockyards, wharfs, warehouses, customs toll-rooms, and several other transactional structures of an urban centre, and blame sea erosion for the total or near absence of such structural remnants at clearly identified port sites of ancient India. In fact, even in the case of Alexandria on the Nile or Ostya Antica Portus on the Tiber, there were only minimum built facilities as the remains would show. Tamralipti during the period of the Mauryan Empire ought to have had one of big wharfs, tariff posts, and various other structures of an urban site. Nevertheless, what emerged after the archaeological excavation hardly showed any sign of a full-blown harbour. While the status of ports even under an empire had been so simple, what to expect by way of relics in places mostly under chiefdoms, where ports were just ferries but with settlements of overseas merchants who had sailed depending on the monsoon wind in and out on their own to procure spices and gems! Since the sailors had to wait till the monsoon wind started blowing back, which took about four to five months, establishing the settlement was inevitable. Naturally, much of the goods with which the ships reached the ports were for the use of the merchants and other mariners themselves who were constrained to stay ashore for over several months.

Camps of Foreign Traders

Archaeological goods with a preponderance of Mediterranean objects excavated recently at Paṭṭaṇam and earlier at Arikamedu make it clear that contemporary ports of southern India were primarily camps of transmarine traders engaged in seasonal exchanges of goods. Among the excavated relics, the Mediterranean ceramic goods, strikingly culture-specific, suggestive of items of personal use such as tableware, containers, and storage jars, dominate at Arikamedu. Terra sigillata, a finer slip variety of Roman pottery with a glossy red surface, was part of the tableware of Roman aristocrats. Shards of Mediterranean ceramics consisting of the Roman terra sigillata and amphorae jars besides the west-Asian torpedo jar as well as turquoise glazed pottery are predominant at Paṭṭaṇam.

Amphorae jars were used as containers of wine, oil, and certain lasting food items. Their presence has been generally made out to be suggestive of imports of olive oil, wine, and garum, of which the first and last hardly had any use-value to the local people, although the wine may have attracted the chieftains. There are remains of huge jars as well, probably used for carrying grains, and hence many considered them as indicative of their import. Overseas merchants and business agents were mainly Greeks, Arabs, Philistines, and a few Romans. Mediterranean merchants were not rice eaters, whose staple was barley. They used wheat as well. None of these grains had any demand in the southern Indian regions where people were primarily users of millet supplemented by rice. *PME* makes a particular reference to the fact that the staple grains of Mediterranean mariners were not locally available and, therefore, they had to be brought in vessels of overseas voyages.[60] Olive oil and garum were the main cooking oil and dietary medium, respectively, of Romans and Greeks. This would mean that those engaged in overseas commerce had to carry with them their staple grains in sufficient quantity, besides the oils, sauces, and beverages.

Remains of Roman terra sigillata, glass bowls, fragments of painted glass objects, and glass pendants discovered at Arikamedu and Paṭṭaṇam sites are suggestive of personal belongings rather than merchandise of exchange. They were part of the personal objects of everyday use of foreign merchants and obviously not meant for exchange unlike what is often made out by some archaeologists and historians. It is reasonable to question the assumption that the items such as grains, olive oil, dry fruits, sauces, and wine were part of the items of import by the overseas merchants. In fact, the

[60] *PME*, 56.

kind of non-mercantile provisions brought in considerable quantity by the overseas vessels from the West clearly suggest that the ports were more than just points of transit halt of foreign traders. They were their camping sites with relatively permanent settlements as evidenced by the findings at Arikamedu and Paṭṭaṇam. *PME* mentions that overseas vessels had to supply the staple grains for the overseas merchants at the ports, for they were not circulated by merchants of the region.[61] It is significant to note that the overseas merchants were arriving in vessels sailing with the monsoon wind blowing towards the north-west coast of the Indian subcontinent by June–July and could sail back only in November–December with the return monsoon wind. This would mean that they were constrained to camping offshore for four to five months during every season.

Except the archaeological indications probably of small warehouses both at Arikamedu and Paṭṭaṇam, remains of permanent structures are conspicuous by their absence. There are no archaeological indications of the establishments of the ruling authorities in any of the excavated port sites. This absence need not be accidental, for what had been in existence according to the socio-economic clues in the extant source material were chiefdom-level political formations precluding bureaucracy. At the same time, autonomous existence and transactions by overseas merchants, trade organizers, and financiers are distinct in the Muziris Papyrus, an important documentary source. That the Papyrus was an agreement signed under Roman law and between the merchant and the moneylender with a third party, probably a Roman financier stationed at Muziris, is a notable factor. This is a clear indication of the autonomy of the port-town as the foreign merchant camp under Roman control in functional terms.[62] From the relatively meagre occurrence of the Indian fine-ware shards, the insignificant presence of indigenous merchants is evident. Similarly,

[61] See discussion in L. Casson, *The Periplus Maris Erythraei* (Princeton: Princeton University Press, 1989), 85, 221.

[62] Muziris Papyrus is reportedly a part of the two separate documents: one pertaining to a maritime loan and the other relating to the security. What has survived is the document that dealt with the security. See L. Casson, 'New Light on Maritime Loans: P. Vindob. G 40822', *Zeitschrift fur Papyrologie und Epigraphik* (Bonn: Verlag Rudolf Habelt) 84 (1990): 195–206.

lack of signs of concentration of stone-working or bead-making in any specific area shows the peripheral role of craftsmen. Local people, seemingly confined to the role of menial service providers, had no influence on the port-town.

The chief manufactures shipped from the ports were beads, gems, and textiles. Some of the craftsmen must have seasonally camped in the ports to give a finish to their manufactures, particularly drilling and polishing the beads. Several agents of the overseas merchants and businessmen must have stayed in the port-towns for longer durations, to mobilize the collection of spices. Even that had not involved much duration because pepper, the predominant spice item, was mainly a wild product, but supplemented by contemporary household agriculture, unlike the long pepper, it was packed and kept in sacks quite before the onset of monsoon. So was the case of ginger, the next important spice, which had to be dried and packed towards the end of summer. As regards several other items collected from the forest too, their acquisition and storing was an immediate pre-monsoon activity.

Ports of Graeco-Roman trade contacts in general had to be settlements of Mediterranean merchants, constrained to stay at the site of shipping, at least for a few months, that is, during the gap between the two monsoon winds. Mediterranean ships arriving at the western coasts of the Indian subcontinent being dependent on monsoon winds, the port's seasonal character, with a time lag of about four to five months, was unavoidable. Overseas traders from the West had no option other than camping at the port until the return monsoon wind would start blowing. Since, in most cases, they had to anchor their ships at the nearest convenient point in the outer sea, due to the lack of a suitable bay or dock at the river mouth due to silting and sand banks, some of them must have stayed on board as well. Either way, all of them had to stay in and around the port site for at least four to five months. It was the bazaar of foreign merchants with their storehouses close to the wharf at the inlet from where boats carried goods to ships offshore. All this goes to suggest that the overseas merchants had to be stationed at the port throughout the season.

Several among the Graeco-Romans like the business agents, shipping contractors, warehouse managers, those engaged in mobilizing and stocking the cargoes must have had to stay even beyond the season. Some of them had to stay more or less on a permanent basis in order to oversee the acquisition and storage of goods. It appears that the Greek witness in the Muziris Papyrus was stationed at Muziris. The prolonged stay of Graeco-Roman people at the port is presupposed by the *Putingarian Table*'s mention of a temple of Augustus at Muziris. Many armed soldiers also must have stayed, guarding the stock of more precious objects like gold, gems, and silks. Moreover, there were other fellow seafaring merchants who included those from Phoenicia, Arabia, Philistine, and Persia. A small number of overland merchants from other parts of the Indian subcontinent also might have been there as itinerants. In short, a port in those days was a point of convergence, not only for overseas merchants like Greeks, Romans, Phoenicians, Philistines, Arabs, and Persians, but also for a few overland merchants from the north, north-west, and central regions of the Indian subcontinent. Archaeological finds at Arikamedu as well as Paṭṭaṇam suggest that the Greeks, Romans, and Arabs had stayed in the port-town.

Not being rice eaters, they had to come with enough provisions and condiments required onboard as well as to live in the alien shore that could supply none of their staples. We have already noted *PME* mentioning about vessels supplying grains to the ports at Limyrike to satisfy the consumption needs of the Graeco-Roman merchant-mariners and business agents settled there, because it was not available in any of the ports in the region.[63] Supply of food grains was an important matter of concern for the Graeco-Roman seamen, for its shortage could have happened quite often due to an unexpectedly longer stay onboard and at the port. Generally, the incoming ships with enough stock of wheat and barley would share their surplus with the vessels facing the contingency of grain shortage. It was not the dietary items alone which the mariners had to bring with them but the storing jars, cooking vessels, tableware, and pieces of furniture as well. They had to keep with them some of their favourite decorative items and ornaments too. Although remains of some of these objects have been found at the excavated sites, one cannot expect archaeological attestation of all these, because normally what survived as relics would be the dumped waste like broken pots and wares. Valuables would be carried by their owners themselves; the rest of the usables

[63] *PME*, 56.

by the local people; and the perishables by nature. Nevertheless, the sundry assembly of relics in the debris of the period between c. 1st century BCE and c. 3rd century CE, found at the prime area of all the excavated ports, is of foreigners, predominantly Graeco-Romans. This clearly suggests that during the period each port on the coasts of peninsular India was virtually a cluster of foreign merchant settlements. In fact, it is not possible to distinguish the port per se from the cluster of foreign merchant settlements, since both were so integral to each other in those days.

Ancient Indian Ships

A few scholars have tried to show that ancient India had a fairly well-developed ship-building technology, which had enabled maritime trade and establishment of merchant settlements in Cambodia, Java, Sumatra, Borneo, Socotra, Japan, China, the Malayan Peninsula, Arabia, Egypt, and Persia. They have mustered the references available in Sanskrit and Pali texts to the maritime activity of the merchant-mariners in ancient India. Since some of these texts belong to the period between c. 300 BCE and c. 300 CE, their references do signify the situation in ancient times.

Although it is uncertain as to how much of the textual contents thereof really applies to ancient times, references in the *jātaka*s do vouch for the prevalence of a seafaring tradition in ancient times.[64] *PME* mentions two types of Indian vessels, *Colandia* (built ones) coasting alone the shore of the Bay of Bengal to Chryse and Sangara (made of single logs bound together) along the coast down to Limyrike.[65] It appears that there were organized merchant-mariners in the Gangetic region, engaged in transporting the goods from the Himalayas, East Asia, and China to the deeper south and southern merchandise including the Mediterranean goods to northern India and to the eastern world. *PME* mentions big fishing boats called

64 R.K. Mukherji, *Indian Ship-building: A History of the Sea-borne Trade and Maritime Activity of the Indians from Earliest Times* (Calcutta: Longmans Green and Co., 1912).

65 *PME*, 30–1.

Tappaga and *Cotymba* of the local fishermen stationed at the very entrance of Barygaza to pilot foreign vessels to the port that was situated in the midst of multiple dangers for any fresh mariners entering the bay.[66] These were seagoing boats but used by the local fishermen, and hence had obviously involved no technology comparable to that of the vessels of overseas voyages.

Such a seafaring tradition seems to have been existent in the northwestern coast of peninsular India too. Merchant-mariners seem to have sailed from Sopara and Barukaccha, coasting along the shores towards the Persian Gulf. It is also likely that they had been coasting down to the deeper south-western shores as well. A square sail ship represented in the famous sculpture of a shipwreck at the Kanheri cave is perhaps the earliest archaeological evidence of imagining the structure and design of a seagoing vessel used in the Arabian Sea.[67] This representation shows two persons on board helplessly praying to the Bōddhisatva Padmapāṇi for rescue and the Bōddhisatva pleased by the devotees, in turn sending two messengers to salvage the former. Sātavāhana coins found on the east coast carry the representation of a ship with two masts reinforced by double stays rigged to an evidently large square sail.[68] Although the widely known coins with the ship motif carry only a single type, those kept in the British Museum include coins with the motif showing variations in the shape and number of mast-heads, besides the depiction of details like a paddle, a buoy, a flag, and so on. They portray the ship with a large square sail attached to two tall masts at the centre of the hull. One of the terracotta seals, with Kharoshṭi letters discovered at Chandraketugarh and a vessel with a single mast depicted on it, is probably indicative of mariners engaged in overseas exchange.[69]

One can expect only an impressionistic representation of the vessel on such objects and it is hard to expect any specific detail or characteristic features in them. This is true of the depictions on pottery

[66] *PME*, 44.

[67] This is mentioned as probably the oldest representation of a sea voyage in Indian sculpture. See Mukherji, *Indian Ship-building*, 35.

[68] Mukherji, *Indian Ship-building*, 119.

[69] M. Chandra, *Trade and Trade Routes in Ancient India* (New Delhi: Abhinav Publications, 1977), 94.

too. A couple of graffito representations on potsherds at the port site of Azhakankuḷam are suggestive of a seagoing vessel, probably a Mediterranean ship.[70] Paintings at the caves 1, 2, and 17 besides the sculpture at the cave 26 of Ajanta, assigned to the 5th–6th centuries CE, have representations of seagoing boats. There is a depiction of a ship on the reverse of a Pallava coin (6th century CE) and one in an Ajanta painting (7th century CE) for us to form an idea about what a seagoing vessel meant to the artists of the time.[71] A medieval text namely *Kṛ'tyakalpataru* contains a lot of information about the art, craft, and technology of ship-building, probably indicative of a tradition continuing from ancient times, indeed, with significant changes over the centuries. However, it is not possible to reliably reconstruct the technology of ship-building of ancient times on the basis of what the text embodies.

South Indian Technology

There is no evidence to show a similar level of maritime tradition anywhere in the deeper south known as Tamilakam. Paratavar, the traditional seafolk of the region, engaged in fishing and salt manufacturing, had no involvement in maritime exchange on their own. Nevertheless, as traditional boatmen, they were engaged in transporting the goods from and to the Yavana ships anchored offshore since most ports were on the river mouth inaccessible to big vessels, due to the absence of a suitable dock.[72] There is no indication in the source material to presume that the traditional seagoing fishing community had developed ship-building technology and navigational skill adequate for deep-sea voyages. In the sources we come across, apart from

70 T.S. Sridhar, D. Thulasiraman, S. Selvaraj, and S. Vasanthi, *Alagankulam: An Ancient Roman Port City of Tamil Nadu* (Chennai: Tamil Nadu Department of Archaeology, 2005), 67–73.

71 W. Elliot, *Coins of Southern India* (London: Trubner, 1885). Also see Mukherji, *Indian Shipping*, 35.

72 *Akanāṉūṟu*, 30:3–6; 126:7–14; and 240:1–7. For the text and commentary, see Nattar, ed., *Akanāṉūṟu*, Vols I and II (1949–50); *Kuṟuntokai*, 348. For the text and commentary, see U.V.S. Iyar, ed., *Kuṟuntokai*, 2nd ed. (Madras: Thyagarajavilasam Publications, 1947).

the small fishing boats, three types of seagoing vessels, *kalam*, *nāvāy*, and *vankam*. In Tamil heroic poems there are references to the naval activities expressed using these terms with a sense of differentiation of their meanings.

In the poems, the term 'kalam' is invariably used to mean a big-sail rigged vessel. The term is generally used in the context of references to the ship in which the Yavanas had come with gold and gone with pepper.[73] Nāvāy (*nauka* in Sanskrit) was another term used to mean a seagoing vessel that transported goods including horses from different countries (*nādus*).[74] Vankam seems to be the vessel of Vanga (Bengal), probably *Colandia* that had been coasting along the shores from the Gangetic bay and Chryse down to the Coromandel ports and back transporting merchandise.[75] Anchorage of these vessels was dependent on a heavy stone tied to a rope.[76] As the names of the vessels and the context of maritime activities along the coast of the Indian subcontinent suggest, contemporary seagoing vessels were either Graeco-Roman or Arab or north Indian. There is no evidence to show that the maritime technology of southern India was

[73] For allusion to sails, see *Akanāṉūṟu*, 149:9–11. For the text and commentary, see N.M.V. Nattar, ed., *Akanāṉūṟu*, Vol. I (1949). *Kalam* is called *marakkalam* as well. See *Puṟanāṉūṟu* 30:10–11. For the text and commentary, see U.V.S. Iyar, ed., *Puṟanāṉūṟu*, 6th ed.

[74] See *Narrinai*, 4:1–4 and 295:5–6. For the text and commentary, see A.N. Iyar, ed., *Nattrinai* (Tirunelveli: The South India Saiva Siddhantha Works Publishing Society Ltd, 1956); *Puṟanāṉūṟu*, 126:14–6. For the text and commentary, see U.V.S. Iyar, ed., *Puṟanāṉūṟu*. Such a vessel is mentioned to have brought gold to the Cēra chief Kuṭṭuvan. See *Maturaikkāñci*, 321–4. For the text and commentary, see U.V.S. Iyar, ed., *Pattuppāṭṭu*, 288–433.

[75] See *Narrinai*, 258:7–10. For the text and commentary, see A.N. Iyar, ed., *Nattrinai*. An *akam* song describes a *vankam* moving day and night with the wind (*Akanāṉūṟu*, 50:1) and another shows surprise at the sight of a vankam arriving 'as if the entire world is floating' (*Akanāṉūṟu*, 255:1–6). For the text and commentary, see N.M.V. Nattar, ed., *Akanāṉūṟu*, Vols I and II.

[76] See N. Subramanian, *The Sangam Polity* (Delhi: Asia Publishing House, 1966), 242n151. Subramanian says that these light houses were not specially built structures serving exclusively the purpose of beckoning ships, but were powerful lamps set up on top of the tallest building on the coast near the harbour.

of a comparable nature. It is clear today in the light of literary and archaeological evidence that the ships from the Indian subcontinent and Arabian coasts were very small compared to the Graeco-Roman standard. Philostratus quotes an Indian sailor's comparative remark on the size of contemporary ships in the Indian Ocean:

> The Egyptians construct ships for our ocean and they send them to sea to exchange Egyptian goods for Indian wares ... the Egyptians build these ships on a scale whereby one of their vessels is equivalent in size to several of those used by the other races.[77]

Nevertheless, there have been arguments that the shipping technology of contemporary Indian seafarers was superior due to their efficient sail and rigging system, compared to that of the Mediterranean navigators. It has been argued that unlike the Indian and Arab ships, Mediterranean ships with their poor rigging system were unsuitable for sailing in rough weather in the Indian Ocean.[78] Extending the arguments on the technical ground further, it has been pointed out that the widely celebrated Graeco-Roman predominance in the Indian Ocean trade was an exaggeration of the colonial historiography. Moreover, the quality of the wood used for building the Mediterranean ships was inferior to the teakwood with which the Indian ships were made. There is a strong presumption that teakwood was shipped to the Red Sea coast for the purpose of building ships.

However, in the light of the available source material, it is clear that the level of the technology of ship-building in the Indian subcontinent was largely unsuitable for cross-oceanic voyages unlike what old-time historians as well as most of those in recent times have

[77] F. Philostratus, *Life of Appolonius of Tyana*, trans. F.C. Conybeare (London: William Heinemann, Loeb Classical Library, 1912), 3.35.

[78] See H.P. Ray, *The Winds of Change: Buddhism and the Maritime Links of Early South Asia* (Delhi: Oxford University Press, 1994). Also 'A Resurvey of Roman Contacts with the East', in *Athens, Aden, Arikamedu: Essays on the Interrelations between India, Arabia and the Eastern Mediterranean*, eds M.F. Boussac and J.F. Salles (New Delhi: Manohar Publishers, 1995), 97–114. It is asserted but without any new supportive evidence; see W. Ball, *Rome in the East: The Transformation of an Empire* (London: Routledge, 2000).

maintained. They have tried to show that contemporary shipping technology of the mariners of the coasts of India was far superior to that of the Mediterranean seafarers, which in the present appraisal is an exaggeration. What had existed was a technology of building ships appropriate only for voyages along the coastal routes in the Bay of Bengal, the Coromandel region, and the Arabian Sea.

5

Exchange Relations in Early Peninsular India

The study of trade or any form of exchange, for that matter, has to be made against its socio-economic aggregate. Analysis of historical socio-economic processes is best done within the Marxist theoretical framework of social formation. It is quite intelligible to conceive forms of economic production as construed by Karl Marx and modes of exchange as conceptualized by Bronislaw Malinowski, Marcel Mauss, and Karl Polanyi. This makes a brief discussion of the salient features of the social formation of the contemporary Indian subcontinent in general and peninsular India in particular, a necessary precondition to understanding the nature of local and long-distance overland as well as overseas exchanges. An overview of the situation in northern India and the Deccan is attempted as a prelude to a closer understanding of the deeper south of the peninsula, which constitutes the main focus.

Situation in Northern India

Interspersed with the large expanse of jungle tracts, there existed many settlements (*gāmas*) with agrarian fields (*khētta*) growing rice in summer and wheat in winter, in the middle reaches of the major river systems of northern India. Other crops included barley and a variety of millets that grew in the respective ecosystems. Along the banks of the rivers Indus, Yamuna, Ganges, and Mahanadi were the numerous gāmas, each of which was a self-sustaining production unit worked by the settlers (*kuṭi-puriśe*) using slaves (*dāsas*), servants (*bhatakas*), artisans (*kārukas*), and craftsmen (*kammakāras*) controlled by a headman or chief called *gāmasamiko* in the Pāli canon, *grāmika* or *grāmamukhya* in the *Arthaśāstra.*[1] *Piṭakas* as well as the *Arthaśāstra* show that to a great extent the specialization of occupations was based on the *kula* (lineage), and hence was hereditary.[2] However, the social hierarchy remained explicable within the theory of the *varṇa* order, for occupational stratification had not meant elaboration of the hierarchy further. Any headman was a prominent Khattya or Brāhmaṇa householder, controlling agrarian fields and thus commanding enough dāsas, bhatakas, and kammakāras.[3] A Vaiśya as a Sēṭṭhi possessing wealth in terms of money and material like a few bullock carts or as a *gahapati* holding khēttas was also a prominent householder, with dāsas, bhatakas, and kammakāras.[4] He and his contingent of dāsas and bhatakas lived in or adjacent to the centres of commerce well known as *paṭṭiṇa* and *nagara*. Contemporary literature as corroborated by archaeology in a few cases shows that a wall, mostly made of mud, bound each of the *grāmas* and nagaras together.[5] Any

[1] These are the terms used in the Pāli canon as well as *Miḷinda Panho*. See D.R. Chanana, *Slavery in Ancient India: As Depicted in Pali and Sanskrit Texts* (New Delhi: People's Publishing House, 1960), 14–22.

[2] *Arthaśāstra* distinguishes *kula* from *jāti*. It appears that the term 'kula' denotes clan with occupational identity. See R.S. Sastri, ed., *Arthaśāstra of Kautilya*, Bibliotheca Sanskrita 37 (Mysore: University of Mysore Oriental Library Publication, 1909), chapter 1, pp. 13–14, verses 3–4.

[3] These generalizations are based on the significations reduced out of the stories narrated in the *piṭaka* texts. See the specific instances quoted in Chanana, *Slavery in Ancient India*, 41–5.

[4] Allusions in the Pāli texts signify the status of Sēṭṭhis possessing any bullock carts and carting rice from the *khētta* to the *paṭṭiṇa/nagara*. A typical example is the one in *Anguttara Nikāya*, I, 381 and *Vinayapiṭaka*, II. 159. See the texts cited in Chanana, *Slavery in Ancient India*, 24–6.

[5] Archaeological excavations at several sites along the Ganges have met with remnants of ramparts seemingly close to what *Arthaśāstra* mentions.

independent householder (gahapati) in a grāma or nagara possessed dāsas and could resort to the service of bhatakas, the extent of which varied depending upon the size of his resources. *Gaha* in the Pāli literature as well as *gṛha* in the *Arthaśāstra* means a house, a fully built structure as distinguished from a hut (*kuṭi*). Any gahapati was invariably a master (*svāmi* or *iśvara*) who could command the services of the *upavāsas* (settlers), also known as *anīśvaras*. *Arthaśāstra* uses the word *svāmya* for the proprietary right over dāsa. *Dāsya*, the state of an individual subjected to the status of an object owned and controlled by the svāmi, was the basic institutional form that facilitated realization of labour for any hard tasks. An archaic practice, probably from the days of the pastoral patriarchs of the *Rig-Veda*, if not earlier, it continued with changes as part of all dominant societies through the *janapadas* and *rāṣtras* to the Mauryan *vijita*.[6] The practice at its historically contingent level imbued any family headman with the status of a svāmi and put his wife/wives and children in the state of dāsya presupposing the right of the former to handle the latter as property, which is testified to by the Pāli texts.[7] A prominent gāmasamiko had control over people and resources in the gāma, the extent of which varied from one to the other, making him a big or a bigger chief. Sometimes he had many gāmas as his own or had many gāmasamikos as his subordinates, forming a janapada under him. A bigger chiefly lineage had a *mahājanapada* under control with a nagara, the most strategic place, as its headquarters. People of a janapada consisted of the four *varṇas* with the gahapatis belonging to the three varṇas: Brāhmaṇa, Kṣatriya, and Vaiśya. Craftsmen like the kārukas, *karmakāras*, *bhṛtakas*, and *dasas* belonged to the Sūdra varṇa. Contemporary literature shows that all of them who constituted the varṇa society were called *āryas*.[8]

See the Chapter II on *janapadanivēśa* of *Arthaśāstra*. For the text and translation, see Sastri, ed., *Arthaśāstra of Kautilya*, 30–1.

6 See the discussions in Chanana, *Slavery in Ancient India*, 41–5.

7 There are several instances signifying the situation in the various stories mentioned in the *piṭakas*. *Arthaśāstra* in its 'Dāsakarmakārakalpa' section indirectly indicates the situation in vogue by stipulating rulings against certain practices.

8 In the *piṭakas* the term *ārya* and *dāsa* are put in binary opposition, to mean 'the free' and 'the slave'. See *Vinayapiṭaka*, III. 161. For the text and translation,

It was not unlikely that a Sūdra could also emerge as a chief by using force, as probably in the case of the Mauryas who are said to have had Sūdra origins. However, dāsas and *dāsis* were *anāryas* and hence outside the varṇa society. Similarly, the forest peoples (*āṭavikas*) in the frontiers of the janapadas were also outside the varṇa society. A powerful forest chieftain could have taken over the control of a janapada through predatory subjugation, thereby setting precedence of the emergence of rulers from beyond the varṇa society.

All-important janapadas were located mostly along the Gangetic plains and on the banks of the rivers Yamuna and Mahanadi. The Indus plains constituted another major region of janapadas. It appears that the Saurashtra region was only partly opened up for agriculture in those times. The banks of the rivers Narmada, Godavari, Krishna, and the Raichur doab were not under the plough for wet-rice agriculture as yet, which accounts for the absence of a mahājanapada in these regions. Agrarian villages might have existed there, but hardly in any organized manner. Human settlements in these regions in the age of the Mauryas seem to have been confined largely to the semi-forested tracts and the strategies of subsistence were compatible to such ecosystems.

Aristocracy

The mainstream society of the period consisted of the ruling personnel (Khattyas) and merchants (Sēṭṭhis) and landholders (Brāhmaṇas)

---

see R. Davids, *Vinayapiṭaka* (London: Pali Text Society, 1921). In *Majjimanikāya* (II. 149) the two terms denote the people of the four *varṇas* as a whole and the alien ones respectively. For the text and translation, see L. Chalers, *Majjhima Nikāya* (Eng. trans.), Vol. II (London: Pali Text Society, 1927). See the contextualization of the references in Chanana, *Slavery in Ancient India*, 55 and note 153. That the term 'ārya' denotes all the four *varṇas* is explicit in the *Arthaśāstra*. The section 'Dāsakarmakārakalpa' prohibits the subjection of any one belonging to the four *varṇas* to dāsya and allows enslavement of any *mlēccha* or *anārya*, obviously peoples outside the varṇa society. The punitive clauses against the offence of enslavement start with the punishment for enslaving a Sūdra. This point has been discussed exhaustively in Chanana, *Slavery in Ancient India*, 87–9. Also see G.M. Bongard-Levin and A.A. Vigasin, 'Society and State in Ancient India', *Indian Historical Review* (ICHR) V, nos 1–2 (1978–9): 23.

in the Yamuna basin, the Ganga valley, and the Mahanadi delta, which formed a broad linguistic unity and socio-cultural homogeneity. The literate from Magadha in the east to Gāndhāra and Kambōja in the north-west and Parinda and Kalinga in the south probably understood one or the other form of Prākṛit such as Māgadhi, Śūrasēni, Gāndhāri, and Ardha-Māgadhi. There was some amount of class differentiation among the people whose distribution had geographical correspondence in the sense that the rich lived in the nagaras and the poor in the grāmas. Further, the number of the rich must have been extremely sparse compared to that of the poor. Among the rich, some were fabulously so, but this economic differentiation does not seem to have evolved beyond the binary stratification anywhere. There was some amount of fluidity about the socio-economic differences among them, which precluded the identifiable presence of an intermediary class. The rich's complex levels of material culture were expressed through the monumental buildings in the nagaras that they owned and the gems, gold, silver, metal ware, and polished ceramics that they possessed as distinguished from the simple folk settlements of the grāmas, characterized by mud huts, plain ceramics, coarse ware, and ordinary beads of sandstone, horns, and terracotta, probably of the dāsas and *karmmakāras*.

The ruling aristocracy (Khattyas) and the rich merchants (Sēṭṭhis) largely controlled the urban complexes through the management of technology that varied from copper smithy and alloy metallurgy to steel casting, polishing ceramics, gem cutting, gold working, advanced architecture, highly developed carpentry, exquisite stone sculpting, boat-making, cart-designing, and town planning, which had reached a very high water mark under the Mauryas. This professional perfection was achieved through the incorporation of local traditions as well as the Macedonian and Greek influences under the state initiative. In the field of primary production, largely the technology of tools and implements of the immediate past continued possibly with some Mauryan imprints in the case of the devices essential for irrigated rice cultivation. It is clear that the technology of crafts manufacture, wood and stone architecture (*vāstu*), and metallurgy (*pākaśāstra* and *sulbadhātuśāstra*) in the Mauryan period was evidently superior to that of the preceding ages, thanks to the organized existence of professional bodies headed by big merchants. *Arthaśāstra* in its chapter on *durganivēśa* (fortification) gives structural details about the buildings such as *rājagṛha* (palaces), *panyagṛha* (merchant warehouses), *kupyagṛha* (wild goods depots), *kōṣṭāgāra* (storehouses), *bandhanāgāra* (prisons), and so on. Most of the surviving Mauryan monuments in stone testify to the astounding progress achieved in wooden architecture too, for they are the latter's stone facsimiles. Various fields of knowledge such as those relating to precious stones (*maṇiāgaśāstra*) explicit in the section on *ratnaparīkṣa* (gem-test) and minerals (*dhātuśāstra*) in the *Arthaśāstra*, health-care (*cikilsa*)—as evidenced by the mention in the Asokan Edict II (*paśucikica* and *manuṣyacikica*)—besides the astronomical mathematics (*jyōtirggaṇita*), grammar (*vyākaraṇa*), and metaphysics that had descended from the *Vēdāngas* had advanced further, obviously under the patronage of the aristocracy.

Literature shows that the rich rivalled against one another in status and ranking. Sources of legitimacy of status being the sectarian religious orders, Khattyas, Sēṭṭhis, and Brāhmaṇas competitively patronized them as they preferred, making them the sites of social contestation. Khattyas, Sēṭṭhis, and Brāhmaṇas celebrated various *samājas* (associations) and endowed the various rituals like *yajñas* (sacrifices), which implied patronage of the respective socio-religious institutions and groups. Sramaṇas and the Vedic Brāhmaṇas were the main sectarian religious groups associated with such institutions. There was competition among the Khattyas, Sēṭṭhis, and Brāhmaṇas against one another for material resources, social status, and cultural power, which they often carried forward to the various religious sects between whom existed bitter rivalry. They seem to have fanatically fought against one another apparently for ideological supremacy, but really for political patronage and the corresponding social hegemony. Asoka found the mutual intolerance among different sects a major problem in the empire. He appointed *dhamma mahāmātras* to take care of the peace and prosperity of all sects and to emphasize the role of the code of conduct (dhamma) in securing them. In Edict XII he asked 'not to extol one's own sect nor disparage another's' explicitly as a measure to avert sectarian conflicts. These pieces of advice were not enough to resolve the conflicts since they were rooted in the social processes rather than the pugnacity of individuals. They were social contestations carried forward to the religious sphere as ideological conflicts of sectarian groups.

It is a well-attested fact that the basic mode of appropriation of labour in the age of the Mauryas was dāsya, which was quite widespread. Each *grahapati* had dāsas and dāsis attached; each grāma had its dāsas and dāsis for hard labour including tilling, the hardest part of the labour processes in agriculture.[9] In both the nagaras and grāmas the poor constituted the largest stratum, which was of the workforce consisting of the dāsas, *bhṛtaka*s, and kārukas of a wide variety identifiable in terms of their object of labour. As in the case of the production of goods and services in all other fields, in the field of arts and crafts too, the basic institutional device for appropriating labour was dāsya. In the nagaras most of the specialized arts and crafts were organized into corporations (guilds) controlled by master craftsmen (Sēṭṭhis). Many artisans and craftsmen who worked under the master craftsmen were dāsas, who figure in the Pāli canon and the *Arthaśāstra* as the dāsa–kammakāra combine.[10] In stone sculpting and woodwork, dāsya must have been the most extensively used social mode for appropriating the labour of the kammakāras, for both were widely activated fields involving hard labour. Monumental constructions and other activities of extremely tough labour such as quarrying and mining, chipping, sculpting, and polishing of hard stones, erecting huge blocks and columns, and so on, presuppose large-scale deployment of dāsa–kammakāras as attached to various *karmmānta*s (manufactories) owned by the aristocracy, particularly, the Sēṭṭhis.[11] Being the sole investors in such enterprises, aristocrats were the chief

[9] Pāli texts contain references to the use of dāsas in agriculture. See Chanana, *Slavery in Ancient India*, 41–52; *Jātaka*, VI. 69. In the *Arthaśāstra*, there are plenty of references to the extensive deployment of dāsas in agriculture. See the 'Dāsakarmakārukalpa' and the 'Adhyakṣapracara' sections of the *Arthaśāstra*. For the text and translation, see Sastri, ed., *Arthasāstra of Kautilya*, 1909.

[10] In the *Arthaśāstra* the dāsas and *karmakāra*s figure as parts of a twin. Probably, it could be due to the comparable plight of both. It also seems to indicate that dāsya as administered by the state was a bit liberalized and made on a par with the status of the *karmakāras*.

[11] Several stories in the *piṭaka*s contain signifiers to the practice of Sēṭṭhis keeping many dāsas with them for all kinds of works (*Vinayapiṭaka*, II.159). For the text and translation, see R. Davids, *Vinayapiṭaka*, II (English trans.) (London: Pali Text Society, 1921).

beneficiaries of trade and commerce. Some of them were big traders who owned and managed huge caravan troupes as well as coasting vessels engaged mostly in the Bay of Bengal.

Exchange Network

Networking the janapadas and situated at strategic points of exchange in the Gangetic region, there flourished in the age of the Nandas and continued to the Mauryan times, several small and big trade centres and their complex settlements headed by Sēṭṭhis. Archaeology has brought to our attention about 130 urban centres between Taxila in the north-west and Perur in the south, the most-developed layer of which might be of the Mauryan period. Many corporations of clans (kulas) were engaged in numerous arts and crafts of full-time specialization and their manufactories (*karmmāntas*) existed there. Urban centres called the paṭṭiṇas and nagaras of the Mauryan period were strategic landscapes spatialized for the circulation of goods in exchange of money based on exchange-value and the notion of profit.[12] In other words, it was trade in our sense of the term. However, in the hinterlands the goods circulated in exchange of goods (*pratipanya*) based on their use-value. Each of the several chiefdoms and the numerous janapadas in the kingdom had entered into ascriptive and customary exchanges of goods-for-goods with its neighbours. Long and far-reaching routes frequented by caravans (*sārthavāhas*) passed through these janapadas and chiefdoms of diverse cultures. Branching off from the grand trunk, there ran numerous sub-routes on land and water linking up the agrarian settlements with marketing centres and the various karmmāntas of urban headquarters (nagaras) facilitating

[12] The references to price and profit in the Pāli texts and the *Arthaśāstra* and the hoards of punch-marked coins help us identify the form of exchange as trade. See the Pāli texts quoted in M. Chandra, *Sārthavāhan*, Translated in Malayalam by K.N. Ezhuthachan (Thrissur: Sahitya Academy, 1975), 23–56. Also his *The World of Courtesans* (New Delhi: Vikas Publishing House, 1973), 18–42. The 'Dāsakarmakārukalpa' and 'Adhyakṣapracāra' sections of the *Arthaśāstra* are full of references to price and profit. References to coins are found throughout the text as part of the punitive clauses stipulating fines. See Chapters 7 and 16 of the text in Sastri, ed., *Arthaśāstra of Kautilya*.

the flow of the select local goods out and non-local goods in over a very wide area.

The exchange network expanded in the Gangetic basin not only along the pre-existing routes, but also by opening up several new routes reaching out to distant points. The most important exchange routes went towards the north-west reaching the Black Sea and the eastern routes went up to Burma and the southern up to Pratiṣṭān.[13] Two major trans-regional trade routes—the northern (*uttarāpatha*) and the southern (*dakṣiṇāpatha*) grand routes—were established during the pre-Mauryan period itself. Archaeology and the *Arthaśāstra* have established the existence of Gangetic links with Taxila in the north as well as Tamilakam in the south and the circulation of the goods across the regions. Trans-regional trade routes expanded along with the spread of the Buddhist Sangha network all over the subcontinent. By the 3rd century BCE, the Sangha had a chain of monastic complexes stretching from the Kashmir valley in the north to Krishna basin in the south-east and from Bihar in the north-east to Maharashtra in the south-west. Bhikkus and the Sēṭṭhis figure in the Buddhist literature as close associates and patrons of the Sangha. Inscriptions in the monasteries show that the Sēṭṭhis were their chief donors. Lists of donors at each monastic complex show that donors came from far and wide and that the *vihāra* was as much a confluence of merchants as of monks. Endowments probably insured the merchants against robbery, which the caravans feared, robbers like Angulimāla being archetypal marauders in the Pāli texts. Trade routes were channels of communication for peoples and cultures of far-flung regions. They facilitated the dissemination of migrants, material goods, technology, knowledge-systems, language, writing, and other aspects of culture under stimulus-diffusion.

The Deccan

Archaeological remains show that the landscape between Vidarbha and the tip of the peninsula was inhabited mainly by peoples whose

[13] See the discussion in R. Thapar, *Asoka and the Decline of the Mauryas*, 3rd ed. (New Delhi: Oxford University Press, 1997), 84.

mortuary practices involved the erection of megaliths like dolmenoid cists, passage–porthole chamber tombs, transepted cists, hood stones, and urns.[14] The goods unearthed from them consist mainly of a wide variety of iron artefacts and pottery besides other metal objects, stone, glass beads, and so on. It is more or less well established now that the dolmenoid cists with the eastern porthole and passage-chambers showing provenance in the lower Krishna basin and extending to the upper Malaprabha valley are the earliest.[15] These descent groups, whose burial goods show the dominance of weapons, were not practitioners of irrigated agriculture, but those who subsisted on agro-pastoralism supplemented by pottery-making, metal-working, stone works, and other craft production. Some of them might have practised wet-rice agriculture, but not extensively.

Archaeological remains on the surface and out of excavations show a continuous history of human settlements in different parts of the Deccan region from the turn of the 1st millennium BCE onwards, adapting to the multiple landscape ecosystems through an array of unevenly evolving techno-economic strategies of subsistence and survival.[16] It was an ensemble structured by the dominance of the

[14] See N.R. Banerjee, *The Iron Age in India* (New Delhi: Munshiram Manoharlal, 1965), 288–91; B.K.G. Rao, *The Megalithic Culture in South India* (Mysore: Prasaranga, 1972); A. Sundara, The *Early Chamber Tombs of South India* (Delhi: University Publishers, 1975); B. Narasaiah, *Neolithic and Megalithic Culture in Tamil Nadu* (Delhi: Sandeep Prakashan, 1980). Earlier it was thought that the megalithic people knew irrigated agriculture. See the discussion in R.E.M. Wheeler, 'Brahmagiri and Chandravalli Excavations', *Ancient India*, no. 4 (1946): 181–308. This assumption is repeated in Rao, *The Megalithic Culture in South India*, 298–91.

[15] See an analytical comprehension of the state-of-the-art research on the topic in S.F. Ratnagar, 'Archaeological Perspectives on Early Indian Societies', in *Recent Perspectives of Early Indian History*, ed. R. Thapar (Bombay: Popular Prakashan, 1995), 30–4.

[16] See H.D. Sankalia and S.B. Deo, *Report on the Excavations at Nasik and Jorwe 1950–1951* (Poona: Deccan College, 1955). H.D. Sankalia, B. Subbarao, and S.B. Deo, *Excavations at Maheshwar and Navdatoli, 1952–53* (Pune: Deccan College Publications, 1958); M.K. Dhavalikar, *First Farmers of the Deccan* (Pune: Ravish Publishers, 1988). Also, V.V.K. Sastry, *The Proto and Early Historical Culture of Andhra Pradesh*, AP Archaeological Series 58 (Hyderabad:

agro-pastoral culture that had a long continuity, of course with certain changes. Agriculture included both shifting and sedentary with the latter mostly centred on arid highland crops like millets and limitedly on fertile lowland crops like rice, wheat, and sugar cane. The socio-economic processes of the region by about the 1st century BCE were primarily of a continuation of the interactive coexistence amongst these unevenly evolved forms of subsistence depended on various levels of the metal technology of iron and high-tin bronze with some sort of specialization in craft production and exchange, but largely within the clan–kin nexus.[17]

The larger section of the population in the region must have belonged to the settlements along the black-soil tracts of the Ghats and upper reaches of the rivers, suitable for agro-pastoral modes of subsistence and it consisted of descent groups and their chiefs of clan–kin ties. Some of them were inhabitants of small fertile pockets of fields around watersheds, living on wet-rice agriculture. It is natural that kinship would be the basis of productive relations among descent groups. Networking across these settlements of the hill tracts rich in forest goods, mineral resources, crafts production, dry-land crops like millet, pastoral goods, and rice, there were trade routes frequented by long-distance itinerant merchants. Trade routes from the north, north-west, and east passed through these habitation areas, collecting the local products in exchange of non-local goods. The local goods largely consisted of forest goods, metal and mineral resources, gems, textiles, and craft-goods while the non-local involved mainly spices meant for overseas exchange.

Exchange and exchange-routes had enabled a circuit of merchants, monks, mendicants, and others, while their convergence at areas of settlements in its turn had led to the rise of monasteries and the growth of urban centres. Human settlements were essential for the

---

Government of Andhra Pradesh, 1983); S.R.K. Pisipaty, *Andhra Culture: An Obscure Phase in the Early Historical Archaeology of Andhra Pradesh* (Delhi: Agam Kala Prakashan, 2010).

[17] For the standard characterization, see A. Parasher-Sen, *Social and Economic History of Early Deccan: Some Interpretations* (New Delhi: Manohar Publishers, 1993).

sustenance of monks, monastic establishments, and their sustainers. While the *upāsakas* in the settlements supported small caves in their vicinity, the big merchants, prominent households, and chieftains endowed bigger establishments. There has always been an exaggeration about the agrarian surplus in the settlements and an over-generalization about its connection to trade, monastic establishments, urban development, and state formation with differences in the precedence of one or the other over the rest.[18] Nevertheless, some of the Buddhist establishments such as Nasik, Junnar, Karle, and Nanaghat were richly endowed by big merchants. It has been suggested that they were probably redistributing the wealth by way of financing long-distance exchange or, in other words, investing the institutional wealth in the field of trade.[19] There are remnants of several Buddhist monuments at different points along the Ghats and the upper reaches of the Godavari–Krishna Rivers as well as their deltas and along the northern Andhra coast.[20] A few of them date back to

[18] For an exaggeration of the material culture, nature, and surplus potential of local settlements as well as for a criticism against generalizations about the connections amongst the various phenomena, see discussion in K.D. Morrison, 'Trade, Urbanism, and Agricultural Expansion: Buddhist Monastic Institutions and the State in Early Historic Western Deccan', *World Archaeology* 27, no. 2 (London: Routledge, 1995): 203–21. Also, P.K. Reddy, 'God, Trade and Worship: A Glimpse into the Region of Early Andhradesa', *East and West* (Istituto Italiano per l'Africa e l'Oriente) 48, nos 3–4 (1998): 291–311.

[19] G.L. Adhya, *Early Indian Economics: Studies in the Economic Life of Northern and Western India* (Bombay: Asia Publishing House, 1966), 98–9.

[20] See J. Burgess, *Report on the Buddhist Cave Temples and Their Inscriptions*, n.s. 4 (repr., New Delhi: Archaeological Survey of India, 1883). For a comprehensive account of sites, see O.C. Kail, *Buddhist Cave Temples of India* (Bombay: D.B. Taraporevala, 1975). Also, I.K. Sarma, *Studies in Early Buddhist Monuments and Brahmi Inscriptions of Andhradesa* (Nagpur: Dattsons Publishers, 1988); D. Mitra, *Buddhist Monuments* (Calcutta: Sahitya Samsad, 1980), 155–7. For an exhaustive chronological list of Buddhist and other religious sites in Andhra, see R. Prasad, 'Cultural Map of Andhradesa from Earliest Ties to AD 300', in *Comprehensive History and Culture of Andhra Pradesh*, Vol. II: *Early Historic Andhra Pradesh*, ed. I.K. Sarma (New Delhi: Tulika Books, 2008), 287–308.

the Mauryan period while most of them belong to the Sātavāhana–Ikshvāku periods (1st century BCE–5th century CE). A few Buddhist monuments were close to a marketing centre or were themselves small townships as exemplified by Prathiṣṭāna (Paithan) on the Godavari, and Amarāvati and Nāgārjunakonda on the Krishna. Ports like Bharukaccha, Sopara, and Kaleina were seasonally active points of exchange where long-distance merchants, craftsmen, and providers of goods and services converged in connection with the Roman trade. Extensive inland trade networks presupposing frequent circuit of itinerant merchants and availability of coins both local and non-local in plenty, presupposing monetized transactions, jointly indicate a wide zone of economic activities and exchanges.[21]

Households of big merchants and local personages of some authority, like the Raṭhikas, Bhōjas, and Peṭenikas, their warriors and the dāsa–bhṛtakas, might have constituted the population in the strategic areas of trade and markets. There were several Brāhamaṇa households too in the plains mostly around the residences of chieftains whom they provided with services of preceptors and Vedic priests. There were specialized merchants like *dhānikas* (corn dealers), *gandhikas* (perfume dealers), *mālakaras* (florists), *suvarnakaras* (gold dealers), *odayantrikas* (irrigation device dealers), and so on, figuring in the cave inscriptions. These dealers, probably organized into *nigamam* (a body like a guild), seem to be itinerants of brief sojourn at points of exchange and hence not integral to the local system of

[21] See P.L. Gupta, 'The Coinage of the Sātavāhana: Types and Their Regional Distribution', in *Coinage of the Sātavāhana and Coins from Excavations*, ed. A.M. Shastri (Nagpur: Nagpur University Press, 1972), 41–62. V.V. Mirashi, 'Wategaon Hoard of Satavahana Coins', JNSI (1972), pt-ii: 205–12. M.R. Rao, *Sātavāhana Coins in the Andhra Pradesh Government Museum*, A.P. Government Series no. 2 (Hyderabad, 1961). S.J. Mangala, 'Coins of the Feudatories and Contemporaries of the Sātavāhana', in *The Age of the Sātavāhana*, 2 vols, ed. A.M. Shastri (New Delhi: Aryan Books International, 1999), 360–90. For a discussion on the nature of urban settlements, see A. Parasher-Sen, 'Urban Settlements in the Deccan and Sātavāhana History', in *The Age of the Sātavāhanas*, Vol. I, ed. A.M. Shastri (New Delhi: Aryan Books International, 1999), 159–89. For a general appreciation of the situation, see H.P. Ray, *Monastery and Guild: Commerce under the Sātavāhana* (New Delhi: Oxford University Press, 1986).

social relations, which was differentiated in terms of status and ranks but was yet to be class-structured. Chiefly households do not seem to have any intermediaries inland placed below them, presupposing that their land control was hardly beyond what could be cultivated by their dāsa–bhṛtaka workforce. They seem to have had no more systematic relations of appropriation with, than predatory control over, the settlements of descent groups either.

The Tamil Region

Our knowledge about the pre-Pallavan social formation of Tamilakam or the Tamil macro-region demarcated by Venkaṭādri in the north and Kanyakumari in the south is almost entirely based on Tamil heroic literature.[22] Literary compositions, Tamil Brāhmi-label inscriptions, and foreign notices indicate the features, structures, processes, and dynamics of a social formation characterized by a combination of several unevenly evolved and kinship-based redistributive economies and structured by the dominance of agro-pastoral means of subsistence.[23] Archaeology of these processes takes us back in time to the centuries of expansion of the Iron Age descent communities.[24] A later

[22] For details about the nature of the composition and structure of the constituents that make the literature, see Kailasapathy, *Tamil Heroic Poetry* (Oxford: Clarendon Press, 1968).

[23] Label inscriptions consist of the Tamil Brāhmi labels belonging to c. 3rd century BCE to 4th century CE. For texts of and detailed comments on the inscriptions, see I. Mahadevan, *Early Tamil Epigraphy from the Earliest Times to the 6th Century AD* (Harvard: Harvard University Press, 2003), 60–5. For details of foreign notices, see the primary as well as secondary sources discussed at length in the first chapter. The foreign notices comprise mainly the Graeco-Roman writings. For relevant excerpts, see K.A.N. Sastri, *Foreign Notices of South India* (Madras: Madras University Press, 1939). For a characterization of the social formation, see R. Gurukkal, *Social Formations in Early South India* (New Delhi: Oxford University Press, 2010).

[24] For details of the Iron Age, see A. Sundara, *The Early Chamber Tombs of South India* (Delhi: University Publishers, 1975); B.K.G. Rao, *Megalithic Culture in South India* (Mysore: Prasaranga, 1972); and L.S. Leshnik, *South Indian 'Megalithic' Burials: The Pāndukal Complex* (Wiesbaden: Franz Steiner Verlag, 1974). C. Maloney, 'Archaeology in South India: Accomplishments

phase of the process, assignable to the period between the closing centuries of the 1st millennium BCE and the first quarter of the 1st millennium CE, is signified in the label inscriptions, Graeco-Roman accounts, and heroic poems.

Modes of human adaptation to the landscape ecosystems of ancient Tamilakam are best represented in the concept of *aintiṇai* or the five physiographical types of Tamil heroic poetics. According to the concept, the Tamil region is conceived as a physiographical assemblage of the five landscape ecotypes, namely *kuṟinji* or the forested hillocks, *mullai* or the pastoral tracts, *pālai* or the parched terrain, *marutam* or the wet-fields, and *neytal* or the littoral, inhabited by hunters, shifting cultivators, pastoralists, cattle-lifters, agriculturists, fisher folk, and salt-makers respectively. These inhabitants were descent groups, namely *kuṟavar, vēṭṭuvar,* and *vēṭar*, who subsisted on hunting/gathering and shifting cultivation; *iṭaiyar* who subsisted on agro-pastoralism; *maṟavar* who lived on predatory means; and *paratavar* who subsisted on fishing and salt manufacturing.[25] Among agro-pastoralists, there were *u̲lavar* (plough agriculturists) and *to̲luvar* (cultivators of dry land called *punam* or *ēnal*). There were artisanal and crafts-folk like the *taccar* (carpenters), *kollar* (smiths), and *kalaṅcai* (potters), besides *vaṇikar* (merchants) of their products. What emerges is an assemblage of coexistence and interaction of various tribes following the means of subsistence determined by the landscape ecosystems (*tiṇais*) that they inhabited.

Findings of previous researches help us conceptualize the above scenario in terms of coexistence and interaction of multiple economies, peoples, and the emergent power structure for characterizing it as a social formation, with hunting/gathering/fishing, agro-pastoralism, wet-rice agriculture, salt manufacturing, craft production, and

---

and Prospects', in *Essays on South India,* ed. B. Stein (New Delhi: Vikas Publications, 1976); Also K. Rajan, *Archaeology of Tamil Nadu (Kongu Country)* (New Delhi: Book India Publishing Co., 1994).

25 See a discussion of the various related aspects in K. Sivathampy, 'Early South Indian Economy: The *Tiṇai* Concept', *Social Scientist* 29 (1974): 20–37. Also R. Gurukkal, 'Forms of Production and Forces of Change: Ancient Tamil Society', *Studies in History,* n.s. 5, no. 2 (1989): 159–75.

exchange as the constituent economies, of course not as mutually exclusive status, but of overlap.[26] Its primary technological base was related to the multiple uses of iron with a marginal place for high-tin bronze. In all the constituent economies of the social formation, productive and distributive relations were based on kinship. As an industry, though paddy cultivation was the most superior in terms of technology and productivity, its relations of production, stuck to kinship, were incompatible to development and hence yet to articulate the conditions for dominance. Agro-pastoralism that combined cattle keeping with shifting cultivation was the dominant economy as borne out by the preponderance of references to cattle raids and allied customs, rites, and rituals. Everything in the socio-cultural regime revolved round this economy and everything was disposed of so as to establish its hegemony over other economies.[27] Such shared practices, ideas, and institutions of the heroic descent groups eventually led to the making of Tamilakam as a region of the Dravidian linguistic and cultural homogeneity.

The nature of social organization of labour can show the level of social stratification, for at once it signifies the level of technology, productivity, and the structure of social relations of appropriation. As already noted, the principal social mode of labour realization was familial and hence based on kinship. Skilled crafts like smelting, metal-working, stone-cutting, bead-making, and pottery were full-time trades of specialists and hence hereditary.[28] Iron had a central place among metals as the most extensively used metal both for making productive tools and defensive weapons. The significance of

[26] Gurukkal, 'Forms of Production', 160–8.

[27] For a detailed consideration of the issue, see Gurukkal, 'Forms of Production', 160–8. Also see his 'Characterising Ancient Society: The Case of South India', Presidential Address, Indian History Congress, Ancient India Section (Patiala, 1998), 24–5. For a revised version, see his *Social Formations in Early South India*, 136–54.

[28] For details of social organization of occupations, see R. Gurukkal, 'From Clan and Lineage to Hereditary Occupation Groups and Caste in Early South India', *Indian Historical Review* xxii, nos 1–2 (1993–4): 22–33. Also see the article reproduced in Gurukkal, *Social Formations in Early South India*, 255–71.

iron in a society of predatory operations for booty capture and redistribution cannot be exaggerated. Further, the practice of burying iron objects along with the dead had pushed a great deal of iron out of circulation presupposing continuous iron-working as a full-time occupation of hereditary specialization. Another activity that had to be regular and extensive was ceramic production due to the brittle nature of the product and its use in everyday life for mundane as well as ritual purposes. Moreover, the variety, fabric, polish, glazing, slips, paintings, texture, and decorative designs of pottery suggest that it was a full-time technology of specialized expertise. Another full-time function of hereditary nature was that of warriors (maṛavar) whose service was essential for every settlement (*ūr*) since its principal mode of appropriation of resources was predatory. Such full-time artisans/craftsmen of hereditary occupations were certainly more in the headquarters of bigger chieftains of the *vēḷīr* and *vēntar* levels, which, as the major redistributive pools of resources, could support more full-time crafts. The familial and kin-based division of labour and the hereditary nature of crafts suggest a social milieu of clan–kin ties with little scope for the rise of complex relations of flexibility enabling development of technology and productivity into a better phase that makes economy differentiated and society stratified.

Tendencies towards social stratification were much more likely at the headquarters of each of the three biggest chiefly lineages—the Cēras, Cōḻas, and Pāṇḍyas. In the marketing centres and coastal towns/ports such as Muciṛi (Muziris), Toṇdi (Tyndis), Korkai, and Pukār, several hereditary craftsmen and specialized functionaries drawn from the hinterlands must have worked as groups of clan–kin ties rather than guild-like organizations transcending kinship. In the centre of the vēntar chiefdoms, differential allocation of new position, status, roles, and ranks within the complex redistributive relationships was quite likely. It is reasonable to presume that it must have led to the beginnings of some kind of notional hierarchy. However, this differentiation does not seem to have given rise to social stratification. No indication of the emergence of a clearly stratified society is seen in the ancient poems that mention only a primordial type of social differentiation represented by the binary between the highborn (*uyarntōr*) that comprised Brāhmaṇas as well as gods and the lowborn (*i<u>l</u>ipirappālar*).[29] It is a fact that the term 'i<u>l</u>ipirappālar' occurs only in the context referring to leather workers or drummers. This need not be denoting the population, although it contrasted with the term 'uyarntōr'. That the second category comprised all people suggests a very flexible kind of social division, and lack of indications to the existence of intermediary positions confirms the fluidity. Similarly, the differentiation in terms of the objective conditions of life was also confined to the binary between the redistributors (*puravalar*) and its dependent benefactors (*iravalar*). In short, it was a society, not altogether complex and clearly stratified, although at the same time not too simple to be egalitarian either. This suggests that contemporary social division was quite fluid and bereft of fixed intermediary positions.

The number of full-time artisans and craftsmen of hereditary occupations was more in the headquarters of bigger chieftains of the vēḷir and vēntar levels. As the major redistributive pools of resources, the chieftains' settlements could support more full-time crafts. Another full-time function of hereditary nature was that of the warriors. Every settlement (ūr) needed full-time warriors since the main mode of political appropriation of resources was predatory. In association with the chiefly households, there were three other full-time hereditary functionaries: the *pāṇar* (bards), *paṛaiyar* (who play a kind of raid drum called *paṛa*), and *tuṭiyar* (who play a small drum called *tuṭi*).

There was a slow emergence of hereditary occupations in the vēntar-level chiefly headquarters, marketing centres, coastal towns, and ports. In the chiefly headquarters, hereditary craftsmen households seem to have existed as people of obligatory service relations with the

[29] There is a different perception in Richard S. Kennedy, 'The King in Early South India as Chieftain and the Emperor', in *Indian Historical Review* 3, no. 1 (1976): 1–15. A better conceptualization is attempted in S. Seneviratne, 'From *Kudi* to *Nadu*: A Suggested Framework for the Study of the Pre-state Political Formations in Early Iron Age South India', *The Sri Lanka Journal of the Humanities* (Kandy: University of Peradeniya) 19, nos 1–2 (1993): 57–77. For a detailed examination of the issue, see R. Gurukkal, 'Antecedents of the State Formation in South India', in *State and Society in Pre-modern South* India, eds R. Champakalakshmi, Kesavan Veluthat, and T.R. Venugopalan (Thrissur, 2002), 39–59.

chieftain. Specialized dealers in arts, crafts, and other products were present in coastal towns, but being mostly part of the long-distance itinerant merchant community, they were not integral to the local people. However, it is likely that the overseas and inland merchants had required servile people at the place of sojourn for various menial jobs. Such people at service under conditions of coercion were workers representing a system of relations of labour transcending kinship. Poems refer to captives working in pearl fisheries. Nevertheless, all this was not enough to give rise to social differentiation and stratification in any significant way. In the process of predatory operations and redistribution, some kind of differential allocation of new position, status, roles, and prestige within the complex redistributive relationships was likely. Differential allocation of positions and roles at the instance of the vēntar-level chiefly authority had a tendency towards formation of a hierarchy. However, the poems do not contain any clues to the existence of a clearly stratified society.[30]

Nevertheless, there were certain contradictions immanent in the working of the social formation, the most striking being the continued articulation of conditions totally uncongenial to the development of plough agriculture, which was the most potential form of production in terms of technology and productivity. Predatory marches of chieftains, their destruction of agrarian settlements as part of the scorched-earth policy in raids, and the dominance of the heroic ideology of raids and booty redistribution provided an utterly adverse environment for the development of agriculture.[31] The redistributive economy did exert pressure on production, but in vain since there was no scope for intensification of agriculture under the kinship-based division of labour. External labour mobilization sufficient to break the fetters of kinship was beyond the capability of the contemporary political apparatus of little coercive ability. This stasis due to development incompatibility between plough technology and relations of

30 For a different perception, see Kennedy, 'The King in Early South India', 1–15.

31 See details given in R. Gurukkal, 'Problems of Agrarian Expansion in Early Iron Age', in *Essays in Ancient Indian Economic History*, ed. B.D. Chattopadhyaya (Delhi: Indian History Congress Publication, 1987), 56–7. This is reprinted in his *Social Formations in Early South India*, 155–65.

kin-labour being an ever intensifying pressure, the social formation was anyway in the process of dissolution.

Forms of Exchange

Human settlements were sparsely distributed and interspersed by forests without proper interconnecting paths, precluding chances of any safe infrastructure in the hinterlands.[32] Therefore, relationships of exchange and interdependence among them were based on reciprocity and redistribution, largely confined to settlements of small neighbouring localities. Organized under spontaneously evolved self-sustaining kin units (ūrs) of production, the descent groups maintained exchange relations with the centrality of institutions like gift, reciprocity, and redistribution. The gift (*koṭai*) was the most significant mode of exchange and the institution through which contemporary society had its resources circulated. However, it was a resource-exhausting institution unless constantly replenished through some stable means. Reciprocity of the informal type was the central mode of exchange among the descent groups of agnatic kin–clan ties and ties of marital affinity. As descent groups became complex, involving formal relationships beyond agnatic kinship or clannish ties, the practice of reciprocity became formalized affecting its pristine nature of being putatively altruistic. There began standardization bringing in differentiation ranging between goods-for-goods exchange and forms of gift-exchange with interests in and expectations of returns, leading to the institutionalization of reciprocity. Poems refer to a kind of commodity loan (*kuṟittumāretirpai* or *kuṟiyetirpai*) to be returned in the same kind and quantity which precludes the notion of interest. Even the exchange of specialized goods was primarily based on the notion of use-value.[33] Nevertheless, it is significant to note that the practice of loan precludes the notion of interest.

It seems that altruistic as well as contingency-driven reciprocity was the usual mode of exchange for all intra-*tiṇai* transactions, while in the case of inter-tiṇai, it was *noṭuttal*, a form of need-based goods-for-goods exchange at sight through higgling and haggling. There were certain

[32] *Puṟanāṉūṟu* 3 provides an allusion illustrative of the situation.

[33] See discussion in Gurukkal, *Social Formations of Early South India*, 146–7.

fixed points of exchange referred to in the poems as *āvaṇam* and *ankāṭi* where people from different ecotypes came for exchange. Each ecotype had its goods of exchange. Descent groups of pastoral tracts had dairy products and millets; those of hillocks had forest goods, mainly honey; and those of the littoral had fish and salt. They converged in the points of exchange in the fertile wet-fields, to exchange their goods for paddy. Artisans and crafts-folk from the different ecotypes exchanged their products for paddy, salt, and fish. Instances of exchanging one kind of fish for another, or salt for fish, or fish for a pearl, and so on, are examples of reciprocity in the case of the neytal-tiṇai. In the case of the marutam-tiṇai it may be paddy for toddy, toddy for rice flakes, sugar cane for rice, and so on. Instances of the people of kuṛinji exchanging honey for toddy, deer-meat for fish, tusk for paddy; or the people of mullai exchanging *varagu* for dry fish, milk for paddy, and so on; or the people of marutam exchanging paddy for fish or salt, and so on, show inter-tiṇai exchanges of the goods-for-goods type. At times in inter-tiṇai transactions, both salt and paddy seem to have functioned as the medium of exchange as well as a measure of value with a relative notion of inter-commodity exchange rates. In fact, paddy and salt were the only two goods with a stable inter-commodity exchange rate. Several poems refer to the exchange of salt with paddy in the marutam where the two were exchanged as goods of equal value and hence were mutually convertible, as the dictum *uppum nellum nērkoḷḷīro* (salt and paddy as measure for measure).

Redistribution was another imported mode of circulation of resources at the intra-tiṇai as well as inter-tiṇai levels. It presupposes a centralized pooling of goods and services, obviously at the chiefly residence in the case of a descent group, for eventual redistribution to those in the clan–kin ties called the nexus of redistributive relationship.[34] Being fundamental to the contemporary system of

[34] See K. Polanyi, *The Great Transformation* (London: Beacon Paper Back, [1944] 1957), 247–9. According to Polanyi, Reciprocity and Redistribution operate as culturally regulated practices based on trust that is inherent in descent groups of strong relationships as a contrast to markets that are self-regulating. See K. Polanyi, 'The Economy as Instituted Process', in K. Polanyi, C. Arensberg, and H.W. Pearson, eds, *Trade and Markets in the Early Empires: Economies in History and Theory* (Glencoe, IL: The Free Press, 1957) 243–70.

resource-sharing, redistribution was the most instituted means all over the region. Both the polity and political economy of the Tamil region were determined and regulated by this instituted means of sharing of resources, often acquired through plunder raids.

It is particularly relevant here to discuss the exchange pattern of the littoral tracts where the main activities were fishing and salt panning by the paratavar, the descent group inhabiting the littoral ecotype and known also as *timilōn* (he who goes out fishing with the small boat, *timil*) and *valaiyōr* (those subsisting on fishing with a net, *vala*). They were the main dealers in fish and salt in early southern India. Certain poetic references are illustrative of fishing, salt manufacturing, and allied exchange practices of the neytal-tiṇai.[35] When a fishing boat was back ashore after a day's catch, the paratavar onboard were surrounded by the kith and kin for their share. Several other claimants like the craftsmen whose services were used for the repair and maintenance of the boat too reached the coast. This was followed by an informal distribution of fish among these people by the headman of the paratavar and then among the fishermen themselves both as altruistic gifts and obligatory reciprocity against the cooperative labour received. What remained as the leftover was carried by their women, as hawkers and peddlers, to exchange it in the neighbourhood. They circulated the fish within the radius of 5 to 6 km from the coast, while the men took it further upstream in boats, but never too far for obvious reasons. Poems mention the *paratavar* girls exchanging fish at the gathering of people in the inlets of the coast. Common sea fish like *ayila, iṛa, koḻuva,* and *cūra* are mentioned in ancient Tamil poems as the types thus locally distributed. Those engaged in fishing in the backwaters and rivers adjacent to the coast were called paratavar, and the common inland freshwater fish mentioned in the source are *kadumīn, varāl,* and *vāḷai*. Generally the circulation of raw sea fish was confined to the neytal and the contiguous marutam tracts only, for it was impossible to transport them beyond before they decayed. Ecotypes such as the mullai and the *kuṛinji* situated far in the interior got them dried and salted.

[35] For a detailed analysis, see M.R.R. Varier, 'Production and Exchange in the Littoral Tracts of Ancient South India', Working Paper, School of Social Sciences, Mahatma Gandhi University, Kottayam, 1998.

There are poetic allusions to the practice of exchanging fish for a variety of goods; for instance, fish for a pot of toddy or for paddy or for honey, roots, deer-meat, sugar cane, rice flakes, or wine. At certain bays where pearl oysters grew, paratavar were engaged in pearl fishing as well as in the collection of cowries and conch shells.[36] A rare variety of pearl *caurṇēyam* collected from the Cūrṇi (Periyar) River and another fine type *kavāṭakam* obtained from Korkai are mentioned in the *Arthaśāstra*. Pearls of fine quality found on the Tamil coast are mentioned by the Graeco-Roman geographers as well.[37] Exchange of cowries and bangles made of conch shells by paratavar girls through haggling was common.

Making of salt out of saline water (*kaḻi*) or salt pans (*cēṛu*) was a full-time enterprise of a section of the paratavar. Salt panning was done by draining in and retaining the sea-water in pans and by leaving the brine to dry in the sun. Salt, an essential good for all, had a central role in the facilitation of inter-tiṇai goods-for-goods exchange with a sense of inter-commodity exchange ratio. Peoples of all other ecotypes in the interior had to procure salt from the littoral tracts, a practice not confined to the Tamil region alone, but routine to the subcontinent as a whole, except for the regions too far off from the sea coast, which had to depend on an alternative source. Salt manufacturing and carting it into the interior ecotypes was, therefore, a major economic activity in the coastal region. While in the intra-tiṇai and inter-tiṇai situations, reciprocity and redistribution were the common forms of exchange in the region, mercantile was the form in the case of the circulation of unavoidable goods like salt in the trans-regional situation. Those engaged in the carting of salt from the pans as part of mercantile distribution were called *umaṇar* whose long journey as caravan troops

[36] See references to right-whirled conch (*valampiri*) in *Akanāṉūṛu*, 201:3–7 and 350:11–13. In *Akanāṉūṛu*, 280:11–14 pearls are mentioned and in 349:1–2 conch bangles. For the text and translation, see N.M.V. Nattar, ed., *Akanāṉūṛu* with commentary, Vols II and III (Tirunelveli: The South India Saiva Siddhantha Works Publishing Society Ltd), 1950–1.

[37] See J. McCrindle, *Ancient India as Described in Classical Literature* (Orient Books; repr., Patna: Eastern Book House, 1987), 144–5. Also see the allusion in *Akanāṉūṛu*, 126:7–14. For the text and commentary, see Nattar, ed., *Akanāṉūṛu* with commentary, Vol. I (1949).

(*umaṇaccāttu*) through the difficult tracts to the foot-hills is picturesquely described to in several poems.[38] Poems referring to carts of umaṇar waiting near the pans to load salt and then, laden with the sacks, leaving for far-off destinations through hazardous and inhospitable tracts is almost like a stock expression in ancient Tamil poems. Salt caravans (umaṇaccāttu) bartered salt at other tiṇais for the products there, which included precious goods such as pepper, elephant tusks, gems, and so on. Caravans, who were themselves armed for self-defence, also had to hire, from place to place, the services of mercenaries for a safe journey. These poetic descriptions to the extensive movement of salt and its circulation in the mercantile mode would have us presuppose the prevalence of similar trans-regional courses in the case of other goods of demand.

In the Brāhmi-label inscriptions of the 3rd to 1st century BCE as well as in the poems there are references to the merchants specialized in the transaction of certain specific merchandises such as salt, grains, cotton fabrics, metallic objects like iron ploughshares, gold ornaments, and gems.[39] They seem to have recorded along with the personal names of the donors of the caverns and rock-beds, the occupational names such as *ponkolavan* (the goldsmith), *pon-vāṇikan* (gold merchant), *uppu-vāṇikan* (salt merchant), *pānita-vāṇikan* (sugar or toddy merchant), *aṛukai-vāṇikan* (cloth merchant), *koḻuvāṇikan* (ploughshare merchant), *eṇṇai-vāṇikan*, and *malai-vaṇṇakkan* (lapidary).[40] These were individual dealers in specific goods, who probably belonged to the community of long-distance merchants, evidently

[38] *Puṛanāṉūṛu*, 102: 1–4 refers to the bullock carts of *umaṇar* loaded with salt moving through undulating marshy routes and their difficulties in retrieving the wheels of their carts clogged/caught in mire. For the text and commentary, see U.V.S. Iyar, ed., *Puṛanāṉūṛu* with commentary, 6th ed. (Madras: Thyagarajavilasam Publications, 1963).

[39] The chronology of the cave labels is fixed with the Arikamedu graffiti of 1st century CE as the point of reference and on the basis of orthographic factors. Labels of all the above cavern sites are assigned to the pre-Arikamedu period, roughly the preceding three centuries before the Christian era. For a detailed discussion, see Mahadevan, *Early Tamil Epigraphy*, 91–5. Labels of all the above cavern sites are assigned to the pre-Arikamedu period, roughly the preceding three centuries before the Christian era.

[40] Mahadevan, *Early Tamil Epigraphy*, 369, 372, 376–7, 381, 417, 419, 441.

prominent as the act of donation shows. The reference to a *kāvuti* (accountant) of the *nikamam* of Veḷḷarai, found on a label inscription of Mānkuḷam, suggests the existence of an organized body, but there is no evidence to state it was of the merchants.[41] However, it is evident from the inscriptions that these merchants were relatively rich, although not comparable to those figuring in the Nasik, Junnar, and Karle caves.

These inscriptions are on the overland merchant routes such as the Madurai–Tiruchchiṛappaḷḷi route, the Tiruppattur–Karaikkuṭi route, the Pudukkōṭṭai–Tiruchchiṛappaḷḷi route, and the Tiruchchiṛappaḷḷi–Erode route. There were several fixed points of exchange at places where the routes intersected or converged and the mode of exchanges was barter based on the use-value of goods (*noṭai*) determined on the spot as a result of higgling–haggling by the retailers. Long-distance merchants were transporters of goods in bulk from the source of supply to distributive points of demand like āvaṇam or ankāṭi (fair place) and the *tuṛai* or *paṭṭinam* (port) from where goods of overseas demand were carried in ships by merchants from the Persian, Arabian, and Mediterranean seaboards. At every port a bazaar that dealt with various artefacts, particularly beads, bangles, garlands, anklets, and so on, was active, catering to the needs of the people who converged there. They must have acquired them through goods-for-goods exchange.

Coins and Currency

In the Indian subcontinent, the history of the use of coins, as archaeologically corroborated, goes back to around the 6th century BCE.[42] Exchange networks of the mahājanapadas in the fertile Gangetic plain with the strategically situated Magadha as their nucleus provided the required political economy for the use of coins. As ruling lineages in the resource-rich Gangetic region of bustling exchange relations

41 Mahadevan, *Early Tamil Epigraphy*, 319. Also see the discussion in R. Champakalakshmi, *Trade, Ideology and Urbanisation in South India 300 BC to AD 1300* (New Delhi: Oxford University Press, 1996), 118–19.

42 K. Dhavalikar, 'The Beginning of Coinage in India', *World Archaeology* 6, no. 3 (London: Taylor & Francis, 1975): 330–8.

began to emerge as dynasties, coins began to be issued, probably more as a royal stamp of authority than an instrument of exchange among merchants. Ancient coins, invariably made of high-value metals, had no role in the day-to-day transactions or in the procurement of goods and services in the daily life. Hence, their circulation was confined primarily to the royal court and major centres of exchange. It appears that they were used mainly by itinerant traders and the personnel of the local ruling power, who constituted the main components of the townsfolk. Coins had no role in the transactions of the inhabitants in the villages, whose exchange relations with traders were marginal and hardly beyond reciprocity.

Coins of Northern India

Rulers of the mahājanapadas seem to have started the coin tradition by issuing punch-marked coins of silver and copper, largely rectangular but mostly of irregular shape as a result of adjusting the rough slices of the metal bar to the correct weight by cutting the edge. These coins called *karṣapaṇa* had circulated in the exchange centres across the subcontinent. Used as means of payment to officials in the royal service and as a medium of exchange primarily among long-distance merchants, the coins were minted in huge quantity. Punch-marked coins continued to be issued extensively in different denominations during the Mauryan period, with the sun sign and a six-armed symbol accompanied by the wheel, human figures, geometrical designs, and motifs of animals, plants, and trees. *Arthaśāstra* mentions *ardha* (half), *pada* (quarter), and *aṣṭabhāga* (one-eighth) as the denominations of karṣapaṇa. By and large these punch-marked coins remained almost a continuum, stylistically the same, except the flans turning thicker and smaller over the centuries. Coins in the subcontinent meant punch-marked coins, and money, the karṣapaṇa even during subsequent periods.[43]

Roman coins were collected from the Andhra region. Coins became diverse during the period of the Sātavāhanas.[44] While punch-marked

[43] In southern India the term for money even today is *kāśu-paṇa* or *kāśu* or *paṇa*, which is either a derivation of the term as it is or piecemeal.

[44] See Rao, *Sātavāhana Coins*. Also, Gupta, 'The Coinage of the Sātavāhana'. For a specific study, see Mirashi, 'Wategaon Hoard of Satavahana Coins'.

coins persisted, fresh coins cast and die-struck, mostly of lead and potin, but supplemented by those made of copper, brass, bronze, and silver were introduced. They carried representations of natural objects like hills, rivers, and trees; animals like lions, tigers, elephants, bulls, horses, and camels; cultural images like the mother goddess (Lakshmi), the Ujjain *chaitya*, and the royal bust; and artefacts like the wheel and the ship. The symbols of three-peaked hills, the Ujjain chaitya, and the lion standing on two legs seem to have been the most widely used symbols. Some of them bear a few legends and inscriptions in the Prākrit language and Brāhmi script conveying the ruler's name. A few coins had a ship motif. Puḷumāvi and Sātakaṛṇi were the rulers who issued coins with the ship motif. Sātavāhana coins had circulated all over the region covering southern Gujarat, Andhra, and northern Karnataka. Another major distributor of coins overlapping the region was the Western Kṣatrapa dynasty that ruled over the Scythian kingdom during the early centuries of the CE.[45] A series of silver coins modelled on the Greek types, but invariably with the name of the king and the date in the Saka Era was issued by the Kṣatrapa rulers. They were in circulation in Gujarat, Rajasthan, Maharashtra, and Andhra regions, often interspersed with the later Sātavāhana coins.

Coins of northern India seem to have reached the Tamil region too, obviously through the long-distance merchants. There were several tributary channels to the pan-Indian exchange routes diverging from Pratiṣṭān to the different parts of the Tamil macro region up to the cape and to the ports like Muciṟi and Toṇḍi as well as the inland markets of the Kerala region. Punch-marked coins of the pre-Mauryan Magadha, the earliest among the archaeologically reported in southern India, travelled with the merchants through these channels.

Gold, silver, and copper coins of Roman emperors from Augustus of the 1st century BCE to Constantine of the 4th century CE found in as many as over eighty hoards come next in antiquity.[46] Some of

45 D.R. Reddy and P.S. Reddy, *Coins of the Satraps of the Sātavāhana Era* (Hyderabad: Numismatic Society of Hyderabad Publication), 1983.

46 Roman coins have been found in India at over 130 sites, with a concentration in the Krishna valley in Andhra and the Coimbatore region in Tamil Nadu. For early notices of finds, see W. Elliot, *Coins of Southern India* (London: Trubner, 1886); R. Sewell, 'Roman Coins Found in India', *Journal of the Royal Asiatic Society* (Cambridge), n.s., XXIII, no. 36 (1904): 591–637.

the southern Indian sites from where hoards of Roman coins have been discovered are Poḷḷāchi (of Augustus and Tiberius), Karur (of Augustus, Antonia, Tiberius, Claudius, and Constantinus), Veḷḷalūr (of Augustus, Darius, Germanius, Tiberius, Caligula, and Claudius), Kalayamuttūr (Darius, Tiberius, Caligula, Claudius, Nero, Domitian, Nerva, Trajan, Hadrian, and Commodius), and Madurai (Domitian, Theodosius, Eudocia, Constans, and Zeno) in Tamil Nadu; and Eyyal (of Tiberius, Claudius, Nero, and Trajan), Vaḷḷuvaḷḷi (Julius Caesar and several others), Panagad, Kōṭṭyathunādu, and Puthenchiṟa (details not available) in Kerala.[47] A significant discovery of Roman copper coins (mainly of Honorius and Arcadius) has been made at the Vaigai bed in Madurai. One-fourth of the total Roman coins found in India date from the time of Augustus and Tiberius. Before the 1st century CE was far advanced, the India trade attained such magnitude as to give concern to thoughtful observers. As stray finds, a few Phoenician, Greek, and Seleucid coins have been reported from Karur.[48]

Coins of Tamilakam

The ruling lineages of Tamilakam, the Pāṇḍyas, Cēras, and Cōḻas, seem to have had issued coins of copper and silver mostly of the punch-marked type, the numismatic details and find-spots of which have been discussed in the second chapter in connection with the review of coins as a source category. Some of them are portrait coins as well. These are identified as issued by the Pāṇḍyas, Cēras, and Cōḻas on the

[47] See R. Sewell, *Lists of* the *Antiquarian Remains in the Presidency of Madras,* Vol. I (Madras: Archaeological Survey of Southern India Publication, 1882), 144, 190, 193, 203, 214, 218, 221–2, 226, 240, 244, 285–6. Find-spots are given in K.V.S. Aiyer, *Historical Sketches of the Dekhan,* Vol. I (Madras: Modern Print Works, 1917), 86–7. The Roman coins recovered from Kerala are discussed in P.L. Gupta, *The Early Coins from Kerala* (Thiruvananthapuram: Government of Kerala, Department of Archaeology, 1965). For a detailed catalogue of Roman coins, see S. Suresh, *Symbols of Trade: Roman and Pseudo-Roman Objects Found in India* (New Delhi: Manohar Publishers, 2004), 18–20.

[48] See R. Krishnamurthy, 'Coins from Phoenicia Found at Karur', *Studies in South Indian Coins,* ed. A.V. Narasimha Murthy, Vol. IV (Tirupati: Sri Venkateswara University, 1994), 19–28. Also his 'Seleucid Coins from Karur', *Journal of Mythic Society* (Bangalore) III, no. 1 (1993): 1–11.

basis of their characteristic symbols found punched on the reverse of the coins. The coins of the Pāṇḍyas carry the fish motif; those of the Cēras, the bow and arrow; and those of the Cōḻas, the tiger. A few coins of the Pāṇḍyas and the Cēras have been found with Brāhmi legends, Peruvaḻūti and Mākōtai or Kuṭṭuvan Kōtai respectively. A few coins assigned to the hill chieftains like Malayamān, identified on the basis of the symbol of a flowing river, have also been reported. Coins with a horse symbol are also assigned to these chieftains. Quantitatively, the Pāṇḍya coins are more and the Cōḻa ones the least. As noted earlier, a few coins of the Pāṇḍyas are known as Peruvaḻūti coins and a few coins of the Cēras as Mākōtai or Kuṭṭuvan Kōtai coins, based on the respective legends in Brāhmi letters with the legend of Mākōtai or Kuṭṭuvan Kōtai in Brāhmi letters.[49]

Coins of Tamilakam remain a puzzle in terms of their discovery, chronology, and function. Most coins have been discovered by one or two numismatists and in the same place, the Amarāvati River bed. Their chronology is what the numismatists guess and their context is presumably that of the ritual offering made to the river. The portrait coins are evidently of the Graeco-Roman times since they are modelled on the Roman silver coins with the portrait of Augustus and Tiberius.

Money, Markets, and Urbanization

Money, markets, and urbanization are modern concepts but used liberally in the context of practices, places, and institutions of exchange in early societies as well. It is often maintained that they appeared simultaneously in all civilizations. These highly loaded terms are widely used in historiography without much thought about their semantic implications. In fact, like several other terms, they have very little relevance to the time, space, and process, which we are discussing. Actually, their semantic function is limited to conveying a relative difference or distinction about the objects, sites, and processes concerned, notwithstanding the problem of their approximation even

[49] R. Krishnamurthy, 'Mākkotai Coins', *Studies in South Indian Coins*, Vol. II (Thiruvananthapuram: State Department of Archaeology, Kerala, 1992), 89–94.

to the irrelevant. Therefore, one has to make clear at the outset how loaded the terms are and to what misconceptions their coining leads.

Approximation in the historicizing of money by postulating its primitive forms in cattle, cowrie shells, and metal pieces, and so on, divests the term of its technical meaning completely. It goes anachronistic too. What economists talk about by way of history of money as part of the self-evident wisdom is seldom based on evidence from the past sources. In ancient times, community relations and cultural contexts were decisive in matters of the medium of exchange. Their representation of the practice and objects thereof in the language of economics hardly helps us capture reality.[50] In order to avoid this, one has to describe the historical context by avoiding terms that are overloaded with technical meanings and implications. In the past, in relatively formal modes, sometimes primary grains and salt in the areas where they were scarce might have commanded other goods in exchange. Salt and paddy/wheat were such valuables of demand in most parts of the Indian subcontinent, which could be exchanged for other goods of choice. Any relatively non-perishable high-value and low-volume goods of great demand would claim other goods in exchange. They could function as a medium of exchange and a measure as well as a store of value. At some point they could also function as the standard for rating the relative value of other goods and establishing inter-good exchange rates.

Coins marked a logical extension of the exchange based on goods of common or wide demand. A coin was invariably made of a valuable material of wide demand in time and place, for it should function as a token of value guaranteeing its exchange for other goods of choice anytime, anywhere, at will. It was the metallic worth or the intrinsic value of the coin which acted as the secret of its power to guarantee. Thus, coins served as 'a general store of purchasing power' and 'a bearer of options of purchase', thanks to its physical value. Coins become money when they are able to discharge these functions mainly on the basis of their status as legal tender, the secret of which is the state power behind them, and the law. Nevertheless, ancient money generally had enough intrinsic value, although objects like cowries, devoid

[50] See discussion in D.R. Graeber, *Debt: The First Five Thousand Years* (Brooklyn, New York: Melville House Publishing, 2011), 21–42.

of material value, had functioned as a medium of exchange and measure of value in primordial societies founded on trust. In complex societies the trust fails unless legally formalized and reinforced by a repressive institution like the state.

Gold and silver coins were used by big merchants in their bulk transactions of goods, but only in situations precluding barter, due to the absence of demand for the goods of one party for the other, but not vice versa.[51] Such situations would constrain the former to give gold or silver coins as valuable materials of wide demand, in exchange for the goods of the latter. Obviously, in the context, gold and coins as objects made of high-value metals functioned as valuable goods or goods of great demand. In *Periplus Maris Erythraei* (*PME*) there is a mention of the exchange of Roman coins in Barygaza, as raw material for the local ruler to mint their coins.[52] Gold and silver coins were often treated as high-value metals that had special demand as goods in certain places. Often coins themselves were goods of demand. In the ancient Tamil poems the Graeco-Roman coins are mentioned as *pon* (gold) brought by the transmarine merchants.[53] Even in coin-based transactions among merchants of ancient and early historic periods, barter was the primary mode of exchange, be it among big merchants themselves or between them and the retailers. Big merchants used gold and silver coins in bulk transactions among themselves when direct barter could not work. Lesser coins made of relatively low-value metals such as potin, bronze, copper, and lead were used in

[51] G.L. Adhya thinks that the onset of coins with the regular issue of them by various ruling houses throughout the subcontinent as suggestive of the stage of trading through barter had largely passed. See his *Early Indian Economics: Studies in the Economic Life of Northern and Western India c. 200 B.C. 300 A.D.* (Bombay: Asia Publishing House, 1966), 95. This is not a tenable argument both in terms of empirical data as well as theoretical knowledge. D.D. Kosambi, referring to the poor coinage of the Sātavāhanas, as reflected in their issue of lead and potin, had rightly observed the situation of the prevalence of barter in the Deccan during the period. See *Introduction to the Study of Indian History* (Bombay: Popular Prakashan, 1958), 257.

[52] *PME*, 49.

[53] *Puṟanāṉūṟu*, 126:15; 149:4; and 343:5. For the text and commentary, see Iyar, ed., *Puṟanāṉūṟu* with commentary. Also see *Akanāṉūṟu*, 201:4. For the text and commentary, see Nattar, ed., *Akanāṉūṟu* with commentary, Vol. I.

their transactions with small merchants. Retail exchanges by small merchants, hawkers, and peddlers hardly involved the use of coins. In short, barter was the primary mode of exchange in contemporary transactions.

During the period, the pattern of exchange among the folk in the Deccan and the immediate south consisted of forms, largely based on the logic of goods-for-goods, precluding the concept of exchange-value/price or the notion of interest/profit. Coins hardly figured in their transactions. Prominent households, mainly the ruling personnel and big merchants who had access to coins, also might not have used them in their day-to-day transactions. They seem to have used the coins as objects of donations to the monasteries and other Buddhist institutions. Both overland and overseas merchants from faraway places like the Gangetic valley and the Mediterranean world had entered into exchange relations with the region, primarily within the economic milieu of barter. In the subcontinent their transactions were based on the norms of use-value rather than exchange-value. It is true that coins were in use in certain contexts, but mostly as part of valuables and hence as goods, rather than money. Roman coins entered the transactions as gold and silver, two valuable metals that could be a convenient store of wealth, material for making ornaments, and a prestigious object of donation to enhance status and ranking.

The occurrence of coins in southern India in hoards perhaps suggests their non-currency status in time, place, and culture. Further, the survival of the Roman coins in hoards, as fresh as from the mint, and several of them with an aperture at the centre or loops on the periphery, is a clear indication of their non-currency status in contemporary society. What the people in the Tamil macro region needed were gold and silver which they used as ornaments and valuables of status and ranking. Hence, the Roman coins were used mainly as objects of treasure per se as their discovery in hoards and appearance as fresh as from the mint suggest. Gold and silver coins were turned into ornaments by putting them on a thread as several pieces found with loops on the edge or aperture at the centre would have us believe. Some of these coins probably stored and inherited as treasure seem to have had circulation after several centuries as the references to *paḻankācu* (old coin) and *tuḷaippon* (gold coin with an aperture) found in some of the early medieval inscriptions of southern India suggest.

It is possible that these coins, often called pal̠ankācu and tuḷaippon, were the *dīnāra* of the Roman Empire.

Nevertheless, it is significant that the mere presence or absence of coins hardly means prevalence or lack of monetization in a society.[54] Ancient Rome had a brisk exchange with China, but as of now there is no numismatic evidence of it. As a contrast to the coasts of the Indian subcontinent, the peoples of the Chinese coasts were monetized, which probably accounts for the non-survival of Roman coins. Similarly, the Graeco-Roman contact with the Scythian region and north-western India is well known from sources, but there is no numismatic evidence of it. As in the case of China, this region was perhaps relatively monetized, as evident from the large number of coins issued by Scythian and Kushān rulers. It has also been pointed out that these rulers were in the habit of melting the Roman coins to re-mint them as their own.[55] In short, it is not the hoards of Roman coins discovered as treasure troves at various sites in southern India which would provide us with a reliable basis to generalize upon the existence of trade and its volume of exchange, although it has been the general practice in the historiography of trade in early India. Coins obtained as dispersed objects from stratified sites are better indicators of how they were used, by whom, when, and in what context.

[54] See, for example, in relation to Sri Lanka, D.P. Weerakkody, 'Roman Coins of Sri Lanka: Some Observations', *The Sri Lanka Journal of the Humanities* (Kandy: University of Peradeniya) 21, nos 1–2 (1995): 1–30. O. Bopearachchi, 'Recent Discoveries of Foreign Coins Hitherto Unknown in the Sri Lankan Context', in G.P.S.H. de Silva and C.G. Uragoda, eds, *Sesquicentennial Commemoration Volume of Royal Asiatic Society of Sri Lnka 1845–1995* (Colombo: Royal Asiatic Society Publication, 1995), 127–39. Also, D.P. Weerakkody, *Taprobane: Ancient Sri Lanka as Known to Greeks and Romans* (Turnhout: Brepols, 1997) and A. Burnett, 'Roman Coins from India and Sri Lanka', in *Origin, Evolution and Circulation of Foreign Coins in the Indian Ocean*, eds D.P. Weerakkody and O. Bopearachchi (New Delhi: Manohar Publishers, 1998), 179–89. Also, F. De Romanis, 'Romanukharattha and Taprobane: Relations between Roe and Sri Lanka in the First Century A.D.', in *Crossings: Early Mediterranean Contact with India*, eds F. De Romanis and A. Tchernia (1997), 157–237.

[55] A. Cunningham, *Coins of Ancient India: From the Earliest Times to the Seventh Century A.D.* (London: B. Quaritch, 1891), 50. Also, E.J. Rapson, *Indian Coins* (London: Trubner & Co., 1897), 4, 16.

Interestingly, they are found invariably at port sites and among debris that seemingly had belonged to merchants. Actually, the presence or absence of coins has to be situated in the overall context of contemporary social formation and the plausible form of exchange, ascertained before any generalization about trade is made.

In the Tamil region, the overall pattern of contemporary internal exchanges, as depicted in the heroic poems, was that of ascriptive and customary exchange practices like reciprocity based on use-value. It was primarily a system of goods-for-goods exchange (*nēr-kol*) based on haggling (noṭuttal) that involved no notion of exchange-value, price, and profit. There were formal points of exchange, the network of which was fairly large and where descent groups of different ecosystems with diverse resources converged for transactions. Poems refer to points of exchange such as *tuṛai* (port) and āvaṇam/ankāṭi (fair place) as well as occasional markets like *nāḷankāṭi* (daily fair place) and *antik-kaṭai* (evening shops). These were places of transactions where the folk converged for goods-for-goods exchange that was based on community relations and norms rather than market conditions. Therefore, the use of the term 'market' to refer to these sites and contexts of exchanges is unsuitable and misleading. In fact, goods of mercantile circulation were confined to essential items like salt and sea fish, which only the littoral could produce. Raw fish being perishable, its distribution was never beyond the distance that the coastal hawkers were able to walk up in a day, while salt and the dried fish had reached far into the interior recesses. Similarly, most inhabitants had required iron implements and the women folk, the variety of horn and shell bangles, iron anklets, and other ornaments of beads made of terracotta, glass, semi-precious stones, and so on. Hardly any goods, other than such artefacts of occasional demand, had required itinerant merchants of long routes. Even merchant goods had their circulation not as part of trade but through other forms of exchange, namely barter, reciprocity, redistribution, and gifts. In short, trade and markets were largely unlikely in the region's economic aggregate of the times.

Likewise, urbanization, despite the absence of any tangible evidence of it in many cases, has been a celebrated topic in the historiography of early India. It has been viewed as a process integral to trade, trade routes, money, and markets. How to define an urban centre with what attributes has been explained in a very convincing manner by Gordon Childe.[56] To summarize the attributes, an urban centre should be a strategic point of convergence of goods and services with enough infrastructure of transport, communication, and governance, sustained by its hinterland of agrarian surplus. The Gangetic region around the 6th century BCE is hailed to have witnessed this process, which scholars glorify as the second urbanization in Indian history.[57] In terms of archaeological indications of exchange of goods, convergence of multicultural peoples, and level of material culture, urban development of the Gangetic region is in no way comparable to those of the Harappan Civilization. Nevertheless, it is a fact that the level of agrarian production, extent of trade, rise of fortified structures, development of a juridico-political apparatus including the militia, and emergence of a ruling aristocracy as evidenced by archaeological remains as well as textual references suggest that the Gangetic region had some urban centres like rājagṛha, Kaushambi, and Vārāṇasi.[58] However, this was not the case with the Deccan and further south of the peninsular India during the early historic period. In the Deccan, urban processes are said to have begun in the 1st century BCE, but with little or no archaeological indication of exchanges, multicultural convergence, and advanced material culture, the most significant constituents of urbanism.[59] There is no evidence of agrarian surplus in

[56] V.G. Childe's theoretical characterization of the urban has wider acceptance, although his identification of the process as a revolution has evoked criticisms. See his 'The Urban Revolution', *The Town Planning Review* 21, no. 1 (1950): 3–17.

[57] See, for instance, D.K. Chakrabarti, 'The Concept of Urban Revolution and the Indian Context', *Puratatva* (Bulletin of the Indian Archaeological Society), no. 6 (1972–3): 27–31.

[58] For details, see R.S. Sharma, *Material Culture and Social Formations in Ancient India* (Delhi: Macmillan India Limited, 1983), 123–6. Also see A. Ghosh, *The City in Early Historical India* (Shimla: Indian Institute of Advanced Studies; repr., New Delhi: Munshiram Manoharlal, 1990), 19–23.

[59] See discussions in H.P. Ray, *Monastery and Guild: Commerce under the Sātavāhana* (New Delhi: Oxford University Press, 1986). Also see Parasher-Sen, *Social and Economic History of Early Deccan*. Often the role of agrarian surplus is overstated; for instance, see the discussion in Morrison, 'Trade, Urbanism, and Agricultural Expansion', 203–21.

the Deccan region where the deltas were not under plough during the period. Plough technology though symbolic of surplus productivity, generation of economic surplus in agrarian societies was a juridico-political process of appropriation. This would mean that the formation of the state was a necessary pre-requisite for urban development. Any investigation using the diagnostic attributes would show that there was no urbanization in the Deccan during the period, and studies arguing the other way round do so under the influence of the uncritically accepted wisdom of historiography.[60]

In early historic social formations, one cannot find the existence of money, markets, and urbanization in their theoretically valid way, wherein forms of exchange were largely non-formal and use-value based.[61] This is not to say that there were no formal centres of exchange and that none of them was a town. Certainly, there were towns on the coast as well as in the interior, but they were not centres with a concentration of ruling personnel, big traders, craftsmen, and artisans who had sustained themselves on what the surrounding villages produced. There is no evidence to show that these towns had their hinterlands of a well-developed agrarian economy integrated by a political formation with institutionalized relations of appropriative control. An urban site was a high-level consumption centre with relatively permanent establishments, authority, governance, institutions, practices, groups, relations, and transactions sustained by the hinterland of sufficient productive surplus.

[60] There is exaggeration about the material culture, nature, and surplus potential of the settlements in most studies. For instance, see D.K. Chakrabarti, 'Post-Mauryan States of Mainland South Asia (c. BC 185–AD 320)', in *The Archaeology of Early Historic South Asia: The Emergence of Cities and States*, ed. F.R. Allchin, Part III (Cambridge: Cambridge University Press, 1995), 274–326; Morrison, 'Trade, Urbanism, and Agricultural Expansion', 203–21. Also, P.K.M. Reddy, 'God, Trade and Worship: A Glimpse into the Region of Early Andhradesa', *East and West* (Rome: Istituto Italiano per l'Africa e l'Oriente) 48, nos 3–4 (1998): 291–311. For details of the so-called urban process, see A. Parasher-Sen, 'Urban Settlements in the Deccan and Sātavāhana History', in *The Age of the Sātavāhanas*, Vol. I, ed. A. Shastri (New Delhi: Aryan Books International, 1999), 159–89.

[61] For a close study of the nature of early urban sites, see Champakalakshmi, *Trade, Ideology and Urbanisation*, 117–30.

Contrasting Political Economies

Classical Graeco-Roman political economy, strongly founded on agrarian surplus and trade revenue, bears a strong comparison with that of the Mauryan Empire. Both had slave-based agrarian production (with cultural differences, of course), extensive trade networks, landed ruling aristocracy, big traders, enormous military strength, and bureaucratic state power over a huge empire with the bulk of the population abysmally poor and rural. Although differences have been pointed out in terms of the extent of dependence on slave labour, intellectual pursuits, crafts production, manufacturing technology, development of science, growth of philosophy, and so on (which in fact are not quite true, mostly), the two are eminently comparable. However, the political economy of the immediate post-Mauryan Gangetic region, the Deccan and the Tamil region, bears absolutely no comparison with that of the classical Mediterranean world.

Political Economy of Roman Empire

Classical Greece and Rome were slavery dependent, aristocratic, agrarian economies of deficit, made up through trade surplus and conquest of grain-rich regions. Crafts production and industry were secondary to agriculture in their economy, but the mining industry had a predominant place, for it could supplement trade in metals, minerals, and marbles. Spanish mines yielded huge amounts of silver and the Iberian and Dalmatian mines enough gold for minting coins and making jewellery. Iron, lead, and tin came from the British mines. Graeco-Roman overseas merchants had bartered all these resources, except jewellery, with the merchants in the ports of the Indian subcontinent. Many craft-production units, specializing in the manufacture of fine ceramics, glassware, jewellery, and textiles, had come up in the cities and towns of the empire. Greek aristocrats were either big estate owners or wealthy merchant-mariners while their Roman counterparts were landed rulers, financiers, and bankers, who considered merchants a notch lower in social status and ranking. The majority of the population, constituting poor farmers, lived in many rural settlements, each of which was clustered around a town. Shortage of grain drove the Roman ruling aristocracy into imperialistic expansion through conquests of the agrarian provinces of Egypt, Sicily, and Tunisia besides regions around the Black Sea. Trade revenue being their supplementary requirement, acquisition of strategic areas of commerce and control of ports became another compulsion for taking to wars and conquests. The result was a large empire founded on the massive stock of plundered wealth and sustained through the returns from the vast agrarian estates, huge overseas trade revenue, and extensive tax money.

The Roman Empire, after the Battle of Actium, was a formidable imperial power with a huge army consisting of about thirty legions (roughly 300,000 soldiers) deployed in several garrisons at all strategic points along the frontier with the reinforcement of forts and bastions. It was a strongly organized juridico-political system headed by the autocratic state power exercised through various institutional structures of political control and documentation procedures of bureaucracy. It was sustained by a well-structured revenue administration and system of taxation, particularly the tariff imposed on luxury goods brought from the eastern world. Compared to the volume of tax collected from the inland traders, what the empire exacted from overseas traders at the rate of a quarter of the total value was enormous. According to an estimate, the total value of goods from the east was one billion sesterces.[62] Naturally, its revenue from overseas transactions with the eastern world was indeed substantial. The institution of tax in cash and the rising consumer demand for luxury goods had constituted the political economy that facilitated overseas trade in the Roman Empire. In fact, the crucial aspect of the political economy of the empire was the state's revenue from the trade in luxury goods, which amounted to 300 million sesterces per year. Naturally, Roman society's ever-increasing demand for luxury was the source of state power as well as the motor of overseas trade.

However, trade in general was not anything central to the economy of the Roman Empire, which was primarily agrarian. Trade and craft production were small compared to its agrarian resource base

[62] For details, see R. McLaughlin, *The Roman Empire and the Indian Ocean: Rome's Dealings with the Ancient Kingdoms of India Africa and Arabia* (Barnsley, South Yorkshire: Pen & Sword, 1914), 226–7.

that was commendable.[63] It is important that the Roman Empire was one of enormous expenditure and huge liabilities as well. The imperial state had to sustain a vast contingent of bureaucracy, a gigantic number of migrant service personnel including legionaries along the Empire, a huge agrarian sector, extensive imports even of basic foods, and the internal circuit of goods. According to an estimate, the empire's annual military expense was 700 million sesterces and the liability by way of the grain-dole offered to 200,000 citizens in Rome was 48 million sesterces. Consumer demand for overseas luxury goods, despite the high revenue out of it, had involved the problem of the drain of gold and silver, which according to Pliny the Elder was to the tune of 100 million sesterces of Roman bullion per year.[64] It is clear from the senator's statement that the only way to check the drain was reducing the craze for the eastern goods that could be procured only in exchange of the Roman bullion. One has to connect this to another critical statement of Pliny the Elder that the merchants were selling the eastern goods in Rome at hundred times their prime price.[65] It is implied here that most of the bullion had gone into the hands of the merchants who were mainly Greeks and Egyptians.

The imperial state conducted the empire under the covenants of Roman law and administered all matters of political economy as much institutionalized and document-based as possible. A slavery-dependent society of high literacy, structured by the dominance of aristocrats with relatively advanced material culture, arts, architecture, literature, science, technology, philosophy, and other scholarly pursuits, the Roman Empire represented an urban civilization of Hellenistic influence. Planned cities, monumental buildings, advanced shipping technology, big ports, contractual firms for shipment/trans-shipment, detailed commercial arrangements, institutionalized financing practices, banking, monetization through high-value metallic currency, large volume of trade, markets with adequate infrastructure,

63 See M.I. Finley, *The Ancient Economy*, 2nd ed. (Berkeley: University of California Press, 1985), 33–4. Also see K. Hopkins, 'Introduction', in *Trade in the Ancient Economy*, eds P. Garnsey, K. Hopkins, and C.R. Whittaker (Berkeley: University of California Press, Los Angeles, 1983), xii.

64 Pliny the Elder, *Natural History*, 12.41.

65 Pliny the Elder, *Natural History*, 6.26.

and well-maintained merchant routes were the main features of the empire's urbanism.

It is evident that the empire had a well-developed system for administering its trade and commerce. Contents of several *ostraca* discovered at the Egyptian ports and certain instructive inscriptions found on the desert route show that there were clear stipulations regarding the tariff rates on exports and imports. There were strict measures for checking the weight and quality of goods imported, assessing their value and taxing them, and processing and distributing them throughout the empire's marketing centres in the case of food-grains and at specific points of demand in Rome and Europe in the case of luxury items. Official arrangements were made for the management of harbours, customs departments, and warehouses. Various methods were evolved to ensure the safety of overseas as well as overland traders and trade routes. It is relevant here to recall the instance of the Augustan fleet destroying the pirates who had been a menace in the Indian Ocean coasts of the eastern Africa and southern Arabia. Overseas traders seem to have been offered armed protection by the soldiers on board, who ensured the safety of the former in alien ports too. Similarly, overland traders' security was guaranteed by the imperial soldiers deployed along the inhospitable desert routes in the Empire.

Augustan conquests had given Rome control not only of vast agrarian tracts of Egypt, but also of its ports, besides mercantile command over South Asian coasts, which was essential to meet the social demand for consumable goods from the east. Mercantile command pumped into the hands of the Roman aristocracy enormous money, enabling them to reinvest it in trade. The Roman aristocracy was rich enough to commission huge overseas vessels to get goods of demand in Rome imported through Philistine, Arab, and Greek merchants. This is not to mean that the entire aristocracy was involved in trade. In fact, it was only the urban elite and not the rural landed who tried their fortunes in trade.[66] Risky, hazardous, and uncertain, the main component of the merchant-mariners onboard were slaves and freedmen of the aristocrats.

[66] A.H.M. Jones, *The Roman Economy: Studies in Ancient Economic and Administrative History* (Oxford: University Press, 1974), 30.

In short, Roman–Indian trade was not accidental but very much a structured outcome of the political economy of the Roman Empire that was characterized by huge wealth, absolute state power, eminently organized militia, an adventurously enterprising aristocracy, a rich entrepreneurial middle class, sustained social demand for consumable overseas goods, and a wide network of trade and market. A fabulously rich aristocracy with an insatiable thirst for luxury goods like muslin, gems, pearls, pepper, and ivory from the coasts of southern India and silk from China was the crucial demand factor in the political economy of classical Roman Empire, in the context of exchange relations with the Indian subcontinent. For the safe transport of these precious objects, the state took the initiative in the development of both overseas and overland routes. Similarly, for strategic reasons of defence and transportation of goods, a wide network of strong roads was established, linking the major centres of exchange in the empire, many of which survive. These roads facilitated quick movement of the imperial force in times of war on the one side and wide distribution of goods, especially food-grains throughout the empire in times of peace on the other.

Roman emperors had issued the world's most developed system of coinage and currency based on coins of gold, silver, bronze, copper, and brass. These coins had reached the entire commercial centres of the Indian Ocean rim-countries, where several ruling lineages tried to imitate, in their own way, the emperors' portrait coins symbolic of imperial political power. As already discussed, several hoards of Roman gold and silver coins have been discovered from southern India. Much more than means of payment and measure of value, Roman coins were stamps of royal authority and imperial political signature wherever they circulated. With a system of coinage and currency well developed, classical Greece and Rome succinctly illustrate the role of money as a driving force of social integration and economic activity.[67]

Graeco-Roman societies were extensively monetized by the 1st century BCE itself and subsequently as the empire expanded, the range of demand for monetary circulation also expanded markedly. Naturally,

[67] W.V. Harris, ed., *The Monetary Systems of the Greeks and Romans* (Oxford: Oxford University Press, 2008), 6.

regional money systems were permitted to operate in coexistence with the Roman coins and currency for the time being, but soon provincial coins encountered acute dearth and got completely replaced by the Roman money. Roman money spread even to the most remote corners of the empire by way of payment to soldiers and means of procurement of defence needs. Coins like the *aureus* and the *denarius* were the main trade currencies draining beyond the borders of the empire. Although coins were the most widely used form of money, bullion was prevalent in transactions outside the city of Rome, and the extensive credit-money had contributed significantly to economic growth by sustaining stability of money supply.[68] However, as in the case of any other civilization, the Graeco-Roman civilization was an ensemble of unevenly developed communities, of which some were even totally non-monetized.[69] Even among many whose services were hired at different points of halt and transit, the mode of payment was barter, as we understand from the Muziris Papyrus. South Indian societies were largely in such a state where the dominant mode of exchange was of goods for goods, as already explained earlier.

Hardly do we need to mention that none of the ruling systems in the immediate post-Mauryan Indian subcontinent holds any comparison with the state system of the classical Roman Empire. There is no comparison between the Roman political economy and the political economy of different regions in the Indian subcontinent. Social formations in the Ganga, Mahanadi, and Narmada valleys or along the lower reaches of the Krishna, Godavari, Kaveri, Vaigai, and Periyar during the period were predominantly agro-pastoral, and political formation, largely of the chiefdom type. It is worth examining the case of a comparable country, conquered by Rome and integrated as part of the empire.

[68] Harris, ed., *The Monetary Systems of the Greeks and Romans.*

[69] The rural folk in ancient Greece and Rome followed the barter system. J.G. Manning says that monetization penetrated under the imperial economy 'since the private economy of the rural asses was still largely characterized by barter while credit was constrained by personal, family, and status relationships'. See his 'Coinage as "Code" in Ptolemaic Egypt', in W.V. Harris, ed., *The Monetary System of the Greeks and Romans* (Oxford: Oxford University Press, 2008), 84–111.

On the contrary, Rome was fabulously rich during the turn of the CE. Augustan conquests had not only given Rome control of Egypt's ports, but also mercantile command over South Asian coasts, which was essential to meet the social demand for consumable goods from the east. Mercantile command pumped into the hands of the Roman aristocracy enormous money, enabling them to reinvest heavily in trade. The Roman aristocracy was rich enough to commission huge overseas vessels to get goods of demand in Rome imported through Philistine, Arab, and Greek merchants. In short, Roman-Indian trade was not a fortuitous event but quite natural to the political economy of the empire, noted for huge wealth, absolute state power, well-organized army, an adventurous aristocracy, extensive exchange networks, and a crazy middle class steadily demanding overseas luxury goods.

Late Iron Age Britain

A comparison between the political economies of early historic southern India and late Iron Age Britain, which were more or less of the same type, has been found quite relevant here.[70] Britain, on the eve of the conquest by Julius Caesar, like southern India, was in the Iron Age/Megalithic and Early Historic phase. Both of them represented a largely undifferentiated economy of semi-tribal, agro-pastoral social formation based on clan–kin ties and ethnic loyalties. What we have discussed at length by way of the features of the social formation in the case of southern India, more or less, apply to Iron Age Britain.[71]

70 For such a comparison, see C.R. Whittaker, 'Conjunctures and Conjectures: Kerala and Roman Trade', *South Asian Studies* 25, no. 1 (2009): 1–18.

71 For the archaeology of the megalithic culture, now frequently referred to as the Iron Age culture in the Tamil South, see B.K.G. Rao, *The Megalithic Culture of South India* (Mysore: Prasaranga, 1972). L.S. Leshnik, *South Indian 'Megalithic' Burials: The Pandukal Complex* (Wiesbaden: Franz Steiner Verlag, 1974). Also A. Sundara, *The Early Chamber Tombs of South India* (Delhi: University Publishers, 1975). For a discussion of the chiefdoms in the late megalithic phase, see R. Gurukkal and M.R.R. Varier, *Cultural History of Kerala*, Vol. I. (Department of Cultural Publications, Government of Kerala, 1999), 238–46.

Contemporary Britain was a chiefdom-level polity in which chieftains of varying strength, living in fortified hills, headed their agro-pastoral descent groups with a dominant warrior section, settled in different landscapes. People lived in settlements scattered in the planes with small patches of farmlands surrounded by forests and meadows. Chieftains regenerated their power through raids and redistribution of the booty among their people of clan–kin ties. Bards, celebrating the might of chieftains and their warriors in raids, legitimized the heroic polity. Chieftains gave feasts and gifts to bards who praised them, warriors who fought for them, and others who depended on them. It was a politico-cultural situation of heroic passions and values. Certain ecologically and culturally contingent nuances apart, this is almost exactly the British version of the early historic or late megalithic Tamilakam, the socio-economic and politico-cultural features of which we have already discussed at length.

A notable event of difference in the case of Britain was the islands' conquest by Rome and annexation to the empire, which had witnessed marches of legions and migrations of peoples. It was not a mere conquest but a systematic annexation involving de facto incorporation of the island into the empire's network of contemporary maritime trade involving a substantial techno-economic impact. Productive and distributive technologies of market-oriented agriculture and mining industry, promoted under the empire's mercantile pressure, seem to have enabled expansion of trade networks and formation of several proto-urban centres. They transformed the dependence of productive and distributive relations on kinship, which in turn made the economy differentiated and society class structured within the time span of a century. Corresponding to such techno-economic and social changes, a class of big landed merchants and ruling aristocracy came up transforming the chiefdom-level polity beyond clan–kin ties and ethnic loyalties into monarchical states like those at St. Albans and Colchester. Kings and the aristocracy generated demand for luxury goods, necessitating overseas trade to procure prestige items in exchange of grain, mine products, and slaves. Britain became a full-fledged trading region with a class of monetized ruling aristocracy representing a political economy of a relatively soaring effective demand.

No Significant Impact

Similar changes did not happen in the political economy of southern India, which continued to be of the same semi-tribal, agro-pastoral social formation for at least four to five centuries more. This is not to suggest that there was no socio-economic change at all in the region for so long a period, but only to point out the stark contrast with what had happened in the history of British political economy. Incessant interactive coexistence among self-sustaining settlements of multiple ecotypes had accomplished a common horizon of shared cultural practices as facilitated by a common language. Overland exchange contacts which involved dissemination of new ideas, knowledge systems, and world views among them had certainly made some changes. Worldviews and knowledge-systems of Brāhmaṇical, Jain, and Buddhist orders did penetrate into the late Iron Age south India, but were of no transforming influence on the politics of plunder raids. Redistributive politics of raids that was detrimental to agriculture persisted. It was amidst these adversities that the people of *mēnpulam* (wet-fields) had to carry on production, and thereby remain absolutely confined to small pockets without much progress till the 7th century CE. Some of the bards, obviously under the influence of the heterodox world views, seem to advise the chieftains to abstain from raids leading to the devastation of cultivated fields and promote agriculture that alone could bring power and fame.[72] Stressing the need for ensuring the protection of the peasants, they exhort the chieftains to maintain peace that is inevitable for the prosperity of the land. Nevertheless, none of these seems to have had any impact on the chiefdoms.

A few poetic references attest that the ideas of state power, bureaucracy, and the institution of periodic exaction were certainly brought to the attention of the ruling lineages in southern India. Some of the scholarly bards, particularly the Brāhmaṇa poets (*pulavar*), seem to have tried to acquaint the chieftains with the political ideas and institutions, probably of the Mauryas. Predatory operations continued and the structure of political organization hardly acquired any momentum towards

[72] Songs under the *turais* of *Ceviyaṛivūru* and *Poruṇmoḻik-kānji* have allusions testifying this. See a discussion of this at length in Gurukkal, *Social Formations of Early South India*, 155–65.

integration of chiefdoms. Not adequately developed, these chiefdoms were not integrated to the Mauryan Empire. Since major institutions like the state never come up as transplant, the chiefdom-level polity remained the same until the dissolution of the social formation.

Long-distance overland exchange relations did carry forces of production and strategies of subsistence from one place to another, modifying and transforming the pre-existing ones as agreeable to the ecosystems and social relations. They must have induced some pressure on the crafts production and industry, especially in metal, glass, gems, and textile. Given the Mediterranean demand for the eastern gems and cotton products, it was quite likely that overseas exchange relations had stimulated mineral-based crafts production and textile manufacturing. Beryl mining and lapidary must have acquired a higher dimension through organized efforts under the pressure of overseas demand. Pearl fishing too was another enterprise that could have received a significant impetus in the same way. However, none of these seems to have brought about any technological and organizational development leading to changes in the kinship basis of contemporary productive relations.

There are indications in the source to the existence of organized professional dealers specialized in gems, metals, minerals, and textile besides experts in lapidary, but hardly do we see any sign of the emergence of a wealthy leadership, owning and controlling all the enterprise. Nevertheless, it does not seem to have led to any change in the clan–kin basis of crafts production and industry. There were long-distance overland merchants operating as locality-specific organized bodies in southern India, whose social prominence is explicit from the label inscriptions that register them as patrons of heterodox monks. They were too small in number to have constituted themselves as a class distinct from the local community of clan–kin ties.

Agrarian industry too was not impacted by long-distance exchange, although we have inscriptional evidence of the existence of grain merchants. Agriculture was largely of the slash-and-burn type operated as a collective activity of the clan concerned and the chieftain as the embodiment of the clan ties held control over the agrarian tracts. It is possible that the chiefly households had some agriculture of crops that had overseas demand. Some of the poetic descriptions show that pepper, the predominant item among spices, was cultivated in the households of chieftains. This may be true of ginger, the next important spice as well. However, this was not enough for exerting any pressure on the kinship basis of productive relations. Such exchange-induced crops' entry into the household agriculture, which was just an extension of the clan farm, was not sufficient to turn the chieftains into a landed group beyond redistributive obligations. Chieftains were rich in their valuables and had people under their command, for they embodied their clans. This would not mean that they formed an aristocratic class of independent status. Being very much within the same material culture of their clans, chieftains did not particularly generate any demand for non-local luxury goods and other techno-economic consumables. It is not accidental that the sources do not indicate the existence of a distinct class, identifiable as the ruling aristocracy. There are no indications in them towards the transformation of the chiefdom into the monarchical state power as we have discussed at length elsewhere in the book.

Forest products and spices too, particularly pepper, which constituted other major items of overseas demand, do not seem to have given rise to a prominent and influential group of cargo suppliers. It is quite possible that Graeco-Roman overseas exchanges had involved formally negotiated relationships with the merchant-mariners of the Indian coasts, but their nature and extent are unclear. Tamil names Cātan and Kaṇan on pottery from the Red Sea port do indicate the outstation service of personnel associated with the Mediterranean commerce, but in what capacity is unknown. As coasting seafarers, the merchants of the Indian littoral were probably collaborating with the Graeco-Roman merchants by transporting the cargoes reaching Tamralipti on the Bay of Bengal from the Gangetic region, Chryse, China, and the rest of the far eastern world to the Tamil ports. Similarly, the overland long-distance merchants of the subcontinent seem to have transported goods from their northern Indian sources including the Himalayas to Bharukaccha. These were more or less the services of cargo providers to overseas traders. It appears that the overland and overseas merchants of northern India were servicing the Mediterranean traders by supplying them with cargoes from different parts for shipping. Sources do not show the emergence of shipping agents, ship-owners, financiers, bankers, and trans-shipping contractors out of these cargo providers. There is no sign of merchants from the Indian coasts setting out on sail as independent seafarers engaged in cross-oceanic voyages for exchange in the Mediterranean world. Perhaps, there was no need for it. Graeco-Roman exchange contacts could not generate it either.

Graeco-Roman traders had brought and bartered a huge quantity of gold and silver coins as well as bullion for the goods of their demand. As pointed out earlier, their impact was marginal since most of these got converted into dead treasure and ornaments, rather than means of payment for improved technology capable of the mobilization of labour beyond clan–kin relations. Had they been acting as money, there would have been some impact of them as a catalyst for mobilization of labour leading to emergence of relations transcending kinship. A certain level of differentiated socio-economic development was essential for the region to acquire the capacity to use coins as money. With a relatively self-sufficient and self-sustaining semi-tribal socio-economic situation being predominant, the rural subcontinent had neither the capability nor the need for it.

Uneconomic and Unnecessary

It was uneconomic for the seafaring merchants of India to venture into cross-oceanic trade on their own, for they had very few items to carry home other than gold and silver in exchange of their precious goods that were invariably of low volume and high value. Mediterranean luxury goods had no effective demand in the Indian subcontinent and items like copper, lead, and alloy metals like tin, which had demand, could not have sustained the exchange economically. Voyages being dependent on monsoon winds, months-long stay ashore on the Red Sea coast would be inevitable and hence they would have been constrained to carry in the ship enough provisions for subsistence. Even then they would have required only small ships for their enterprise, which were utterly unsuitable and extremely risky for cross-oceanic voyages. It was a very risky business also because it involved journey through pirate-infested sea route and inhospitable desert routes. Further, it was an enormously expensive enterprise requiring deployment of multiple agencies, firms, and contractors for various services. Due to such uneconomic and adverse factors, even during the medieval period, merchant-mariners of the Indian coasts preferred to depend upon intermediaries like the Arabs and Turks, rather than plunging themselves into the risk of plying the trade on their own.

It was unnecessary for the merchant-mariners of India to conduct the extremely life-risking and hugely expensive exchange in the alien land, for there were neither any internal economic pressures or push-factors nor any external attractions or pull-factors. We have already discussed the state of affairs in the social formation, which precluded the political economy of demand for techno-economic or luxury goods from far-off places. Those minimum goods like copper, lead, and tin, which had some demand among the artisan community, were anyway not required in huge quantity, for the metal-crafts industry of contemporary southern India was confined to a small number of hereditary craftsmen's households catering primarily to chiefly needs. Since users of metal wares and implements made of copper and bronze were not in plenty, the industry's raw-material requirement was not a pressure on local merchants. In short, there was hardly anything so inevitable for the people of contemporary Indian subcontinent to be obtained through overseas voyages by their own merchants.

As far as the Mediterranean world was concerned, the situation was just the reverse, for the aristocratic demand for several luxury goods from the eastern lands was amazingly huge, and hence its trade extremely profitable. Therefore, it was, indeed, quite worth for the Mediterranean merchant-mariners to throw themselves adventurously into the life-risking voyages across the Indian Ocean for trading in precious goods. On the contrary, such an adventure was utterly unnecessary for the merchants from the Indian subcontinent since their Graeco-Roman counterparts were reaching ashore with gold and other items of local demand. For the former, such an expensive commerce necessitating various institutional and organizational arrangements as well as involvements of agencies and firms like bankers, financiers, ship-owners, trans-shipping contractors, and so on, was not feasible either, for obvious reasons. In short, in the strict sense, the term 'trade' is inappropriate to the context of contemporary Sātavāhana and Tamil political economy. There has been little discussion of such questions relating to the political economy of contemporary Indian societies. With the result, the predominance of Indian overseas trade and her maritime civilization based on spice export, particularly of pepper, has always been a case taken for granted in the country's historiography.

6

Polity, Statecraft, and Overseas Exchange

State and long-distance trade are often mentioned as being interconnected, for trade, unlike other forms of exchange which have prehistoric antiquity, presupposes the presence of a differentiated economy, social hierarchy, literacy, monetization, military power, and evolved political institutions. It has been argued that the state consumption combined with a shift from exaction in kind to monetary payments spawned the development of markets, increasing division of labour and growth.[1] Behind the Graeco-Roman trade, there were several juridico-political formations like the imperial Roman state, its powerful legions, fleets, bureaucracy, and codified Law; and socio-economic developments such as a differentiated economy, stratified society, aristocracy, high literacy, extensive monetization, financiers, bankers, contractual institutions, many seafaring professionals, and adventurous traders. Trade was an enterprise under the patronage of the empire that was responsible for providing protection to the caravans overland and mariners overseas by policing the desert and

[1] K. Hopkins, 'Introduction', in *Trade in the Ancient Economy*, eds P. Garnsey, K. Hopkins, and C.R. Whittaker (Berkeley and Los Angeles: University of California Press, 1983), ix–xxv.

checking the Bedouin raids.[2] Historians, who credited the Indian subcontinent with extensive operation of overland as well as overseas trade, hardly seem to have examined whether the regions thereof had attained the manifestation of such features. We hope we have done it in the foregone pages, and what remains is a brief review of the political formation in the case of northern India and of the peninsular regions at some length. It is relevant here to consider trade and statecraft in the Mauryan Empire, its first most evolved phase in the history of the subcontinent, as the point of reference to demonstrate the difference in the case of the nature of exchange practices under the post-Mauryan political formations.

Gangetic Polity

The polity in the Gangetic region was characterized by several self-sustaining small and big chiefdoms, called *janapadas* and *mahājanapadas* respectively, which were complex redistributive systems of uneven sizes sustained on raiding cattle, caravans, and crops. Following a few centuries of continuity and change in the predatory politics of these chiefdoms, institutions and structures of control over peoples and resources began to emerge in the mahājanapadas of chiefly lineages and their confederacies, graduating into monarchy. Magadha emerged as the most powerful among the mahājanapadas and soon a state (*rājya*) with plenty of metals, minerals, and agrarian resources. It became the centre of convergence for merchants who built up an extensive network of exchange relations across the mahājanapadas. Predatory marches of chieftains, migrations of people, diffusion of relatively advanced agrarian technologies, re-organization of the clannish division of labour into families of hereditary specialization, expansion of agriculture, production of surplus, class differentiation,

2 See the discussion of the Oriental luxury trade going through both Egypt and Palmyra in G.K. Young, *Rome's Eastern Trade: International Commerce and Imperial Policy, 31 BC–AD 305* (London and New York: Routledge, 2001), chapters 2 and 4.

and extensive network of long-distance trade were the changes of sequential nature.[3]

The Magadhan state dissolved itself into the Maurya-*vijita* or the Mauryan Empire. Massive military campaigns unleashing the horrors of arson and massacre were inevitable for it. Several chiefdoms controlling large inhospitable regions of agro-pastoral economies persisted within the vijita, for they were ready to be allegiant and helpful towards the *vijigīṣu*. There existed the chiefdoms like the Parinda in the centre, the Risṭika, Nābhapankti, and Nābhaka in the north within the vijita, and the Yōna, the Gāndhāra, and the Kambōja in the north-west as *pratyanta* or *anta*, which were outside this linguistic unity of the Prākrit.[4] Irrespective of the linguistic unity or difference, all these chiefdoms were independent social formations structured by the dominance of agro-pastoral means of subsistence.

Historians have shown the Mauryan system of administration as having 'an extremely centralised character, with the higher functionaries as far as possible under the direct control of the ruler', with 'all the powers of the state and the management of the state centralised and carried out entirely from the capital', or as of a partly centralized character, with 'strict control of the state at the heart of the empire and separatist tendencies in the far-flung provinces', or as of a decentralized character with 'central power trying to bring under its sole authority pre-constituted entities to which it leaves a greater or lesser degree of autonomy'.[5] Such attributes apart, the character of the state

[3] For a detailed study of the process of the state formation, see Romila Thapar, *From Lineage to State, Social Formations of Mid-first Millennium BC in the Ganga Valley* (New Delhi: Oxford University Press, 1984), 70–115.

[4] See Edict XIII. For the translation of the text of Edict XIII, see Romila Thapar, *Asoka and the Decline of the Mauryas* (New Delhi: Oxford University Press, 1961), 256.

[5] See Thapar, *Asoka and the Decline of the Mauryas*, 207. Also, B.M. Barua, *Asoka and His Inscriptions*, 2 vols (Calcutta: New Age Publishers Ltd, 1946), 146; R.K. Mookerji, *Chandragupta Maurya and His Times*, 4th ed. (Madras: Motilal Banarsidass Publishers, 1966), 54; G.M. Bongard-Levin, *India in the Mauryan Period* (in Russian) (Moscow: Nauka Publishers, 1973). The representative expressions are borrowed from G. Fussman, 'Central and Provincial Administration in Ancient India: The Problem of the Mauryan Empire', *Indian Historical Review* XIV, nos 1–2 (1987–8): 46.

that the Mauryas yearned to construct is evident in the excerpts from Megasthenes, Asokan edicts, and the *Arthaśāstra*. It was absolute monarchy which, as Romila Thapar qualified, was 'as centralised as was possible during that period'. Perhaps, the nature of the working of the state as appraised according to positivist logic could well be as construed by Mookerji, or Bongard-Levin, or G. Fussman, for evidence is amenable to support all of them.

In order to assess the efficacy of the administrative means, we should know, at least tenuously, how they might have worked in the context of the socio-economic and cultural processes of their times. We should be able to conceptualize the peoples, their ecosystems, material processes of existence, levels of institutional and structural development, and patterns of distribution of power and their socio-spatial praxis to imagine what the administrative means meant to and worked in them. While the means of state power appealed to several people directly, it did to several others indirectly or symbolically. However, the Mauryan king, with his massive warrior force with weapons (*āyudhas*) like *chakras*, *yantras*, *āvaraṇas*, *upakaraṇas*, *yānas*, and *vāhanas* staging devastating marches, was symbolic of a shuddering horror to the peoples at all levels. Megasthenes praised the well-organized royal force (*sainya*), permanent, professional, and completely loyal to the king, reinforced by a strong arsenal rich in a wide variety of weapons manufactured by specialized craftsmen and battle-trained animals, especially the elephant contingent, as the most effective instrument of the Mauryan state.[6] A hierarchy of bureaucracy with servants from the highest to the lowest levels must have signified the might of the king to the peoples. However, it is a fact that a state system never rests solely on might. There are always strategies of peaceful persuasion, as exemplified by the paternal language of the Edicts of Asoka. Nevertheless, in most of the cases, the edicts must have evoked fear as well in the minds of the people. Asoka himself asks not to be afraid of him which could have, in fact, enhanced their

[6] See Diodorus Siculus, Book II:41, Loeb Classical Library ed. (Cambridge: Harvard University Press, 1935); Strabo, *Geography*, Vol. VII, Book 15:1, 47, 48, trans. H.L. Jones, Loeb Classical Library ed. (Cambridge: Harvard University Press, 1928); Arrien, *Indica*, Book VII:2–4, trans. P.A. Brunt, Loeb Classical Library ed. (Cambridge: Harvard University Press, 1983).

fear. Terrorizing the land through the technique of scorched earth and creation of long-lasting fear in the minds of the settlers was a major means of control in ancient times. Almost everything about the king including the wells sunk and trees planted were symbolic of his might. We get a feel of how the chiefdoms in the south such as Satyaputas, Cōḻas, Pāṇḍyas, and Cēras had seen the Maurya from some of the allusions in ancient Tamil poems, such as *vampa moriya* (the great Maurya), *vinporu neṭunkuṭaikkoṭittēr moriyar* (the Mauryas with chariots holding huge sky-touching umbrella and flag), and *vinporu neṭuvarai iyal tēr moriyar* (Mauryas with sky-touching chariot).[7]

Terrorizing was integral to predatory campaigns too, but unlike them, the Mauryas unleashed conquests involving territorial annexation and periodic exaction of revenue. It meant a forceful superimposition of the Mauryan power over the pre-existing structures of surplus appropriation. The Mauryas had replaced the head of these pre-existing structures with their kinsmen (*kumāras*) or trustworthy nobles (*āryaputras*) or a paid high official (*rajūka*) in most of the cases. Asoka claims (Pillar Edict IV) to have entrusted hundred thousands of his peoples to *rajūka*s with full powers of *abhihāra* (to reward) and *daṇda* (to punish) as they would wish, so that they would discharge their functions quietly and fearlessly for the well-being of the people (janapadas). He says that his rajūkas were eager to obey him and that he had appointed them to look after the people exactly as a nurse would do in the case of the child entrusted with her. Certain passages in the edicts show how Asoka spoke softly on the matters of piety and reminded the addressees of the consequences of his wrath. In Edict XIII he warns that he has power even in his remorse, and asks the offenders to repent, lest they be killed.

What we find by way of prescriptions of the state power in the *Arthaśāstra* are: (*a*) an elaborate cluster of salaried servants from the highest like *amātya, samahartta*, rajūka, *adhyakṣa, yukta, upayukta, nibandhaka*s, and so on, to the lowest levels; (*b*) secret

[7] *Akanāṉūṟu*, 69:10, 251:12, 281:8. For the text and translation, see N.M.V. Nattar, ed., *Akanāṉūṟu* with commentary, Vols I and II (Tirunelveli: The South India Saiva Siddhantha Works Publishing Society Ltd, 1949–50); *Puṟanāṉūṟu*, 175:6. For the text and translation, see U.V.S. Iyar, ed., *Puṟanāṉūṟu* with commentary, 6th ed. (Madras: Thyagarajavilasam Publications, 1963).

agents (*gūḍhapuruṣas*) recruited sometimes from among students (*kāpatikas*), renouncers ousted from their orders (*udasthitas*), householders (*gṛhapati-vyanjanas*), traders (*vaidēhaka-vyanjanas*), ascetics (*tāpasa-vyanjanas*), fiery persons (*tīkṣṇas*), poisonous chemical dealers (*rasadas*), and mendicants (*bhikṣus*); (*c*) frontier bastions like *antapāla-durgas*; (*d*) the fourfold military contingents called the sainyas; (*e*) the loyal and allegiant frontiers men dwelling in the forests (*āṭavikas*); (*f*) the numerous royal informers and messengers (*dūtas*); (*g*) and the variety of infrastructures like traderoutes (*vaṇik-pathas*), buildings (*āgāras*), instruments (yantras), conveyances (vāhanas), prescriptive knowledge texts (*sāstras*), inscriptions (*likhitas*), and records (*pustakas*), and so on. An elaborate and stable means ensuring stability in all the important matters such as revenue and political power was the emperor's contingent of paid officers. Excerpts from Megasthenes corroborate the *Arthaśāstra* prescription of the system of salaried servants.[8] *Arthaśāstra* enumerates numerous adhyakṣas who exacted, remitted, and got accounted the wealth from the respective fields like trade, agriculture, forests, mines, and so on, at the instance of the *samāhartta*. Some of them appear in the Edicts of Asoka. Megasthenes confirms the practice of deploying gūḍhapuruṣas to obtain information about the state of affairs in different parts of the empire, secretly.[9] Edict XII mentions about Asoka's extensive espionage system. Extensive spy work might have been necessary only at a few janapadas of fast development and competitive power relations besides the *nagaras* and *paṭṭiṇas* of brisk exchanges, crowded by all kinds of peoples.

There is no reason to disbelieve that these administrative means were available to Chandragupta and Bindusāra and that the means could keep them as emperors by suppressing conflicts and quelling enemies. That these means were not enough for Asoka is evident from the new means strategically evolved by him such as the edicts, the *dhamma*, actions of piety, charitable structures and establishments, and so on. The royal circuit (*anusamyana*) was an important administrative means used by Asoka quite extensively to guard the

[8] Siculus, Book II:41, Strabo, *Geography*, Vol. VII, Book 15:1, 36, 47, 50, 55.
[9] Strabo, *Geography*, Vol. VII, Book 15:48; Arrien, *Indica*, Book XII, 2–4.

empire. A few Edicts of Asoka show that he had the habit of sending his representatives on anusamyana once in five years all over the empire and that the kumāras/āryaputras had it once in three years in their respective areas. Edict III mentions the quinquennial circuits of the yuktas, rajūkas, and *prādēśikas* all over the vijita. This is felt as a long interval to a modern mind with its sense of time, space, and techniques of administration conditioned by the high technology of transport and communication. But that would never have been the case of the people whose spatio-temporal sense was based on the movement on foot. A terrorizing event could have remained fresh in their minds easily for a period of five years. Far more important is the nature of the socio-economic processes at each place.

Writing was an important means to realize extensive social control for the Mauryas, especially Asoka, whose edicts show that the governance was based on written communication and that writing was widely used. There is plenty of evidence in the edicts as well as in the *Arthaśāstra* to prove that contemporary governance was based on archival consciousness. What the Sārnāth Pillar Edict contains is a royal order that prevents anybody tending to violate the Sangha. It asks the official concerned to keep a copy of the order with him and a copy with the *upāsakas*. All high officials were to maintain a detailed inventory about the business they transacted. Accounting of the details of the day-to-day transactions, particularly the matters of revenue and resources, by the *panyadhyakṣa* stipulated by Kautilya is unbelievably meticulous.[10] Significantly, the entire realm of transactions was governed by the legitimacy and validity of written deeds. A document-conscious approach was common among the big merchants and high officials. In fact, the writing skills in all probability were confined to the royal officials, merchants, and monks. There is no doubt that the Sēṭṭhis and high officials did read and write. We do not know whether all the *grāmikas* were able to read and write, but most of them were, as the punitive clause in the *Arthaśāstra* against the making of fraudulent documents (*kapaṭalēkhya*) by the

[10] See the precise nature of accounting as is evident in several contexts. The most representative is *Samāhartrusamudāyaprasthāna, adhyāya* 6 in the 'Adhyakṣapracāra' section of the *Arthaśāstra*.

householder (*kuṭumbi*), the head of office (adhyakṣa), the prominent (*mukhya*), and the lord (*swāmi*) would have us believe.[11]

The Asokan edicts were inscribed at strategic points where peoples gathered, but the large majority of them had no direct access to them. In fact, the edicts were not addressed to the people but to other rulers (Edict II), the king's officials (Edicts III, VI), and sons and grandsons (Edicts V, VI, XIII). It is true that the people were to be told about their contents. They all knew the writings as royal edicts and they knew their contents as explained to them by the royal officials like the *mahāmātras*. What the peoples had possibly retained for years was only an oral version of the inscribed messages, which to them were symbolic of power. Edicts were mostly proclamations of dhamma (IX, XI, XII), his achievements (II, IV, V), the success of the propagation of dhamma (V, VII, VIII), his virtuous acts (II, V), declarations of piety (VII, VIII, X), orders to the officials (III, VI), and exhortations to his successors (V, VI, XIII). A few were orders by the king and most of them contained pieces of advice. Writing as symbolic of the repressive dimension of political power is explicit in the case of the edicts carrying orders to be obeyed. Asoka meant permanency of the messages by inscribing them on stone.

However, it appears that private records were not extensive during the Mauryan period, for there is no indication of the emergence of any land-related rights and privileges necessitating documentary authentication. Normally, the use of writing implicating a relatively wider society would be linked to the emergence of a class with superior rights arbitrarily superimposed on the conventional by the king effecting transformation in production relations. Such rights would be too non-local, disparate, and diverse to be absorbed as part of the local tradition or to be sustained by the social memory. *Arthaśāstra* mentions the practice of allotting arable lands to sharecroppers (*ardhasītikas*) for a lifetime and the practice of granting land to Brāhmaṇas and royal officials as non-transferable rewards during the period. These do imply superimposition of new rights and

[11] *Sarvādhikaraṇarakṣaṇa* in the *Arthaśāstra*'s ninth chapter on *Kaṇṭakaśodhana*. For the text and translation, see R.S. Sastri, ed., *Arthaśāstra of Kautilya*, Bibliotheca Sanskrita 37 (Mysore: University of Mysore Oriental Library Publication Series, 1909).

privileges over the customary, the orders of which must have been kept in the royal archives.

Writing had acquired an unprecedented dynamic to spread across the region as a symbol of power, legitimacy, authority, authenticity, and truth. Normally, in such a document-based system of administration of transactional relations, there would be a lot of records of revenue, particularly accounts relating to trade and commerce. In that sense, the volume of written documents generated during the Mauryan period by way of documents relating to trade revenue accounts and copies of various licence documents issued to business agents, financiers, and big merchants maintained by the adhyakṣas concerned, and receipts of tolls and customs tariffs given to their remitters by the royal service personnel must have been amazingly extensive. Nevertheless, nothing has survived due to the obvious fact that such accounts, documents, and receipts of dated value must have been written on perishable material.

Trade and Trade Routes

This state power that was an institutional expression of the political economy of the period remained all-pervasive along the arterial routes of the movements of merchants, monks, and mendicants. Literary references to and sculptural representations of the extensive use of bullock carts indicate the level of contemporary technology of transport, the quickest form of which was represented by the horse-drawn chariot. The horse was symbolic of power as well as speed of transport and communication. Mauryas must have had some system for quick transport and communication through horsemen and charioteers. However, to places quite far off from the capital, quick transport of goods and conveyance of messages were not possible. Asoka seems to have made some arrangements to overcome this to a certain extent, as his Edict VI claims:

> In the past the quick dispatch of business and the receipt of reports did not take place at all times. But I have now arranged it thus. At all times, whether I am eating, or am in the women's apartments, or in my inner apartments, or in the cattle shed, or in my carriage, or in my gardens—wherever I may be, my informants should keep me in touch

> with public business. Thus everywhere I transact public business. And whatever I may order by word of mouth, whether it concerns a donation, or a proclamation, or whatever urgent matter is entrusted to my officers, if there is any dispute or deliberations about it in the Council, it is to be reported to me immediately, at all places and at all times.

Caravans were the main carriers of goods as well as messages to distant points along the trade routes, the maintenance of which was, therefore, a matter of top priority for the Mauryas. Asoka was keen in maintaining all the major routes of earlier times and in opening up new ones. Trade networks across settlements in the plains as well as in the metal- and mineral-rich hillocks flourished better under the imperial protection of the Mauryas. Two major networks of routes, namely the *uttarāpatha* (northern routes) and *dakṣiṇāpatha* (southern routes) were expanded and maintained by them. Megasthenes has mentioned about a royal department constituted specifically for the construction and upkeep of trade routes.[12] In short, the state's recognition of the importance in the regular maintenance of trade routes (*vaṇikapathas*) as part of a strategic means of territorial control cannot be exaggerated in the case of the Mauryan Empire.

It is a matter widely recognized that the state had taken care of improving the merchant routes by planting shade trees, sinking wells to ensure the availability of drinking water, and establishing way-side inns for the caravan troupes to safely halt. This would mean that tolls were collected regularly from the caravan troupes who were the beneficiaries. *Arthaśāstra* gives the picture of a fairly well-established system of financing, practice of borrowing, exaction of interest, assessment of profit, and an institutionalized mode of exaction of taxes from the businessmen and traders. Overseas trade administration also seems to have been well organized with clear stipulations of rules regarding the imposition of tariffs on the outgoing and incoming of goods. Trade routes that linked the important points of exchange had acted not only as roads for the transport of goods and services but also as channels of political communication. It is natural that the Mauryas were eager enough to monopolize the control of these channels, both for the immediate revenue advantages and for the long-term purpose of the military troupe-movement in times of strategic needs.

12 See Strabo, *Geography*, XV, 50.

As regards the statecraft of the maintenance of the trade networks in the plains as well as in the metal- and mineral-rich hillocks connected to the two huge long-distance routes uttarāpatha and dakṣiṇāpatha was often based on the strategy of coercion of the agro-pastoral chiefdoms. Being in the milieu of goods-for-goods exchange and redistribution, the economic aspirations of the chiefdoms hardly clashed with those of the empire, which had revolved around the revenue from trade and state-owned agriculture. Subdued by the Mauryan power, the chiefdoms might have easily agreed to guard the caravans (*sārthavāhas*) traversing through the trade routes that cut across, and the mines of metals and minerals, which belonged to their regions, from the raids of robbers and marauding tribes.

This does not mean that the forest dwellers were always subservient and the caravans, and hence immune to plunder raids. Edict XIII has a passage indicating that the āṭavikas were coerced to obey the norms of the king. Asoka seems to have coerced them to be obedient always for not being killed. Therefore, the clans in the forests (āṭavikas) were largely obedient and seem to have served the janapadas in the vijita as frontier guards. *Arthaśāstra* prescribes the *vanacaras* (forest clans) like *vagurikas*, *sabaras*, *puḷindas* or the outskirts-dwellers like the *candāḷas* fit to be entrusted with the task of keeping the frontiers between the royal bastions (antapāladurga) and the opening to the villages at the boundary of a janapada (*janapadānta*).[13] There are mentions in the text about the āṭavika-sainya (army made of forest clans) as a warrior contingent of the king indicating the way the chiefdoms were diplomatically allied to the state. It was the state that had the highest number of dāsas, extensively employed in mines and agricultural fields (*sitas*).[14] *Dāsis* were used in large numbers in the security and secret services of the

[13] See the 'Janapadanivēśa' section in the *Arthaśāstra*. For the text and translation, see R.S. Sastri, ed., *Arthaśāstra of Kautilya*, chapter 2.

[14] D.R. Chanana, *Slavery in Ancient India* (New Delhi: People's Publishing House, 1960), 41–52. In the *Arthaśāstra*, it is obvious from the references in the 'Dāsakarmmakārakalpa' section as well as the 'Adhyakṣapracāra', *adhyāya* 24 of the *Arthaśāstra* that *dāsas* were extensively used in agriculture. For the text and translation, see Sastri, ed., *Arthaśāstra of Kautilya*, chapter 2.

state and they could be purchased from foreign lands also and given training as royal bodyguards.[15]

The Deccan Polity

Discussions of polity in the historiography of peninsular India have largely been centred on the rise and fall of dynasties rather than on the formation of political structures and power relations.[16] Having made little difference between lineages and dynasties or chieftains and kings, most historians have treated the Andhra/Sātavāhana as an important dynasty of the immediate post-Mauryan India (1st century BCE and 3rd century CE) in the light of the Purānic mention of their genealogy under the label of the Andhra kings, numismatic evidence, certain archaeological monuments, and a few epigraphs.[17] Similarly, the Cēras, Pāṇḍyas, and Cōḻas of about the same period, celebrated in the Tamil heroic poems, have been taken for dynasties and kings by most historians.[18] They have used the terms 'kingdom' and 'empire' rather than 'state' in their discussions of polity, largely with the notion of one differing from the other in relation to the extent of territory, power, and authority. At the same time, they have not used the term 'chiefdom' much, and always served the purpose by coining the terms 'province' or 'locality'. The term 'chief' in their discussion

15 Sastri, ed., *Arthaśāstra of Kautilya*, chapter 2.

16 Most points discussed at different parts of the following section are reproduced from R. Gurukkal, 'Antecedents of the State (Polity) Formation in Early South India', Paper presented in the International Symposium, Toyo Bunko Oriental Manuscript Library, Tokyo, March 2014.

17 V.V. Mirashi, *The History and Inscriptions of the Sātavāhana and the Western Kshatrapas, Maharashtra State Board for Literature and Culture* (Bombay: Maharashtra State Board for Literature and Culture, 1981).

18 Tamil heroic literature refers to what is popularly known as the corpus of Sangam literature. The corpus includes, in its most archaic stratum, some of the anthologies grouped under *Eṭṭuttokai* (The Eight Anthologies) and *Pattuppāṭṭu* (The Ten Idylls), roughly belonging to the 2nd century BCE and 3rd century CE. U.V.S. Iyer has edited and published the texts of idylls and anthologies belonging to the Tamil heroic tradition, during 1955–7. Also see K. Kailasapathy, *Tamil Heroic Poetry* (Oxford: Clarendon Press, 1968).

appears generally with the prefix 'feudatory' to denote him as a subordinate under the king, rather than a relatively autonomous ruler. Nevertheless, a king is always mentioned as the rightful ruler of an autonomous territory, namely the kingdom, rather than a subordinate at the mercy of the emperor. As a result, the term 'empire', which denoted a higher form only in scale, has been widely applied to the kingdom as well.

Political Formation

Differences discernible between the chiefdom and the kingdom or between the kingdom and the empire in terms of the structure, function, and other attributes are theoretical constructs of our times. They are not part of contemporary experience.[19] But theoretical constructs are inevitable for comprehending the formations, processes, and internal dynamics, which constitute the object of historical study. Big and small chiefdoms of descent groups seem to have characterized the Deccan and its immediate south during the Mauryan period as exemplified by the Bhōja, Āndhra, Kalinga, and Piṭinika. These four were within the vijita of the Mauryan Empire. This is a situation precluding the existence of a class society structured by the dominance of a ruling aristocracy, institutionalized into a system of governance based on periodic exaction of productive surplus from the region. It is not strange that there is no evidence of the continuation of the Mauryan system of administration. In fact, most of the prominent households were possibly of higher civil as well as military functionaries of the Mauryan Empire. Once the Empire declined and disintegrated, the heirs of the old-time official personnel might have

[19] D.R. Chanakya was perhaps the first to present an analytical abstraction of the state attributes in the context of traditional India. He abstracts the attributes as *saptānga*: *swāmi*, *amātya*, *janapada*, Durga, *kōsa*, *daṇḍa*, and *mitra*. See discussion in R.S. Sharma, *Aspects of Political Ideas and Institutions in Ancient India* (repr., New Delhi: Motilal Banarsidass Publishers, 1996), 31–48. Modern analysis has generated an impressive body of theoretical literature ever since the publication of H.J.M. Claessen and P. Skalnik, eds, *The Early State* (The Hague: Mouton Publishers, 1978). See H.J.M. Claessen, R. Hegestejn, and P. van de Velde, eds, *Social Evolution & History* (Volgograd: Uchitel Publishing House) 7, no. 1 (2008): 1–268.

become people of chiefly status. Having no superior authority above to delegate any powers to them, they might have virtually become small chieftains of their localities. Some of them, depending upon the strength of the people and resources at their command, were bigger chieftains and the biggest among them had dominion over a larger region. Such a situation is evidently that of the pre-state, best represented universally by the tribal chiefdoms of unilineal descent, which vary in their organizational pattern of power relations across tribes, clans, and lineages.[20]

Although the existence of the state is unlikely in such a situation, the Sātavāhana political formation has been widely recognized as a metropolitan state in Indian historiography. Sātavāhanas appear to have been a chiefly lineage with Brahmanical pretentions in the central Deccan, wielding control over the southern trade route as its lords (*dakṣiṇāpatha-pati*), but without any consolidated political authority, probably till the ascendancy of Gautamiputra Sātakarṇi who could transcend the *gōtra* nexus and assert himself as a king.[21] An inscription in the Nasik Cave records his land-grant to the monastery at the Trirasmi hill, founded by his mother Gautami, indicative of a system of archiving charities of political significance.[22] Another inscription

[20] See the discussion in M.H. Fried, *The Evolution of Political Society* (New York: Random House, 1967), 236–341. Also, E.R. Service, *Origins of the State and Civilization* (New York: W.W. Norton & Co. Inc., 1975), 14–16. For details of the tribal polity, see M.D. Sahlins, *Tribesmen* (Englewood Cliffs, NJ: Prentice-Hall, 1968), 22–5. See variations in tribal polity discussed in the introduction to J. Middleton and D. Tait, eds, *Tribes without Rulers* (repr., London: Routledge & Kegan Paul Ltd., 1970), 1–32.

[21] See the brief but clinching discussion in B.D. Chattopadhyaya, 'Transition to the Early Historical Phase in the Deccan: A Note', in *Archaeology and History: Essays in Memory of Shri A. Ghosh*, eds B.M. Pande and B.D. Chattopadhyaya (Delhi: Agam Kala Prakashan, 1987), 727–35. This has been reproduced in his *Studying Early India: Archaeology, Texts, and Historical Issues* (New Delhi: Permanent Black, 2003), 39–47. For a view almost the same but arrived at differently, see Y. Subbarayalu, 'Contacts between the North and the South: An Epigraphical Perspective', Foundation Day Lecture (New Delhi: ICHR, 2012).

[22] See cave inscription 11, L.3–5 in Mirashi, *The History and Inscriptions*, 170.

(No. 18) in the cave, which contains Gautami's praise of her son Sātakarṇi includes among his merits 'the judicious spending of the rightfully exacted tax' (*dhamōpajita karaviniyōga karasa*) as one of his glorious attributes. This is a pointer to the existence of taxation of a formal nature for meeting the cost of governance, one of the most crucial features of the state. In the same cave, an inscription (No. 13) of the same king registers a royal order issued by word-of-mouth at the site requiring its intimation to amātya Sāmaka of Govardhana. It indicates a rudimentary bureaucratic apparatus and document-based governance, yet another vital feature of the state, to have evolved by the time. There are inscriptional references to Sātakarṇi and his successors paying attention to the maintenance of the *varṇa* system, probably a need in the wake of *varṇasamkara* and the emergence of *sankīrṇajāti*. Maybe, it is a sin of political overseeing of the stabilization of a caste-based social order. It appears to be a phase witnessing dissolution of the kinship base of productive relations into class base as reinforced by the fetters of caste hierarchy.[23]

Lords of the Southern Routes

Control of trade routes and points of exchange was probably a main source of revenue of the Sātavāhanas as the title Dakshiṇāpathīśvara (the divine lords of the southern trade routes) would have us believe. This would mean that the ruler was responsible for offering protection to the caravans all along their journey and entitled to a fee for the service. There is a mention in *Periplus Maris Erythraei* (*PME*) about the ruler making arrangements for the safe entry of the foreign vessels to the port of Barygaza by deploying big fishing boats to serve as pilots:

> ... native fishermen in the King's service, stationed at the very entrance in well-manned large boats called *tappaga* and *cotymba*, go up the coast as far as Syrastrene, from which they pilot vessels to Barygaza. And they steer them straight from the mouth of the bay between the shoals

[23] This stage has been described as 'the duality' wherein the pre-state features co-existed with certain new ones in the gradual process of development. See Service, *Origins of the State and Civilisation*, 20.

with their crews; and they tow them to fixed stations, going up with the beginning of the flood, and lying through the ebb at anchorages and in basins.[24]

Who the ruler was is not clear from the mention, but he was concerned enough to provide assistance to the mariners to safely make their way to a port not easily accessible. Being the lords of the route, the Sātavāhanas must have collected tolls from the wayfarers, especially the cargo movers and merchants. That the Sātavāhanas owed their prosperity to trade is a view justifiably maintained by most historians according to whom the period witnessed a remarkable growth of inland as well as overseas commerce in the Deccan. Several cave inscriptions of the Buddhist monastic establishments at Nasik, Karle, and Junnar register donations by merchants. Some of them seem to have included Graeco-Romans as well, who are often considered to have been converts to Buddhism.[25] Being sailors dependent on monsoon winds, these people had enough time ashore waiting for the return monsoon wind and some of them must have settled for longer duration for mobilizing the cargoes. It is not unlikely that a few of such people, in frequent contact with the overland itinerant merchants who were upāsakas of Buddhism, perhaps under their influence, got attracted to the way of life.

Sātavāhana country was known to the Graeco-Roman geographers and navigators as a landscape rich in forest goods. *PME* referring to the coast along the Konkan beyond Barygaza describes the Deccan plateau and mentions the richness of the forested mountains with wild animals. There were several inland points of exchange acting as the feeders of the main Sātavāhana port, namely Kalliena, where the Graeco-Roman merchant mariners had their sojourn, bartering alloys like arsenic and tin besides Italian bronze artefacts (relatively cheap compared to the local high-tin bronze objects) and fine-quality coral, as the stray archaeological finds at the domestic site of Kolhapur testify. They indicate that there was some demand for Italian bronze

24 *PME*, 44.

25 Conversion is unlikely, for Buddhism was not a proselytizing religion. However, it is quite possible that some of the Greek and Italian mariners had become upāsakas who were in contact with the craftsmen and traders.

objects, coral, and gems in the Deccan, obviously among the prominent householders of Pratiṣṭān. Nevertheless, there seems to have emerged no ruling aristocracy large enough to generate much demand for Mediterranean luxury goods.

Indian historiography has noted that the Indo-Roman trade had reached its zenith during the Sātavāhana period, and despite the subjugation of the Kalliena port by Nahapana for a short while, the rulers and merchants benefited immensely by the overseas exchanges. It has been pointed out that Nahapana acquiring control over Barygaza, the hub of overseas exchanges, was able to own the revenue benefits out of the major part of contemporary overseas commerce on the western coast of the Indian subcontinent.[26] Therefore, it is reasonable to presume that the material basis of the conflict between the Sākas and Sātavāhanas was the revenue out of overseas trade. It is a fact that a lot of gold and silver had reached the coffers of the Sātavāhanas, as revenue out of contemporary overland as well as overseas exchanges. Some of the Sātavāhana coins carry the representation of a ship, which is a reflection of the indication of overseas trade on the statecraft. However, we do not have details about the tariff system and regulatory measures relating to the flow of goods in and out by way of overseas trade. In a few inscriptions of the Nasik Caves there are indications of the presence of debtors and creditors, although we do not know who the debtors and creditors were and for what purpose they transacted money. One of the inscriptions in the caves mentions the rate of interest paid by a body of textile dealers to a moneylender as between 9 and 12 per cent. Nevertheless, we do not find any inscriptional or other evidence of the existence of any bureaucratic arrangement compared to the *Arthaśāstra* prescriptions or for the pursuance of precedents set by the Mauryas or the practising of the directions provided for in the *Dharma Śāstras*. There is no indication for the prevalence of any organized trade revenue administrative system either.

We do not see the Sātavāhanas taking the initiative in the expansion of the wet-zone agriculture and alluvial deltas of the major rivers

[26] It is said that overseas trading vessels were diverted from Kalleina to Barygaza after Nahapana seized it from the early Sātavāhanas. See *PME* 41 and 52 that give us some hints into the nature of political power in the coastal region of western India. Also see discussion in Adhya, *Early Indian Economics*, 21.

in their kingdom, which were not brought under the plough during their reign, obviously due to insufficiency of population pressure and lack of non-kin labour in productive relations. It took the rulers of the Deccan a few centuries to have the deltas converted into extensive fields of paddy, wheat, and sugarcane cultivation. Naturally, an integrated society, predominantly class-structured, became a reality only two or three centuries later.

The Tamil Polity

Let us now examine the political formation of Tamilakam (the region between Venkaṭādri and Kanyakumari) as represented by the pre-Pallavan Cēras, Pāṇḍyas, and Cōḻas. As already discussed, our historical understanding of the features of the pre-Pallavan social formation, the socio-economic, juridico-political, and cultural combine, is almost entirely based on the Tamil heroic literature.[27] We have already discussed the socio-economic and cultural characteristics of the chiefdoms in a previous chapter. What we seek to discuss in the present context are the features, structures, processes, and dynamics of the political formation of the chiefdom in the light of the main sources such as references in the heroic poems, the Tamil Brāhmi-label inscriptions, and notices in the accounts of foreign geographers.[28]

Minor Chiefdoms

There are different levels of chiefly status represented in the poems that contain clues to the pattern of distribution of power, from the simple to the complex, along the small and big descent communities.

[27] See R. Gurukkal, 'Forms of Production and Forces of Change in Ancient Tamil Society', *Studies in History* 2, n.s. (1989). It is reproduced in his *Social Formations in Early South India* (New Delhi: Oxford University Press, 2010), 136–54.

[28] Label inscriptions consist of the Tamil Brāhmi labels belonging to c. 3rd century BCE to 4th century CE. For texts of and detailed comments on the inscriptions, see I. Mahadevan, *Early Tamil Epigraphy from the Earliest Times to the Sixth Century A.D.*, Harvard Oriental Series 62 (Harvard: Harvard University Press, 2003), 60–5.

The heroic poems allude to coexistence and interaction of these unevenly evolved chiefly systems that can be broadly classified into three: the *kiḻār*, *vēḷir*, and *vēntar*.

Kiḻār is the primary category of chief-ship figuring in the poems as the *Ūr-kiḻār* or *Ūr-mannar* who were generally lowland chiefs of small settlements, mostly in the dryland zone (*vanpulam*).[29] A poem praises the kiḻār of Īrntūr, a settlement of vanpulam with marginal resources, depending primarily on plunder raids, as the enemy of hunger who would summon his blacksmith on seeing a hungry bard and order a new lance to arm him for a raid to appease the bard's hunger.[30] Kiḻār-level chieftains were mostly hunter-chiefs either of the *vētar* or *kuṛavar* descent communities, although some had sway over agrarian tracts and were more resourceful.[31] All had to participate in the predatory campaigns of the bigger chiefs and fight for them, while a few of them had also to sing their praise. Some of them were designated as *ēnāti* (*sēnāpati*) of the highest category of chiefs (vēntar). Chieftains of non-agrarian tracts were easily exhausted of their resources as shown elsewhere.

All chieftains had to resort to plundering as an alternative to replenish their resources for gift-giving. Numerous are the examples illustrating the plunder–gift continuum in the cattle-raid songs in *Puṛanānūṛu*. Plunder-raids were, in fact, the instituted means for pooling the resources under the authority of a chieftain and redistribute them in the form of gifts. Plundering raids being fundamental to the maintenance of the contemporary economy, all ideas and institutions in the broad superstructure helped the plunder-based redistribution function effectively. All chieftains could not have persisted on giving gifts solely out of what they received by way of voluntary offerings from their people, which was insufficient. Chieftains of the various descent groups were the principal gift-givers who commanded the resources of both the arid zone (vanpulam) and wet-fields (*mēnpulam*). Recipients of gifts were bards (*pāṇar* and *pulavar*), warrior chiefs (*maṛavar*), and other dependants (*iravalar*) who moved around the big

[29] *Puṛanānūṛu*, 177:17, 181:4. For the text and translation, see U.V.S. Iyar, ed., *Puṛanānūṛu*.

[30] *Puṛanānūṛu*, 180.

[31] *Puṛanānūṛu*, 176, 376, 381–8.

and small ruling lineages. Pulavar (scholarly bards) are mentioned to have received gifts of gold, chariots, and elephants from the principal ruling lineages (*mūvēntar*) and other powerful chieftains, which cannot be literally so. It could be just a bardic stock expression of the ideal. Warrior headmen are mentioned to have received primarily predatory control over village settlements as gifts for their services in raids of the mūvēntar, which is a mention of the ideal too. During rare occasions, the ideal could have been the real as well. Lesser bards sang in praise of anybody who could give something to them, for they were extremely poor.[32] Poets praise the generosity of the gift-givers by referring to their readiness to give away as gifts even the seeds reserved for sowing. Though this also appears to be a stock expression of the poets, it occurs only in poems praising the chieftains of dry and non-productive tracts.

The level of power represented by the vēḷir seems to be the most archaic and lineage-conscious. A hill chief called Irunko-*vēḷ*, one of the traditional five vēḷs, is mentioned in a poem as *vēṭarkōmān*, the chief of the vētar (hunter), who belonged to a long line of 49 generations of chiefs.[33] Poems show that the vēḷir chieftains, heading the descent communities called vētar, *iṭaiyar*, and kuṛavar, held sway over the forested hills of the *kuṛinji* and the *mullai* tracts of pastoral forest hills. Venkaṭamalai, Kanṭīraimalai, Kollimalai, Mutiraimalai, Kutiraimalai, Paṛmpumalai, Potiyilmalai, Pāyalmalai, Ē̱lilmalai, and Nānjilmalai are the famous millet-rich hill chiefdoms celebrated in the poems.[34]

32 See allusions in *Puṛanānūṛu*, 376, 382, 398, and 400, expressing the acute poverty of the lesser bards. Allusions in *Puṛanānūṛu* 192 and 393 show how poorly/sparsely dressed a *pāṇa* was. *Puṛanānūṛu*, 139 portrays the miserable lot of a *viṛali*, the woman of the pāṇa folk. At times, the bards seem to have used viṛali, who would sing and dance, to secure gifts from the chieftains. See *Puṛanānūṛu*, 109. There are many allusions to the poverty of minor chieftains who were depended upon by the lesser bards. *Puṛanānūṛu*, 127, 327 to 331 and 333 are some of the poems displaying the resource scarcity of the minor chieftains. Interestingly, all these chieftains are those commanding tracts in vanpulam.

33 *Puṛnānūṛu*, 201:11–12 and 202:12–14. For text and commentary, see the volume edited by U.V.S. Iyar.

34 *Puṛnānūṛu*, 143, 168. For text and commentary, see the volume edited by U.V.S. Iyar.

Ē<u>l</u>ilmalai was the most prominent hill chiefdom of Kerala and the lineage of Nannan, the hunter-chief of vēṭar (*vēṭarkōmān*). Another chiefdom closely linked to the southern end of Kerala was Potiyilmalai. Pāri, the chief of Paṛampumalai; Ōri, the chief of Kollimalai, Kāri who killed Ōri and became the chief of his hill; E<u>l</u>ini, the chief of Kutiraimalai; Pēkan, the chief of Vankalmalai; and Kumaṇan, the chief of Mutiraimalai, are the most celebrated hunter-chiefs of the vētar or kuṛavar communities.[35] Sometimes, the hill chiefs are called *vēṭṭuvar*. This would suggest that the term *vēḷ* derives from *vēṭ*, meaning hunter. However, all the vēḷir were not hill chiefs: for instance, E<u>l</u>ini, the chief of Veṭṭāṛu, was a vēḷ in control of agrarian lowlands.

They had to resort to plunder raids to compensate their economic deficits, and they seem to have maintained predatory control over the agrarian zones in their proximity.[36] Some of them seem to have exchanged forest goods to procure prestige goods like gold coins, precious stones, and horses, which the poems mention as *yāṇar* (new resources). The hill of Irunko-vēḷ is praised in a poem as gold-yielding, implying its richness in the forest resources like ivory, monkeys, animal skins, and sandalwood, which brought gold in exchange, and obviously Roman coins.[37] Paṛampumalai is called *yāṇaraṛā aviyan malai*, the hill with the potential of new resources.[38] Piṭṭan *korran* of Mutiraimalai is called *kaṭumān* korran, the victorious chieftain possessing horses. Chieftains with control over such hills of rare resource potential and possessing prestige objects had a higher status and ranking. Some of them had control over agrarian tracts too as exemplified by the *Ay* chief who had owned the rich hillock, fertile plains, horses, and chariots. His house was called *koil* or *nakar* (palace), suggestive of a higher status. Nevertheless, the range of the redistributive relationship of a hill chief was limited, though a few bards from distant places

[35] *Puṛnānūṛu*, 158. For text and commentary, see the volume edited by U.V.S. Iyar.

[36] *Puṛnānūṛu*, 110, 168, to cite only a few. For text and commentary, see the volume edited by U.V.S. Iyar.

[37] *Puṛnānūṛu*, 202:7–8. For text and commentary, see the volume edited by U.V.S. Iyar.

[38] *Puṛnānūṛu*, 116:13–14. For text and commentary, see the volume edited by U.V.S. Iyar.

met him occasionally. His predatory range too was small, enabling only small-scale raids. With no relations transcending kinship in the system of production and circulation, the political power of this category of chief-ship remained subsumed within the kinship system.

Major Chiefdoms

The next category of political power is that of the vēntar represented by the three major chiefly lineages (mūvēntar or *mūvar*), namely the Cēras, Pāṇḍyas, and Cōḻas. They had their core areas in Karur, Madurai, and Uṛaiyur respectively, and the peripheral strategic points near the ports of Muciṛi, Korkai, and Puhar respectively. The Cēras held sway over the kuṛinji-dominated zones of the Western Ghats towards the sea; the Pāṇḍyas, over the mullai-, *pālai-*, and *neytal*-dominated zones in the south central region of Tamilakam; and the Cōḻas, over the *marutam*-dominated Kāvēri region. There was no notion of precisely demarcated territory and poems would fix the Himalayas as the northern boundary of each *vēntan* whose control beyond the core, where it waned and constantly fluctuated, had to be frequently refreshed through predatory campaigns.

The Cēras are referred to in the poems as *kānaka-nāṭan* (the chief of the forested *nāṭu*) or *malaiyan* (the chief of *malai* or hill) which is suggestive of their ecological region. A poet praising *Cēramān Kōtai Mārpan* expresses confusion about how the chief should really be addressed.[39] The poet asks whether the chief could be called *nāṭan* as he had marutam lands or *ūran* as he had kuṛinji lands or *cērpan* as he had coastal tracts. This would suggest that the Cēra region, their resource base, was a mixture of diverse ecological zones with the predominance of hills and forests, with forest wealth as the main resource. A poem refers to the hill products (*malaittāram*) and sea products (*kaṭal-tāram*) of Cēran Cenkuṭṭuvan and the gold that reached ashore by boats.[40] The Pāṇḍyas too had a mixed ecological region dominated by pastoral and coastal tracts. A Pāṇḍyan chieftain

[39] *Puṛnāṇūṛu*, 49:2–4. For text and commentary, see the volume edited by U.V.S. Iyar.

[40] *Puṛnāṇūṛu*, 343:1–10. For text and commentary, see the volume edited by U.V.S. Iyar.

calls himself the head of the land of numerous new resources, *yāṇar maiyar koman.*[41] The Cōḻa who is well known as *kāviri kiḻavan* in the poems had his land in the Kāvēri delta, rich in paddy and sugarcane.[42]

How the vēntar category of chieftains appropriated resources is the most pertinent question here. Their core areas were not bigger than an *ūr* and the surrounding areas were held by numerous other chiefs. It is implicit that their mechanism of appropriation too was predatory. There are indications in the poems to the expansion of the predatory control beyond their original ūr (*mutūr*) obviously through the process of subjugation.[43] A poem shows Cēramān Kuṭṭuvan Kōta sitting as the *uṭaiyōr* (lord) of a mutūr in the place of its original chief, probably suggesting subjugation. The subjugation process seems to have involved three different methods: subordination with tributary obligations, expulsion, and marital alliance. There are many references in the poems to all these methods of enlarging the domain of the vēntar. The chiefs of Nānjilmalai, Pāyarmalai, and Veṭṭāṟu were Cēra vēntar's subordinates with the obligation to fight in times of raid.[44] A few poems praise the chiefs, Tirukuṭṭuvan, Tirukkiḷḷi, and Tirukkaṇṇan as the ēnāti of the Cēra. Similarly, Paṇṇan, the *kiḻān* of Ciṟukuṭi, and Aruvantai, the kiḻān of Ampar, were Cōḻa subordinates with tributary and military obligations. Nākan, the *kiḻavan* of Nalai, and Nampi Neṭunceḻiyan are mentioned as Pāṇḍya subordinates with obligations of a warrior. Sometimes, chiefs in the fringes were subordinated by two vēntar chiefs, letting the obligation shift from one to the other.

In addition to such subordinates, there were many village chiefs called *cīṟūr-mannar*, mostly, *maṟava* headmen, who functioned as the warrior headmen of the vēntar. The vēntar sometimes made them village chiefs (Ūr-mannar) as a reward for the latter's obligatory service (*viṭutoḻil*) in the predatory campaign. This seems to have enabled the

41 *Puṟnāṉūṟu*, 71:11–12. For text and commentary, see the volume edited by U.V.S. Iyar.

42 *Puṟnāṉūṟu*, 58:1 calls the chief *kāviri kiḻavan;* 61:5–6 mention him as the chieftain of the land of paddy. For the text and commentary, see the volume edited by U.V.S. Iyar.

43 *Puṟnāṉūṟu*, 54:1–2.

44 *Puṟnāṉūṟu*, 139:6–12.

maṟava headmen to gain predatory control over ūrs. Several poems are in praise of such warrior chiefs who were ready to rush to their vēntar in times of emergency and die fighting for him. It appears that in the expanded area, control was maintained by stationing the kinsmen of the vēntar at different points for collateral management of resources as necessitated by the limitations of contemporary transport and communication facilities. The poems show that the people in the subjugated areas could remain fearless only by parting with the vēntar a share of their resources, in the form of *tiṟai* or *koḷ* (tributes) in kind. Often the vēntar had to raid the settlements to exact tiṟai, for the bigger chieftains always preferred to resist, rather than volunteering to pay the tributes.

Ancient Tamil poems address vēntar as *kāvalar* (protector) of the *kuṭi* or *kuṭimākkaḷ*, the settlers. Pāṇḍya Neṭunceḻiyan refers to his kuṭimākkaḷ as *en niḻal vāḻnar* (those living under my shade). This would presuppose the exaction of some goods in return from the kuṭimākkaḷ for the protection offered to them. In the case of the Cōḻa, it is clear that the vēntar used to exact *puravu* (crop) from the kuṭi. All the three vēntar are referred to in the poems with the term *iṟaivan*, meaning 'he who exacts', although there is no clear evidence of periodic exaction in fixed measure or quantity by any of them. Therefore, it seems that the vēntar had exacted their share of resources through predatory operations and voluntary offerings. Poems of the *ceviyaṟivūṟutuṟai* and *poruṇmoḻikāñcittuṟai* advise the vēntar how to protect the settlements and maintain them as productive, and how to appropriate their surplus in a sustainable manner. They ask the chieftains not to behave like an elephant in the crop field, destroying far more than what it eats, but to follow the way of a bee sucking honey without harming the flower. These are poems by the pulavar (scholarly bards), several of whom were Brāhmaṇas who knew the instituted modes of periodic exaction in developed kingdoms elsewhere. The returns from exchange relations must have enabled the vēntar to possess gold and other prestige items. However, it is not clear how they were involved in the process of exchange and how they exacted benefit out of it.

Several passages in the heroic poems refer to *koṭai* (gift-giving or redistribution) among the dependants within a determinate pattern of community relationships, as a major activity of the vēntar, like the vēḷir and kiḻār chieftains. Plunder was indispensable for them also since their redistributive network was much more elaborate and complex than what they could have afforded with their actual resources. They had a large body of dependants such as their kinsmen (*kiḻaiṅjar*), scholarly bards (pulavar), warrior chiefs (maṛavar, kiḻār, and *mannar*), warriors (maṛavar), bards (pāṇar and *poruṇar*), and magico-religious functionaries. The poetic flower symbolism of *veṭci* (cattle raid), *karantai* (cattle recovery), *vanji* (chieftain's raid), *kānji* (chieftain's schematic resistance of a raid), and *tumpai* (preparation for raid) show how institutionalized and common the plunder was. There is no evidence of the vēntar maintaining a ready troop of warriors like a standing army. Nor is there any evidence of a systematically organized militia under the vēntar, though the term ēnāṭi (sēnāpati) occurs in connection with the titles of a few headmen, as noted earlier. In fact, the chieftains had only a set of people belonging to the fighter clan with kinship ties who could be mobilized instantaṇeously by the beating of a battle drum. A poem refers to the *maravar* of Cōḻa Nalankiḷḷi as *paṭaimākkal*, meaning fighters. The need for frequent redistribution and the strain of raids should have acted as a compulsion on the vēntar to intensify production, but it appears from the pieces of advice in the poems exhorting the chieftains to show more care and attention to agriculture, that they were not productively inclined. It is evident that ideas glorifying plunder and redistribution were governing their actions. Karikāla Cōḻa's efforts to dig reservoirs (*kuḷa-tōṭṭu*) and to raise flood banks of the Kāvēri River are indeed indications of the chieftains' initiative in irrigation, more an exception than a rule.

The structure of the vēntar-level political power was more complex than that under the vēḷir since its redistributive social relationship was elaborate. It involved some kind of a simple hierarchy from vēntar to the kuṭi, with kilār or mannar as intermediaries, but cutting across kinship and distancing the vēntar from the kuṭi. However, during the pre-raid or post-raid feasting (*uṇṭāṭṭu*), the vēntar did drink and dine with the fighters (maṛavar) at his residence. A complex redistributive political economy based on raids precludes the formation of a structured polity with defined positions and functions: the only institution of some political character mentioned in the poems is *avaiyam* (*sabha*) which seems to have functioned as an assisting body of the vēntar. Members of this body seem to have been mainly the warrior chiefs and the pulavar (the scholarly bards). However, the image of a king was quite well-known to the bards who eulogized the mūvēntar as crowned kings, albeit without any correspondence to reality. However, even the pulavar do not seem to be glorifying the vēntar as accomplished rulers with the *saptānga* attributes.

Cēras are the only line of chieftains bestowed with a collection of eulogizing songs, *Patirruppattu,* solely dedicated to them, indicative of their prominence. They contain invaluable clues to the structure of political power, nature of authority, and sources of legitimacy. Many of the features that the anthology attributes to the Cēras are applicable to the other vēntar also. Like others, the Cēras are praised as performers of *velvi* (Vedic sacrifices), devotees of Korravai, the war goddess, and worshippers of Murukan (Karthikeya). However, unlike the case of the other two of the mūvēntar, the poems equate the Cēras with the Vedic gods such as Sūrya, Agni, Marut, *pancabhūtas*, the constellations, and the *navagrahas*, remindful of the *lōkapāla* theory of the Itihāsa–Purāṇa tradition.[45] Poets eulogize the Cēras as wearing garlands made of seven crowns.[46] A poem says that Ko-perumcēral Irupoṛai protects his *kuṭimākkaḷ* exactly how a mother fosters her child, and this reminds us of the concept in the second edict of Asoka (Separate Edict 2) that equates the relation between the king and his subjects with that of a parent and his children. However, the 'mother' metaphor is very important in the context of the kinship basis of contemporary polity.

Their claim to identity with the Brāhmaṇic tradition shows its increasing influence on the political power. It is clear from the poetic expressions and descriptions in *Patirruppattu* relating to the nature of the political authority of the Cēras that they were seeking to legitimize it by drawing ideas heavily from Vedic Itihāsic Purāṇic Śāstraic Brahmaṇism. Their authority is characterized in terms of Purāṇic–Śāstraic notions and status legitimized by comparing and associating them with epic characters. A poem claims that Cēramān Perumcōrrutiyan conquered the land of the Pāṇḍavas and hosted

[45] See *Patirrppattu,* second *pattu,* verse 5. For the text and translation, see A.D. Pillai, ed., *Patirruppattu* with the text and commentary (Tirunelveli: The South India Saiva Siddhantha Works Publishing Society Ltd, 1949).

[46] *Ptirruppattu,* II.6, V.5.

a feast for both the Pāṇḍavas and Kauravas after the Bhārata war.[47] There are references in the poems to the Cēras possessing an army of the classical fourfold division, conquering many rulers and subjecting them to a subordinate position. In several songs, the Cēras are described as the overlord of all monarchs in the land between the Himalayas and Kanyakumari.

Such epic, Śāstraic, Purāṇic claims are common to the other vēntar too. Several are the stated examples of high-sounding claims that seek to legitimize the status of the vēntar. All the vēntar are mentioned to have incised their emblems on the Himalayas and hoisted flags on its peaks. Each one of them is said to have ruled the land surrounded by the Himalayas and the seas. A poem eulogizes Pāṇḍya Māran Vaḻūti as ferocious enough to frighten the north Indian kings.[48] However, most poems hold the authority of the mūvēntar over Tamilakam as a matter of tacit recognition. It is maintained in the poems that the whole of Tamilakam belonged to them. However, the concept of territory was not distinct from the ideal based on an overall general perception of the landscape as demarcated by the eastern hill and the western sea. It is significant that the Edicts of Asoka referred to them not as individual rulers but as clans of kindred descendants, as expressions like *Satiyaputo* and *Kēraḷaputo* suggest. There seems to be a difference between the image that the poets attribute to the vēntar and the reality about what they were. We know that the whole of Tamilakam did not belong to them and there were other tribute-receiving chiefs like Atiyamān who were close to the vēntar in status. A poem in praise of Neṭumān Añci warns all the chiefs of agrarian settlements to rush to him with tiṛai if they wished to retain their ūrs with them.[49] Many of the hill chiefs were uncompromisingly opposed to the vēntar. Pāri of Paṛampumalai, who offered strong resistance to the vēntar, though he was subsequently defeated and killed, is a good example.

Actually, vēntar too were chiefs but the crucial difference was their greater command over resource, larger redistributive intercommunity relationship, and better access to cultural sources of legitimization. They were surrounded by Brāhmaṇa pulavar of the Vedic tradition

47 *Puṛnānūṛu*, 2.

48 *Puṛnānūṛu*, 52.

49 *Puṛnānūṛu*, 97.

and a few were well informed of the Śāstraic–Purāṇic notions of kingship. But a predatory chieftain, whose status and power were linked with the range of the redistributive community network, could have hardly gone by Śāstraic prescriptions. A poem by a scholarly bard reminds Pāṇḍya Nanmāran of the fact that *aṛaneṛi mutarrē aracin korram* meaning 'greatness of royalty' remained with the primacy of *dharma*.[50] All songs in *Ceviyaṛivūṛutuṛai* contain ideas of this type, which sounded exotic in a milieu of plunder raids and redistribution and the vēntar continued to depend upon heroism and gift-giving. *Pāṇas* (bards) and their heroic compositions were the main strength behind their name, fame, and legitimacy. They kept the image of the vēntar by roaming around the land with their songs in praise of the latter's exploits. The *Panārruppaṭai* category of poems itself exemplifies the instituted nature of such circuits.

The above discussion enables an abstraction of the broad trends in the political process. Before we identify the forces of change in the process and understand their direction, the structure of the polity has to be made a little clearer. The basic constituent of the structure was kuṭi or family. A particular kuṭimākkaḷ or a host of families of one particular group and their *kōmān* or *perumakan* (chief) constituted the simplest unit that signified an organized settlement or ūr bound by kinship. This could spontaneously evolve as nāṭu through the process of the expansion of one and the same kuṭimākkaḷ through their agnatic and affinal relatives as exemplified by the hill chiefdoms. A collection of kinship-based ūrs of a variety of kuṭimākkaḷ integrated under a chief as his nāṭu signifies the subsequent structure of complex relations transcending kinship, as exemplified by the lowland chiefdoms. Within such nāṭu units, the structure of the ūr also involved complex relations when an alien chief and his kuṭi were superimposed on it. In short, the disintegration of the kinship base of the ūr was the crux of the process of change in the total structure.

Contemporary political process was linked up with predatory operations and redistribution of booty. Predatory marches of chiefs, their ravaging of settlements, arbitrary redistribution of the ūr, and the consequent migration and subsequent immigration were the characteristic features of the period under review. Formation of

50 *Puṛnānūṛu*, 55.

dispersed settlements in the place of nuclear units of kinship groups was a major consequence of these events. Redistribution of resources beyond the clan–kin ties had certain crucial consequences. It appears that at some point in time the institution of redistribution involved gifts of ūr to warrior chiefs, obviously predatory control rather than ownership. Scholarly Brāhmaṇas being part of the redistributive social relationship, such gifts seem to have been made to them too, though not extensively.[51] Generally, Brāhmaṇa households of the time were those depending on agro-pastoral wealth as exemplified by the case of Kauṇiyan Viṇṇan Tāyan of Pūnjārrūr.[52] However, not being cultivators, the land gifted to Brāhmaṇas had to be tilled by others, and it implied the emergence of a new system of relations in production transcending kinship.

Tamil Rulers and Overseas Exchange

Graeco-Roman writings refer to rulers of Limyrike in the context of describing the ports and marts of the region, in order to indicate under whose dominion each of them was situated. Nevertheless, none of them mentions any of the rulers by name. We know that the Asokan edicts address the rulers of the Tamil South as Satyaputas and Kēralaputas (sons of their lineages), suggesting that they were not rulers significant enough to be recognized as individual monarchs. Graeco-Roman accounts also call the rulers by their lineage names as exemplified by the expressions like Caprobotras (Kēraḷaputas) and Pāṇḍyan. Nevertheless, it is evident that the seafaring merchants who reached the coast of India were aware of the respective political authority that exercised control over the area of each port or mart. There are direct references in their writings about some of these rulers to have taken diplomatic initiatives in establishing formal exchange relations with the Roman Empire by sending emissaries to the emperor. Strabo mentions embassies sent by the Pāṇḍyan ruler to Augustus. As regards the mention of embassies sent to the emperor, there remains so much of confusion about the period, personnel, and

[51] Pāṇḍyan Mutukuṭumi Peruvaḻūti's gift of a village as an *ēkabhōga brahmadēya* mentioned in the Veḷvikuṭi Plates is an example.

[52] *Puṛnāṇūṛu*, 166.

purpose. It is almost like a legend in the sense that the whole reference is mixed up with various anecdotes of no certainty, combining mutually distant places and disparate periods into a medley of the fantastic. An excerpt cited below would vouch for it:

> From one place in India and from one king, Pāndion, but according to other writers, Poros, there came to Caesar Augustus' gifts and an embassy accompanied by the Indian sophist who committed himself to flames at Athens, like Kalanos, who had exhibited a similar spectacle in the presence of Alexander. If, however, one should dismiss these accounts and observe the records of the country prior to the expedition of Alexander, one would find things still more obscure.[53]

Some of the Greek historians like Dion Cassius, Florus, and Orosius mention emissaries sent to Roman Emperors, Augustus, and Trajan. But just as Emperor Asoka found most regions controlled by chieftains known after their descent groups, rather than established monarchs of personal identity to be reckoned with, these Greek historians seem to have found them heads of tribes like barbarians.[54] Historian Dion Cassius (180 CE) writes:

> ... ever so many embassies came to him from various barbarians, including the Indi [Indians]. And he gave spectacles on one hundred and twenty-three days, in the course of which some eleven thousand animals, both wild and tame, were slain, and ten thousand gladiators fought.[55]

It appears that the story of sending embassies by some of the rulers from certain regions of the Indian subcontinent is baseless. Actually, it is a matter of contradiction as well as incompatibility. It is evident that there was an irresistible socio-economic compulsion for

[53] J.W. McCrindle, *Ancient India as Described in Classical Literature* (repr., Patna: Eastern Book House, 1987), 9, paragraph 4.

[54] *Dio's Roman History*, Vol. IX, trans. E. Cary, Loeb Classical Library 117 (Harvard: Harvard University Press, 1904–27); *Florus: Epitome of Roman History*, Vol. IV, trans. E.S. Forster, Loeb Classical Library ed. (Harvard: Harvard University Press, 1929), 12.

[55] Dio Cassius, *Roman History* Book, IX, 73.

the Mediterranean traders to go out to the east at any rate and acquire spices as well as other luxury goods. They would anyway have gone over to the eastern ports. It is quite unlikely that the rulers of the regions in the Indian subcontinent had sent emissaries to persuade the emperor to have exchange relations, for it was unnecessary, and hence the contradiction. Another factor is that the regional rulers of the Indian subcontinent were of the chiefdom-level political formation precluding the possibility of sending diplomatic emissaries to the emperor, and hence the anachronism. Further, contemporary exchanges were not imports and exports under scheduled commerce between countries facilitated by state-level negotiations to have dispatch of embassies.

A Pāṇḍyan queen's delegation to the Augustan Rome, widely quoted in all the books, is just a story. An embassy presumed to have been sent for the formalization of exchange relations and promotion of transmarine commerce between the Pāṇḍya country and Roman Empire is, in fact, anachronistic and naturally not borne out by evidence.[56] Therefore, historians today do not believe in the episode of this Pāṇḍyan embassy to Rome. *PME*, after describing the ports of Barygaza and Sopara as the gateway to the west coast of India, mentions the ports and marts of Limyrike, with navigational information regarding sea routes, landmarks, geographical location, and countries. Further it provides business particulars such as which port provides what sorts of merchandise and political details such as who rules the region of each port and where whose dominion ends. In the context, both Cerabotros (Kēraḷaputras) and Pāṇḍyas figure as rulers of Limyrike, in whose countries, respectively, the most famous ports of Muziris and Nelcynda were located.

Tamil rulers benefited by overseas exchanges that brought ashore a good deal of gold and silver. However, as in the case of the Sātavāhanas, there is no evidence of the Tamil rulers evolving any administrative authority over the ports and establishing regulatory control over the movement of commercial goods by means of the imposition of tariff rules too. If the evidence of the Sātavāhanas comes from the inscriptions of the Buddhist establishments, the data support for the Tamil

[56] Strabo, *Geography*, XV, 1–4. For interpretation and contextualization, see C.R. Whittaker, 'Conjunctures and Conjectures: Kerala and Roman Trade', *South Asian Studies* 25, no. 1 (2009): 1–18.

rulers comes from the ancient Tamil poems. Poetic allusions show that the Yavana (Graeco-Roman) merchants had brought a lot of gold to the lands of the chieftains which, indeed, made them rich. However, the political economy of the chiefdom was such that the chieftains could have used the acquired gold and silver for enhancing their status and ranking through redistribution. Acquisition of such prestige goods and strengthening of redistributive relations could hardly have brought about any fundamental change in the political economy of the chiefdom.

Consciousness about the benefit of overseas contacts is explicit in the initiatives taken by bigger chieftains in the promotion of overseas exchange traffic in the ports of their dominion. A poetic reference in ancient Tamil literature praises the Cēras for the measures adopted to check the problem of piracy on the west coast and the 'arrangements of lights' on the shore for the ships to make out the coast during night. Nevertheless, it was not within the capacity of the chiefly infrastructure to extend services beyond the bare minimum and, hence, it is not accidental that there exists no evidence of the chieftains' interest in the protection of trade and trade routes acquiring institutional manifestations. There is no evidence to show that the chieftains had governed the ports, except the fact that their dominion over the regions in which these ports were situated was a matter of tacit recognition. Systematic governance was not within the capability of chiefdom-level political formations precluding bureaucracy. Naturally, overseas merchants, trade organizers, and financiers were largely autonomous in the conduct of their business as is evident in the Muziris Papyrus, an agreement signed under Roman law and between the merchant and the moneylender with a third party (obviously a Roman trade manager) stationed at Muziris.[57]

In fact, the chieftains were aware of the fact that powerful rulers had always bothered to ensure a regular upkeep and maintenance of the road infrastructure and trade routes. In ancient Tamil poems the

[57] As mentioned earlier, the Muziris Papyrus is reportedly a part of the two separate documents: one pertaining to a maritime loan and another relating to the security. What has survived is the document that dealt with the security. See L. Casson, 'New Light on Maritime Loans: P. Vindob. G 40822', in *Zeitschrift fur Papyrologie und Epigraphik* 84 (1990): 195–206.

references to the Mauryas are all in association with the roads cut and levelled along the hills for an easy ride of their huge chariots.[58] Several songs in the anthologies refer to the hazardous journey of merchants and caravans through forests and arid planes with no facilities of protection from wayside robbers.[59] This exposes the nature of the political formations that precluded any organizational capability of protection and maintenance of traders and trade routes.

Chieftains and Seafaring

What these chiefdoms must have done by way of patronage to the overland as well as overseas exchanges of the time is a question quite relevant to the context. We do not have much evidence to discuss this, for archaeology is silent in the matter and foreign notices hardly give any clues to what the overseas merchants received by way of patronage or favour. *PME* abounds in references to access impediments in the case of most ports in the north-western coast of the Indian subcontinent, due to either physiographical or ecological problems like shoals, hidden reefs, fast currents, silt formation, sand dunes, and so on. Almost all ports were in the interior without adequate bays for the ships to dock and hence they had to be anchored offshore. Pliny the Elder mentions how inconvenient and inhospitable Muziris, the *primum emporium* of Limyrike, was to the mariners because of its being in the interior and under the threat of pirates in the proximity. It is evident that the rulers were not able to maintain the ports in the regions of their dominion, with necessary infrastructure, obviously wanting instrumentalities of the state.

In the case of the Sātavāhanas, we have no indication in the source material as to whether the ruler had taken any initiative in improving

[58] See *Akanāṉūṟu*, 69:10, 251:12, 281:8. For the text and translation, see N.M.V. Nattar, ed., *Akanāṉūṟu* with commentary, Vols I and II; *Puṟanāṉūṟu*, 175:6. For the text and translation, see U.V.S. Iyar, ed., *Puṟanāṉūṟu* with commentary, 6th ed.

[59] *Puṟanāṉūṟu*, 60, 116, 310, 313. For the text and translation, see U.V.S. Iyar, ed., *Puṟanāṉūṟu* with commentary, 6th ed; *Akanāṉūṟu*, 190. For the text and translation, see N.M.V. Nattar, ed., *Akanāṉūṟu* with commentary, Vols I and II.

the conditions of the ports of the western Deccan. There are some poetic references in the case of the Tamil chieftains to have provided some facilities like the big lamp put up at a high point on the shore, serving the purpose of a lighthouse for the overseas vessels, namely *vankam, kalam,* and *nāvāy*, to make their way to the port.[60] Similarly, there are allusions to some of the chieftains who are said to have routed the pirates out into the deeper sea. Among the heroic exploits of some of the chieftains extolled by the poets, their naval strength in successfully combating the enemies in the sea comes up a few times. From the poetic allusions we understand that it was the Yavana soldiers who had ensured the security of the ports which, in fact, were primarily settlements of foreign merchants and sites of their cargo-houses. What emerges from the lack of care for the maintenance of the ports by the rulers is not only the non-existence of the state power but also the absence of any priority for it, because the need was not theirs but of the overseas merchants, especially the Graeco-Roman navigators. But not being a part of the Roman Empire, the imperial agency was not able to do anything for the upkeep of the ports.

Poetic embellishments notwithstanding, it is hard to believe that a Tamil chief was able to commission a sea-going vessel, do all arrangements of agents and managers, offer protection to the transport of his cargoes along the desert and exchange them. Chieftains hardly stand in comparison with the Roman aristocrats who were able to commission vessels for maritime trade. Though of varying degrees of resource strength, the chieftains were, indeed, far above the people, but by being part of the kin–clan ties which embodied their tribes/clans rather than constituting a class by themselves. However, the chieftains being in command of forest eco-zones rich in spices, ivory, peacock, gems, and so on, and some of them of the coastal tracts with pearls and textile, the major merchandise of the ancient overseas trade, they must have acquired a good quantity of gold and silver as

[60] See *Narriṇai*, 175, l.3. For the text and translation, see A.N. Iyar, ed., *Nattrinai* (Tirunelveli: The South India Saiva Siddhantha Works Publishing Society Ltd, 1956); *Akanānūṟu*, 255:1–6. For the text and translation, see N.M.V. Nattar, ed., *Akanānūṟu* with commentary, Vols I and II. We are not sure whether the arrangement of light was a structured lighthouse. Reference to a proper lighthouse occurs in *Cilappatikāram*, which is a later text.

valuables which could be exchanged for better status and ranking. These valuables do not seem to have facilitated a more productive circulation of resources and effective mobilization of labour, by which the redistributive society could have evolved into a class-stratified one. It is not accidental that there is no indication of the chiefly political authority undergoing transformation into a state power.

Classical Graeco-Roman world and peninsular India bear no comparison in matters of society, economy, culture, and polity. We have discussed the features of society and economy in one of the previous chapters and those of the polity above. Chieftains had material and human resources as clan heads who embodied their clanfolk. Their control over the resources and people was thus contingent upon redistributive obligations. Therefore, chieftains hardly constituted an autonomous aristocratic class by themselves with an increasing demand for non-local luxury goods and other techno-economic consumables. Naturally, sources do not contain any indications of the rise of monarchical state power during the period.

Exchanges and incessant interaction among the self-sustaining entities with one another accomplished a common horizon of shared cultural practices as facilitated by a common language. As a result, there was dissemination of knowledge systems and world views, particularly of the Brahmanical as well as Sramanic orders, into the late Iron Age/megalithic people in southern India. However, it seems to have had no transforming influence on the politics of plunder raids. Predatory marches of chieftains, their destruction of agrarian settlements as part of the scorched-earth policy in raids, and the dominance of the heroic ideology of raids and booty redistribution, utterly uncongenial to the expansion of agriculture, persisted.[61] It was amidst these adversities that the people of *mēnpulam* had to carry on production, and thereby remain absolutely confined to small pockets without much progress till the 7th century CE. Some of the bards, obviously under the influence of the heterodox world views, seem to advise the chieftains to abstain from raids leading to the devastation

[61] See details given in R. Gurukkal, 'Problems of Agrarian Expansion in Early Iron Age', in *Essays in Ancient Indian Economic History*, ed. B.D. Chattopadhyaya (Delhi: Indian History Congress Publications, 1987), 56–7. This is reprinted in his *Social Formations in Early South India*, 155–65.

of cultivated fields and promote agriculture that alone could bring power and fame.[62] Stressing the need for ensuring the protection of the peasants, they exhort the chieftains to maintain peace that is inevitable for the prosperity of the land. Nevertheless, none of these seems to have had any impact on the chiefdoms.

A few poetic allusions attest that the ideas of state power, bureaucracy, and the institution of periodic exaction were certainly brought to the attention of the ruling lineages in southern India. Some of the scholarly bards, particularly the Brāhmaṇa poets (pulavar), seem to have tried to acquaint the chieftains with the political ideas and institutions, probably of the Mauryas. Predatory operations continued and the structure of political organization hardly acquired any momentum towards integration of chiefdoms. Not adequately developed, these chiefdoms were not integrated to the Mauryan Empire. Since major institutions like the state never come up as transplant, the chiefdom-level polity remained the same until the dissolution of the social formation. In fact, the redistributive economy did exert some pressure on production as poetic allusions like the one to Karikāla's construction of Anicut would have us presume, but in vain since there was no scope for intensification of agriculture under the kinship-based division of labour.

In short, the political formation had not attained institutional and infrastructural development sufficient to administer contemporary overseas exchange relations. However, out of the couple of Tamil Brāhmi-label inscriptions from the Egyptian port of Berenike showing the presence of Tamils there, one mentions *koṟṟap-pumān*, a chieftain.[63] This is quite significant an evidence suggestive of some sort of involvement that a Tamil chieftain had in the maritime transactions of the time. This isolated evidence apart, we do not have any other indications of the Tamil chieftains' participation in overseas exchanges. There are certain allusions in the heroic poems, which

[62] Songs under the *turais* of *Ceviyaṟivūru* and *Poruṇmoḻik-kāñji* have allusions testifying this. See a discussion of this at length in Gurukkal, *Social Formations of Early South India*, 155–65.

[63] For details, see R. Salomon, 'Epigraphic Remains of Indian Traders in Egypt', *Journal of the American Oriental Society* 111, no. 4 (1991): 731–6.

are often cited as evidence of the active involvement of the Tamil chieftains in maritime activities. These references, largely to the naval skill of the chieftains in combating their enemies, are often misunderstood as evidence of their involvement in overseas commerce. None of the poetic references shows the chieftains playing any role in the organization of contemporary overseas exchanges. It is relevant here to have a critical re-evaluation of these poetic passages allegedly referring to the chieftains' direct participation in transmarine commerce. A passage, often quoted as a very important evidence of the Cēra chieftain's direct involvement in overseas trade, is from a poem in praise of Malayamān Tirumuṭik-Kāri, a hill chieftain:

cinamikaṭanai vānavan kuṭakaṭar
polantaru nāvāyōṭṭiya vavvaḻip-
piṛakalan celkalā tanaiyē mattai[64]

Literally, the passage means: '[I]t is impossible to go behind a gold giving ship sailing in the western sea of the Cēra.' It is used as a simile to express the poet's impossibility in finding themes and expressions to praise the chieftain who has been already sung by an eminent poet. Since he has not left anything unsung about the attributes of the hero, the poet is helpless. It becomes impossible for him to sing just as it is impossible for a boat to follow a (Roman) ship in the western sea of the Cēra, which brings gold. Literary, scholars and historians have wrongly translated the passage as 'the helplessness of a ship, unable to move by being behind the gold giving ship navigated by the Cēra in the Western Sea'. They have shown it as strong evidence of the Tamil chieftain's participation in the overseas trade of their times. Another well-known passage is from a small poem that praises Karikār Peruvaḷattān, a Cōḻa chieftain, as a possessor of a continent of many virulent elephants and as one who belonged to the lineage of a great navigator who could move the battleship stuck in the sea without wind, by calling the wind and commanding it:

64 *Puṛanānūṛu*, 126:14–16. For the text and translation, see U.V.S. Iyar, ed., *Puṛanānūṛu* with commentary, 6th ed.

naḷiyirumunnīr nāvāyōṭṭi
Valitoḻilāndavuravōn maṛuka
kaliyiyal yākkaṇa karikāl vaḷava[65]

Scholars have taken the passage to mean that the chieftain was an expert mariner with a long ancestry of having mastered the movement of the wind, and interpreted it as an indication of their engagement in overseas trade. Actually, there is no such implication in the verse that alludes only to the chieftain's expertise in navigating a coasting boat in the context of naval encounters. It has nothing to do with the expertise in overseas voyages for the purpose of trade. There are a few more allusions to the chieftain's navigational skill in riding the battle-boat to chase the enemies out into the deep sea. Uniformly, the reference is to the chieftain's rare ability to drive the enemies away into the outer sea. Often the phrase (a stock one) that occurs is *katalōṭṭiya*, literally meaning only 'driven in the sea', but its actual signification is of driving out of the enemies back into the outer sea.[66] It is a stock expression signifying the skill of the chieftain in navigating the battle-boat swiftly and efficiently for the successful chasing away of the enemy boats far into the outer sea. A chieftain's title itself is *kaṭal piṛakōṭṭiya velkeḻu kuṭṭuvan*, meaning Kuṭṭuvan who drove the enemies back into the outer sea. All these suggestive of the Tamil chieftains' fame as masters of the sea with rare expertise in seafaring are taken to be showing the plausibility of their participation in overseas commerce. But none of the poetic allusions provides clinching evidence of the direct involvement of the Tamil chieftains in the conduct of overseas trade.

The absence of evidence of the organization of overseas commerce under the chieftains is natural, for obvious socio-economic and political reasons. It is hard to imagine them to have had any direct role in the overseas exchange that was a heavily collaborative enterprise by big aristocrats as financiers, bankers, ship-owners, and various

65 *Puṛanāṉūṛu*, 66:1–3. For the text and translation, see U.V.S. Iyar, ed., *Puṛanāṉūṛu* with commentary, 6th ed.

66 See *Patirruppattu*, fifth pattu (ten), pāṭṭu (song) 6:12–13: '... *tiraipparappir paṭukaṭalōṭṭiya velpukaḻ kuṭṭuvan*'. For the text and translation, see Pillai, ed., *Patirruppattu* with the text and commentary.

contractual firms. Contemporary Graeco-Roman trade had required networking which involved deployment of several agents and managers, transport of goods over sea, desert, and river routes, unloading, weighing, reloading, and leaving the goods under the ownership and seal, paying cameleers, boatmen, and so on. It required a differentiated economy, class-structured society, and the entailing state power, codified jurisprudence, documentation-based bureaucratic administration, systematic taxation, and well-billeted legions. Chieftains had no organizational and institutional infrastructure for all this. Moreover, it is explicit from the Muziris Papyrus, a business contract of detailed stipulations executed under the Roman Law, that contemporary overseas transactions had required a document-based, law-bound, juridico-political set-up of an empire. It gives an idea about the juridico-political system that governed contemporary transactions. Conditions that the document stipulates in case of the failure of repayment of the loan on the specified date show the juridical power that makes the borrower agree for severe actions against him. A well-evolved and structured state power is evident as the sanction behind the stipulations provided for in the loan agreement. Where the document underlines that there shall be no legal action against the lender for the execution of such drastic measures against the debtor, the de facto nature of the juridical power is explicit.[67]

Contemporary modes of internal exchange relations and the nature of regional political economy necessitate a rethinking about the nature of exchange relations of the merchants of the Indian subcontinent with the Graeco-Roman mariners from the Mediterranean world. Loose generalizations by earlier scholars notwithstanding, it is a fact that there is no clear evidence of ancient Tamils organizing trade with Rome. Evidences are for the coming of foreign traders, particularly the Graeco-Romans in their vessels for shipping the goods. It was hardly trade for the Tamil society, for trade would mean profit-oriented exchange using the medium of money. Mere presence of coins is not enough to confirm a monetized society. There should be evidence of the use of money both as a means of payment and measure

[67] D. Rathbone, 'The "Muziris" Papyrus (SB XVIII 13167): Financing Roman Trade with India', in *Alexandrian Studies II in Honour of Mostafa el Abbadi* (Alexandria: Societé Archéologique d'Alexandrie, 2000), 39–50.

of value which sources hardly vouch for in the case of ancient Tamil society. On the contrary, there are plenty of indications in the sources to the fact that the society was largely non-monetized, and that the Roman coins functioned as part of social valuables and not as money. It appears that they had no role in the organization of overseas commerce due to various reasons in which the absence of the state was a decisive one.[68]

A Comparative Appraisal

It is extremely difficult to characterize the political structure of a complex of unevenly evolved chiefdoms that defy labelling under any of the known models. In the sense that the state means a centralized political authority of due sanction and legitimacy within a defined territory with an organized standing army, a regular taxation system, and a bureaucracy, we cannot identify any of chiefdoms as the state. As far as the chiefdoms in the Deccan and the Tamil region are concerned, what we discern is not the structure of an easily explicable pre-state either, although various levels of the political formation signify different stages of pre-state developments (Map 6.1). Further, there is an overlap of these stages at all levels, adding to its complexity. In the Sātavāhana polity of the post-Sātakarṇi phase, some of the features of institutional development of the state are evident. Likewise, in the polity of the vēntar category of chieftains, some of the ideas and institutions resembling the state are found as distinguished from the other categories of chieftains of the hills and forests, explicitly of the lesser level of political formation coexisting in the region.

In short, during the period under review (1st century BCE–3rd century CE), most people in the Deccan and the Tamil macro region were integral to descent groups adapted to multiple landscape ecosystems with appropriate strategies of subsistence that included plough agriculture in a relatively limited way, but largely under the dominance of the agro-pastoral. There was extensive trade network across

[68] For a detailed consideration of the issue, see R. Gurukkal, 'Classical Indo-Roman Trade a Misnomer in Political Economy', *Economic and Political Weekly* XLVIII, nos 26 and 27 (2013): 67–78.

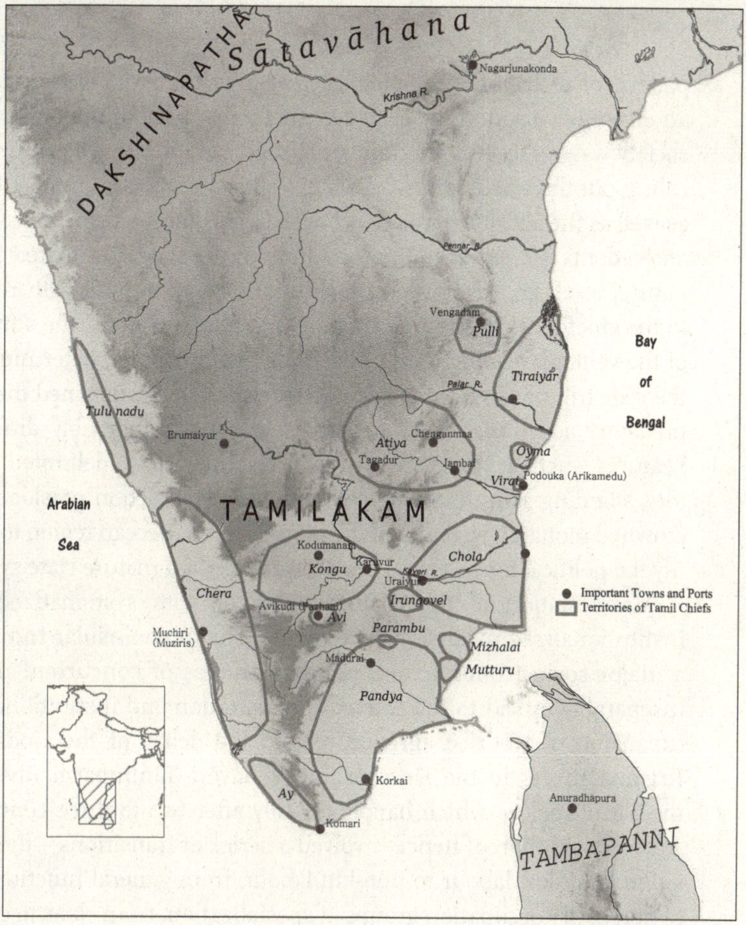

Map 6.1 Chiefdoms of Peninsular India

Source: Author.
Note: Map not to scale.

settlements, frequent circulation of long-distance itinerant merchants, local chieftains, Buddhist monks, mendicants and others, widely distributed monastic establishments, specialized craft production, centres of exchange, and monetized transactions in the Deccan region. All these features, except Buddhist monastic institutions, were true of the Tamil macro region too but probably on a lesser scale. Socio-economic processes in the Deccan and the Tamil macro region indicate that the pattern of distribution of political power in the regions represented an ensemble of unevenly evolving chiefdoms. In both the regions the society was yet to become class-structured even in the 3rd century CE, ruling out the existence of the state. Political processes in the Deccan as well as the Tamil macro region were largely those of chiefdoms with antecedents not closer to the formation of the state. Compared to the nature, level, and dynamic of institutional development with respect to the chiefdoms in the Andhra and the Kalinga regions, the situation of the vēntar-level chiefdom in the Tamil macro region, determined by the redistributive economy and social relationships sustained through predatory accumulation of resources, was not remarkably different. Features such as class-structured social hierarchy, delimited territory, standing army, bureaucracy, and periodic exaction presided by a crowned monarch were not manifest even in the Deccan region to identify the political formation of the Sātavāhanas as a mature state system.

Manifestation of the mature statecraft with systematized and institutionalized means of trade regulations in peninsular India was a major socio-economic and political process of concurrent nature inseparably linked to the extensive penetration and institutionalized expansion of wet-rice agriculture into the deltas of the Godavari–Krishna Rivers in the Deccan and of Kāvēri–Tāmṛaparṇi Rivers in the Tamil region, which happened only after two to three centuries. Antecedents thereof hence involved a series of transitions—the transition from kin labour to non-kin labour, from general functionaries to hereditary occupation groups of specialization, from clans to castes, from descent community settlements to structured agrarian villages, and from chiefdom to the state.

Compared to the Sātavāhanas, the mūvēntar seem to have had a lesser range of control over trade and trade routes, for the Tamil macro region, unlike the Deccan, was not extensively networked by merchants, monks, and monastic establishments. Many songs in the anthologies refer to the hazardous nature of the long journey of merchants and caravans through forests and arid planes of no protection from wayside robbers.[69] This is a pointer to the nature of the political

[69] *Puṛanānūṟu*, 60:8–9; 116:7–9; and 313:5–6. For the text and translation, see U.V.S. Iyar, ed., *Puṛanānūṟu* with commentary, 6th ed.; *Akanānūṟu*, 89:10–14; 167:7–9; and 191:1–12. For the text and translation, see N.M.V. Nattar,

formations that lacked instituted arrangements for protecting and maintaining trade and trade routes. They seem to have been actively involved in promoting overseas exchange by seeking to prevent pirates and making 'arrangement of lights' on the shore for guiding the ships sailing towards the coast at night. But there is no evidence of their overseeing the flow of merchandise in and out with the imposition of tariff rules. Overseas exchange must have benefited them by providing them with prestige goods that could enhance their status both through their possession as treasure as well as redistribution. But this could hardly have led to any fundamental transformation in their political structure, for it had no impact on the social mode of labour realization or productive relations of the time.

Since there was no empire in contemporary India, the trade contacts of the Roman Empire could have been based only on a relationship of imbalance in matters of exchange. What features an empire presupposes in political economy—techno-economic infrastructure, imperial force, bureaucracy and juridico-political institutions—are what we underline here. Their absence or variations upset the balance in the relationship of exchange. Actually, it is anachronistic to talk about Indo-Roman trade in the light of the characterization of the political economy of the ancient Tamil South, and the expression is, therefore, a misnomer. Being a chiefdom-level society, there was no ruling aristocracy either to have been capable of being financiers or bankers or business agency for investing in overseas commerce or merchant bodies rich enough for commissioning seagoing vessels on their own. Whether chieftains could have constituted an aristocratic group by themselves is the relevant question then. Indeed, chieftains were rich in their valuables and had people under their command but all of a contingent network of redistributive obligations within the kin–clan ties. Such a group of chiefly distinction, embodying the clan wealth but subsumed by the clan ties, cannot be equated to an autonomous aristocratic class of ever increasing demand for non-local techno-economic consumables and luxurious goods.

---

ed., *Akanāṉūṟu* with commentary, Vol. II; *Paṭṭiṉappālai*, 254–7. For the text and translation, see U.V.S. Iyar, ed., *Pattuppāṭṭu* with the commentary of Nāccinārkkiṉṉiyar, 6th ed. (Madras: Thyagarajavilasam Publications, 1961), 513–63.

7

Afterword

In the preceding chapters we have discussed the nature of the eastern Mediterranean exchange relations with the coasts of the Indian subcontinent, with a view to seeing as to whether what has been generally represented as Indo-Roman trade in Indian historiography is tenable in the light of the extant source material and at the instance of interpretation with the relevant theoretical preoccupation. What we have attempted is a historiographical reconsideration and an interpretational reappraisal of the nature of 'classical Indo-Roman Trade', using the theory of social formation, critical political economy, and economic anthropology of exchange.

It is a fact that in the historiography of overseas trade, the sentimental notion of 'Indo-Roman trade' prevails even when the history of 'Roman–Indian trade' is chosen as the subject matter of discussion. Most writings on the history of early Indian trade are with little or no explanatory methodological preoccupation with tasks such as analysis of the homology between the nature of the social formation and the structure of exchange practices, and critical engagement in comparative political economy. We have found in the study that what Karl Marx and Bronislaw Malinowski had pointed out long ago—there is a direct correspondence between the form of social organization and its pattern of production, distribution, and exchange—holds good, offering us enormous insights in understanding the nature of exchange relations in the past. They help us explain as to how trade differs from other forms of exchange in pre-capitalist social formations.

The use of the term 'trade' in historiography, as if it applies uniformly to all kinds of transactions in time and place, leads to many anachronistic correlations, causations, and generalizations about the nature of early forms of exchange. We cannot anymore afford to overlook in historiography the significance of differentiating trade from other forms of exchange, by holding on to the wrong presumption that trade is a phenomenon of universality and relationship of uniformity beyond time and space. Similarly, with insights of economic anthropology and archaeology, it is indispensable to theoretically differentiate the concept of value involved in the non-market modes of exchange among descent groups, not only from the monetized market mode but also from the incompatible notions of value involved in the exchange between the monetized and non-monetized peoples. It is not possible to understand the concept of value embedded in exchange relations among the people of uneven economies and social organizations without a critical anthropological perspective about the limitations of the principles of neoclassical economics and without freeing our thoughts from its basic presumptions.

What turns out to be explicit in the present attempt is that historical studies of exchanges based on an awareness of the above differences can discover new evidence in the source material and ensure historiographical advance in matters relating to the characterization of 'classical Indo-Roman trade', a mystified subject, debated by historians. In the process it gets exposed that some of the historians of trade go about counterbalancing the paucity of evidence by making overstatements and disputable generalizations consciously, while many others rather mechanically adduce even new finds to reinforce the old notions uncritically accepted under the influence of the dominant historiography. Most non-Indian historians specializing in the subject largely accept the dominant presumptions of Indian historiography due to the delicacy in challenging them. Serious challenges, they are aware, would implicate them as colonialist and brand their arguments as Eurocentric. A few of them, despite being knowledgeable in economic anthropology that helps comprehend the nature of contemporary exchange relations, do repeat obsolete notions, wanting linguistic competency to overcome the limitations of translations of ancient texts, particularly those in ancient Tamil. This is true of the large majority of our new generation of researchers in the subject, who are suffering from the added disadvantage of having no social theoretical competency. It is high time that they realized the fact that they have a lot to learn from Marx, Malinowski, Marcel Mauss, and Karl Polanyi.

Having done a re-evaluation of the extant literary source material and the recent archaeological finds in critical political economy perspective, we are convinced that the popular historiographical presumptions about the nature of exchange relations of the classical Roman times and the role of merchant communities of the Indian subcontinent are not borne out by history. What emerges out of our critical reappraisal of them is that the so-called classical Indo-Roman trade was not even 'Roman–Indian trade' but an ensemble of different forms of exchange in which trade was just one and confined to Rome. Contrary to the popular presumption, contemporary Graeco-Roman exchange was one of serious imbalance due to glaring contrasts between the social formations of Rome and the regions of the Indian subcontinent. This imbalance was inevitable to contemporary transactions that were primarily between an empire and a region of chiefdoms. Further, most inferences made by both the Western and Indian archaeologists about South Indian merchants' direct participation in overseas exchange are socio-economically untenable, incompatible, and anachronistic.

An important factor often ignored is that contemporary Mediterranean exchange of goods from the eastern world was a heavily collaborative, highly systematized, an extensively networked, document-based contractual activity, with precise notions of weights and measures as well as clearly stipulated rates of rent, interest, price, and profit accounted for in terms of money. It is not taken seriously too that a fairly well developed state power with structured juridico-political institutions and practices is presupposed by the operation of such transactions. Theoretically, an evolved state apparatus is the structured institutional outcome of a differentiated economy, class-stratified society, and ruling aristocracy of conflicting interests. It is anachronistic to presume that contemporary social formations of peninsular India had satisfied them. Although, there is no indication in the source material of the Sātavāhanas or any claim by historians for the direct participation of the rulers in the conduct of overseas commerce, the role of the Tamils in it has been strongly put forward in south Indian historiography, in the light of poetic allusions (mostly based on wrong interpretations). Tamil merchant bodies, largely in the milieu of clan–kin ties and a redistributive economy, hardly had the required techno-economic, organizational, institutional, and structural capabilities to run overseas exchanges. Communities yet to transform themselves into a class-structured society precluded the possibility of any individuals coming up to commission a trans-oceanic vessel or to finance transmarine trade.

Some of the widely heard arguments are about a few Tamil chieftains celebrated in the poems as masters of the sea to have led seafaring merchants to the Red Sea ports for the conduct of trade with the Mediterranean world. It is true that the chieftain who embodied the descent group had wealth and people of the chiefdom at his disposal. Nevertheless, he could not have organized and controlled contemporary Mediterranean trade, an enterprise involving elaborate networking of and negotiations with various business agents, haulage contractors, cargo movers, and goods distributors. It is incompatible and anachronistic to presume that contemporary Tamil chiefdoms, largely in the milieu of clan–kin ties and a redistributive economy, had the required techno-economic, organizational, institutional, and structural capabilities. If the Tamils were to run transmarine trade on their own, they should have, at the outset, either hired or owned ships fit for crossing the Indian Ocean. Then they should have sailed utilizing the south-east monsoon wind at least till the Horn of Africa, if not right up to the Red Sea ports of Berenike or Myos Hormos, and returned after six months with the north-west monsoon wind. They should have had carried with them rice and other provisions sufficient for the considerably long stay on board as well as ashore and made arrangements thereof. Such capabilities are utterly unlikely in a chiefdom-level society and polity.

Nevertheless, it is true that some archaeological remains in the form of shards of Indian pottery have been found at these ports, some of which were of the Tamils as the Brāhmi labels indicate. Who these Tamils were and what role they had played in the exchange is unclear. Had they been merchants, they must have been cargo suppliers to Mediterranean ships or some service providers to the mariners in them. There is no possibility of them being merchant-mariners of their own ships, for there is no evidence of the existence of the ship-building technology appropriate for cross-oceanic voyages anywhere in contemporary India. Extant archaeological indications in the form of fragments of cotton sail at the Red Sea ports are not enough to support the presumption. Nevertheless, the coasting voyages along the pre-Roman route by certain adventurous seafaring merchants in their big boats made of teakwood and rigged with cotton sail were quite likely. Contacts along the coasting routes from north-west India to the Persian Gulf and South Arabia up to Aden by merchant-mariners of long and short sojourns at various points are well attested by ceramic archaeology based on typology, material composition, and source of specific wares. Their exchanges were purely merchant-driven slow enterprise of barter based on use-value in which the ruling aristocracy had no role, and hence they were scarcely comparable to the bustling commerce, based on exchange-value, of the empire. These merchants, largely hailing from the north-west India and mostly confined up to the seaboards of the eastern Arabia, had anyhow seldom braved beyond the port of Aden.

It is not accidental that we lack evidence of the merchant-mariners of India engaged in cross-oceanic trade with the Red Sea coast and beyond, because they could not have crossed the Indian Ocean, for want of the appropriate technology to build huge ships capable of withstanding the rough sea during the monsoon. It is possible that some Tamils had accompanied the traders in the Mediterranean ships, perhaps as merchant middlemen and providers of trade goods and services on board, for it would not have necessitated organizational and institutional capabilities.

In short, the expression 'Indo-Roman trade' popularized by Indian historiography, is inappropriate, for what had happened was largely Roman trade, in the organization and control of which the rulers and merchants of the Indian subcontinent had no role. A further argument is that most inferences made in the light of recent archaeological and epigraphic material, both by Western and Indian archaeologists, about south Indian merchants' or chieftains' direct participation in overseas exchange are socio-economically untenable, incompatible, and anachronistic. It is true that a substantial quantity of gold and silver had reached the coastal regions of the subcontinent through barter. But mainly these precious metals had formed part of the treasure and ornaments, rather than being a catalyst for the mobilization of labour, organization of productive relations transcending kinship, expansion of agriculture into the deltas, and accumulation of productive surplus leading to economic differentiation, social stratification, and formation of the state. In short, the impact of Graeco-Roman exchange relations on the unevenly evolved societies of the Indian subcontinent was marginal.

Exchange relations of ancient and early historic times were largely built up and maintained over centuries by a huge network of merchant bodies, both overland and overseas merchants of widely separated lands and cultures. Mostly merchant bodies themselves managed their transactions, of course fighting against the robbers and entering into understanding with local chieftains of the regions they passed through, often with very valuable goods. It is inappropriate to conceive these transactions as imports and exports between countries. However, societies with a differentiated economy, class-stratification, presence of a ruling aristocracy, and enough business agents capable of commissioning sea-going vessels could have conducted such scheduled commerce. Only in the regions forming part of big empires, there existed a kind of scheduled commerce with tariffs and tolls exacted as part of the revenue administration of rulers who had naturally made some arrangements for the maintenance of ports, marts, and exchange routes as well as for the security of caravans and mariners. Further, the mode of exchange was largely barter and never trade as such, which was feasible only in ports and marts under the ruling aristocracy with class-stratified societies of effective demand for goods from alien cultures. What turns up as strikingly significant here is that the whole historical imagination about Indo-Roman trade and India's maritime civilization celebrated in Indian historiography is a misnomer.

Bibliography

Adhya, G.L. (1966), *Early Indian Economics: Studies in the Economic Life of Northern and Western India, c. 200 B.C.–300 A.D.* Bombay: Asia Publishing House.

Agrawal, D.P., R.V. Krishnamurthy, and S. Kusumgar (1978), 'New Data on the Copper Hoards and the Daimabad Bronzes'. *Man and Environment* II: 41–6.

Aiyer, K.V.S. (1917), *Historical Sketches of the Dekhan*, Vol. I. Madras: Modern Print Works.

Ancient India (AI) ([1946] 1983), no. 2. New Delhi: Archaeological Survey of India [ASI].

AI ([1959] 1986), no. 15. New Delhi: ASI.

Arrien (1983), *Indica*, Book VII: 2–4. Translated by P.A. Brunt, Loeb Classical Library ed. Cambridge: Harvard University Press.

Avanzini, A. (2007), 'Sumhuram: A Hadrami Port on the Indian Ocean'. In *The Indian Ocean in the Ancient Period: Definite Places, Translocal Exchange*, edited by E.H. Seland, 29–31. Oxford: International Series, Archaeopress.

Bagnall, R.S., C. Helms, and A.M.F.W. Verhoogt (2000), *Documents from Berenike 1: Greek Ostraka from the 1996–1998 Seasons*. Bruxelles: Fondation Égyptologique Reine Élisabeth.

Ball, W. (2000), *Rome in the East: The Transformation of an Empire*. London and New York: Routledge.

Bang, P.F. (2008), *The Roman Bazaar: A Comparative Study of Trade and Markets in a Tributary Empire*. New York: Cambridge University Press.

Banerjee, N.R. (1965), *The Iron Age in India*. New Delhi: Munshiram Manoharlal.

Banerjee, N.R. and K.V.S. Rajan (1959), 'Sanur 1950 to 1952: A Megalithic Site in District Chinglepet'. *Ancient India* 15, no. 15: 4–8.

Begley, V. (1983), 'Arikamedu Reconsidered'. *American Journal of Archaeology* 87, no. 4: 461–81.

——— (1988), 'Rouletted Ware at Aricamedu: A New Approach'. *American Journal of Archaeology* (Boston: Archaeological Institute of America) 92, no. 3: 427–40.

Begley, V. and R.D. De Puma, eds (1991), *Rome and India: The Ancient Sea Trade*. Madison: University of Wisconsin Press.

Begley, V., P. Francis Jr., N. Karashima, K.V. Raman, S.E. Sidebotham, K.W. Slane, and E.L. Will, eds (1996), *The Ancient Port of Arikamedu: New Investigation and Researches 1989–1992*, Vol. 1. Pondicherry: Centre d'histoire et d'archéologie, École française d'Extrême-Orient.

——— (2004), *Arikamedu: Ancient Port City*, Vol. II. Pondicherry: École Française d'Extreme-Orient.

——— (2004), *The Ancient Port of Arikamedu: New Excavations and Researches 1989–1992*. Paris: Centre d'histoire et d'archéologie, École française d'Extrême-Orient.

Bhandarkar, R.G. (2001), *Early History of the Deccan*. Reprint, Delhi: Asian Educational Services.

Blue, L., R.J. Whitewright, and R. Thomas (2011), 'Ships and Ships' Fittings'. In *Myos Hormos—Quseir al-Qadim Roman and Islamic Ports on the Red Sea*, edited by D.P.S. Peacock and L. Blue, Vol. 2: *Finds from the Excavations 1999–2003*, BAR International Series 2286, 179–80. Oxford: Archaeopress.

Blue, L., R. Tomber, and S. Abraham, eds (2009), *Migration, Trade and Peoples*. The British Association for South Asian Studies, Part 1: 'Indian Ocean Commerce and the Archaeology of Western India', 29–41. London.

Bohannan, P. and G. Dalton, eds (1962), *Markets in Africa*. Evanston, IL: Northwestern University Press.

Bongard-Levin, G.M. (1973), *India in the Mauryan Period* (in Russian). Moscow: Nauka Publishers.

Bopearachchi, O. (1995), 'Recent Discoveries of Foreign Coins Hitherto Unknown in the Sri Lankan Context'. In *Sesquicentennial Commemoration Volume of Royal Asiatic Society of Sri Lanka 1845–1995*, edited by G.P.S.H. de Silva and C.G. Uragoda, 127–39. Colombo: Royal Asiatic Society Publication.

Bridget, A. and F.R. Allchin (1968), *The Birth of Indian Civilisation: India and Pakistan before 500 B.C.* Baltimore: Penguin Books.

Buhler, G. ([1886] 1984), *The Laws of Manu*. Oxford University Press. Reprint, Delhi: Motilal Banarsidass Publishers.

Burgess, J. (1883), *Report on the Buddhist Cave Temples and Their Inscriptions*, n.s. 4. New Delhi: Archaeological Survey of India.

Burnett, A. (1998), 'Roman Coins from India and Sri Lanka'. In *Origin, Evolution and Circulation of Foreign Coins in the Indian Ocean*, edited by D.P.M. Weerakkody and O. Bopearachchi, 179–89. New Delhi: Manohar Publishers.

Caldwell, R. (1856), 'Introduction'. In *A Comparative Grammar of the Dravidian or South-Indian Family of Languages*, 97. London: Harrison and Sons.

Cappers, R.T.J. (2006), *Roman Food Prints at Berenike: Archaeological Evidence of Subsistence and Trade in the Eastern Desert of Egypt*. Los Angeles: Costen Institute of Archaeology Monograph Series 55.

Carey, E., trans. (1904–27), *Dio's Roman History*, Vol. IX, Loeb Classical Library 117 (Harvard: Harvard University Press).

Carey, M. and E.H. Warmington (1963), *The Ancient Explorers*. Harmondsworth, Middlesex: Penguin Books Ltd.

Casal, J.M. (1949), *Fouilles de Virampatnam-Arikamedu* (Excavation of Virampattanam-Arikamedu). Paris: Imprimerie Nationale.

Casson, L. ([1959] 1991), *The Ancient Mariners: Seafarers and Sea Fighters of the Mediterranean in Ancient Times*. Victor Golancz, 2nd ed. Princeton: Princeton University Press.

——— (1984), 'The Sea Route to India: Periplus Maris Erythraei 57', *The Classical Quarterly*, n.s. 34, no. 2: 473–9.

——— (1986), 'P Vindob G 40822 and the Shipping of Goods from India', *BASP*, 23, nos 33–4: 73–9.

——— (1989), *The Periplus Maris Erythraei: Text with Introduction, Translation, and Commentary*. Princeton: Princeton University Press.

——— (1990), 'New Light on Maritime Loans: P. Vindob. G 40822'. *Zeitschrift fur Papyrologie und Epigraphik* (Bonn: Verlag Rudolf Habelt) 84, no. 3 (1990): 195–206.

——— (1991), 'Ancient Naval Technology and the Route to India'. In V. Begley and R.D. de Puma, eds, *Rome and India: The Ancient Sea Trade*, 8–11. Madison: University of Wisconsin Press.

——— ([1974] 1994), *Travel in the Ancient World*, 2nd ed. Baltimore: John Hopkins University Press.

——— (1995), *Ships and Seamanship in the Ancient World*. Baltimore: John Hopkins University Press.

Catsambis, A., B. Ford, and D. Hamilton, eds (2011), *The Oxford Handbook of Maritime Archaeology*. Oxford: Oxford University Press.

Chakrabarti, D.K. (1972–3), 'The Concept of Urban Revolution and the Indian Context'. *Purātatva* (Bulletin of the Indian Archaeological Society), no. 6: 27–31.

Chakraborty, H.P. (1966), *Trade and Commerce of Ancient India*. Kolkata: Academic Publishers.

Champakalakshmi, R. (1975–6), 'Archaeology and Tamil Literary Tradition'. *Puratatva* 8: 112.

——— (1996), *Trade, Ideology and Urbanization, South India 300 BC to AD 1300*. New Delhi: Oxford University Press.

Chanana, D.R. (1960), *Slavery in Ancient India: As Depicted in Pali and Sanskrit Texts*. New Delhi: People's Publishing House.

Chandra, M. (1977), *Trade and Trade Routes in Ancient India*. New Delhi: Abhinav Publications.

Charlesworth, M.P. (1928), *Trade-Routes and Commerce of the Roman Empire*. London: Cambridge University Press.

——— (1951), 'Roman Trade with India: A Resurvey'. In *Studies in Roman Economic and Social History in Honour of Allan Chester Johnson*, edited by P.R. Colman-Norton, 131–43. Princeton, NJ: Princeton University Press.

Chattopadhyaya, B.D. (1977), *Coins and Currency Systems in South India*. New Delhi: Munshiram Manoharlal Oriental Book Publishers.

——— (1987), 'Transition to the Early Historical Phase in the Deccan: A Note'. In *Archaeology and History: Essays in Memory of Shri A. Ghosh*, edited by B.M. Pande and B.D. Chattopadhyaya, 727–35. Delhi: Agam Kala Prakashan.

Cherian, P.J. (2007–10), *Interim Report of Pattanam Excavations*. Thiruvananthapuram: Kerala Council for Historical Research.

——— (2011), *Report on the Fifth Season Excavation at Pattanam*. Thiruvananthapuram: KCHR.

Cherian, P.J., G.V. Raviprasad, Koushik Datta, Dinesh Kumar Ray, V. Selvakumar, and K.P. Shajan (2009), 'Chronology of Pattanam: A Multi-cultural Port Site on the Malabar Coast'. *Current Science* (Bangalore) 97, no. 2: 236–40.

Cherian, P.J., V. Selvakumar, and K.P. Shajan (2007), 'Evidence for the Ancient Port of Muziri at Pattanam, Kerala'. *Chemmozhi* (Chennai: Centre of Excellence for Classical Tamil) 2, no. 1: 26–7.

Childe, V.G. (1950), 'The Urban Revolution'. *The Town Planning Review* 21, no. 1: 3–17.

Cunningham, A. (1891), *Coins of Ancient India: From the Earliest Times to the Seventh Century A.D.* (London: B. Quaritch).

Dalton, G. (1971), 'Traditional, Tribal and Peasant Economies: An Introductory Survey of Peasant Economy'. In *Modules in Anthropology*, edited by C.B. McCaleb, 28–34. Reading, MA: Addison-Wesley.

——— (1977), 'Aboriginal Economies in Stateless Societies'. In *Exchange Systems in Prehistory*, edited by T.K. Earle and J.E. Ericson, 191–212. New York: Academic Press.

Davids, R. (1921), *Vinayapiṭaka*, II (English trans.). London: Pali Text Society.

De Romanis, F. (1997), 'Rome and the *Nótia* of India: Relations between Rome and South India from BC to the Flavian Period'. In *Crossings: Early Mediterranean Contacts with India*, edited by F. De Romanis and A. Tchernia, 80–160. New Delhi: Manohar Publishers and Italian Embassy Cultural Centre.

——— (1997), 'Romanukharattha and Taprobane: Relations between Roe and Sri Lanka in the First Century A.D.'. In *Crossings: Early Mediterranean Contact with India*, edited by F. De Romanis and A. Tchernia, 157–237.

——— (2008), 'Muziris Trade in the Roman Economy'. In *The Living Dead and the Lost Knowledge*. Thiruvananthapuram: Department of Archaeology, Government of Kerala.

——— (2012), 'Playing Sudoku on the Verso of the *Muziris Papyrus*: Pepper, Malabathron and Tortoise Shell in the Cargo of the *Hermapollon*'. *Journal of Ancient Indian History* (Calcutta) 27: 75–101.

Dhavalikar, K. (1975), 'The Beginning of Coinage in India'. *World Archaeology* 6, no. 3 (London: Taylor & Francis, Ltd): 330–8.

Dhavalikar, M.K. (1988), *First Farmers of the Deccan*. Pune: Ravish Publishers.

Dikshitar, V.R.R. (1947), *Origin and Spread of the Tamils*, Adayar Library Series No. 58. Madras: Adayar Library.

Elliot, W. (1857–8), 'On the Sepulchral Remains of Southern India'. *Report of the British Association for Advancement of Science Transactions* XIX (O.S.): 227.

——— (1886), *Coins of Southern India*. London: Trubner.

Fauconnier, B. (2012), 'Graeco-Roman Merchants in the Indian Ocean: Revealing a Multi-cultural Trade'. *Topoi. Orient-Occident* (Université Lumière Lyon) 16, Supplement 11: 75–109.

Finley, M.I. (1985), *The Ancient Economy*, 2nd ed. Berkeley: University of California Press.

Firth, R. (1959), *Economics of the New Zealand Maori*. New Zealand: R.E. Owen, Government Printer.

Fitzpatrick, M.P. (2011), 'Provincialising Rome: The Indian Ocean Trade Network and Roman Imperialism'. *Journal of World History* 22, no. 1: 27–54.

Ford, L.A., A.M. Pollard, R.A.E. Coningham, and B. Stern (2005), 'A Geochemical Investigation of the Origin of Rouletted and Other Related South Asian Fine Wares'. *Antiquity* 79, no. 306: 909–20.

Florus, Lucius Annaeus (1929), *Epitome of Roman History*, translated by E.S. Forster, Loeb Classical Library edition. Harvard: Harvard University Press.

Francis, P. (1991), 'Beadmaking at Arikamedu and Beyond'. *World Archaeology* 23, no. 1: 28–43.

——— (2002), 'South Indian Stone Bead Making'. In *Asia's Maritime Bead Trade: 300 B.C. to the Present*, edited by P. Francis, 112–25. Honolulu: University of Hawaii Press.

French, D.H. and C.S. Lightfoot, eds (1989), *The Eastern Frontier of the Roman Empire: Proceedings of a Colloquium Held at Ankara in September 1988*. Oxford: British Archaeological Reports.

Fried, M.H. (1967), *The Evolution of Political Society*. New York: Random House.

Fuks, A. (1951), 'Notes on the Archive of Nicanor'. *Journal of Juristic Papyrology* 5: 207–16.

Fussman, G. (1991), 'Le Periple et l'histoire politique del'Inde'. *Journal Asiatique* (Paris) 279, no. 3/4 (1991): 37–8.

——— (1997), 'The *Periplus* and the Political History of India'. In *Crossings: Early Mediterranean Contacts with India*, edited by F. De Romanis and A. Tchernia, 66–71. New Delhi: Manohar Publishers and Italian Embassy Cultural Centre.

——— (1987–8) 'Central and Provincial Administration in Ancient India: The Problem of the Mauryan Empire'. *Indian Historical Review* XIV, nos 1–2: 46.

Garnsey, P., K. Hopkins, and C.R. Whittaker, eds (1983), *Trade in the Ancient Economy*. Berkeley, LA: University of California Press.

Ghosh, A. (1990), *The City in Early Historical India*. Shimla: Indian Institute of Advanced Studies. Reprint, New Delhi: Munshiram Manoharlal.

Godelier, M. (1977), *Perspectives in Marxist Anthropology*. New York: Cambridge University Press.

Graeber, D.R. (2001), *Toward an Anthropological Theory of Value: The False Coin of Our Own Dreams*. New York: Palgrave.

——— (2011), *Debt: The First Five Thousand Years*. Brooklyn, NY: Melville House Publishing.

Gregory, C.A. (1982), *Gifts and Commodities*. London: Academic Press.

——— (1994), 'Exchange and Reciprocity'. In *Companion Encyclopaedia of Anthropology: Humanity, Culture and Social Life*, edited by T. Ingold, 911–39. London: Routledge.

Gregory, C.A. (1997), *Savage Money: The Anthropology and Politics of Commodity Exchange*. Amsterdam: Harwood Academic.

Gupta, P.L. (1965), *The Early Coins from Kerala*. Thiruvananthapuram: Government of Kerala, Department of Archaeology.

——— (1972), 'The Coinage of the Sātavāhana: Types and Their Regional Distribution'. In *Coinage of the Sātavāhana and Coins from Excavations*, edited by A.M. Shastri (Nagpur: Nagpur University Press), 41–62.

Gurukkal, R. (1987), 'Problems of Agrarian Expansion in Early Iron Age'. In *Essays in Ancient Indian Economic History*, edited by B.D. Chattopadhyaya (Delhi: Indian History Congress Publications), 56–7.

——— (1989), 'Forms of Production and Forest of Change in Ancient Tamil Society'. *Studies in History*, n.s. V, no. 2: 159–75.

——— (1993–4), 'From Clan and Lineage to Hereditary Occupation Groups and Caste in Early South India'. *Indian Historical Review* (ICHR Publications) XXII, nos 1–2: 22–33.

——— (2002), 'Antecedents of the State Formation in South India'. In *State and Society in Pre-modern South India*, edited by R. Champakalakshmi, Kesavan Veluthat, and T.R. Venugopalan, 39–59. Thrissur: Cosmo Books.

——— (2010), *Social Formations in Early South India*. New Delhi: Oxford University Press.

——— (2013), 'Classical Indo-Roman Trade: A Misnomer in Political Economy'. *Economic and Political Weekly* XLVIII, nos 26 and 27: 67–78.

——— (2014), 'Classical Indo-Roman Trade: A Historiographical Reconsideration'. *Indian Historical Review* 40, no. 2: 181–206.

Gurukkal, R. and D. Whittaker (2001), 'In Search of Muziris'. *Journal of Roman Archaeology* (Cambridge: Cambridge University Press) 14: 335–50.

Gurukkal, R. and M.R.R. Varier (1999), *Cultural History of Kerala*, Vol. I. Thiruvananthapuram: Department of Cultural Publications, Government of Kerala.

Handley, F.J.L. (2011), 'The Textiles: A Preliminary Report'. In *Myos Hormos—Quseir Al-Qadim: A Roman and Islamic Port on the Red Sea Coast of Egypt*, edited by D.P.L. Peacock and L. Blue, Vol. 2, *Finds from the 1999–2003 Seasons*, BAR International Series 2286, 321–34. Oxford: Archaeopress.

Harris, W.V., ed. (2008), *The Monetary Systems of the Greeks and Romans*. Oxford: Oxford University Press.

Healy, J.F. (1991), *Pliny the Elder, Natural History: A Selection*. London: Penguin Classics.

Hegde, K.T.M (1985), 'Scientific Studies in Archaeology'. In *Recent Advances in Indian Archaeology*, edited by S.B. Deo and K. Paddayy, 100–4. Pune: Deccan College Publications.

Herskovits, M.J. (1940), *The Economic Life of the Primitive People*. London and New York: Knopf Publishers.

Hill, J.E. (2009), *Through the Jade Gate to Rome: A Study of the Silk Routes during the Later Han Dynasty, First and Second Centuries CE*. Lexington: Book Surge.

Hopkins, K. (1983), 'Introduction'. In *Trade in the Ancient Economy*, edited by P. Garnsey, K. Hopkins, and C.R. Whittaker, x–xviii. Berkeley, LA: University of California Press.

——— (2002), 'Rome, Taxes, Rents and Trade'. In *The Ancient Economy*, edited by W. Scheidel and S. Von Reden, 190–230. Edinburgh: Edinburgh University Press.

Humphrey, C. and S. Hugh-Jones (1992), *Barter, Exchange, and Value: An Anthropological Approach*. Cambridge: Cambridge University Press.

Indian Archaeology—A Review [IAR] 1961–62 (1964), edited by A. Ghosh. New Delhi: Archaeological Survey of India (ASI).

IAR 1962–63 (1965), New Delhi: ASI.

IAR 1963–64 (1967), New Delhi: ASI.

IAR 1964–65 (1969), New Delhi: ASI.

IAR 1965–66 (1973), New Delhi: ASI.

IAR 1954–55 ([1955] 1993), New Delhi: ASI.

IAR 1955–56 ([1956] 1993), New Delhi: ASI.

IAR 1956–57 ([1957] 1993), New Delhi: ASI.

IAR 1957–58 ([1958] 1993), New Delhi: ASI.

Interim Report of Paṭṭaṇam Excavations. Thiruvananthapuram: KCHR Publication, 2007–10.

Iyar, A.N., ed. (1956), *Nattrinai*. Tirunelveli: The South India Saiva Siddhantha Works Publishing Society Ltd.

Iyar, U.V.S., ed. (1947), *Kuṛuntokai*, 2nd ed. Madras: Thyagarajavilasam Publications.

——— (1961), *Pattuppāṭṭu* with the commentary of Nāccinārkkiṉṉiyar, 6th ed. Madras: Thyagarajavilasam Publications, 288–433.

——— (1963), *Puṛanāṉūṟu* with old commentary, 6th ed. Madras: Thyagarajavilasam Publications.

Janssens, K.H.A., ed. (2013), *Modern Methods for Analysing Historical Glass*. London: John Wiley & Sons Ltd.

Jayaswal, K.P. ([1929–30] 1983), 'The Hathigumbha Inscription of Kharavela'. In *Epigraphia Indica*, edited by H. Sastri, XX, 72–4. Reprint, New Delhi: Archaeological Survey of India.

Jones, A.H.M. (1974), *The Roman Economy: Studies in Ancient Economic and Administrative History*. Oxford: Oxford University Press.

Judd, T. (2007), 'The Trade with India through the Eastern Desert of Egypt under the Roman Empire'. Rev. version, Special Paper, University of Liverpool, England, pp. 1–18.

Kail, O.C. (1975), *Buddhist Cave Temples of India*. Bombay: D.B. Taraporevala.

Kailasapathy, K. (1968), *Tamil Heroic Poetry*. Oxford: Clarendon Press.

Karanth, R.V., K. Krishnan, and K.T.M. Hegde (1986), 'Petrography of Lime Plaster'. *Journal of Archaeological Science* 13, no. 6: 543–51.

Kasinathan, N., A. Abdul Majeed, D. Thulasiraman, and S. Vasanthi (1992), *Alagankulam: A Preliminary Report*. Madras: State Department of Archaeology.

Kelly, G. (2009), 'Craft Production and Technology during the Iron Age to Early Historic Transition at Kodumanal, Tamil Nadu', *Tamil Civilization*, 23 (October–December): 1–14.

Kennedy, R.S. (1976), 'The King in Early South India as Chieftain and the Emperor'. *Indian Historical Review* 3, no. 1: 1–15.

Kennet, D. (2009), *Report on the TGP from Pattanam Excavation 2007 Season*. Thiruvananthapuram: Kerala Council for Historical Research.

Kessler, D. and P. Temin (2007), 'The Organization of the Grain Trade in the Early Roman Empire'. *Economic History Review* 60, no. 2: 313–32.

Krishnamurthy, R. (1991), *Pāndyar Peruvaḻuti-nāṇayangal* (Coins of the Pāṇḍyan Peruvaḻūti). Madras: Garnet Publications.

——— (1991), *Cankakāla Cōḻar Nāṇayangal* (Cōḻa Coins of the Sangam Age). Madras: Garnet Publications.

——— (1992), 'Mākkōtai Coins'. In *Studies in South Indian Coins*, edited by A.V.N. Murthy, Vol. II, 89–94. Chennai: New Era Publications.

——— (1994), *Late Roman Copper Coins from South India: Karūur, Madurai and Tirukkoilūr*. Chennai: Garnet Publishers.

——— (1997), *Sangam Age Tamil Coins*. Madras: Garnet Publications.

Leshnik, L.S. (1974), *South Indian 'Megalithic' Burials: The Pāndukal Complex*. Wiesbaden: Franz Steiner Verlag.

Levi A. and M. Levi (1967), *Itineraria picta: Contributo allo studio della Tabula Peutingeriana* (Picturesque Itineraries: Contribution to the Study of Peutinger Tables). Rome: L'Erma di Bretschneider.

Luders, H. (1912), 'A List of Brahmi Inscriptions from Earliest Times to about A.D. 400 with the Exception of those of Aśoka', Appendix to *Epigraphia Indica*, edited by S. Konow, Vol. X-1909-10. Calcutta: Government Printing.

Mahadevan, I. (2003), *Early Tamil Epigraphy from the Earliest Times to the Sixth Century A.D.*, Harvard Oriental Series 62. Harvard: Harvard University Press.

Mahalingam, T.V. (1970), *Report on the Excavations in the Lower Kavery Valley*. Madras: Madras University Press.

Majumdar, R.C. (1960), *Classical Accounts of India*. Calcutta: Firma K.L. Mukhopadhyay Publishers.

——— (2003), *Ancient India*, 210–16. Reprint, New Delhi: Motilal Banarsidass Publishers.

Malinowski, B. (1922), *Argonauts of the Western Pacific: An Account of Native Enterprise and Adventure in the Archipelagos of Melanesian New Guinea*. London: Routledge & Kegan Paul.

Mangala, S.J. (1999), 'Coins of the Feudatories and Contemporaries of the Sātavāhana'. In *The Age of the Sātavāhana*, edited by A.M. Shastri, 2 vols (New Delhi: Aryan Books International), 360–90.

Maloney, C. (1976), 'Archaeology in South India: Accomplishments and Prospects'. In *Essays on South India*, edited by Burton Stein, 1–40. New Delhi: Vikas Publishing House.

Manning, J.G. (2008), 'Coinage as "Code" in Ptolemaic Egypt'. In *The Monetary System of the Greeks and Romans*, edited by W.V. Harris. Oxford: Oxford University Press.

Marx, K. (1959), *Economic and Philosophical Manuscript, 1844*, translated by M. Milligan. Moscow: Progressive Publishers.

——— (1990), *Capital*, Vol. I. London: Penguin Classics.

Mathew, A. and S. Raju, 'Inching towards *Nelcynda*', *Rational Discourse* (Thiruvalla: Marthoma College Publications) XII, nos 1 and 2: 5–17.

Mauss, M. (1954), *The Gift: Forms and Functions of Exchange in Archaic Societies*. London: Cohen & West.

McCrindle, J.W. (1927), *Ancient India as Described by Ptolemy*. Reprint, New Delhi: Munshiram Manoharlal.

——— (1987), *Ancient India as Described in Classical Literature*. Orient Books; repr., Patna: Eastern Book House, 144–5.

McLaughlin, R. (2010), *Rome and the Distant East: Trade Routes to the Ancient Lands of Arabia, India and China*. London: Bloomsbury Publishing.

——— (2014), *The Roman Empire and the Indian Ocean: Rome's Dealings with the Ancient Kingdoms of India Africa and Arabia*. Barnsley, South Yorkshire: Pen & Sword.

Meredith, D. (1954), 'Eastern Desert of Egypt: Notes on Inscriptions: 2, Mons Claudianus Nos. 22–40', *Chronique d'Egypte* 29: 103–23.

——— (1953), 'Annius Plocamus: Two Inscriptions from the Berenice Road'. *Journal of Roman Studies* (Cambridge) 43, nos 1–2: 38–40.

Middleton, J. and D. Tait, eds (1970), *Tribes Without Rulers*. London: Routledge & Kegan Paul Ltd.

Miller, J.I. (1969), *The Spice Trade of the Roman Empire 29 B.C.–A.D. 641*. Oxford: Clarendon Press.

Mirashi, V.V. (1981), *The History and Inscriptions of Satavahanas and Kshatrapas.* Bombay: Maharashtra State Board for Literature and Culture.

Mirashi, V.V. (1972), 'Wategaon Hoard of Satavahana Coins', JNSI, pt-ii: 205–12.

Mitra, D. (1971), *Buddhist Monuments.* Calcutta: Sahitya Samsad.

Mookerji, R.K. (1966), *Chandragupta Maurya and His Times,* 4th ed. Madras: Motilal Banarsidass Publishers.

Morley, N. (2007), *Trade in Classical Antiquity.* Cambridge: Cambridge University Press.

Morrison, K.D. (1995), 'Trade, Urbanism, and Agricultural Expansion: Buddhist Monastic Institutions and the State in Early Historic Western Deccan', *World Archaeology* 27, no. 2 (London: Routledge): 203–21.

Mukherji, R.K. (1912), *Indian Ship-building: A History of the Sea-borne Trade and Maritime Activity of the Indians from Earliest Times.* Calcutta: Longmans Green and Co.

Nair, B. (1977), *The Problem of Dravidian Origins: A Linguistic Archaeological and Anthropological Approach.* Madras: Madras University Press.

Narasaiah, B. (1980), *Neolithic and Megalithic Culture in Tamil Nadu.* Delhi: Sandeep Prakashan.

Narayanan, M.G.S. (1977), 'New Light on Chilappatikaram and the Date of Kunavayirkottam'. In *Re-interpretations in South Indian History,* 66–82. Trivandrum.

Orosius (2010), *Seven Books of History against the Pagans,* translated by A.T. Fear. Liverpool: Liverpool University Press.

Panikkar, K.M. (1945), *India and the Indian Ocean: An Essay on the Influence of Sea Power on Indian History.* London: G. Allen & Unwin Ltd.

——— ([1947] 1985), *India through the Ages,* originally published in London. Delhi: Discovery Publishing House.

Parasher-Sen, A. (1993), *Social and Economic History of Early Deccan: Some Interpretations.* New Delhi: Manohar Publishers.

——— (1999), 'Urban Settlements in the Deccan and Sātavāhana History'. In *The Age of the Sātavāhanas,* edited by A.M. Shastri, Vol. I, 159–89. New Delhi: Aryan Books International.

Parker, C. (1990), 'Classical Antiquity: The Maritime Dimension', *Antiquity* (Cambridge) 64, no. 243: 335–46.

Pavan, A. (2011), 'Sumhuram as International Centre: The Imported Pottery'. In *Along the Aroma and Spice Routes: The Harbour of Sumhuram, Its and the Trade between the Mediterranean, Arabia and India,* edited by A. Avanzini, 99–112. Roma: L'Erma di Bretschneider.

Pavan, A. and H. Schenk (2013), 'Crossing the Indian Ocean before the Periplus: A Comparison of Pottery Assemblages at the Sites of Sumhuram (Oman) and Tissamaharama (Sri Lanka)'. *Arabian Archaeology and Epigraphy* (Australia: Sydney University) 23, no. 2: 191–201.

Peacock, D. and L. Blue, eds (2006), *Myos Hormos—Quseir al-Qadim, Roman and Islamic Ports on the Red Sea*, Vol. 1: *Survey of the Excavations 1999–2003*, University of Southampton Series in Archaeology, 6. Oxford, GB: Archaeopress.

——— (2011), *Myos Hormos—Quseir al-Qadim, Roman and Islamic ports on the Red Sea*, Vol. 2: *Finds from the Excavations 1999–2003*, University of Southampton Series in Archaeology, 6. Oxford, GB: Archaeopress.

Peter, M. (2010), 'Revisiting Indian Rouletted Ware and the Impact of Indian Ocean Trade in Early Historic South Asia'. *Antiquity* (London: Cambridge University Press) 84, no. 326: 1043–54.

Philostratus, F. (1912), *Life of Appollonius of Tyana*, translated by F.C. Conybeare. London: William Heinemann, Loeb Classical Library, 3.35.

Pillai, A.D., ed. (1949), *Patirruppattu*. Tirunelveli: The South India Saiva Siddhantha Works Publishing Society Ltd.

Pillai, V.K. ([1904] 1997), *The Tamils Eighteen Hundred Years Ago*. Madras: Madras University Press.

Pillay, K.K.P. (1963), *South India and Ceylon*. Madras: Madras University Press.

Pisipaty, S.R.K. (2010), *Andhra Culture: An Obscure Phase in the Early Historical Archaeology of Andhra Pradesh*. Delhi: Agam Kala Prakashan.

Pliny the Elder (1938–63), *Natural History*, 10 volumes, Vol. VI, translated by H. Rackham, 104. Cambridge: Harvard University Press.

——— (1991), *Natural History*, translated by J.F. Healy. London: Penguin Books.

Polanyi, K. (1957), 'The Economy as Instituted Process'. In *Trade and Market in Early Empires*, edited by K. Polanyi, C.M. Arensberg, and H.W. Pearson, 241–70. Illinois: Glencoe III: The Free Press.

——— ([1944] 1957), *The Great Transformation*. London: Beacon Paper Back.

Polanyi, K., C. Arensberg, and H.W. Pearson, eds (1957), *Trade and Markets in the Early Empires: Economies in History and Theory* (Glencoe, IL: The Free Press, 1957), 243–70.

Potter, D.S. and D.J. Mattingly, eds (1999), *Life, Death and Entertainment in the Roman Empire*. Michigan: University of Michigan Press.

Prasad, P.C. (1977), *Foreign Trade and Commerce in Ancient India*. New Delhi: Abhinav Publications.

Prasad, R. (2008), 'Cultural Map of Andhradesa from Earliest Ties to AD 300'. In *Comprehensive History and Culture of Andhra Pradesh*, Vol. II: *Early Historic Andhra Pradesh*, edited by I.K. Sarma, 287–308 (New Delhi: Tulika Books, 2008).

Rajan, K. (1994), *Archaeology of Tamil Nadu (Kongu Country)*. New Delhi: Book India Publishing Co.

Rajan, K. (1998), 'Traditional Bead Making Industry in Tamil Nadu'. *Purātattva* (Ghaziabad: Indian Archaeological Society) 28: 59–63.

——— (1998), 'Further Excavations at Kodumanal'. *Man and Environment* (Pune: Indian Society for Prehistoric and Quarternary Studies) 23, no. 2: 65–76.

——— (2004), 'Traditional Gemstone Cutting Technology of Kongu Region in Tamil Nadu'. *Indian Journal of History of Science* 39, no. 4: 385–414.

Rao, B.K.G. (1972), *Megalithic Culture in South India*. Mysore: Prasaranga.

Rao, M.R. (1961), *Sātavāhana Coins in the Andhra Pradesh Government Museum*, A.P. Government Series No. 2. Hyderabad.

Rapson, E.J. (1897), *Indian Coins*. London: Trubner & Co.

Rathbone, D. (2000), 'The "Muziris" Papyrus (SB XVIII 13167): Financing Roman Trade with India'. In *Alexandrian Studies II in Honour of Mostafa el Abbadi*, 39–50. Alexandria: Societé Archéologique d'Alexandrie.

Ratnagar, S.F. (1981), *Encounters: The Westerly Trade of Harappan Civilisation*. New Delhi: Oxford University Press.

——— (1995), 'Archaeological Perspectives on Early Indian Societies'. In *Recent Perspectives of Early Indian History*, edited by R. Thapar, 1–52. Bombay: Popular Prakashan.

——— (2007), *Makers and Shapers: Early Indian Technology in the Home, Village and Urban Workshop*. New Delhi: Tulika Books.

Rawlinson, H.G. (1916), *Intercourse between India and the Western World*. Cambridge: Cambridge University Press.

Ray, H.P. (1986), *Monastery and Guild: Commerce under the Sātavāhana*. New Delhi: Oxford University Press.

——— (1994), 'The Western Indian Ocean and the Early Maritime Links of the Indian'. *Indian Economic and Social History Review* 31, no. 1: 65–88.

——— (1994), *The Winds of Change: Buddhism and the Maritime Links of Early South Asia*. New Delhi: Oxford University Press.

——— (1995), 'A Resurvey of Roman contacts with the East'. *Athens, Aden, Arikamedu: Essays on the Interrelations between India, Arabia and the Eastern Mediterranean*, edited by M.F. Boussac and J.F. Salles, 97–114. New Delhi: Manohar Publishers.

——— (1996), 'Early Coastal Trade in the Bay of Bengal'. In *The Indian Ocean in Antiquity*, edited by J. Reade, 351–64. London: Kegan Paul.

——— (2003), *Trade and Trade Routes between India and China c. 14 BC–AD 1500*. Kolkata: Progressive Publishers.

Rea, A. (1902–3), 'Adichchanallur Excavations'. In *Annual Report of the Archaeological Department Southern Circle, Madras and Coorg*, 11–14. Madras: Archaeological Survey of India, Southern Circle.

Reddy, D.R. and P.S. Reddy (1983), *Coins of the Satraps of the Sātavāhana Era*. Hyderabad: Numismatic Society of Hyderabad Publication.

Reddy, P.K. (1998), 'God, Trade and Worship: A Glimpse into the Region of Early Andhradesa'. *East and West* (Rome: Istituto Italiano per l'Africa e l'Oriente) 48, nos 3–4: 291–311.

Renfrew, C. (1975), 'Trade as Action at a Distance: Questions of Integration and Communication'. In *Ancient Civilisation and Trade*, edited by J.A. Sabloff and L.C.C. Karloski, 3–59. Albuquerque: University of New Mexico Press.

——— (1977), 'Alternative Models for Exchange and Spatial Distribution', in *Exchange Systems in Prehistory*, edited by T.K. Earle and J.E. Ericson, 71–89. New York: Academic Press.

Rostovtzeff, M. (1957), *Social and Economic History of the Roman Empire*, 2 vols, revised by P.M. Fraser. Oxford: Oxford University Press.

Sahlins, M. (1968), *Tribesmen*. Englewood Cliffs, NJ: Prentice-Hall.

——— (1972), *Stone Age Economics*. Chicago and New York: Aldine-Atherton Inc.

Salomon, R. (1991), 'Epigraphic Remains of Indian Traders in Egypt'. *Journal of the American Oriental Society* 111, no. 4: 731–36.

Sankalia, H.D. and S.B. Deo (1955), *Report on the Excavations at Nasik and Jorwe 1950–1951*. Pune: Deccan College Publications.

Sankalia, H.D., B. Subbarao, and S.B. Deo (1958), *Excavations at Maheshwar and Navdatoli, 1952–53*. Pune: Deccan College Publications.

Sarma, I.K. (1988), *Studies in Early Buddhist Monuments and Brahmi Inscriptions of Andhradesa*. Nagpur: Dattsons Publishers.

Sastri, K.A.N. (1939), *Foreign Notices of South India*. Madras: Madras University Press.

——— (1972), *The Sangam Literature: Its Cults and Cultures*. Madras: Swathy Publishers.

Sastri, R.S., ed. (1909), *Arthaśāstra* of Kautilya, Bibliotheca Sanskrita 37. Mysore: University of Mysore Oriental Library Publication Series.

Sastry, V.V.K. (1983), *The Proto and Early Historical Culture of Andhra Pradesh*, AP Archaeological Series 58. Hyderabad: Government of Andhra Pradesh.

Scheidel, W. and Von Reden, S., eds (2002), *The Ancient Economy*. Edinburgh: Edinburgh University Press.

Schneider, H.K. (1980), *Livestock and Equality in East Africa: The Economic Basis for Social Structure*. Bloomington and London: Indiana University Press.

Schoff, W.H., trans. and ed. (1912), *The Periplus of the Erythraean Sea: Travel and Trade in the Indian Ocean by a Merchant of the First Century*. New York: Longmans, Green and Co.

Senart, E. (1906), 'The Inscriptions in the Caves at Nasik'. In *Epigraphia Indica*, Vol. VIII, edited by E. Hultzsch, 59–96. Calcutta: Superintendent, Government Printing.

Selvakumar, V., K.P. Shajan, and R. Tomber (2009), 'Archaeological Investigations at Pattanam, Kerala: New Evidence for the Location of Ancient Muziris'. In *Migration, Trade and Peoples*, edited by L. Blue, R. Tomber, and S. Abraham, The British Association for South Asian Studies, Part 1, 'Indian Ocean Commerce and the Archaeology of Western India', 29–41. London: British Academy Publications.

Selvakumar, V., P.K. Gopi, and K.P. Shajan (2005), 'Trial Excavations at Pattanam, Paravur Taluk, Ernakulam District, Kerala—A Preliminary Report'. *Journal of the Centre for Heritage Studies* 2 (Tripunithura: Centre for Heritage Studies Publication): 57–66.

Seneviratne, S. (1993), 'From *Kudi* to *Nadu*: A Suggested Framework for the Study of the Pre-state Political Formations in Early Iron Age South India'. *The Sri Lanka Journal of the Humanities* (Kandy: University of Peradeniya) 19, nos 1–2: 57–77.

Service, E.R. (1975), *Origins and the State and Civilisation*. New York: W.W. Norton & Co. Inc.

Sewell, R. (1882), *Lists of* the *Antiquarian Remains in the Presidency of Madras*, Vol. I. Madras: Archaeological Survey of Southern India Publication.

——— (1904), 'Roman Coins Found in India'. *Journal of the Royal Asiatic Society of Great Britain & Ireland* (Cambridge: Cambridge University Press), n.s., XXIII, no. 36: 591–637.

K.P. Shajan, V. Sevakumar, and P.J. Cherian (2004), 'Locating the Ancient Port of Muziris: Fresh findings from Paṭṭaṇam'. *Journal of Roman Archaeology* (Cambridge: Cambridge University Press) 17 (2004): 312–20.

Shajan, K.P. and V. Selvakumar (2007), 'Pattanam: The First Iron Age Early Historic Settlement of Kerala'. In *Archaeology in Kerala: Past and Present*, edited by M.R. Manmathan. Kozhikode: Feroke College Publications.

Shanmugam, P. (2003), *Cankakāla Kācu Iyal* (Numismatics of the Sangam Age Coins). Chennai: International Institute of Tamil Studies.

Sharma, R.S. (1996), *Aspects of Political Ideas and Institutions in Ancient India*. Reprint, New Delhi: Motilal Banarsidass Publishers.

Sastri, H.K., ed. (1926), *Epigraphia Indica*, Vol. XVIII, 1925–26. Calcutta: Government Printing.

Siculus, Diodorus (1935), Book II: 41, Loeb Classical Library ed. Cambridge: Harvard University Press.

Sidebotham, S.E. (1989), 'Ports of the Red Sea and the Arabia–India Trade'. In *The Eastern Frontier of the Roman Empire: Proceedings of a Colloquium*

Held at Ankara in September 1988, edited by D.H. French and C.S. Lightfoot, 485–513. Oxford: British Archaeological Reports.

——— (2011), *Berenike and the Ancient Maritime Spice Route*, California World History Library, 18. California: University of California Press.

Sidebotham, S.E., M. Hense, and H.M. Nouwens (2008), *The Red Land: The Illustrated Archaeology of Egypt's Eastern Desert*. Cairo: The American University in Cairo Press.

Sidebotham, S.E. and W.Z. Wendrich, eds (1999), *Berenike 1997. Report of the 1997 Excavations at Berenike and the Survey of the Eastern Desert, Including Excavations at Shenshef*, CNWS Special Series 3. Leiden: Research School CNWS, School of Asian, African and Amerindian Studies.

——— (2000), *Report of the 1998 Excavations at Barenike and the Survey of the Egyptian Eastern Desert, Including Excavations at Wadi Kalalat*. Leiden: Research School of Asian, African and Amerindian Studies (CNWS) Publication.

——— (2002), 'Berenike: A Ptolemaic Roman Port on the Ancient Maritime Spice and Incense Route'. *Minerva*, 13, no. 3.

Sivathamby, K. (1974), 'Early South Indian Economy: The *Tiṇai* Concept'. *Social Scientist* (New Delhi) 3, no. 29: 20–37.

Smith, A. ([1776] 1950), *An Inquiry into the Nature and Causes of the Wealth of Nations*, sixth ed., 2 vols. London: Methuen.

Smith, V.A. (1924), *The Early History of India*, 4th ed., 400. London: Oxford University Press.

Sridhar, T.S., D. Thulasiraman, S. Selvaraj, and S. Vasanthi (2005), *Alagankulam: An Ancient Roman Port City of Tamil Nadu*. Chennai: Tamil Nadu Department of Archaeology.

Srinivasan, S. (2006), 'Megalithic High-tin Bronzes: Ethnoarchaeological and Archaeometallurgical Insights on Manufacture and Possible Artistic and Musical Significance'. *Man and Environment* XXXI, no. 2: 1–8.

——— (2010), 'Megalithic High-tin Bronzes and India's Living Prehistory'. In *50 Years of Archaeology in Southeast Asia: Essays in Honour of Ian Glover*, edited by B. Bellina, E. Bacus, and O. Pryce, 260–71. Bangkok: River Books.

——— (2013), 'Megalithic and Surviving Binary High-tin Bronze Traditions in Southern India: Tracing Binary Bronze Usage to Harappan Times'. *Transactions of the Indian Institute of Metals* 66, nos 5–6: 731–7.

Srivastava, B. (1968), *Trade and Commerce in Ancient India: From the Earliest Times to c. A.D. 300*. Varanasi: Chowkhamba Sanskrit Series Office.

Strabo (1917–32), *Geography*, translated by H.L. Jones, eight volumes. Cambridge: Harvard University Press.

Strauch, I. and M.D. Bukharin (2004), 'Indian Inscriptions from the Cave Hoq on Soquotra (Yemen)'. *Annali dell 'Instituto Orientale di Napoli* (AION) 64: 121–38.

Subbarayalu, Y. (1992), Unpublished Report on Kodumanal Excavation. Thanjavur: Tamil University.

——— (2008), 'Pottery Inscriptions of Tamil Nadu—A Comparative View'. In *Airavati: Felicitation Volume in Honour of Iravatham Mahadevan*, edited by R. Kalaikkovan and M. Maldini. Chennai: Varalaru.com.

——— (2012), 'Contacts between the North and the South: An Epigraphical Perspective', Foundation Day Lecture. New Delhi: ICHR.

Subramanian, N. (1966), *The Sagam Polity*. Delhi: Asia Publishing House.

Sundara, A. (1975), *The Early Chamber Tombs of South India: A Study of the Iron Age Megalithic Monuments of North Karnataka*. Delhi: University Publishers.

Suresh, B. (2007), *Arikamedu: Its Place in the Ancient Rome–India Contacts*, 70–1. New Delhi: Embassy of Italy and Manohar Publishers.

Suresh, S. (2004), *Symbols of Trade: Roman and Pseudo-Roman Objects Found in India*. New Delhi: Manohar Publishers.

Tchernia, A. (1997), 'Winds and Coins: From the Supposed Discovery of the Monsoon to the *Denarii* of Tiberius'. In *Crossings: Early Mediterranean Contacts with India*, edited by F. De Romanis and A. Tchernia, 238–49. New Delhi: Manohar Publishers and Italian Embassy Cultural Centre.

Thapar, Romila (1961), *Asoka and the Decline of the Mauryas* (New Delhi: Oxford University Press, 1961), 256.

——— (1978), '*Dāna* and *Dakshiṇa* as Forms of Exchange'. In *Ancient Indian Social History*, 94–108. New Delhi: Orient Blackswan.

——— (1984), *From Lineage to State, Social Formations of Mid-first Millennium BC in the Ganga Valley*. New Delhi: Oxford University Press.

——— (1992), 'Black Gold: South Asia and the Roman Maritime Trade', *South Asia*, n.s. 15, no. 2: 1–27.

——— (1997), *Asoka and the Decline of the Mauryas*, 3rd ed. New Delhi: Oxford University Press.

——— (1997), 'Early Mediterranean Contacts with India: An Overview'. In *Crossings: Early Mediterranean Contacts with India*, edited by F. De Romanis and A. Tchernia, 11–40. New Delhi: Manohar Publishers and Italian Embassy Cultural Centre.

Tomber, R. (2000), 'Indo-Roman Trade: The Ceramic Evidence from Egypt', *Antiquity* 74, no. 285 (Cambridge: Cambridge University Press): 624–31.

——— (2005), 'Amphorae from Pattanam', *Journal of the Centre for Heritage Studies* (Tripunithura) 2: 67–8.

Thapar, Romila (2008), *Indo-Roman Trade: From Pots to Pepper*. London: Gerald Duckworth & Co. Ltd.

——— (2008), 'The Imported Pottery at Pattanam: External Contacts and Trading Partners'. In *The Living Dead and the Lost Knowledge*. Thiruvananthapuram: Department of Archaeology, Government of Kerala.

——— (2012), 'From the Roman Red Sea to Beyond the Empire: Egyptian Ports and Their Trading Partners'. *British Museum Studies in Ancient Egypt and Sudan* 18: 201–15.

van der Veen, Marijke (2011). *Consumption, Trade and Innovation: Exploring the Botanical Remains from the Roman and Islamic Ports at Quesir al-Qadim, Egypt*. Frankfurt am Main: Africa Magna Verlag.

van der Veen, Marijke, A. Cox, and J. Morales (2011), 'The Plant Remains Evidence of Trade and Cuisine'. In *Myos Hormos—Quseir al-Qadim, Roman and Islamic Ports on the Red Sea*, Vol. 2: *Finds from the Excavations 1999–2003*, edited by D.P.S. Pracock and L. Blue, University of Southampton Series in Archaeology No. 6, 227–34. Oxford: Archaeopress, 2011.

Varier, M.R.R. (1998), 'Production and Exchange in the Littoral Tracts of Ancient South India', Working Paper (Kottayam: School of Social Sciences, Mahatma Gandhi University).

——— (2008), 'Graffiti and Brāhmi Letters from Pattanam: A Note on Continuity and Change in the Art of Writing'. In *The Living Dead and the Lost Knowledge*, 35–6. Thiruvananthapuram: Department of Archaeology, Government of Kerala.

Vasanthi, S., S. Selvaraj, D. Thulasiraman, and T. Śrītar (2005), *Alagankulam: An Ancient Roman Port City of Tamil Nadu*. Chennai: State Department of Archaeology, Government of Tamil Nadu.

Veyne, P. (2002), *The Roman Empire*. California: Harvard University Press.

Warmington, E.H. (1928), *The Commerce between the Roman Empire and India*, 2nd ed. Cambridge: Cambridge University Press.

Weerakkody, D.P.M. (1995), 'Roman Coins of Sri Lanka: Some Observations'. *The Sri Lanka Journal of the Humanities* (Kandy: University of Peradeniya) 21, nos 1–2: 1–30.

——— (1997), *Taprobane: Ancient Sri Lanka as known to Greeks and Romans*. Turnhout: Brepols.

Wheeler, R.E.M. (1946), 'Arikamedu'. *Ancient India* (New Delhi: Archaeological Survey of India) 1, no. 2: 17–124.

——— (1947), 'Brahmagiri and Chandravalli Excavations'. *Ancient India* 1, no. 4: 221–2.

——— (1954), *Rome Beyond the Imperial Frontiers*, 124–5. London: Bell and Sons.

Whitewright, R.J. (2007), 'How Fast Is Fast? Technology, Trade and Speed under Sail in the Roman Red Sea'. In *Natural Resources and Cultural Connections of the Red Sea*, edited by J. Starkey, P. Starkey, and T. Wilkinson, Red Sea Project III, British Archaeological Reports, International Series 1661, 77–87. Oxford: Archaeopress.

——— (2007), 'Roman Rigging Material from the Red Sea Port of Myos Hormos'. *The International Journal of Nautical Archaeology* 36, no. 2: 282–92.

——— (2008), *Maritime Technological Change in the Ancient Mediterranean: The Invention of the Lateen Sail*, Vols 1 and 2. Unpublished PhD dissertation, University of Southampton.

Whittaker, C.R. (2004), *Rome and Its Frontiers: The Dynamics of the Empire*. New York: Routledge.

——— (2009), 'Conjuctures and Conjuctures: Kerala and Roman Trade'. *South Asian Studies* 25, no. 1: 1–9.

Wild, F.C. (Spring 2002), 'The Webbing from Berenike: A Classification'. *Archaeological Textiles News Letter*, 34: 9–16.

Wild, J.P. and F.C. Wild (2001), 'Sails from the Roman Port of Berenike'. *International Journal of Nautical Archaeology* 30, no. 2: 211–20.

Young, G.K. (2001), *Rome's Eastern Trade. International Commerce and Imperial Policy 31 BC–AD 305*. London and New York: Routledge.

Index

Bay of Bengal, 69, 80, 137, 194, 199, 207, 246
bead-making, 27–8, 33, 135, 178, 187, 192, 215
Becare village, 64, 66, 160–1, 167, 168–70
Berenike (Red Sea port), 1, 35–6, 45, 96, 104, 110, 125, 132, 139, 295; ships built at, 149; terracotta objects unearthed at, 143
Bhandarkar, R.G., 95
Bharukaccha. See Barygaza (Bharukaccha)
Bhāskara Ravi, King, 166
Bindusāra, King, 254
black and red ware (BRW), pottery of, 25, 27, 29, 176
black pepper (*piper nigrum*), 32, 36, 44, 128–32, 146, 162
Black Sea, 58, 147, 208, 237
Bodynaykanur, 49
Brāhmi-label inscriptions, 18, 24, 223
Brihat Samhita, 53
Broach. *See* Barygaza (Bharukaccha)
bronze-making, 27, 135
Buddhist inscriptions, 17, 39–42
Buddhist monastic institutions, 264, 289
Burgess, James, 91

Caesar, Julius, 48, 97, 227, 242
caityas (Buddhist shrines), 159
Camara, 160–1, 174
Cammoni village, 74
camps of foreign traders. *See* foreign traders, camps of
candāḷas, 259
Cankam literature, 82, 84
Cape of Guardafui, 117
Cape of Spices, 71
capitalist society, 7
Caprobotras (Kēraḷaputas), 277
caravan transport, 35, 37, 143
cardamom (*ellettaria cardamomum*), 32, 124, 129, 131–2
cargo carried by ancient ships, amount of, 142
Caspian Sea, 58
Cassius, Dion, 60–1, 278
Casson, L., 102
Cenkamēdu, 176–7
Cēra coins, 49–51
Cerabotros, kingdom of, 76–7, 279
ceramic goods, 37, 38–9, 166, 183, 186–7, 190
Ceviyaṛivūṛutuṛai, 272, 276
Chakraborti, H.P., 100
Champa, 92, 112
Champakalakshmi, R., 102
Chanakya, D.R., 261n19
Chandra, Moti, 100
Chandragupta, King, 254
channel linking, of Nile with Red Sea, 110
Charlesworth, M.P., 97
chiefdoms of Peninsular India, 289 (map); *See also* Tamil chieftains
Childe, Gordon, 234
Chinese writings, on Mediterranean trade, 82
Chryse Island, 77–9
cīṛūr-mannar, 271
clan–kin relations, 8, 186, 210, 216, 220, 242–3, 245, 247, 277, 295
Claudius, Emperor, 48, 68, 127, 227
Cleopatra III, Queen, 114
coastal traders of India, 174
code of conduct (*dhamma*), 205
coins and currency, 47–52, 224–8;
Cēra coins, 49–51;
Cōḻa coins, 51–2;

copper coins, 34, 47–8, 52, 225; *dīnāra*, 48, 232; of Eyyāl collection, 48; gold coins, 47, 125, 133, 230; *karṣapaṇa*, 225; of Northern India, 225–7; *paḻankācu* (old coin), 48, 231; Pāṇḍyan coins, 49; Phoenician coins, 47; punch-marked coins, 47, 49, 225; purchasing power, 229; Roman coins, 47, 95–6, 225–7; Satāvāhana coins, 47, 226, 265; silver coins, 47, 125, 225; as source for studying history of ancient economy and exchange, 47; Tamilakam coins, 47, 227–8; *tuḷaippon*, 48, 231
Cōḻa country, 34, 161, 174–5; coins of, 51–2
Colandia (Indian vessel), 79–80, 127, 176, 194, 197
Colchis (Korkai) port, 78–9, 160
Comari port, 78–9, 170
commodities of exchange value, 10
Compendia, 65
copper coins: of Northern India, 225; of Roman Empire, 34, 52
Coromandel coast, ports on, 169–76
Coṭṭonāra, 77–8
Cotymba boat, 75, 157, 195, 263
craftsmen: hereditary, 180; south Indian, 178
critical political economy, concept of, 6
Cuḷḷi River, 87
Cunningham, Alexander, 91
customs duty, 43, 45; Alexandrian Tariff, 128; clearance of, 143; imposition of, 128; tokens (*ostraca*) of, 37

Dachinabades, 158
dakṣiṇāpatha-pati, 262
Damaskenos, Nikolaos, 60
daṇda, 253
Darius, Emperor, 48, 110, 227
Davids, Rhys, 92
De Romanis, F., 102, 104
de Saint-Martin, M. Vivien, 91
Deccan region, exchange networks in, 208–13; agro-pastoral culture, 210; clan–kin ties, 210; inland trade networks, 212; Sātavāhana–Ikshvāku periods, 212
Deccan region, polity in, 260–6; caste-based social order, 263; conflict between Sākas and Sātavāhanas, 265; cost of governance, 263; Indo-Roman trade and, 264–5; lords of the southern trade routes, 263–6; Nasik Cave records on, 262, 265; political formation, 261–3; power relations across tribes, 262; Sātavāhana political formation, 262; taxation system, 263; *varṇa* system, 263
dhamma, 254
dhamma mahāmātras, 205
dharma, 276
Dharma Śāstras, 265
Dhēnukakaṭaka, 40
dīnāra, of Roman Empire, 232
Dio, Cassius, 61
Dipavamśa, 53
division of labour, 216, 218, 249–50, 284
Dravidian language, 108

economic enterprises, 6
economic value, neoclassical theory of, 12
Egypt, 237; Augustus' conquest of, 3, 95, 101, 116; Greek mariner from,

69; records of Mediterranean trade, 44–6
Egyptian turquoise glazed ware, 187
elasticity of demand, 10
Elliot, W., 47
Elphinstone, Mount Stuart, 92
Eros, Caius Numidius, 116, 140
Erythraean Sea, 69
Eṭṭuttokai, 82–4
Eudoxus of Cyzicus, 58, 114
exchange of goods: agreement regarding, 61; from eastern world, 294
exchange relations: coins and currency, use of, 224–8; contrasting political economies, 236–48; Deccan region, 208–13; Graeco–Roman system of, 45–6, 63, 81, 138; between India and Graeco-Roman, 94; Mediterranean, 102; methodology for analysis of, 15–18; money, markets, and urbanization, 228–35; Roman Empire–southern India, 52; and situation in Northern India, 200–8; social theory of, 5; Tamil region, 213–24; between West Asia and Indian subcontinent, 39
exchange-value, notion of, 10

fair price, 11, 138
Florus, Pius Annius, 60, 278
foreign traders, camps of, 189–94; acquisition and storage of goods, 193; autonomy of, 191; items of import, 190; non-mercantile provisions at, 191; olive oil and *garum*, use of, 190; personal belongings, 190; seasonal exchanges of goods, 190; supply of food grains, 190, 193; warehouses, 191
forest peoples (*āṭavikas*), 203

Ganges River, 62, 72, 75, 77–80, 90, 127, 129–30, 175, 201
Gangetic region, polity in, 250–7
gem cutting, 187, 204
gift-exchange, 8, 219
Godavari–Krishna delta, 211, 290
gold-yielding ships, of Cēra chieftain, 86–7
goods of self-subsistence, 125
goods-for-goods exchange, 8, 125, 128–36, 189, 219, 222; in Mauryan Empire, 259; standardized system of, 9; in Tamil region, 233
grahapati, 206
Graeco-Romans: of Alexandria, 123; contacts with China, 82; cross-oceanic voyages in Indian Ocean, 115; expansion of, 123–8; maritime activities in the Indian Ocean, 126; monopoly in Indian Ocean, 126; navigators, 150; overseas exchange network, 124; overseas trade, 20, 32, 88; political economy, 236; presence in the Indian Ocean, 103–5; seafarers, 103; settlements in India, 91, 96; ships, 4, 83, 88, 141, 146, 149, 182; tableware, 187; trade component of, 145; writings on ancient Mediterranean trade, 54–82
grāmikas, 255
Gulf of Aden, 69–70, 108, 119
Gulf of Cambay, 69, 71, 74, 117, 151
Gulf of Mannar, 79
Gulf of Suez, 119

Kadalundi River, 161
kalam (seagoing vessel), 197, 282
Kaleina, 212
Kalittokai, 83
Kalliena port, 154, 159, 264–5
Kānchipuram, 24, 29, 34
Kane, 117
Kanyakumari, 161, 173, 213, 266, 275
kapaṭalēkhya, 255, 258
Karaikkādu, 176
karṣapaṇa (coin), 225; denominations of, 225
Karle, Buddhist inscriptions at, 39
karmmakāras, 204, 206–7
Karur, 29, 47–8, 50–2, 177, 227, 270
katalōṭṭiya, 286
Kaushambi, 112, 234
Kautilya, 255
Kāvēri–Tāmṛaparṇi delta, 290
Keprobotos, 160, 162
Kēraḷaputo, 275
Khor Rori, South Arabia, 38
Kiepert, Heinrich, 91
kiḷār, 267
kingship, Śāstraic–Purāṇic notions of, 276
knowledge systems, dissemination of, 283
Kodumaṇal (Kodumaṇam) village, 27–8
Kodungallur (Cranganore), 166
Kolhapur, 264
Konkan port, 159, 264
Koptos, 37, 143
Koptos Tariff (Egyptian stone inscription), 45
Korkai port, 28–9, 33, 88–9, 173
Kōṭṭaimedu, 32, 176
Kuṛumtokai, 84
Kushana period, Roman influence on India during, 95
lapidary, 187, 245; craftsmen in, 178; ethno-archaeological evidence of, 177–8
Lassen, Christian, 91
legal agreement, between debtors and creditors, 144
legalization of goods, procedures of, 37, 45, 143
Leucos Limen port, 37
Leuke Come, port of, 119, 141
Levant, 108
Life of Appollonius of Tynana, 81
Limyrike, 76, 78, 81, 119, 127, 129, 136, 159–60, 173, 193–4, 277, 279, 281
literary sources, for understanding ancient maritime trade, 52–4
loan contract, maritime, 123
long-distance traders, 28, 47
luxury goods: demand for, 237, 291; tariff duty on, 142; trade in, 117, 139–41

Madurai, 40–1, 47, 48–9, 52, 227, 270
māduram (muslin fabric), 82, 172
Mahanadi River, 201, 203–4, 241
mahājanapadas, 202, 250
mahāmātras, 256
Maṇimala River, 169
Majumdar, R.C., 97–9
makaṭpārkāñcittuṛai, 84
Malinowski, Bronislaw, 7, 11, 13, 107, 200, 292, 294
Manusmṛiti, 53, 92
Map of Ancient India, 91
Marakkāṇam, 176
marine insurance, 53
Marinos of Tyre, 80
maritime civilization, 1, 17, 100, 106, 248–9

maritime routes from India, ancient, 108
market, concept of, 228–35
Marugālttalai, 41
Marx, Karl, 7, 200, 292
Mathura, 112
Maturaikkāñci, 89, 173
Mauryan Empire, 172, 189, 245, 284; administrative system, 251–2, 258; agro-pastoral economies, 251, 254, 258; appropriation of labour, 206; bureaucracy, hierarchy of, 252; conquests involving territorial annexation, 253; *Dharma Śāstras*, 265; document-based system of administration, 257; exaction of revenue, 253; horsemen and charioteers, 257; land-related rights and privileges, 256; maintenance of the trade networks, 259; military campaigns, 251; military functionaries of, 261; overseas trade administration, 258; predatory campaigns, 253; socio-economic and cultural processes, 252; trade and statecraft in, 250; trade networks, 258; trade revenue, 257; transport and communication in, 255, 257; *vijita*, 251; warrior force, 252; written communication, 255; *See also* Persian Empire; Roman Empire
Mauss, Marcel, 11–13, 107, 200, 294
Medamoud, 140
Mediterranean ceramics, 32, 34, 161, 166, 183, 186, 190
Mediterranean exchange relations, 2, 18, 20, 102, 106, 165, 292
Mediterranean maritime relations, with peninsular India: Alexandrian Tariff, 128–9; antecedents of contacts, 109–13; goods of exchange, 128–36; Graeco-Roman expansion and, 123–8; Hippalus' discovery, 113–18; history of, 108; Mediterranean ships, 145–50; modes of exchange, 136–8; nature of trade, 138–45; politics of claims, 109; routes of exchange, 111; wind-based voyages, 118–23
Mediterranean Sea, 99, 145, 147
Mediterranean seafarers, 103, 112, 153, 188, 199; of cross-oceanic voyages, 188; non-mercantile provisions, 191; staple grains of, 190
Mediterranean ships, 145–50
Mediterranean trade contacts, history of: archaeological sources, 23–52; historiography, 91–107; literary sources, 52–90
medium of exchange, 10, 136–9, 220, 225, 229–30
Megasthenes, 54, 56–7, 63, 252, 254, 258
mercantile navigation, in Arabian Sea, 110
mercantile transactions, 139; document-based, 143
metal working, 187, 209, 215
metal-crafts industry, of south India, 248
monetary payments, 249
money: concept of, 228–35; as medium of exchange, 136–8
monsoon winds: discovery of, 69, 102, 113–18; navigation based on, 3, 69–70, 105; for trans-oceanic voyages, 69–70, 118–23, 188

Muciṛi port, 87
Mukherji, R.K., 94, 133
Mullaippāṭṭu, 89
Muza, 111
Muziris Papyrus, 42–4, 141, 143, 191, 193, 280, 287
Muziris port, 28, 77, 131, 160, 162–7, 183; temple of Augustus, 193
Myos Hormos (Quseir al-Qadim), 1, 35–8, 45, 58, 69, 96, 110, 125, 132, 139–40, 147, 149–51, 295

Nābhaka, 251
Nābhapankti, 251
nagaras, 189, 201–2, 204, 206–7, 254
Nāgārjunakonda, 212
Nahapana (Saka ruler), 159, 265
Nākkida, 161, 169
Nammadus River, 74, 157
Nanmāran, Pāṇḍya, 276
Naoura, 160–1
Narmada River, 71, 74
Naṟṟiṇai, 84
Nasik, Buddhist inscriptions at, 39
nation state, concept of, 13, 15
Nāṭṭamēdu, 176
Naura, 76, 154, 160
naval technology: of ancient India, 5, 20; for cross-oceanic voyage, 117
nāvāy (seagoing vessel), 197
navigation, based on monsoon winds, 3, 69–70
Nelcynda, 66, 76–7, 129, 134, 154, 160–1, 166, 167–9, 279
Nelcyndes tribe, 167
neoclassical economics, principles of, 12, 293
Neṭunceḻiyan, Pāṇḍya, 272
Nicanor Archive, 37, 46, 137n51, 139, 143
Nile River, 3, 35, 43, 59, 96, 98, 110, 116, 119, 121, 189
Nilgiri 'circles' and 'burrows', 25
Northern India, exchange relations in, 200–8;
agrarian fields (*khētta*), 200; appropriation of labour, 206; aristocracy, 203–7; class differentiation among the people, 204; crops, 201; network of, 207–8; settlements (*gāmas*), 200; *vaṛṇa* society, 202–3

Okelis, port of, 117, 121
oriental goods, social demand for, 124
Orosius, Paulus, 60, 278
ostraca, 37–8, 45–6, 139–40, 143, 239
Ostya Antica Portus, 189
overseas routes: between Arabian Peninsula and India, 117; between China and India, 112; between Mediterranean and Indian coasts, 120 (map)
overseas trade: Augustan patronage of, 116; historiography of, 292; revolution of, 101–2
Oxus, 58
Ozene city, 76

pack-animal caravans, 109
Palar River, 71
Pālaiyamkōṭṭai, 41
Pālār River, 34
Palmyra, 32, 58, 121
Pampa River, 161, 169
Pāṇḍya country, 33
Panikkar, K.M., 99
Pāṇḍya Ceḻiyan–Cēra battle, 87–8
pāndyakavāṭakam (pearl), 82
Pāṇḍyan coins, 49

Sopara (Opara), 134, 158–9; South Indian technologies, 196–9; southern ports, 159–61; stay of Graeco-Roman people at, 192–3; Tyndis, 161–2; wharf and warehouse, 182
Poseidonius, 114
pottery of Indian subcontinent, 38
Prākrit language, 226
Prasad, P.C., 100
Prathiṣṭāna (Paithan), 212
precious goods, trade in, 77, 90, 96, 223, 247–8
prices, determination of, 10
Ptolemaic dynasty, 97
Ptolemy II, Emperor, 35
Ptolemy VIII, King, 114
Ptolemy's *Geography*, 19, 54, 80–1, 91, 161, 174
Puṛanāṇūṛu, 85, 162, 164, 267
Pugaḷur cavern, labels of, 41
puḷindas, 259
Pukār port, 28–9, 90, 175
punch-marked coins, 19, 24, 26, 47, 49, 207, 225–6
Puskalavati, 112
Putingarian Table, 193

Qana, South Arabia, 38
Quseir al-Qadim, 1, 35, 37, 121

rājagṛha, 234
rajūkas, 253
Rawlinson, H.G., 94
realgar and orpiment, 77, 135
Red Sea, 147
Red Sea ports, 35–8, 108, 117, 131, 137, 295; goods that moved in and out of, 128
redistributive community network, 276
redistributive relationship, 8, 216, 218, 220, 269
Rig-Veda, 202
Risṭika, 251
rock crystals, 4, 27, 124, 129, 178
Roman coins, 34, 47, 240; in India, 95–6, 225–7; melting of, 232; monetization of, 240; re-minting of, 232
Roman Egypt, 20, 123–4, 137, 145, 153
Roman Empire, 64, 103, 153, 282, 291; annual military expense, 238; coinage and currency (*See* Roman coins); demand for luxury goods, 125, 238; exchange relations with south India, 52; fall of, 94; Hellenistic influence, 238; influence on India during Kushana period, 95; monetary system, 96; overseas trade, 237; points of exchange in, 121; *See also* Mauryan Empire; Persian Empire
Roman trade: political economy of, 2; with Southern India, 93; *See also* Indo-Roman trade
Roman/Egyptian financiers, 137

sabaras, 259
sail technology, 150–3
salt panning, 221–2
Samudda Vaṇija (sea trader), 52
Sangam Literature, 5
sangara, 80, 127, 131, 176, 194
sankīrṇajāti, 263
Sanskrit language, 108
Sārnāth Pillar Edict, 255
Sastri, K.A. Nilakanta, 98–9
Satavāhanas, 159, 290, 294; coins, 47, 195, 226
Sātakarṇi, Gautamiputra, 262

86; versification, technique of, 84
Tamil polity, 266–88; benefit of overseas contacts, 280; chieftains and seafaring, 281–8; clan–kin ties, 277; cultural sources of legitimization, 275; distribution of power, pattern of, 266; and exchange relations with Roman Empire, 277; internal exchange relations, 287; major chiefdoms, 270–7; minor chiefdoms, 266–70; political organization, 284; predatory campaign, 271; role in organization of Indo-Roman trade, 5; *saptānga* attributes, 274; standing army, 273; Tamil rulers and overseas exchange, 277–81
Tamil region, exchange networks in, 213–24; agrarian settlements, destruction of, 218; agro-pastoralism, 215; clan–kin ties, 216, 219–20; forms of, 219–24; hereditary occupations and, 217; human adaptation, modes of, 214; inter-commodity exchange rates, 220; intra-*tiṇai* transactions, 219; kinship-based redistributive economies, 213; paddy cultivation, 215; practice of reciprocity, 219; social organization of labour, 215; social stratification, 216; Tamil Brāhmi-label inscriptions and foreign notices on, 213
Tamilakam, 196, 208; coins of, 227–8; political formation of, 266; pre-Pallavan social formation of, 213
Tamil Brāhmi-label inscriptions, 41
Tāmṛaparṇi River, 34
Tamralipti, 112, 182, 189, 246
Tappaga (boat), 75, 157, 195, 263
Taprobane, 67–9, 80, 140, 173–4
tariff duties, 140–1
Taxila, 112, 207–8
Tchernia, A., 102
techno-economic consumables, demand for, 291
terracotta, 178; containers, 39
textile weaving, 187
Thapar, Romila, 9, 252
Tiber River, 189
tin tēr poṛaiyan tonḍi, 84
Tiruchchiṛappaḷḷi, 41
Tirukkoilur, 51–2, 176–7
Tiruvakkarai, 176
Tiruvalla taluk, 168
toḳens (*ostraca*) of customs duty, 37
Tolkkāppiyam, 84
Tomber, R., 104
trade revenue, 236–7, 257, 265
trade routes, 117–18, 257–60; coastal and cross-oceanic routes, 122 (map); *dakṣiṇāpatha* (southern routes), 258–9; between India and China, 112; lords of the southern trade routes, 263–6; maintenance of, 258; between the Mediterranean and Indian Coasts, 120(map); raids of robbers and marauding tribes, 259; silk route, 111–12; *uttarāpatha* (northern routes), 258–9; *vaṇikapatha*s, 258
Trajan, Emperor, 48, 60, 62, 227, 278
trans-oceanic voyages: by Graeco-Romans, 115; ideal time for, 119; in Indian Ocean, 115; use of monsoon winds for, 69–70, 118–23

About the Author

Rajan Gurukkal is Sundararajan Visiting Professor at the Centre for Contemporary Studies, Indian Institute of Science, Bengaluru, India. He earned his PhD from Jawaharlal Nehru University, New Delhi, India. He was also the Vice Chancellor, Mahatma Gandhi University, Kottayam, Kerala, India. His publications include *Social Formations of Early South India* (Oxford University Press, 2010), *Cultural History of Kerala*, vol. I (1999), and *The Kerala Temple and the Early Medieval Agrarian System* (1992).